BOSS OF BOSSES:

NICHOLAS MORELLO Murdered Aug. 15, 1930 by "Buster" from Chicago *(not further identified).*

SALVATORE MARANZANO Murdered Sept. 11, 1931 by hired killers including Sam Levine for Vito Genovese and Salvatore Lucania *(Charles Luciano).*

MARANZANO GROUP

Boss:
Salvatore Maranzano
Underboss:
Angelo Caruso

Boss:
Thomas Reina
Murdered Feb. 26, 1930 by unidentified killer of Masseria Group.
Underboss:
Thomas Gagliano
Boss:
Joseph Pinzolo
Placed in Gagliano Group by Masseria. Murdered Aug. or Sept. 1930 by Girolamo Santuccio for the Gagliano Group.

ONTROL AFTER MARANZANO

Boss:
Joseph Profaci
Died of natural causes 1962.

Boss:
Giuseppe Magliocco
Died of natural causes in 1963.
Underboss:
Salvatore Mussachio

Boss:
Joseph Colombo, Sr.
Shot and incapacitated June 28, 1971.
Underboss:
Charles Mineo
Consigliere:
Joseph Yacovelli

Acting Boss:
Joseph Yacovelli
Surrendered leadership 1972.

Acting Boss:
Vincent Aloi

Boss:
Joseph Bonanno
Deposed 1964.
Underboss:
Carmine Galante

Boss:
Frank Labruzzo
Invalidated by the commission in 1965.
Underboss:
John Morale

Boss:
Gaspar Di Gregorio
Retired after suffering heart attack in 1968.

Boss:
Paul Sciacca
Retired due to ill health 1970.

Boss:
Natale Evola
Underboss:
Philip Rastelli
Consigliere:
Joseph DeFilippo

Boss:
Thomas Gagliano
Died of natural causes 1953.
Underboss:
Gaetano Lucchese

Boss:
Gaetano Lucchese
Died of natural causes 1967.
Underboss:
Stefano LaSalle

Boss:
Carmine Tramunti
Underboss:
Stefano LaSalle
Consigliere:
Vincent Rao

Mafia, U.S.A.

Mafia,

Edited by Nicholas Gage

U.S.A.

A PLAYBOY PRESS BOOK

Contents

5

THE MAFIA AT HOME

FRIENDS IN HIGH PLACES

DOLLARS AND DEATH

Acknowledgments

"Joe Valachi's Big Contract." Reprinted by permission of G. P. Putnam's Sons from *The Valachi Papers* by Peter Maas. Copyright © 1968 by Peter Maas.

"The Hit." Reprinted with the permission of Farrar, Straus & Giroux, Inc. from *The Prosecutor* by James Mills. Copyright © 1968, 1969 by James Mills (published in paperback by Pocket Books).

"The Mafia in Sicily." Reprinted by permission of G. P. Putnam's Sons from *The Honored Society* by Norman Lewis. Copyright © 1964 by Norman Lewis.

"How the Mafia Came to America" and "Lucky Luciano–Boss for All Seasons." Reprinted with the permission of Farrar, Straus & Giroux, Inc. from *The Brotherhood of Evil* by Frederic Sondern. Copyright © 1959 by Frederic Sondern, Jr.

"The Purge of the Greasers." From *The Secret Rulers* by Fred J. Cook. Copyright © 1966 by Fred J. Cook. Reprinted by permission of Hawthorn Books, Inc., 70 Fifth Avenue, New York 10011.

"After Luciano" and "Rules to Live By." From *The Crime Confederation* by Ralph Salerno and John S. Tompkins. Copyright © 1969 by Ralph Salerno and John S. Tompkins. Reprinted by permission of Doubleday & Company, Inc.

"Joseph Joe Colombo—Impulsive Innovator" originally appeared under the title "Mafia: Back to the Bad Old Days" in *Time* magazine. Reprinted by permission from *Time, The Weekly Newsmagazine*. Copyright © 1971 by Time, Inc.

7

"The Power Structure." From pp. 111–119, 126–138 in *Theft of the Nation: The Structure and Operations of Organized Crime in America* by Donald R. Cressey. Copyright © 1969 by Donald R. Cressey. Reprinted by permission of Harper & Row, Publishers, Inc.

"Mafia Women" and "Frank Sinatra is a Pal." From *The Mafia Is Not an Equal Opportunity Employer* by Nicholas Gage. Copyright © 1971 by Nicholas Gage. Used with permission of McGraw-Hill Book Company.

"Mrs. Trigger Mike." Reprinted with permission of The Macmillan Company from *Syndicate Wife* by Hank Messick. Copyright © 1968 by Hank Messick.

"A Family Gathering." Reprinted by permission of The World Publishing Company from *Honor Thy Father* by Gay Talese. Copyright © 1971 by Gay Talese.

"Pal Joey—A Study in Gangster Chic" by Charlotte Curtis appeared in *Harper's Bazaar* under the title "The Last Delicious Days of Joey Gallo." Copyright © 1971 and used by courtesy of *Harper's Bazaar*.

"A Good Friend at City Hall." Reprinted with the permission of Farrar, Straus & Giroux, Inc. from *A Percentage of the Take* by Walter Goodman. Copyright © 1971 by Walter Goodman.

"The Mafia in the Supermarket" originally appeared as a series of articles by Joe Demma and Tom Renner, entitled "Organized Crime and Supermarkets," in *Newsday*. Copyright © 1971, Newsday, Inc. Reprinted by permission.

"Muscling In" and "On the Waterfront" by Stanley Penn originally appeared in *The Wall Street Journal* under the titles "Mafia & Business—How Organized Crime Muscles In on Firms In Legitimate Fields" and "On the Waterfront—A Banana Trucker Gets Preference at Docks; Does Mafia Link Help?" Copyright © 1969. Reprinted by permission of The Wall Street Journal.

"In Hollywood." Reprinted from *Crime on the Waterfronts* by Malcolm Johnson. Copyright © 1950 by Malcolm Johnson.

"The Businessman as Victim." Reprinted by permission from "How to Lock Out the Mafia" by Charles Grutzner in the *Harvard Business Review*. Copyright © 1970 by the President and Fellows of Harvard College. All rights reserved.

"A Family Business" by Fred J. Cook. Copyright © 1972 by The New York Times Company. Reprinted by permission.

Introduction

Everyone is a Mafia expert these days. Reading about the latest Mafia assassination provides a bit of excitement, a peek into the mysterious workings of another world. Those sharp-dressing, tough-looking hoods with their colorful nicknames and their scorn for authority appeal to the daydreamer in all of us, and the Mafia seems to be riding a wave of popularity, its wars and heroes chronicled in dozens of books, movies, magazine articles and television programs. In fact, so much lore and literature has grown up around the Mafia that it's easy to think of Mafiosi as picaresque heroes on the order of the James brothers or Robin Hood and his merry men. Mob wars are often treated in print as a particularly American pastime like baseball. The success of such books as Mario Puzo's *The Godfather* and Gay Talese's *Honor Thy Father* demonstrates that this country is in the grip of Mafia fever; as one toy manufacturer put it, the Mafia is "hot" these days. Gangster chic is supplanting radical chic, and any hostess who can produce a guest of honor with Mafia connections is certain to have people grappling for invitations to her party.

Unfortunately, the Mafia does not hand out press releases, thus there is more than a little disagreement on what the Mafia really is and what it's up to lately. For example, on March 3, 1972, *Life* magazine, which had previously carried numerous pieces on the Mafia, published an article that was headlined in very large type: "The Decline and Fall of the Mafia." The slightly nostalgic theme of the piece was stated early on: "Italian-style organized crime in this country is finished." Yet only a month later, on April 7, Joseph Gallo, leader of one of the rival factions within the Mafia family of Joe Colombo, Sr., was shot dead in Umberto's Clam House in Manhattan's Little Italy in the early-morning hours. Joey had been celebrating his 43rd birthday in the company of his wife, step-daughter and friends and was just ordering second helpings when four gunmen entered through a side door. Joey, who had been carelessly sitting with his back to the door, began to shout, "You son of a bitch," but was interrupted by gunfire. He lurched out the door with two bullets in him. A third bullet then fatally severed his aorta. As he died, Gallo's blood turned the pavement red just as, almost a year earlier, the blood of Joseph Colombo had stained the pavement of Columbus Circle during the second annual Italian-American Unity Day rally.

Gallo's death signaled another major campaign in the internal battle for control of the Colombo Mafia family. As Gallo lay in state in a $5,000 bronze casket surrounded by floral tributes, it all began to seem like a replay of something out of the Profaci-Gallo war of the early 1960s, or the Castellammarese War of the 1930s, or the Battle for Chicago during the 1920s. Long black limousines disgorged overcoated occupants who shielded their faces from the cameras outside the Guido funeral home, while inside, Joe Gallo's sister Carmella bent over his coffin and screamed, "The streets will run red with blood, Joey!"

She was right. Within five weeks a total of ten men had died in gangland style. Some were Gallo men. Some were Colombo men. Most of them were in their middle thirties. It began to appear that reports of the demise of the Mafia had been a trifle exaggerated.

This theory, put forth by *Life* magazine, that the Mafia, like the whooping crane, is in imminent danger of becoming extinct, is enjoying the greatest vogue lately. The theory is based on the fact that offspring of Mafia bosses are much more inclined to become professors, like the son of Sam DeCavalcante, or accountants, like the son of Vito Genovese, than Mafia dons. And the theory is partly right. What it doesn't take into account, however, is the number of young petty hoods (like the Gallos and Joe

Colombo originally were) who are eager to become Mafia-connected. The ages of the victims in the latest Gallo-Colombo shoot-out proves that not all Mafiosi are aging Sicilians with fingers too crippled by arthritis to pull a trigger.

The second most prevalent misconception arising from the existence of the Mafia is that most Italians are involved in organized crime. It's little wonder that before he was shot Joe Colombo, Sr., attracted so many thousands of irate Italian-Americans to his Italian-American Civil Rights League. In fact, only a tiny fraction of the 22 million Italian-Americans in this country are involved in crime; there are racketeers from nearly every other ethnic group as well. But whenever mobsters are portrayed in books and films, they always seem to have Italian names and Italian-made shoes with pointed toes. As a result, words like *Mafia* and *Cosa Nostra*, indentifying Italians with organized crime, set many law-abiding Italian-Americans to gnashing their teeth. Italian-born Joseph Valachi, the most famous underworld informer, was amazed to hear that his testimony about his Mafia experiences had raised a clamor of protest from Italian-Americans who felt that he was smearing them and their ancestors. "I'm not talking about Italians," Valachi explained, "I'm talking about criminals."

Every ethnic group in this country has had its share of gangsters. In Chicago during Prohibition, rival gangs of Poles, Jews, Irish, Sicilians and groups of mixed background bloodied the streets with more than 200 gangland murders in four years until, finally, a peace conference was held at the Hotel Sherman. The names of the participants reflect the ethnic variety of organized crime; sitting around the table were Al Capone, Bugs Moran, Maxie Eisen, Christian Bertche, William Skidmore, Jack Zuta and Frank Foster. And one of the most fascinating men in organized crime today is Meyer Lansky, a non-Mafioso who began as a gun-for-hire in partnership with Bugsy Siegel and ultimately came to be considered the financial genius of the underworld. Lansky is primarily responsible for the sophisticated manner in which underworld funds are presently siphoned out of the country into European bank accounts and then returned as "laundered" cash to be loaned to legitimate businesses.

However, while it is true that many ethnic groups have their own piece of the pie, there is no doubt that in certain metropolitan areas like New York, Buffalo, Chicago, Detroit and Philadelphia the Mafia has a virtual monopoly. This book is therefore devoted not to organized crime as a whole, but to the Mafia, undoubtedly the most powerful and the most interesting segment of the underworld. Who are they? What are they like?

Even though Mafiosi undoubtedly love their parents and their children, tell good jokes, show great loyalty to their friends and sometimes even read good literature (both Joey Gallo and his brother Larry aspired after "culture"), they unfortunately cannot be domesticated by a few Park Avenue dinner parties. It's easy to say, "After all, they only kill each other" (to paraphrase Bugsy Siegel), but gang wars inevitably claim a certain number of victims who just happened to be walking down the wrong street at the wrong time. And once killing becomes a way of life, it's hard to draw the line.

Take Albert Anastasia who, before he was assassinated in the barbershop of the Park Sheraton Hotel in Manhattan, was one of the Mafia's most feared killers. Once, according to Joseph Valachi, Anastasia was watching television when he saw an interview with a young man who had happened to recognize bank robber Willie Sutton on the street and pointed him out to police. Anastasia didn't even know Sutton, but he ordered the young man wiped out because, as Anastasia put it, "I can't stand squealers." (After the execution was carried out, Anastasia had his own gunman bumped off to cover his tracks.)

It is also not true that Mafiosi will not harm women and children; more than one Mafia wife has spoken indiscreetly about her husband's activities and died as a result. One with more than average gumption was Constance Rastelli, wife of New York Mafioso Philip Rastelli. She became so incensed when she discovered that her husband was playing around that she began to talk to federal authorities who were investigating a half-dozen major Mafia figures for narcotics violations. They doubted her sincerity until she told them the address at which police were keeping an important witness in top-secret protective custody and added that the Mafia planned to murder the witness. Constance saved the witness's life, but before the government could provide her with adequate protection, she was shot to death.

In the film, *The Godfather*, the members of the Corleone family, when they dispatched a rival or an enemy, always did so neatly and efficiently, and the victim was generally a pretty unsympathetic type anyway. In real life, the Mafia still specializes in torture and slow death. Time and again wiretaps have picked up conversations between Mafiosi discussing their macabre handiwork with glee. And not too many years ago an underworld informant described the following conversation during which two "soldiers" in the "family" of Chicago Mafia boss Sam Giancana—James Torello and Fiore Buccieri—were telling a friend about killing a man named William Jackson who weighed 350 pounds.

Torello: "Jackson was hung up on that meat hook. He was so fucking heavy he bent it. He was on that thing three days before he croaked."

Buccieri (giggling): "Jackie, you shoulda seen the guy. Like an *elephant*, he was, and when Jimmy hit him in the balls with that electric prod . . ."

Torello: "He was floppin' around on that hook, Jackie. We tossed water on him to give the prod a better charge, and he's screamin'. . . ."

In spite of such grim activities, the Mafia still seems a very distant threat. After all, much of the public believes, the only real victims of the Mafia are their own kind—the wayward and the corrupt, those who become involved with gambling, loansharking and narcotics.

The truth is that it would be hard to find anyone in this country who does not pay annual dues to the Mafia. It has been a policy of the organization, ever since Prohibition, to move more and more into legitimate businesses. Mafia groups have gone into such diverse businesses as diaper services, dress manufacturing, meat processing, construction, trucking and garbage collection. On May 9, 1972, the *New York Times* reported that organized crime was increasing the price of every pound of meat sold in New York 15 percent by making supermarket chains and wholesale suppliers pay for labor peace. Even though salaries in the meat industry are lower in New York, New Yorkers were paying up to 60 cents more per pound for meat than consumers in, say, Chicago. "There's no logical reason for such a discrepancy," said Representative John Melcher. "Somebody is getting a big bite of it somewhere."

It's not just the consumer's pocketbook that suffers from Mafia infiltration; his health may be endangered as well. In one classic example a meat company produced frankfurters from the carcasses of diseased cows, horses and sheep which were intended only as feed for minks on mink ranches. The tainted frankfurters were okayed by certain inspectors from the Department of Agriculture who had been bribed.

In another instance two New Jersey Mafiosi, Jerry and Gene Catena, and the members of their Mafia family got a contract to sell a certain detergent to supermarkets. They set about it so zealously that when the product failed tests made by the A&P and the supermarket chain refused to stock it, five A&P stores were destroyed by fire and two A&P managers were shot to death.

Slum dwellers suffer most of all at the hands of the Mafia. In a recent year, for example, gambling and narcotics drained an estimated $343 million from New York City's three main ghettos. That was $70 million more than the state poured into those same areas in welfare during that year.

But the most insidious way in which the Mafia victimizes all of us is through the corruption of police and public officials. It was during Prohibition that men like Lucky Luciano and Frank Costello learned how easy it is to bribe officials and they applied the lesson well. During the 1950s the public learned that entire communities in Kentucky, Florida, New York, Indiana and Louisiana were "owned" by racketeers. In 1971 Attorney General John Mitchell announced that in the previous three years more than 170 state and local public officeholders or former officials, including the former mayor of Newark, New Jersey, had been indicted or convicted on various corruption charges involving organized crime. And things seem to be getting worse, not better. In 1972 an investigation of a police gambling unit in Brooklyn found that 70 percent of the police in the special unit were taking payments from organized-crime gamblers. So pervasive is the power of the "fix" that it extends from the cop on the beat to the highest government officials. Wrote Robert Kennedy: "When the racketeer bribes local officials and secures immunity from police action, the price exacted by corrupt law enforcement—incalculable in dollars—is paid . . . by the public." Joseph Valachi had a more ominous prediction: "Someday," he said, "the Mob is going to put a man in the White House and he's not going to know it until they present him with the bill."

If the Mafia were a legitimate corporation, it would top the list of *Fortune* magazine's Five Hundred largest companies. Its profits are many millions of dollars a year. Nevertheless, there are many who insist—and this is the most dangerous myth of all about the Mafia—that it simply does not exist. The concept of the Mafia, the argument goes, is a shameless canard perpetrated by journalists and novelists who need something to write about. Many honest and well-meaning individuals hold to this theory even though the body of evidence that the Mafia does exist in this country is overwhelming.

The Mafia came to the United States with the first wave of Sicilian immigrants at the end of the last century. The first recorded Mafia killing in this country was in 1889 in New Orleans. A grand jury investigating the gang war that followed reported: "The range of our researches has developed the existence of the secret organization styled 'Mafia.' The evidence comes from several sources fully competent in themselves to attest its truth, while the fact is supported by the long record of bloodcurdling crimes, it being almost impossible to discover the perpetrators or to secure witnesses."

In Brooklyn in 1917 a Mafia boss named Nicholas Morello was executed on the orders of the head of a rival Italian organization, and one of the gunmen, Tony Notaro, ultimately turned informer and described Mafia rituals and organization.

Another insider to reveal the inner workings of the Mafia was a Sicilian named Nicola Gentile who came to the United States in 1903 at the age of 19 and, after serving in Mafia familes in Pittsburgh, Cleveland and Kansas City, returned to Sicily in the Thirties. He retired in the Fifties and began writing a long rambling memoir in Italian. Although his reminiscences were never published, parts of them were quoted in the Italian press, along with interviews with Gentile.

The most famous Mafia informer was, of course, Joseph Valachi, who was imprisoned in Atlanta penitentiary along with his onetime boss, Vito Genovese. One day Valachi began to suspect that Vito was planning his death. Although Valachi had not turned informer as Genovese believed, he ultimately did after he beat a fellow prisoner to death because he thought the man was about to kill him on Genovese's orders. His sensational testimony before the Senate Rackets Committee on nationwide television in the early

Sixties introduced the entire country to the structure and workings of what he called La Cosa Nostra. The information he provided contained much detail not available through other sources; it has been incorporated in many accounts of Mafia activities, including several in this volume. (None of the members call it the Mafia anymore. The name varies from one part of the country to the next—Cosa Nostra, The Outfit, The Arm, The Office. The public, however, sticks to the old-fashioned term, Mafia.)

After the shooting of Joe Gallo, still another Mafia informer—a man named Joseph Luparelli—turned himself in. Like Valachi, he was in fear for his life. He said he had been one of five men (connected with the Mafia family of Joseph Colombo) who engineered the shooting of Joe Gallo in Umberto's Clam House.

In addition to the testimony of informers, there are tapes of conversations between Mafiosi picked up by federal "bugs." For several years, for example, the F.B.I. had bugs in the offices of Sam DeCavalcante, the New Jersey Mafia boss, and Raymond Patriarca, the New England boss, that yielded thousands of pages of information about the structure of Mafia families and the operation of their rackets. These bugs, however, were placed without court authorization and were inadmissible as evidence.

If you take the testimony of Mafia members turned informers over the years and add evidence obtained through wiretaps and revelations by secret informers, including an occasional angry Mafia wife, the structure of the Mafia in this country begins to emerge.

There are 26 Mafia families flourishing in 21 metropolitan areas in the United States. New York has five families, set up in 1931 by Salvatore Maranzano, the last Mafia "Boss of Bosses." and presently headed by Carlo Gambino, Joseph Colombo, Sr., Natale Evola, Gerardo Catena and Carmine Tramunti. Other Mafia families exist in New England; Buffalo; Chicago; Detroit; Los Angeles; Philadelphia; New Jersey; San Francisco; San Jose, California; New Orleans; Miami; Cleveland; Denver; Erie, Pennsylvania; Milwaukee; Kansas City; Pittsburgh; Saint Louis; Madison, Wisconsin; Springfield, Illinois; and Rockford, Illinois. There are an estimated 5,000 full-fledged members of the Mafia (2,000 of them in New York), and every family has a growing number of "associates," including gangsters not of Italian extraction. Each Mafia family has its own specialties, but the most widespread and profitable Mafia enterprises are:

Narcotics: In the Middle East opium poppies are sold on the black market. The juice of the pods is dried and sold by the kilogram (2.2 pounds). It finds its way to Marseille where it is refined into heroin and sold for $3,500 a kilo. By the time it reaches the streets of America, the kilo is worth $225,000. It's that kind of profit that has inspired the Mob to control the heroin market, and this enterprise alone brings them more than $350 million in revenue a year. There have been reports that other ethnic groups, including blacks, Puerto Ricans and Cubans, are moving into the narcotics rackets, but the fact is that the Mafia is still bankrolling the drug traffic and pocketing most of the profits. They have only removed their own men from the high-risk, high-visibility operations on the streets and given such jobs to the hungrier and more eager minority groups.

Loansharking: This racket brings the Mafia the best dollar-for-dollar profits. Any man who for whatever reason cannot get a loan through legitimate channels can get a loan from the Mob at an interest rate that is usually 20 percent a week. Many ghetto inhabitants thus find themselves on an unending merry-go-round of borrowing more each week just to pay off the interest they owe and they never manage to pay back the principle. But it's not just slumdwellers gamblers and businessmen who need cash overnight for an opportunity they just can't pass up also turn to the Mob for money.

Loansharking brings in several billion a year, and if certain of these borrowers can't pay up in the end, the Mafia doesn't mind. That's the way it collects legitimate businesses or favors—from powerful men who find themselves deeply in debt to the organization. James Marcus, former water commissioner of New York City, overextended himself in some business deals and took out an underworld loan at annual interest of 104 percent. When he could not repay it, he ended up deeply involved in graft, and the Mafia had yet another friend in high places.

Gambling: The meat and potatoes of the Mafia is gambling. When the repeal of Prohibition eliminated the vast profits in boot-legging liquor, the Mafia turned its attention to all forms of gambling, including some that it had formerly considered too insignificant to bother with. The size of the gambling profits is suggested by the fact that Americans wager about $20 billion a year on lotteries, horse racing and sports events.

James Baldwin once called the numbers "the American dream in blackface." Nearly 75 percent of all slumdwellers past childhood wager an average of three to five dollars a week in nickle and dime bets on the numbers, hoping for the 600-to-1 payoff. Their friendly neighborhood numbers-runner collects their bets every day and takes the money to the Mafia "bank" nearby. The bettor hopes to succeed in guessing the three digits that match the day's "handle," usually taken from the total dollars bet that day at a selected racetrack. The underworld used to scorn the numbers, calling it "nigger pool," but today an estimated two billion a year is milked out of the ghettos and into the coffers of the Mob through numbers alone.

Bookmaking is almost as profitable, so the Mafia provides many services for bookmakers although not all of them are Mafia members. Even those who work as independents use the Mafia to lay off, or spread the risk, on the bets they're holding. They also pay the Mafia for protection from police interference.

Fixing athletic events is another way the Mafia can make money from gambling. Even if they cannot succeed in fixing an event, they can gather information about the health and condition of the players and put it to good use in setting odds.

"Skimming" is another popular practice, especially in places like Las Vegas where gambling is legal. It involves raking off a certain amount of the cash receipts every night before recording the take in the ledgers. The only problem with skimming is finding a place to stash the cash. It is often kept temporarily in the specially built-in hiding places called "plants" found in the homes of most Mafia bosses.

Labor Racketeering: Unions present many opportunities for profit. The most common one is to charge employers a price for labor peace. In the East the Mafia has infiltrated many unions involved with entertainment, restaurant employees and longshoremen. Sometimes a Mafia boss finds it useful to have whole unions at his disposal when he wants to make a point. For example, when Carlo Gambino was backing Joe Colombo and his Italian-American

Civil Rights League, the longshoremen were given the day off to attend the League's Unity Day rally. But the next year, when Gambino had withdrawn his support and Colombo was marked for execution, the longshoremen were informed that they would not have the day off.

Frank Costello was a Mafia boss who was particularly known for his power with the unions. One day as he was enjoying his daily steambath at a Manhattan hotel, the manager approached him and asked him if he would avoid the hotel's baths in the future because it was making the other clients nervous. The next day not a single chambermaid, waiter, janitor, elevator operator or cook showed up for work at the hotel. Costello had made his point, and within hours the general manager of the hotel was on the phone to Costello, frantically begging him to return to the steambaths.

With rackets like these bringing in revenues that can be reckoned in billions, the Mafia is undoubtedly one of the biggest businesses in the country. But it is also the least known, despite the fact that, in addition to the best sellers, there have been many specialized books on such aspects of the Mafia as its structure and hierarchy, or its foundations in Sicily. The problem is that each man who writes about the Mafia writes from his own limited perspective. He may be a police investigator who has spent 20 years studying underworld interrelationships in his city but knows little about the organization elsewhere. Or he may be a former member of the Mafia, like Joseph Valachi, who can describe the organization, but only from the small corner of it he knows. Certain aspects of the Mafia, such as its gang wars or the meeting at Apalachin, New York, have been thoroughly written about, but others, such as the spread of the Mafia into legitimate business, have not been adequately explored.

The purpose of this book is to give the widest and most accurate possible portrait of the Mafia, and we have chosen to do so by selecting the best works written about it. For the sections treating the history and the structure of the Mafia, we have relied mainly on excerpts from books. But to make the picture as up-to-date as possible, the information about the Mafia's rackets, its movement into legitimate business and its latest internal rivalries has been selected from the best magazine and newspaper articles devoted to these subjects. When a particular facet of the Mafia seemed worthy of further exploration, such as the startling story of how the Mafia corrupted many of New Jersey's major political leaders, we commissioned pieces specifically for this book.

The result, we hope, is a total portrait of the Mafia. It presents the men of the Honored Society on the job—with murder contracts, new and old rackets and deadly rivalries—and off the job— with their wives, their mistresses, their social ambitions. It reveals some friends of the Mafia in high places and zeroes in on some of the men who have created the Mafia of today. Anyone who reads through this book will come away with a full picture of the most powerful and most secret corporation in the country— Mafia, U.S.A.

The Face of the Mafia

ON A WINTRY SUNDAY AFTERNOON a while ago a New York detective was sitting in a restaurant at La Guardia Airport having coffee with a friend passing through New York when a well-dressed Mafioso with receding gray hair approached their table. The soft-spoken Mafioso greeted the detective, whom he knew from many courtroom encounters, warmly and politely, asked after his health and his family and left, wishing him well.

When told who the man was, the detective's friend mused, "That fellow didn't seem like a gangster. Is he a bookmaker or a numbers-runner for the Mafia?"

"No," the detective replied. "He's a hit man. He kills people."

Many things about the Mafia and its members are misleading. Many famous Mafia bosses like Frank Costello, Lucky Luciano and Joe Colombo have shown a genial face to the public, and the organization itself, steeped in folklore and mystery, can seem quaintly romantic. But the real face of the Mafia at work is a lot less pleasant; the Mafia has one particularly unusual business practice that is hard to ignore—killing people.

The opening chapters in this book show the Mafia at work killing people. In the first one, writer Peter Maas tells Joe Valachi's recollections about the most important murder contract Valachi ever carried out for his Mafia bosses.

In the second chapter James Mills describes in detail the fate of Ernest (The Hawk) Rupolo, a Mafioso who talked too much and died regretting it. The stomach-turning way in which Rupolo died is typical of many Mafia executions; the organization does not go in for quick, neat murders when there is time and opportunity for torture first.

21

1

Joe Valachi's Big Contract

PETER MAAS

In early September, 1952, Joseph Valachi was summoned by his capo Tony Bender (nee Anthony Strollo). It resulted in his most important Cosa Nostra contract. They met for dinner, he said, in a Greenwich Village restaurant on Thompson Street called Rocco's. After a few minutes of perfunctory chitchat, Bender got down to business. A soldier in the Thomas Lucchese Family, Eugenio Giannini, had turned out to be an informer for the Bureau of Narcotics. "Gene has been talking to the junk agents," Bender said. "The old man [Vito Genovese] has got the word personally from Charlie Lucky. Charlie says Gene is the smartest stool pigeon that ever lived. He has been talking to the junk agents for years. He has got to be hit, him and anybody with him."

The news about Giannini was correct. He was a Narcotics Bureau informer. In 1942 he had been picked up on a heroin conspiracy charge and served fifteen months for it. Later, like many other informers used by the Bureau of Narcotics, the FBI, and so on, Giannini moved in a twilight zone, continuing his own underworld activities while passing on choice tidbits about his colleagues from time to time. Furthermore, as was the case with every informant until Valachi, he discussed only specific individuals and crimes, never the Cosa Nostra itself. The idea, from his point of view, was that if he happened to be caught in one of his illegal operations, he could always claim that he was on an intelligence-

gathering mission or, if need be, fall back on his previous cooperation—and future potential—to escape punishment. For the law enforcement agency involved, an informer like Giannini always
represents a judgment decision: Is the intelligence he supplies
worth overlooking what he might be engaged in at a given
moment?

In 1950 Giannini had left for Europe with two projects in
hand. One was smuggling U.S. medical supplies like sulfa and peni-
cillin into Italy where they were in high demand in an economy
still struggling to recover from World War II. Another com-
modity in equally high demand at the time in both Italy and France
was U.S. currency, and Giannini did his best to satisfy it, although
his banknotes, of course, were counterfeit. He intended to use part
of the proceeds from these enterprises to finance the purchase of
heroin for distribution, and even bigger profits, back in America.
Toward this end, as he lived it up on the Continent with assorted
mistresses, Giannini made contact with Luciano in Naples and on
the side began tipping off the Narcotics Bureau about various aspects of the deported chieftain's traffic in drugs. Meanwhile, the
head of the bureau's European office, Charles Siragusa, began putting together from other sources a picture of Giannini's own elaborate smuggling plans, and the problem of what to do with the
prize informant was going to have to be faced fairly soon.

Then there was an unexpected development. The Italian
police suddenly arrested Giannini on charges of dealing in counterfeit dollars and tossed him in jail to await trial. He managed to
sneak out a letter to Siragusa, graphically describing the filth, heat,
flies, and bedbugs that featured his new surroundings, and demanded that the Narcotics Bureau arrange his release. At the same
time it was learned that Giannini was still plotting from his cell
to ship at least ten kilograms of heroin into the United States, so
the bureau decided to let him cool his heels for a while. In despera-
tion Giannini wrote another letter to Siragusa, specifically citing
the information he had passed on regarding Charlie Lucky. While
Valachi does not know how Luciano discovered that Giannini was
an informer, the Cosa Nostra has intelligence sources of its own,
and it is likely that this letter did him in.

Eventually Giannini went on trial on the counterfeiting
charges and, when the chief witness against him suddenly changed

his testimony, was acquitted for lack of evidence. Giannini then flew back to New York, where the Bureau of Narcotics kept him under close surveillance.

It was not long after this that Valachi had his meeting with Bender. Ordinarily Giannini would have been a matter for the Lucchese Family to handle, but as part of Genovese's continuing campaign to assert himself, he was, as Bender told Valachi, "anxious to throw the first punch," and the fact that Luciano was the injured party gave him the opening he needed.

Valachi had known Giannini for years. As a matter of fact, Giannini owed him money borrowed just before he had gone to Europe. It was precisely because of this debt, as it turned out, that Valachi was picked for the contract. When Bender told him that Giannini had to be eliminated, Valachi replied, "Well, there goes a couple of thousand that he owes me."

"Yes," Bender said. "I heard it was something like that. You know, Gene is just back from Italy, and he is moving around, and we can't seem to find him. If you hear anything, call me. Don't start thinking about trying to save that money."

The inference was clear, although Valachi went on with the game. "Can't find him?" he echoed.

"That's right. It could be Gene is on to something."

"Well, I'll find him. Does that satisfy you?"

"I will have to talk to the old man about that."

The next night Bender informed him that Genovese was quite pleased with the offer. "Finding" Giannini, in the euphemistic exchange that had taken place, meant killing him. As Valachi explained to me, "I got no choice. I have to volunteer for the contract. If I don't and something goes wrong, they can blame me because he owes me money and they can accuse me of tipping Gene off. That's why I answered Tony the way I did. If they can't find him, I will. Now you know how this Cosa Nostra is."

Valachi's next step was to locate Giannini. As he suspected, it was not very difficult. He simply telephoned him at home at about 10 P.M. Working on the assumption that Giannini would think he was calling about the loan, he spoke just long enough for his quarry to identify his voice and then said, "Meet me on the corner."

The "corner" he referred to was the intersection of Castle

Hill and Westchester Avenues in the Bronx near the Lido, a club Valachi owned. Apparently these directions were sufficient for Giannini. He replied, "I'll be over in twenty minutes."

Valachi waited in a doorway in the dark and watched Giannini drive up. Then he saw another car stop down the block. When Giannini started to say something about paying him back as soon as he had some cash, Valachi silenced him and hustled him into a bar on the corner. "Forget about the money," he said. "I think you got a tail. What do you have, agents following you?"

"Jeez, they must be watching you."

"Maybe they are," Valachi said diplomatically. "Let's pass it up for now. I'll give you a ring in a couple of days."

Giannini left the bar the way they had come in. Valachi waited for a moment and then used a side door. Standing in the shadow, he saw his suspicions confirmed; as Giannini drove off, the second car pulled out as well.

The Giannini contract was a classic instance of how the Cosa Nostra power structure removes itself from the actual commission of a crime. The impetus for the murder came from Luciano, who would be, of course, in Italy all the time. Genovese ordered it, but he would be nowhere near the scene when it happened. Nor would Tony Bender who transmitted the command. Even Valachi, who was responsible for carrying out the contract, would not be physically present. How it was to be done and whom he used was entirely up to him, and he selected three East Harlem "kids," as he called them, rising hoodlums who were in line for membership in the Genovese Family, for the actual execution. Two were brothers, Joseph and Pasquale (Pat) Pagano; the third was Valachi's own nephew, Fiore (Fury) Siano, the son of one of his sisters.

Always painstaking in an affair of this sort, the presence of agents from the Bureau of Narcotics made him infinitely more cautious. A few days after his abortive meeting with Giannini, he called him again and set up a rendezvous at another bar near the Lido, called the Casbah. Valachi brought along one of his three recruits for the job, Joseph Pagano, to, as he says, "kill two birds with one stone." The first reason was to enable Pagano to get a good look at his victim; the second to put Giannini at ease the next time he saw Pagano. There was also a third reason for the meeting. Valachi had purposely not suggested the Lido because he wanted to find out if Giannini was still being followed. Thus he and Pagano waited across the street as Giannini entered the bar, and once more he spotted a tail. Then Valachi and Pagano entered the bar separately. He introduced Pagano to Giannini and said, "Gee, Gene, every time I call you, you got somebody covering you."

Giannini expressed astonishment. "I'm glad you tipped me," he said. "I can't understand it."

"Ah, forget it. Let's have a drink."

The two men chatted on for a few minutes, Valachi asking him about his sojourn in Europe, when Giannini suddenly said, "Jesus, I had the creeps last night."

"What do you mean?" Valachi recalls saying.

"I don't know. It's hard to explain. I feel like I'm going to be killed."

"What are you talking about?" Valachi quickly said. "Why do you say a thing like that?"

"It's just the way I feel."

To break the mood, Valachi called over a girl in the bar who had once worked for him in the Lido, introduced Giannini to her as "my old pal," and bought another round of drinks. Then he drew Giannini aside and said, "Listen, you got to cheer up. Why don't you go out with her and have a good time?"

"Joe, I'm a little short. That's why I ain't paid you. I got a deal working, but I'm broke right now."

Valachi promptly handed Giannini $100. "Go ahead and enjoy yourself."

He stayed for another drink before telling Pagano, "Let's go." Giannini remained with the girl when they left. As they walked to Valachi's car, Pagano said, "I can't get over it, the way he was saying he was going to get hit. Well, it must be true he's talking. Twice you call him, and twice he has a tail."

After making certain that he was not being followed, Valachi dropped Pagano off in East Harlem. The next afternoon he contacted the girl he had left with Giannini and learned from her that the condemned man had mentioned something about a "game" in Harlem. Valachi passed this intelligence on to the Paganos and Siano. A few days later one of them—he thinks it was Joseph Pagano—reported back that Giannini was working "at a drop" on Second Avenue for a dice game around the corner on East 112th Street. "I'll explain what working 'at a drop' means," Valachi notes. "The crapshooters go to this place, which is the drop, before they go to the game. In other words, the game was about half a block away. The fellow who is working the drop looks over the players, and if he sees they are okay, he escorts them to the game at such-and-such address or such-and-such room in a hotel."

Upon receiving this information, Valachi immediately asked, "What about the agents?"

"We didn't see any. He must have beefed about it or something."

"Okay, that's what we have to know."

There was, however, a further complication when Valachi discovered that it was a Cosa Nostra dice game run by a member of the Lucchese Family, Paul (Paulie Ham) Correale. He had previously sent Pagano to Greenwich Village to pick up the guns for the killing from Tony Bender. Now he had to resolve the matter of the site. He found his lieutenant at an after-hours place, the Gold Key Club in midtown Manhattan, which, according to Valachi, was owned by Bender. Since the Gold Key Club was often under police surveillance, Valachi took his usual precautions in going there, parking his car some distance away and switching to a cab to avoid having his license number noted.

Before he could speak, Bender snapped, "What the hell's the holdup? Let's get this thing over with. I hope you're not trying to save your money."

"Tony, listen to me," Valachi protested, "there have been junk agents all over this guy." Then he brought up the problem of the drop. "The game belongs to Paulie Ham," he said. "Is it okay to get Gene there?"

"Well, you're right about this. I'll have to talk to the old man. I will make sure. Call me up here tomorrow night. You don't have to come down. Just call me up, and I will have an answer for you."

Valachi telephoned as directed, and Bender said, "It's okay."

For Giannini now, despite all of Valachi's machinations, time was running out. He would get one small reprieve. Valachi's plan for the assassination was to have one man stationed in a getaway car on 111th Street, a block south of the game. The other two, after completing their mission, were to cut through one tenement on 112th Street, exit out of another building facing 111th Street and into the car. On the night of September 18, 1952, Valachi rode with the Pagano brothers and Siano to inspect the area. Everything seemed set. Giannini was standing on the sidewalk in front of the drop, and no agents could be found in the immediate area. Then, just as he was about to leave them, Valachi recalls asking Pat Pagano if he had made certain that there were no locked doors barring the escape route.

"No, I—"

"That's it," Valachi broke in angrily. "Go home and sleep. Check those halls tomorrow. What's the matter with you kids? Are you crazy? You ain't doing a thing until you're sure. I'm responsible for this."

The next afternoon, assured that this final safety measure had been taken, Valachi gave the go-ahead. He told Siano that he would be waiting for news of what happened at a restaurant on 114th Street and Second Avenue. In telephoning him, he added, Giannini was to be referred to as a girl. Then he reminded Siano that as soon as the shooting was finished, the pistols were to be dropped into the East River off the Third Avenue Bridge.

Valachi, to fix his own alibi, arranged to have dinner with three friends in the restaurant. Around midnight, Siano telephoned and said, "The girl hasn't shown up yet."

"Okay, I'm going up to my place."

Valachi then asked his dinner companions to drive him to the Lido. There, around 4 A.M., as he remembers, he received another call. It was all over. "We saw her," Siano said. "We're going on a trip for a couple of days."

"Fine," Valachi replied and went home to bed.

(New York City police records show that at 6 A.M. on September 20, 1952, the body of Eugenio Giannini, age forty-two, of 282 West 234th Street, was found in the gutter in front of 221 East 107th Street. The cause of death was gunshot wounds in the head by persons unknown. Further investigation indicated that the shooting actually took place on Second Avenue near East 112th Street. The deceased had narcotics arrests both for violation of state and federal laws, and it was learned through confidential sources that he had been an informant for the Federal Bureau of Narcotics.)

At the time the Narcotics Bureau believed that Giannini had been slain not because he was an informant, but because he had tried to bilk his associates out of most of their share of the heroin he was then engaged in smuggling into the country. There was some justification for this. According to the bureau's information, ten kilos were involved in the transaction. Undercover agents discovered, during the course of their investigation, that Giannini had quietly dispatched his brother-in-law to Italy to bring in six kilos on his own. This led to the brother-in-law's arrest in Salerno with the heroin in hand about a month before Giannini was murdered.

Once it had been established that the victim had been taken to 107th Street after being shot, there also was conjecture in the Bureau of Narcotics that this was simply a neat symbolic gesture since, until Valachi pieced together the organization of the Cosa Nostra, what would become known as the Lucchese Family was called the East 107th Street Mob.

Valachi was as curious about the body being removed. The first he heard about it was over the radio when he woke up that morning. The reason for it was not quite so esoteric, and for a while it appeared to an outraged Valachi that he was headed for another table as a result.

"The guys running the game," Genovese told him a few days later, "claim they had to move the body to save it. They are pretty mad. They say it cost ten grand to pay off the cops."

For a moment Valachi thought that Bender had not cleared the site of the killing, but Genovese confirmed that he had given his approval. "I just want to find out what this is all about," he said. "So find out."

Valachi reported back to Genovese full of righteous indignation. "You know those guys that said they took Gene out of the neighborhood to throw the heat off the game? Well, they're lying."

"What do you mean?"

"There were a couple of boys working at the drop with Gene. When they found him, they thought he still had a chance. They were rushing him to the hospital!"

"Is that the way to the hospital?"

"Of course it is," Valachi said. "You don't know the neighborhood like I do. They are going to Fifth Avenue Hospital. (Actually Flower and Fifth Avenue Hospital, located at 106th Street and Fifth Avenue.) They have to drive down Second Avenue, and naturally they turn at 107th, as it's a westbound street and it takes them right to the hospital. On the way they realize Gene is dead, and they dump him off. Now they want to play heroes. They want everyone to think they knew Gene was dead and they took a chance being caught just to get his body away from the crap game. I won't go for it. Every time I'm told to do something, it's a mess, and I'm in the middle."

"Where did you get this from?"

"From the kids, Fiore and the Paganos."

"Well, don't worry, I'll take care of it."

With all of his old mistrust of Genovese flaring up again, Valachi decided to take no chance. He buttonholed Thomas Lucchese, Giannini's Family boss, at "somebody's wake" soon afterward and said, "Tommy, a lot of your boys are acting cold to me about this. I don't care how they feel, but you and me go back a long way. I want to know how you feel. Do you think I went crazy and did it myself without orders?"

"Forget about it," Lucchese said. "Everything is fine. It wasn't your fault. The guy got what he deserved."

(One of the three men Valachi says he used in the Giannini murder, his nephew, Fiore Siano, suddenly vanished about nine months after it became known that he was talking. According to intelligence gathered by the New York City police, "Siano disappeared about the end of April or the beginning of May, 1964. He has not been seen since three unknown males took him out of Patsy's Pizzeria, 2287 First Avenue, during the aforementioned period. Siano is believed dead. The rumor is that his body was disposed of in such a manner as to prevent it from being discovered." Siano liked to shoot pool, and I spoke to one of the players in the last game he was known to have been in. In what is certainly the understatement of the year, the player recalls, "Fiore seemed moody, like he had something on his mind." Of the Pagano brothers, Joseph was sentenced to five years in 1965 for his part in what was described as a classic case of Cosa Nostra infiltration of a legitimate business; Pasquale Pagano, characterized by the Bureau of Narcotics as an "up-and-coming" underworld figure, has been in and out of prison and is currently at liberty. Valachi's testimony against them, without corroboration, is legally insufficient. Indeed, the Giannini murder illustrates the near impossibility of the successful prosecution of a gangland slaying. The police were called immediately after the shooting, but nobody saw anything. An elderly janitor was found cleaning the sidewalk. When a bloodstain still on the pavement was pointed out to him, he said, "Blood?")

2
The Hit

JAMES MILLS

The body is that of a middle-aged white man, 5'9" tall, scale weight not yet determined. There is a heavy rope ligature looped around the neck. The wrists are tied together with an intricate series of turns of a yellow woven plastic cord which also encircles the abdomen. [*In the New York City morgue, the medical examiner stands over the body of a man found floating in shallow water at a Queens County beach. . . . As he examines the body, he dictates his findings to a stenographer.*] There is also a rope around the abdomen tied with several knots, and this yellow cord passes through it. The rope projecting from the abdominal ligature is a heavy triple-stranded one, and to one end of this was tied two concrete blocks, which are also tied together with similar heavy rope and yellow cord and chain. . . .

I identified him in the morgue. Identified him! I couldn't *even* identify him. It was just—like a skeleton with some stuff on it. [*Willie Rupolo, a bookie, talks about his brother Ernie, who had been a Mafia gunman and professional killer before his body was found on the beach.*] I told them, "To tell you it's my brother, I can't. Not the way he looks. Not what you're showing me. When I saw him he had the cinder blocks on him. And the rope around. I can't understand it. That's an awful thing. That's what I can't see, why they had to do it like that. It's not even a clean knockoff.

33

It's, I don't know, savages. Shot him, stabbed him, I can't understand it. To kill him, that's one thing. But not like that. Not only me, but even the others in the underworld, his own friends, they can't figure it. If you live by the gun, you die by the gun. But do it right. Wait outside his home or something and hit him when he comes out, but not like they did it. If you want to get rid of him, hit him clean. Like get him in a car, hit him, and throw him out of the car. What's all this here rigamajig? I don't know if they saw television, or what."

. . . The iron chain, fairly heavy, is at present rusted and covered with sand, as is the body. This chain is also attached to the ankles. There is a considerable amount of mud and sand, still moist, on the body and in the clothes, and also some broken mollusk shells. . . .

He was brought up by his mother to be another Al Capone. He'd come home and give his mother money, and she knew it had to be from something bad, and that pleased her. Because she was always after him to be another Al Capone. [*Harold Fox, a retired New York City detective, knew the dead man and calls him by his underworld nickname, The Hawk.*] I said to him, Hawk, you come from good people, how'd you ever get mixed up in this? And he said, his mother, she told him he could be another Al Capone. The Capones had lots of money. He'd come here from Chicago, and he had lots of money. The mother knew people he gave money to, and he'd say how he left Brooklyn and became a bigshot in Chicago. She figured if Al Capone could do it, why couldn't her son do it?

Ernie had dreams, you know, that someday he was gonna be the head of the Mafia. And I says, "You couldn't! You can't tell *me* what to do. How're you going to tell anyone else what to do?" That was my answer. [*Eleanor Cordero, the dead man's common-law wife for the six and a half years before his murder, talks to friends.*] And he'd say to me, "You don't know what you're talking about. If it wasn't for me, they'd kill you." Because like I hated his friends. They were ready to shoot me on sight any time they ever saw me because I couldn't stand any one of them. He'd bring them up to dinner, you know, parties and dinners and this and that. I didn't want them in my house.

I told Ernie, "The only reason they hang around is because you're a good-time Charlie, and if you weren't buying them drinks and dinner and everything else, you wouldn't even see them. They haven't got two dimes to rub together so they're kissing your ass. Roy Roy and Butch and all those other bastards."

Ernie used to tell me, "But they're my friends. They'd lay down their lives for me."

And I said, "The only thing they'd do for you is kill you."

. . . The yellow cord is tied around the right shoe and ankle. There are also several loops of heavy chain. . . .

So I couldn't even identify my brother. I explained to them that for me to make a positive identification would be hard, that there was a doubt, because what I really saw was—well, you couldn't tell if it was a human being or what. So I gave them information about a mesh in his stomach, that he had an operation for a hernia and there was a mesh screen in his stomach. And I told them, you'll find a bullet in him because he's been walking around with a bullet in him for years and years, and they could never take a chance of trying to take that bullet out.

And I identified the shoes he wore, and the pants. I can't miss them, those were my pants. That day he was wearing my clothes. The zipper was broken on his pants. He was in my store, a real hot muggy day. He went to the bathroom and he must have pulled the zipper and he came out and he says, "I broke the zipper, now how can I walk around?"

And I says, "Sit down, my wife'll be here in a minute. She'll fix it. Or take a pair of my pants, a pair of my slacks." And I says, "Don't worry about it." Because every time he had a fight with his wife Eleanor and he needed to sleep some place he used to ring my bell, three and four in the morning, and he'd say, "I want to sleep here."

And I'd say, "Go ahead, brother." Because he wouldn't go to no other brother, but he'd come to me. Then when he made up he'd go back. So a lot of times, he'd be wearing my socks or my shoes.

That day he's there in my store and he's got Roy Roy with him and he says to Roy Roy, "I gotta go to my brother's house and change my pants." And Roy Roy drove him to my house with me following in the Caddy. They come upstairs and I gave him a pair of my slacks and a sport shirt. He was broke so I gave him $20. I'll never forget it. I took $20 out of the register in the store. I says, "Here, put this in your pocket." And then when he got found in the river, he had $50 on him.

So when they were leaving, Roy Roy invited me to come with them for a drink at the Coco Poodle, and I says no I was too tired and that I'd have to make it some other night.

And that was the last I saw of him, when he left with Roy Roy. I never saw him again. That's the last I saw my brother. The next day I waited for my brother. I don't see him. I don't see the kid no more.

. . . There is evidence of an old hernia operation with the presence of a small fragment of recognizable tantalum mesh and some black sutures. There is a pair of trousers, extensively torn, with a leather belt now pulled down to the left knee and leg. The fabric is ripped. The zipper is partly open. On removing the shoes and socks, the epidermis of the feet, which is macerated, comes away with the socks. . . .

When I was about 10, in school in Brooklyn, I liked the teacher, I was her pet, and I schemed up something that I could annoy her, to make her pay attention more to me. [*Some years before his murder, The Hawk sat with Detective Fox and talked into a tape recorder about his past crimes.*] And what I did scheme was I looked up her name in the phone book and I started to call her up at night. I called her up night after night, and every time a different story about what had happened to a pupil in school, where he got run over or he's sick. And she would get grief over it and say, "Who is this calling?" Well, I never told her who was calling, but one day the call was traced and I was caught in the phone booth by two detectives, and they took me to the station house where they made me face the teacher. And she was shocked to know it was me. And I couldn't face her. I was ashamed. I was brought to court, she had signed a complaint, and I was given six weeks in the New York Catholic Protectory in the Bronx.

And then I went back to school, and the teacher told me that she was sorry she had to sign the complaint, that she didn't know that it was gonna be me. And I said I was sorry for what I did, I was punished for it, and that's all.

And I stood in school awhile and then when I was 12 I had in mind to get out of school. I schemed for my birth certificate to be forged. I erased my date of birth, I made myself 15 years old, and I brought it to the school, brought it to the board of health, and the school fell for it, and the board of health fell for it, and I got my working papers and got out of school. I got out of school and I started what I always wanted to do, a career of crime.

I started by burglarizing. We called it the bucket racket, myself and one other boy about 18. What we used to do is ring a bell, and if a woman came out we'd have a car outside and we'd say, "Can we have a bucket of water, the car's steaming." And if nobody answered the bell, we'd break in. We'd ransack the house, go for the bedrooms, jewelry, money. The jewelry, we'd get rid of it, take it to a pawnshop or sell it to people out on the street that we knew. I was 12. We did about seventy-five or a hundred burglaries. Then I was arrested, me and this other fella. Then I was 13, but I told them I was 16 and they believed me. I got a suspended sentence of three years.

So I kept on burglarizing. There were three of us now. I was arrested again, coming out of a house. We were all shot at by detectives, caught red-handed. I was sentenced to one day to three years in the New York City reformatory. I was still 13. I did ten months. Then I went out, and this time I went on with crime, but no burglaries. I did robberies with three other fellas, older than me. I bought a gun off another hoodlum. I was 14.

One day we were given chase by two cops in a radio car. While they were chasing us, we threw the guns out of the car. They got up to us, stopped us, searched us, and took us in. I was held for violation of parole and went back for another eight months.

Then I went back to the neighborhood. I was out a couple of weeks, and I got a letter from my brother, that he was in trouble, to go and see him at Raymond Street jail. He was in trouble for robbery. He asked me to help him out, to go to New York [*Manhattan*] and get in touch with these fellas that he associated with, to join them, to join their oufit, to help my brother, join them in what they were doing, committing robberies. I went to New York, I joined them, and any robbery we did I put my share on the side for my brother, to help him with his lawyer. So what happened was that my brother received five to ten years in state prison, and I was shot, which I almost died.

When I used to go out with these fellas, one of the fellas was taking a share out for a girl he was living with at this apartment. There were four of us. He wanted to put the girl in for a share. And he did put her in a few times. So I had an argument with him. I told him I wouldn't take it from him. I called him names. So I was going on and on and he told me to shut up, "Or I'll shoot you right in the head." And I told him, foolishly, that he hadn't got the guts enough to shoot me in the head.

Well, the first thing you knew, I was shot. As I'm falling down, the girl started screaming, the other two fellas scrambled out, and this fella told the girl, "Let's throw him out the window." So she hollered, "No," and that's all I could remember.

So I hated Ernie's friends, but he always said, "No, Eleanor, you're wrong, you're wrong." I told him all they'd do was hurt him. Like when his eye was shot out. His version to me about how he lost his eye, they were in a hotel, and he was with some people, and somebody was bothering somebody else's girl, and he told the guy not to bother her. And the guy says to him, "Shut up. Mind your own business or I'll let you have it." And Ernie says, "You punk, I wouldn't care what you did." And the guy turned around and he opened a drawer and he took a .45 out and shot him. And he falls over the table, and the last thing he remembered the radio was playing "My Blue Heaven" and they said, "Let's throw him out the window." Ernie told me, "I wasn't even dead and I hear these guys saying, 'Let's throw him out the window.' They didn't kill me by shooting me so they're gonna throw me out the window."

After my brother lost his eye, and his face was disfigured, he didn't care for his life anymore. That's what really turned the kid. When he looked at himself in the mirror—and before he was a real good-looking kid—he just went berserk. He went berserk. And the smart guys who was coming up, they knew that this kid is going to be a good kid for us to use, in other words that's what

I call it, to use him, so we'll put him on the payroll, and give him this, and make him stop this here stealing or anything like that, and he became under their wing. Because when he had both his eyes he was doing a lot of robberies, and that's how he got the name "The Hawk." He never missed anything. He had eyes like a hawk. So they made him stop the stealing and they gave him contracts. And that's all he did after that. He was just a hit man, since he was 16.

. . . Examination of the head discloses considerable maceration and separation and loss of the skin of the nose, with fracture of the nasal bones. The right eyeball is absent, and the socket is scarred. . . .

Ernie used to call me, "My Heaven." He'd call me on the phone, "What are you doing, My Heaven?"

"Nothing."

"All right," he'd say, and he'd call and call and call. He was always calling up. He'd leave to go to Brooklyn and he'd call up from the station, he'd call up when he got to Brooklyn, he'd call up when he reached the bar he was at, he'd call up at least ten times a day.

On Sundays he'd be home and he'd baby-sit and I'd go antique-hunting all day with my niece. You know, we'd go driving around. He would give me the world if he had it. If he went to the *moon*, he'd come back and say, "What are you doing?" I would throw him out and say, "That is it, this is the end!" I would move away from him, right? And two days later, there he'd be. I would move, I would disgrace him, embarrass him. He'd be having dinner with people and I'd walk in, "Give me money and get out of my life." You know—insult him, degrade him. And he would always be there.

. . . When the scalp is examined there are two entrance bullet wounds found on the right posterior parietal region. More posteriorly there is a third bullet perforation, an exit wound. The brain tissue, which is liquefied and pultaceous and green in color, oozes through this large exit wound, and during the manipulation of the head a tarnished, 380 metal-jacketed bullet emerged from this hole with liquefied brain. . . .

I was shot right in the eye. When I gain consciousness in the hospital I seen this fella that shot me and a girl brought in front of me with a squad of detectives, and they told me, "Here's the fella that shot you. We know he did it, now tell us yourself."

I said, "I don't know him and I don't know the girl. Leave me alone." I didn't want to get revenge on him that way. I figured if I recuperate, I'll take care of him myself.

So when I got out I looked for him, but I couldn't catch up with him, and later every time I was out of jail, he was in jail. Every time I was in jail, he was out.

Then after a while I had an opportunity to meet one of the two fellas that was in the room and ran out and left me when I was shot. And they was supposed to be friends of mine. I never forgot that. I met him in a hangout, playing dice. I got alongside of him, and I started gambling against him. He told me, he says, "Don't bet the way you're betting. It's foolish. I'm going to take your money."

I says, "There's no friendship in gambling. If you take my money, you take it." Which he did.

So when I lost my money, I went downstairs from the hangout and I went down in the cellar where I used to have guns hid down there. I took one gun, went back to the hangout where the dice game was, and I stuck up the game. I told the fellas in there that it's not meant for them, that it's meant for the fella in the corner. Well, they were satisfied to hear that. So I asked him, I said, "I want all your money and make sure you produce it." Well, at first he didn't give it to me, he says no. I says, "I'll count three. If you don't give it to me by three I'm going to shoot you in the leg, and the second shot, you ain't gonna feel it."

So I count three, and he didn't produce the money, so I shot him between the legs. But I didn't hit his legs, I grazed them. When I did that, he took his money out of his pockets, put it with the money he had in his hands, and he give it to me and he pleaded with me, "Don't shoot me, don't shoot me no more." And that was that. I went downstairs, put the gun away, and went across the street in the poolroom and stood around.

The Hawk was a fella you couldn't help like. He had a helluva personality. You'd never have known that he was the bastard he was. Even though I was a detective, he used to talk to me a lot, and he was very sincere. But he wanted to be a bigshot. When he did something he'd go to his mother to give her some of the money to show he amounted to something. And then he'd go to his wife—that was his first wife, not Eleanor—and she'd say, "What's wrong? What happened?" and he'd say, "I just put a slug in someone." And she'd put cold towels on his head and settle him down and put him to bed.

People used to tell me, "Eleanor, I don't know how you get away with it. I've seen that guy *kill* people for less than that, the way you talk to him."

And I'd say, why that son of a bitch couldn't fight his way out of a paper bag. Because this was the way he treated *me*, but he could *terrify* anyone else. And I could never believe that he could terrify anybody else, because I'd walk in and give him a smack and that would be the end of it.

Like I'm sitting in this bar once, and I'm sitting there, and I'm drinking. I'm drinking with one of *his* girl friends, I want you to know. But she's not supposed to be his girl friend. She's *my* friend now. I've got the money on the bar, so she's my friend now. And I say, "That son of a bitch, he'll never leave me alone. I can't stand it anymore." And now it's getting late—two, three in the morning.

And so all of a sudden she says to me, "He's here!"

And I says, "So what, he'll never kill me because when he kills me then he hasn't got me anymore, right? Don't worry about it."

So that bar emptied out like in two seconds flat, and he comes in. And he puts a gun right in my back, and he says, "Are you coming home?"

And I says, "No," and I was drunk. "I'm not coming," I says. "And if you don't take that gun out of my back I'm gonna take this glass and I'm gonna smash your *other* eye out."

And he says, "You're very brave, aren't you?"

And I says, "You're damned right. A punk like you, I could wipe the floor up with you any time."

And he says, "I'll get you when you come home."

"Leave me alone!" I says. "Get out!"

And he says, "I'll get you when you come home."

I says, "And I'm coming home with a whole frigging army." I says, "I'm calling Mr. Nits."

Now at this time Mr. Nits, this cop, was out to get Ernie for bookmaking. So Ernie says, "Yeah. That's something you would do."

I says, "So you know I'm gonna do it, so shut up and get out of here."

And he left. And the whole bar left, and I was there alone. All these good people, these stand-up guys. Let there be a little trouble, they all disappear.

And now I go parading home, and I walk in the house and he's there. I says, "So? What do you want now?"

He says, "You think you can get away with all this?"

I says, "Look, kill me. After I'm dead go aggravate somebody else. Because my life isn't worth living anyway."

I mean these scenes were like commonplace. We'd fight, I'd kick him out, and then he'd call with stories, you know, and I used to feel sorry for him and I'd say, "All right, come on home," and I'd go and I'd get him wherever he was and bring him back home.

After I stuck up the guy in the dice game, I joined this outlaw outfit, fellas that were against the racketeers, that knew that the bigshots and racketeers had everything sewed up, that would take money off different people. So we figured we'd take it off them, off the racketeers. We'd stick them up.

And there was a funny thing happened one time. This one guy was known as a top hoodlum, a very tough guy, very respected and all that. I and another fella cornered him in a hallway one day. We got $800, $900 from him. It took us exactly two or three seconds at the most. And during that time we had a laugh because he lost control of himself. What I mean is self-control.

We got called on the carpet many a time. We were warned, by the top men. They'd tell us to lay off what we were doing. But we'd deny it, and we always told them, "You don't know what you're talking about." Because we all—five of us—used masks, and they weren't so sure it was us. We felt very bitter toward them, because anything you tried to do, they would come over and say, "That's *my* spot. This is *my* store. Don't touch *that* fella. Don't touch *this* bookmaker." You couldn't do nothin'.

My brother was a hit man for them. And they were afraid of him. They figured if they were gonna hit *him*, they'd better do a good job. You know, that's the reputation the kid had. That's why the kid kept walking around. And then the kid was good. I mean the only time he went bad was goin' to people he shouldn't of gone to, grabbin' people by the throat, takin' money off them.

Like he walked in behind a bar, Dino's Bar,. and he asked for money and got refused. He went behind the bar, he took the money out of the register, gave everybody drinks. That's the type of guy he was. "If you don't wanna give me no money, I'll take it."

In the later years he was not a thief, he'd just grab you for your money. In other words, he didn't go out on stickups, he didn't go out on burglaries, he just, "I'll get my money, I'll walk into this guy and I'll get my money." He'd go to a bookmaker, put a pistol to his head, "I want a thousand." He'd go into a shy, he knew the guy was shying, that he had money, and "I want $5,000." That's the type of kid he was, "I want $5,000 or you don't operate." So he'd bring a couple of hoods with him, and he'd make sure he got the $5,000. So he always got the money.

But he knew it couldn't go on like that forever. He knew he was gonna get hit sooner or later. He used to tell me when he got drunk. He'd say, "You know, Willie, I'm living on borrowed time. How much more do you think I can go around takin' people, takin' people, takin' people?"

. . . The entrance of the bullet which popped out of the scalp is the mouth. The bullet, in penetrating the mouth, grazes the tongue and produces a rather deep furrow. The track then continues backward and upward through the base of the skull. . . .

It sounds ridiculous, but it really was like this, back and forth, six, seven times a year he'd move in and out. One time I put all his clothes down the incinerator. I said, "I quit. I don't care if you walk around with your ass hanging out. Don't come back."

And he would come back. His brother Willie said one time, "Eleanor, if he knew that you were going to hit him over the head with an ax when he walked through that door, he'd walk through the door anyway, as long as it was *you* hit him over the head with the ax."

One time he's not living with me again and he runs into some guy who says he had a couple of drinks with me. And now he comes home, he's going to *murder* me! This is it. He's killing me now. And a friend came home with him. So his friend told me later they had gone into the kitchen, he got a big kitchen knife, and he was gonna cut me up to ribbons.

So anyway I went to bed. You know, like he's telling me he's going to kill me, he's going to murder me, and I says, "Oh, yeah? Go frig you, too." And I'm getting undressed and I'm going to bed because he's telling me this all the time. So I'm lying in bed and I'm going to sleep. I'm *tired*, right?

I hear something going on outside, but I don't know what's going on out there. I don't even care. I'm just going to sleep. But he comes in and says he's gonna give me a beating. For some reason he forgot about the knife. He picks up the coffee table and he comes *charging* into the bedroom and—CRASH!

I says, "*Now* you've had it." I says, "I've been waiting five years for you to put a finger on me. That's *it*."

I pick up the phone next to the bed, dial operator. "*I'm getting murdered!*" I scream at the operator. So I get connected with the police, the 66th precinct. I say, "*This son of a bitch is killing me!*" I says, "*Hurry up!*" I says, "*I'll be dead before you get here!*"

Now they come charging over, up the fire escape and everything else, and now they've got him, right?

And I says, "I don't care *what* you do." I says, "*Look* at this, look what he did to my leg, look at this." I says, "He's gonna *die* for this. That did it. Get him out. I don't care *where* he goes, just get him out of here."

They took him down in the elevator and off he went. They let him go. So Ernie took it on the lam for a couple of days. And now I have him. He hit me, right? And, oh, how the presents start coming, and, oh, I really had it made then. He came with hundred-dollar bills, "Honey, buy yourself something." *Nothing* was too good for me.

. . . There is also a bullet perforation with macerated edges on the anterior surface of the neck below the chin on the left side. This bullet also is a 380 deformed missile, and drops out of a segment of the spinal canal. . . .

So we were very bitter about the bigshots and we kept on taking money from them, and this went on several months. And then one day I'm in a poolroom and a squad of detectives come down and arrest me for a robbery. I didn't really know what they were talking about until I got in·the station house. And the tipster of that robbery was there and he says, "That's the man."

So really the tipster didn't know that I really didn't take part in that robbery. I was supposed to go, and he always thought I went on the robbery, but I didn't go. But I was given a share of the loot, for friendship's sake. I wasn't worried about anything because I wasn't identified by the people who were stuck up, but I laid in Raymond Street jail almost nine months.

One of the fellas that had done a little talking himself but admitted that I was not on the stickup, but that I was supposed to go, that I was given an even share of the money, came down to me when we were in jail and told me that the tipster was the one that did all the talking, and that he'll take care of him.

I said, "I don't care what you do, you're just as bad as him." So they took care of the tipster. They cut him up in jail. He got twenty-seven stitches on his face. He's still disfigured to this day.

Then I got a contract by an organization to put two fellas on the spot, two hoodlums [*Willie Gallo and Ferdinand "The Shadow" Boccia*]. But I refused the job. I told them, I says, "I wouldn't put no one on the spot for you people. If there's any killing to do, I'll take the contract myself. I will kill them myself."

You see, puttin' a fella on the spot, a hoodlum, it isn't something that you'll be well-liked by the underworld. It's somethin' really low, when you put somebody on the spot. And any men that would put their own kind on the spot—I'm talking about hoodlums—not many of them are living today who put the finger on them, because they themselves are destroyed, because you did a thing like that.

So I got the contract to kill them. And there was another fella with me in on the contract. The contract went on for a few months. It was well planned. Nothing could go wrong. There was plenty of time and plenty of money involved. I had one of the fellas that was going to die most of the time, sometimes I had the two of them. And lots of times they were lucky, that they missed by inches. Something would go wrong. You know how that is.

Well, the time finally came that everything was clear. I had one of the fellas [*Willie Gallo*] that was gonna die with me, and the other fella that was gonna do the killing with me. We gave this fella a dinner, we drank, a woman—in other words we gave him a good time. When the party was all over we knew what we were gonna do. We walked out, we drove to a certain block, I took a gun out of my pocket, I put it to this fella's head, and I keep firing and it don't go off.

So the fella told me, "What are you doin'?"

I says, "Well, I'm only kidding you."

"Kidding!" he says.

"That's all I was doin'," I told him.

Well, he was a little drunk, he thought that probably I *was* kidding.

He says, "The way you're marked? You carrying a gun with you? Put it away."

Well, I was going to ask to go and put the gun away anyway, and I'd be right back, but not really to put it away, to put some oil on the gun. Which I did. And I tried out the gun, and it went off. And I went back to where my partner and him were waiting for me, and I says, "Okay, I put the gun away." I told him, "Let's go a few blocks. We're going to meet a certain party." He okayed it. He says all right. He was wobbling a little bit from the liquor.

So when we got to this certain spot, I let it go off. So between I and my partner, we gave him seven shots. We thought he was dead. The only thing he said was, "Oh, Mom," and that's all. We figured we left him for dead.

Well, we went to sleep for a couple of hours and the next day we went down to see this organization where they were at. Well, they didn't like the idea, that the fella had lived. They knew the other thing was taken care of, the other fella was killed, a few hours before this one was shot. Well, they did a little yelling because it was done wrong, but we just listened.

Then they sent us to some of their people in another state. We were there for a while, and my friend that was with me was afraid. He figured that we didn't do it right, that we were gonna get killed in that state. I told him, "No, they wouldn't kill us. What do you think that for?" Well, the next day I was taken to a doctor, to be operated on for my eye, to get a glass eye put in. And after the operation, which didn't work anyway, I went back to where we were hiding, and that night my friend told me, "I'm sorry, I have to leave you alone." He says, "I'm going home, back to the neighborhood." He says, "I don't trust these people."

I says, "Wait till I get better. I'll come with you. Don't leave me this way."

What really had got him scared is when we were alone in the hideout he happened to open up a closet and he seen machine guns, shotguns, and pistols layin' around there like nothin', and that made him scared.

So he really did what I didn't expect him to do. He really left me alone. So if there was anybody to be killed there, I would have been killed alone. So I was there after that two weeks. All I did was ate, drank, and had a good time up in the hideout.

And then I was sent back to New York. I was given information that the fella I shot talked on me and my partner, told everything he knew, that we shot him. And that he's living yet, that he's still in the Kings County Hospital, still in serious condition. They told me that they'll take care of it, to come back, that they'll take care of things.

But before I went to New York, I went to Brooklyn. And when I got there I met a fella, the same fella I caught in a dice game. The same fella that was in the room when I got shot. The same fella that I shot in the dice game.

He came over to me, he shook hands with me, and he says, "I'm sorry for what happened, let's be friends."

I said, "It's all right with me."

He says, "Where are you going now?"

I says, "I'm going to New York."

He was the only person that knew I was going to New York, beside the organization. Well, I took the train and I went to New York. I got off at Canal Street. When I got upstairs, it was no coincidence, there was a squad of detectives waiting for me, just turning the corner. And they grabbed me and threw me right in the car.

I was brought in front of the man I shot in Kings County Hospital. He identified me. The detectives told me he had made a death-bed statement, and "You're just lucky he's living yet. We don't know if he'll still live."

He wanted to talk to me.

He asked me, "Why did you shoot me?"

I told him, I said, "Why did you talk on me?"

He said, "But that ain't the question I'm asking."

I says, "What's the difference what I shot you for? You could of got revenge later on, instead of talking, saying that I shot you."

Now the reason for that was this, that he was no lily himself. He was a gunman himself. He held a gun in his hand many a time.

Ernie would get up in the morning—I never got up one day in six and a half years before twelve o'clock—Ernie would get up in the morning, shut the bedroom door, change the baby, wash the baby, get Ellen's lunch, then he'd get Ellen's breakfast ready, do everything, wash the floors, clean the house, make my coffee, and knock on the door.

"It's twelve o'clock, honey. Do you want to get up?" He'd come in, stroke my hair, and say, "Do you want to get up?"

And I'd get up and I'd drag myself to the kitchen table, and I'd say, "Ohhhh, I'm so tired." Because I would of been up all night waiting for him to come home. He never really told me too much about what he was doing. I mean he wouldn't tell me anything to make me nervous or worried or anything like that. He'd come home, he'd say, "There was trouble tonight," or this happened or that happened, and I'd listen with one ear. I knew he was bookmaking, and he shylocked for a while. And this son of a bitch ran off with the money. That was another episode. This Fat Nick. I used to tell Ernie, "This bastard's gonna run away with your money."

And he says, "Oh, he wouldn't dare do that. He's afraid of me."

And I said, "You wait and see. This is the man who's gonna run away with your money." And he did. He really did. He ran away with the money. He *loved* wine, women, and song. His nickname was King Farouk, because he liked to live like King Farouk. He was a big fat thing. And I didn't trust him as far as you could see. And I used to tell Ernie, "He's gonna run away with your money." And sure enough he did.

This guy that was a gunman himself, that was supposed to be a tough guy—well, he says that he's not going to identify me in court. But he lied. He did identify me in magistrate court, and I was held for the grand jury.

While I was waiting trial in Raymond Street jail, I had a lawyer hired by the organization. He came over to see me in jail, and he told me not to worry about nothin', that everything would be fixed up, just to take it easy. Well, I was there about two months. And then I was brought to trial, and before my trial started the judge talked to me in his chambers with my lawyer and with my partner, and he told me, "If I was you, I wouldn't gamble on this case. If you take a plea of assault in the second unarmed I will give you two and a half to five years."

Well, I just listened and then my lawyer grabbed me on the side, and he says, "Don't take no plea. Everything is fixed up. You're going out this afternoon."

So I told the judge, "No, your honor. I want to stand trial. I'm innocent."

"Well," he says to me, he says, "once that trial starts there's nobody gonna stop it. Remember that."

Well, he kept his word. The trial started, the man I shot got on the stand, and he *buried* me. He told the truth, how I shot him, and everything. So I was found guilty of assault in the first degree. I was found guilty in five minutes by the jury. The judge gave me and my partner ten to twenty years in state prison.

So we went back to Raymond Street jail, waiting to get transferred to state prison. While we were waiting, we were called again to go back to court for resentencing. Well, during that time we were told that they're gonna try and fix up that we get a light sentence. So we believed it. And when they took us back to court, the judge told us, "The reason I got you back for resentencing was that your counsel was not present when I sentenced you the other day, and that's illegal according to law, so for that I'm gonna take one year off. I'm giving you nine to twenty years."

So I was sent to state prison, and the same baloney used to go on. We used to get word not to worry, that when a different governor comes in we'll be out. All that, you know. Years go by and by and you still live on hope. And live on their baloney stories that they give you.

And many a night I would stay up, and think what really went on, and how foolish I was. Sometimes I would look in the mirror and look at myself, and that was part of my crime career, by looking in the mirror and seeing the way I was. I seen that I was a different person. And plenty of times I used to spit at the mirror. I used to hate myself.

My brother was arrested when he shot that there Gallo, Willie Gallo, and he did nine to twenty he did on that. He did twelve years on that. That's the job he muffed. Him and that there, what's his name. They got the contract to kill Willie Gallo, and they muffed it, the guy lived. He was in most of them contracts at his young age. On the Gallo one I don't think he was 17. The guy lived and put the finger on him and he went away for nine to twenty. They shot him. They used about twelve bullets. They put gasoline on him and his clothes caught on fire and then a milkman went by, and it was in the snow, and turned him around in the snow and saved him. [*Willie's version of this murder differs slightly from The Hawk's account.*] And then he went to the hospital and while he's laying in the hospital they got told to lam and they went to Baltimore, and when he comes back three or four weeks later the detectives are waiting for him at the station.

Ernie knew, he knew. I'd say he knew it for about six months, that he was gonna get killed. I didn't believe him. Would you believe it if somebody just came out and told you, "Honey, they're gonna kill me"?

He wouldn't get in the car with me for six months before he got killed. He was always with these bums, Jerry and Roy Roy, and he'd always get some jerk to drive him around. And I'd say, "Hey, what's the matter with this guy? I've been driving him around for years and now all of a sudden he'll never get in the car with me anymore."

And Willie, my brother-in-law, said to me, "He never gets in the car with you because he's afraid they're going to kill him and they're going to kill you, too, if you're with him. So he won't drive with you."

And here's another funny thing. Ernie had a lot of papers that this woman was holding, and he always told me about these papers. He says, "They'll never do anything because I've got these papers that this woman is holding in her safe." He goes there about, I'd say, two weeks before he gets killed to get this stuff from her.

Now all these years this woman is holding this stuff for him, these papers and whatever the hell it was, that Ernie always felt secure that he had all this stuff. He used to tell me, "She's holding this in the safe." He used to tell me, "Don't worry."

Now, he goes there that day—I'll never forget it—he calls her up, he calls her daughter up, and he makes the appointment to go there.

And there was nothing there.

So she says to him, maybe they're in the safe, in the place like, you know, where all the records are and stuff. They go over there, but they're not there, and now all of a sudden all this stuff she's holding for Ernie like for about seven or eight years is gone. And two weeks later, so was Ernie.

. . . An old bullet is found just to the left of the midline, encapsulated in fibrous tissues. There are six bullet tracks in all. . . .

I did eight years and six months of the sentence, and I went home. Everything was strange. I hung around a while, felt around a while. They contacted me and they told me things had been tough, that they had been double-crossed. Well, I couldn't get so fresh with them. I was alone, and just out. A lot of things happen while you're away so long. I just yessed them, and they told me things are tough, and I've got to be careful now that I'm on parole.

Well, one day I got myself into another swindle. This fella here, he was double-crossing everybody, double-crossing his own organization. He would give tips to certain card games and dice games, and get in with these people, and then would turn on them, and rob them.

And he was trying to set me up, and a couple of other fellas, and I turned around and I went to certain people and I told them about it, and they said the next time he comes in just hit him right in the head. If he comes in with another proposition.

Well, it just happens that one night he pulls his brand-new car in front of my place, gets out of the car, comes in my store, sits me down, and tells me he's got a good thing. Well, I was waiting for him to come. I says, "All right, what's the good thing?"

And he explained it to me. He says, "We'll make a good buck on it."

Well, I turned around, I says excuse me a minute. And I went in back of my store, put a gun in my pocket, and came out and just kept talking to him. And I says, "Well, okay. We do it."

And in the meantime there was a fella come in I knew, drunk like a pig. Well, I had an idea to get in the guy's car with the drunken fella. I told the guy, I says, "Look, let's get this drunken fella out of here. We'll take him home. We'll talk in the car." He says, all right.

Well, when we get inside the car, the drunken fella gets in the center. And I get by the door. So I'm directing him where to go. "Go up this block, turn right, turn left." Well, when we get to a certain spot, the car is going slow, and I says, "Take it easy here."

So I take out the gun, and I told him in Italian, I says, "I'm sorry this is gonna happen. It was gonna be either you or me."

Well, he started hollerin', and sayin', "Please, what are you doin' to me?"

I says, "Well, I'm gonna shoot you right in the head."

So the car was going slow. He couldn't even step on the motor, his legs were shakin'. Instead he turns the wheel on the sidewalk a little. And I shot him twice, right in the face.

And the drunken fella is what saved the guy's life. When I fired the two shots, this drunken fella opened the door and run like a rabbit. He's hollerin', "Don't shoot at me! Don't shoot at me!" So that threw me off. And I had to go back and shoot the guy two more times.

And then I took a handkerchief out of my pocket, took all the fingerprints I could off, closed the door, and went back to my business.

Well, it wasn't long. The next day I was arrested. The man was dying. He identified me in the hospital, told them everything what I did. And here's another fella that's supposed to be a tough guy, a big racketeer, a man that was known as a killer in the mob. He couldn't meet his maker either.

So I did seven years more. It was another one of them cases where everything is "fixed up." And it was all a lot of hooey.

You know how other people, they lie in bed and tell each other how much they love each other? Well, Ernie used to lie there and tell me all these murder stories. This guy he shot. And it was his *friend*, he told me. And he said the guy was *good*-looking. He said, "Honey," he said, "he was the best-looking guy. He was *really* a good-looking guy." And he says, "He was my best friend."

So they call Ernie down—Vito [Genovese], I guess—and they say he's gotta hit this guy.

"But he's my best friend."

"Hey, it's you or him. Get rid of him."

So now they're out, and they're wining. And he tells me, "We're out having a good time, big dinner, drinking and everything else, and who comes along but this guy Kip."

He couldn't get rid of this fellow Kip. And Kip is drunk out of his mind. So Ernie tells me, "I can't get rid of Kip. I gotta get rid of this guy. I gotta get rid of him, and I don't know what I'm gonna do." He says, "I can't go home. I gotta kill this guy."

I said, "How could you *do* such a thing?"

So he said, well, what happened, they're in a car, they're all drunk out of their minds, right? Kip is in the front seat, but he had passed out, he was so drunk. And Ernie tells me, he says, "We drive up this block, and I take out the piece, and I empty the gun at the guy."

He says Kip wakes up—he sobered up in a minute—and says to Ernie, "Ernie, what did you do?"

"Shut up!" Ernie says. "Don't say a word."

And they take the guy and they threw the guy out of the car. And Kip is petrified, so Ernie drove him home, and he went in, and Ernie went home.

He tells me the guy didn't die. I say, "Didn't die! With all those bullets in him?"

"Yeah," he says. "He crawled all the way to 60th Street, to the bar," he says. "And he *lasted* till seven in the morning. And I don't know if it was the milkman, or the guy came to open the bar, but he sees him laying right in the door. The guy *crawled* all the way there."

Now they pick up Ernie, and the guy says Ernie did it. They take Ernie to the hospital. Ernie tells me, "I run to the bed, I get down on my knees," and he tells the guy, "Who did this to you? I'll get him if it's the last thing I do."

And the guy says, "*You* did it!"

Ernie told me, "I almost came down with a heart attack." Ernie says to the guy, "What's the matter with you? I'm your *friend*. I wouldn't do such a thing."

And Ernie's telling me the whole scene, how he raced into the hospital room, he's kneeling next to the bed, and he's telling the guy, "Who *did* this to you?" And he's the one who did it, right?

And then there was the other one my brother muffed. Where he shot the guy, that there bigshot, what's-his-name. That's when my brother blew his top against the organization, because the bigshot's brother opened up on him after he had promised him no murder rap. My brother muffed it and then he went home, and this guy went to the hospital and he opened up right away. So they picked my brother up at home and went to the hospital and the bigshot fingered him from his bed, his death bed, and the kid says to him, "I'm your friend. I didn't hurt you." And they locked the kid up.

So then what happened, the bigshot's brother went to see him, and he says, "Look, what are you going to do? You gonna rat?" And the bigshot says, "What, are you crazy? No, I'm gonna change my story."

So all the bigshots sit down. They went to my mother's house, and they told my mother, "Look, don't worry. He will be saved. He'll walk out of the courtroom. The guy's taking the stand and just gonna say he had it in for the kid, that's why he said he did it."

So now my brother's wife, my mother, my father, they went up to the court. So this guy takes the stand. Now, the night before they had all met at my mother's house, all the bigshots, Genovese's men, and all of them says, "Don't worry about it. The kid'll walk out."

So now this is a big boss, and he takes the stand, and the first thing he says, "That's the hired killer."

So that's why my brother blew his top on the organization.

THE HAWK POINTS CLAW AT GENOVESE

The Hawk, a one-eyed perpetually sneering trigger man, leaned from the witness box in Kings County Court today, pointed his finger at Vito Genovese, Manhattan racketeer, and identified him as one of the men who hired him to help murder (The Shadow) Boccia in September, 1934.

Genovese shifted slightly in his chair and stared at The Hawk. Perspiration glistened on the face of both men and The Hawk, who wears a patch of adhesive tape over his right eye socket, yanked at the knot in his tie and unbuttoned the collar of his shirt.

"What was your occupation at that time?" Judge Samuel S. Leibowitz asked The Hawk.

"I was a gambler," he replied.

"And a killer?" queried the judge.

"Oh, sure," The Hawk declared.

The Hawk, questioned by Julius A. Helfand, Assistant District Attorney, revealed that he met Genovese in a Brooklyn restaurant in March, 1934.

There he was introduced to Genovese by Michael Miranda who described Genovese as the "*don vin done*," which in the Italian underworld lingo means "the big man—the great man."

—*New York World-Telegram*
June 7, 1946

. . . In addition to the bullet tracks, there are multiple stab wounds, seven on the left anterior surface of the chest and four on the right. Two of the four wounds on the right penetrate the chest. . . .

That Friday, the last time I ever saw him, he was in the kitchen, leaning up against the refrigerator, and he tells me, "Honey, they're gonna kill your daddy."

He wasn't living home then, but he was coming home every day. You know, all that same garbage, back and forth. And I says, "Oh, another crazy story to get back in the house." I says, "Don't worry." I says, "If they kill you, I'll make sure that whoever did it goes to jail."

He says, "Yeah. Don't say that," and on and on.

Now, the next day, Saturday, he's supposed to bring me money. So he calls up Saturday morning, and he's in a bar on Fort Hamilton Parkway somewhere and he tells me about a fire. He says, "I almost died last night in a fire. Two guys came to the door and I wouldn't let them in and they were screaming and

I was cursing." He says, "Your daddy was out in the street in his underwear." He was telling me all that was going on.

I says, "Ernie, why do you think up these fantastic tales? Anything to get back in the house." Then he says, "I'm meeting the guys. I'm gonna have the money for you." And I says, "All right."

So he kept calling all day. You couldn't go to the bathroom without him calling, "Where were you, what are you doing?" So he's calling. He didn't get the money, he didn't get the money.

Now it's Sunday and he's calling, and the last time he calls is Sunday night because I'm moving and they shut the phone off Sunday night. He calls Sunday night and, "I'll be there, I'll be there with the money," and on and on.

Now I don't hear from him Monday, right? Because I have no phone, and he obviously didn't get the money because he didn't come. Tuesday I don't hear from him. Wednesday morning I move. Now I figured, "Oh, this dope is gonna show up." By Thursday when he doesn't show up, I call my sister.

"Did you hear from Ernie?"

She says, "No."

I says, "Gee, that's funny. I was so sure he was coming with the money."

So Thursday passes by. Now Friday comes and I says, "Something happened. This has never happened in six and a half years, because this man *never* stayed away a week no matter *what* happened."

All right. Now it's Friday, I don't see him. What's going on? I haven't heard from him since Sunday. By this time he would have had my sister on the cross, "Where is she, what's going on?"

So now I start calling. And calling. And calling. Calling Roy Roy's mother. She says, "He went away, he went away for a few days."

"He went away for a few days? What do you mean he went away for a few days? Where did he go?"

Roy Roy's mother says, "I don't know. He's coming home, he's coming home, he's coming home."

I called everybody. Everybody Ernie ever knew, I have on the phone. Nobody saw him. Now I call Frances back, Roy Roy's mother. I says, "Look, I'm telling you now," I says, "you better get Roy Roy to the phone. I'm telling you Ernie is *dead*."

. . . Of the seven wounds on the left anterior surface of the chest, four penetrate backwards at various points, cutting through the costal cartilages and also through the interspaces. Of these four, three perforate the left lung. . . .

SINGING "HAWK" NEAR LIBERTY

Ernest (The Hawk) Rupolo, killer-for-hire of the gangster decade '30s, was on his way to liberty from Dannemora Prison yesterday in proceedings before Judge Samuel Leibowitz. This was in accordance with a 1946 promise made by the Brooklyn District Attorney's Office in return for evidence against his alleged underworld paymaster, Vito Genovese, of Murder, Inc. fame.

All concerned in the release, including "The Hawk" himself, agreed he is now marked for murder himself and cannot expect to survive long. He had been serving a nine-to-twenty-year sentence.

With the promised aid of Brooklyn authorities and the expected collaboration of State Parole Board members, Rupolo will make a desperate effort to disappear completely.

—*New York Daily Mirror*
September 24, 1949

So my brother blew his top on the organization. He exposed the big bosses. "I was hired killer for Genovese. I was hired killer for Mike Miranda. I was hired killer for this here." So he's supposed to get killed by this mob, because there is no forgiving. According to the code of the greaseballs he was supposed to be killed.

But the kid *made* some of the bosses. Because they used him a lot when he was young, and they always depended on him to do the jobs that he was told to do. So they sat down on this here— should he walk the streets or not? And they forgave him. They said, "Well, this kid did twelve years, solid years, for us." So for that he got a reprieve. In fact, Mike Miranda says to him, "Take care of yourself, kid. Don't worry about nothin'. If you need anything come to me."

That's why he ran wild the way he did. A guy like him, what he did, if he wasn't so well liked by them—and if it wasn't for the work he done for them so some became top bosses today—he wouldn't of lived two minutes.

They never tried to hit the kid. They were scared because,

believe me, if someone went after him and he had an idea where it come from, he'd go right up to their doorstep, right to the boss. He didn't care who it was, he'd go right to the boss and wait on his doorstep to kill him. He wouldn't give them a second chance. That's the way the kid was. Let's face it. He didn't care for nothin'.

He used to come to my place every day and eat with my father, myself, and my wife, every day. That's how I knew that when he didn't come in for lunch that day, I knew something was wrong. I knew foul play some place.

And because of the fire. Ten days or a week before, the kid came down to my place and I said, "Where you going?"

"To church to light a candle."

"Why?"

"Because I'm not supposed to be here today."

And I says, "Well, what happened?"

"I don't know," he says. "My whole sofa caught on fire. A good thing the landlord come in and I got out of there. I could have burned to death."

And I says, "What happened?"

And he says, "There was a couple of guys knockin' for me to open the door. And I says, the hell with them, and I was high, and I just laid down and tried to go to sleep." And he says, "Those guys must have thrown a match or a cigarette on my sofa, and it was lucky I wasn't burned alive."

All that time he didn't think nothin'. He just thought it was a couple of drunks looking to get laid upstairs. There were some sporting girls, you know, some whores living upstairs, and that's what he thought at the time. If he had of ever thought like that was, you know, to do something to him, he never would have gone back to the place. Not him.

And then later, after they found the body, I thought back and I figured, well, it *was* something, that they had been looking to get him out of there at that time, and try to do away with him. And when they failed to get him out of there, to walk him out of there or something, I figure they looked to burn him, that's what I figure.

I don't think Genovese had a thing to do with killing my brother. You see, Ernie knew Sonny [*John "Sonny" Franzese, a*

Long Island Mafioso] from when they were kids. And he hated him. Because he said, "While I was away doing sixteen years that bastard was out making money." Sonny never did a day, so Ernie figured Sonny was reaping the harvest while he was away doing time. They hated each other. They really, really did.

Now I think Ernie was stepping on Sonny's feet. Ernie couldn't make money in Brooklyn anymore and he needed money and he figured he'd go out to Queens and start in in Queens in whatever Sonny was doing—bookmaking, muscling in on bars, whatever. And Sonny didn't want that.

What I think happened, I think Ernie was drinking all day, right? And now he's pretty—he's not with it anymore. He's like in a fog. They go to Willie's house, Ernie and Willie and Roy Roy. My personal feeling is that Roy Roy had an appointment to meet somebody and that he stalled at Willie's house. And then Roy Roy told Ernie he'd drop him off somewhere, or something like that. And then he was killed on the way. Roy Roy met some people and they told Ernie they would drive him home, and they killed him in the car.

. . . On the left lateral surface of the chest there are seven more stab wounds. These are up to six inches in depth. . . .

When they finally did hit my brother, Roy Roy had to be the one to set him up. He drove for him. He was the only one he'd of gone with. That's what they do. They take your best friend and he has to do what they say, even if he *is* your best friend. And they make him walk you into something, take you out, wine you and dine you, and then walk you into it. Roy Roy had to be the one.

But the stab wounds. I don't know. That's what I'm sick over. I seen this here before. Like a lot of bodies, they were never brought up. Like Joe Jelly. They say, "Oh, they threw him in the river. They ripped his stomach and threw him in the river so he won't come up."

It's only a miracle that my brother did come up. Because there's a lot of people—like they say Tony Bender's body's never been found, and they say, "Well, sure, they must have threw him in the river."

That's the only way I can see it. Like that's why they slit a guy's belly. They figure the water won't bring him up. This is just one chance in a million that my brother did come up. Because people who've been hit in the last ten or twelve years, their bodies were never found. Nobody knew, just rumors, talking, "He must be in the river somewhere." Because if a body is either buried or in the river, they figure it won't come up and you won't see it no more.

. . . On the anterior abdominal wall there are six large incised stab wounds, all above the navel and from four to six inches in length. . . .

"I'm telling you Ernie is *dead!*" I says to Frances.

"What makes you say that?" she yells.

"I *know* he's dead. I know he's dead, because if he wasn't dead he would have been breaking my door down by now."

"Don't say that!" she yells at me. "I'm lighting candles for you. He'll be all right," and this and that.

I says, "All right." So she gives me a time to call to get Roy Roy on the phone. And sure enough, I call and I get Roy Roy on the phone. So I says, "Roy Roy, where's Ernie?"

He says, "He's on the lam in New Jersey."

I says, "Don't give me that garbage. You're talking to me!" I says, "You *know* if he was on the lam in New Jersey, he's not going to New Jersey without me, if he had to take me there in chains." I says, "Just tell me where he is."

"What are you worried about?" he says. "You're always throwing him out anyway."

And I says, "That's none of your damned business. I live my life. I want to do what I want to do. But don't tell *me* this guy isn't going to call *me* for a week," I says, "because you *know* better than that."

So he says, "I don't know where he is."

I says, "Roy Roy, you're the last one that saw him alive."

"*Don't say that!*" He got hysterical when I said that.

So I says, "I *am* saying it. And where is he?"

He says, "I don't know, I don't know where he is."

I says, "I'm going to call you up tomorrow morning and if

you don't come up with Ernie by then I'm coming to Brooklyn. And that's it. That's gonna be *it*."

So I called back the next day, and Roy Roy's not around. And I went right to Willie's store, you know, the luncheonette.

"Where's Ernie?"

Nobody saw him.

So I says, "Willie, don't give me any of that garbage." I says, "Where is he?"

He says, "I don't know. He moved out of his room. Roy Roy moved him out."

And I says, "I don't want to hear that garbage! Who saw him and where did he go?"

"All I know is he left the house that night. My wife told him, don't leave, it's raining. He says, no, he had to go, he had to go."

I says, "All right."

So then I see Ernie's jacket hanging in the store. "What's his jacket doing here?"

So he says, "Oh," he says, "it was hot. He left his jacket here."

I says, "Was he drunk?"

He says, "No."

Now Ernie had reached the point where he couldn't drink anymore. He'd have four drinks and he was stoned. I said, "Did he have his teeth in his mouth?"

He says, "No."

I says, "He was drunk. Where did he go?"

He says, "I don't know. They dropped me off. Roy Roy said he was going to take him to the train." He says, "That's all I know."

I says, "Okay. That's all you know?"

"Right."

"Willie, you don't know *anything* else?"

"No."

So I says I'm going right to the police station. Now by this time I'm crying. I says, "He's *dead*, I'm telling you he's *dead*."

All right. I walked into the 66th. I'm crying like a maniac by now, and I said, "Ernie's dead."

And the cops laughed at me. They said, "You're just looking for him because you want some money, right, Eleanor?"

I says, "No, I'm telling you now, he's dead." Because I had called them a million times before—"Get that bum out of my house!" So now they figure I'm just looking for him. I says, "No, I'm serious." So they said they had to report it to Missing Persons. So I says, "But look for him. Look for him all over. Because I know he's *dead*. If he's not dead, they've got him tied up somewhere. I didn't hear from him for a *week*."

So they said all right. And I said, "I'll call you later."

From there, now, I go to his apartment on Berkely Place. Now Willie told me he had moved out of Berkely Place, that he's not there. But I look through the window and see his jewelry box on the dresser.

Now I'm wild. I says, "Oh, my God," and I'm banging on doors and I'm kicking. I go up and I start ringing all the doorbells in the building. Who saw him? One guy was telling me about the fire, and I says, "Well, it was *true*, about the fire."

But nobody saw him after that day. "We didn't see him. We didn't see him. We didn't see him."

I says, "Well, now I *know* he's really dead."

I get back home and I say, "He's gone. He's finished. But where? That's the question." He didn't come back because he didn't have the money, right? But I know that would have lasted two or three days, then he would have said, the hell with the money, I'm going to see her anyway.

And I'm calling. I call everybody and anybody. Nobody saw Ernie. I'm calling two or three times a day to the 66th, to Missing Persons. I don't hear anything, and I'm bothering everybody.

Until the day that detective rang the doorbell. I opened the door, and his first words to me, he says, "You're right."

I said, "Where is he?" I figured they found him in some empty lot somewhere.

He says, "We have him in the 100th precinct."

I says, "I don't know where that is."

He says, "Rockaway. Come with me."

And that was it.

. . . Cause of death: bullet wounds of head, brain, neck, and spine. Multiple stab wounds of the chest, lungs, heart, and abdomen. Homicidal.

Roots of Evil

T HE MAFIA IS A VINE that has spread shoots and tentacles across the United States, but its roots are firmly entrenched in the dusty, sun-baked soil of Sicily. It was there that the Mafia was born centuries ago, and the rituals, the secrecy and the code of ethics of Mafia, U.S.A., still closely approximate those of the old country. To understand what kind of men the Mafia attracts and how the organization maintains its unique power over them, it is necessary to know something of Mafia history. That is the purpose of the four pieces that make up the following section.

In the first chapter, writer Norman Lewis describes how the Mafia was born among the oppressed peasants of Sicily as an honored society, dedicated to fighting the oppressors of Sicily's people. He explains how originally noble purposes were perverted into those of a criminal organization, devoted to exploiting the very people it was founded to protect.

The second chapter, by Frederic Sondern, Jr., deals with the first impact of the Mafia on this country. The Mafia arrived with the first waves of Sicilian immigrants near the end of the last century and in those early days the organization preyed exclusively on fellow Italians who suffered it in silence to protect their families and their lives.

All the important early leaders of the Mafia in the United

States were native Sicilians who brought with them the traditions and prejudices of the old-world Mafia. For example, they were firmly opposed to forming alliances with gangsters from other ethnic groups, no matter how great the financial benefits might be. Younger Mafiosi, reared in America, scornfully referred to these old-timers as "greasers" or "Mustache Petes."

Finally, on the night of September 10, 1931, the balance of power changed hands. In this single night, the young Turks within the organization staged a bloody coup and efficiently wiped out around 40 of the Mustache Petes, taking control of the Mafia. The night of September 10 came to be known as "The Night of the Sicilian Vespers." The third chapter in this section, by Fred J. Cook, a respected journalist who has studied the Mafia for many years, outlines how the coup was planned and carried out so brutally and so effectively that it dramatically changed the development of organized crime in America.

The evolution of the Mafia since the purge of the old guard in 1931 is traced by Ralph Salerno and John Tompkins in the fourth chapter of this section. Salerno was for many years a specialist on the Mafia in the New York City Police Department. Since his retirement he has advised and assisted private and government groups engaged in the fight against organized crime. In the chapter printed here, Salerno describes the haphazard effort of local, state and federal law-enforcement agencies against the Mafia in the last 40 years. Although he was himself part of the law-enforcement establishment for many years, Salerno does not hesitate to point out its weaknesses in dealing with organized crime in general and the Mafia in particular.

3
The Mafia in Sicily

NORMAN LEWIS

Sicily—the America of the ancient world—has been a colony exploited by the use of slave labor, either openly or in a disguised form, for two thousand years. The Roman armies marched to the conquest of Gaul and Britain on bread made from corn grown by Sicilian slaves. When, with the fall of Rome, the Papacy took over the great Sicilian estates, it was the chain gangs of Sicilian peasant laborers that provided three-fourths of its wealth. Sicily was exploited by Norman, German, Frenchman, Aragonese, Spaniard, and finally the Bourbons, but nearly always from a distance. After the Germans there was no central government, no monarch, no court, no resident hierarchy. So long as the corn was shipped out of Sicilian ports each year, nothing else mattered. Defining the seemingly endless ice age of feudalism in Sicily, Filangieri, the social historian, said that an overbearing despotism had grown up to separate the Crown from the people. As a result, Sicily was a political hermaphrodite, neither monarchy nor republic, "which suffered from all the dependency of the former, while lacking the advantages of a constitution, and all the turbulence of the latter, although deprived of its liberties."

And then, just at the time when the first stirrings of the modern world were visible elsewhere in Europe, another tragic yoke was laid upon the Sicilian neck by the establishment of the Inquisition. And in Sicily, through the remoteness of the Crown, its effects were even more deadening than in Spain itself. More and more to the modern observer the Holy Office appears as a device concerned primarily with economic situations, and only secondarily with matters of faith. Drawing its revenues from heresy, it saw to it that heresy was abundant. In Spain heresy provided an excuse for the ruin and annihilation of a class of rich Christianized merchants of Jewish or Moorish origin. In Sicily its objectives were all-embracing, although vaguer. Heresy started as religious dissent, but as religious dissenters—understandably enough—were remarkably few, the Inquisition widened its scope to include a miscellany of bigamists, "philosophers," usurers, sodomites, priests who married their concubines, and finally opponents of any kind, who automatically became classed as heretics. Membership of the Inquisition, like that of an exclusive club, was open only to the aristocracy, and in Sicily the barons enrolled themselves with enthusiasm as familiars. All convictions were accompanied by forfeiture of property, and the Inquisition gave no receipts. In procedural matters the scales were heavily weighted against those whose reputation for original thought or whose conspicuous possessions happened to attract the Holy Office's attention. Arrests were made on suspicion, often as the result of anonymous denunciation. The accused was presumed guilty and the functions of prosecutor and judge were combined. Women, children and slaves could be called as witnesses for the prosecution, but not for the defense. Nor could the victim be allowed a lawyer to plead his case, as this would have been tantamount to opposing the Inquisition and, as such, an act of heresy.

The familiars of the Inquisition dominated Sicily for three centuries. Until the time of their disbanding in 1787 there were never less than two thousand of these psalm-singing marauders, each in command of his own band of retainers—all of whom enjoyed the same extralegal privileges. They stripped rich men of their property, and sentenced them to *murus largus*—the most comfortable kind of incarceration the day had to offer. The poor were punished for their lack of seizable goods by torture and *murus strictus*, which meant that they were flung, fettered, into a deep dungeon and endured "the bread and water of affliction" until they died. Horrified by these excesses, which he was quite powerless to check, the Spanish Viceroy, the Duke of Medinaceli, wrote:

"It would take a year to describe the things they do. Unheard of things—the most hideous and frightful enormities." The poor man's only shield was the Mafia and the vendetta. Justice was not to be come by, but the association of men of honor, silent, persistent and inflexible, could at least exact a bloody retribution for the loss of a wife or daughter, or the burning down of a house. Colafanni, an authority on the period, sums up: "The Mafia in Sicily under the Bourbons provided the only means for the poor and humble to make themselves respected. . . . To the Mafia, then, went all the rebels, all those that had suffered injuries, all the victims."

It was in the school of the vendetta, too, that the traditional character of the *mafioso* was formed. The common man, a victim of absolute power, had to learn to stomach insult or injury with apparent indifference so that vengeance could be delayed until the opportunity for its consummation presented itself. The *mafioso* therefore developed a kind of self-control closely resembling that quality known as *giri* by the Japanese, and so much admired by them. A true man of honor never weakened his position or armed his enemy in advance by outbursts of passion or of fear. When he sustained some grave injury he made a pact with himself to be revenged, and thereafter would wait patiently and unemotionally half a lifetime if necessary until his moment came—often seemingly on excellent terms with the man he proposed to destroy.

But when a man lost his head, threw Mafia-inculcated secrecy and caution to the wind and struck back openly, his only chance of salvation was to take to the maquis. For this reason there was never a time when Sicily was without its bandits. At the end of the Second World War thirty separate armed bands terrorized western Sicily, while even in the late winter of 1962-63 motorized bandits were still staging highway robberies on the main provincial highway between Castellammare and Ballestrade. A hundred and fifty years ago the Bourbon authorities decided to deal with this situation by creating the first pseudo-police force. The only qualification for enrollment in the Armed Companies, as they were called, was ruthlessness. Many of these upholders of the law were ferocious criminals reprieved from the gallows and allowed to rehabilitate themselves in this way. What the familiars of the Inquisition had overlooked, the Armed Companies took. After the depredations carried out in the name of religion, Sicilians were now doomed to suffer voicelessly under the agents of the state. Since then they have quite simply turned their backs on authority of any kind. For this reason the police charged with the investigation of the highway robberies of February 1963 met with nothing but the most intractable hostility from local villagers, while even the victims of the robberies appear not to have been specially helpful. For this reason, when a man is found lying seriously wounded, possibly dying, and the police appeal to him to identify his aggressor, the reply is usually couched in a formula: "If I die, may God forgive me, as I forgive the one who did this. If I manage to pull through, I know how to settle my own accounts."

This is the famous Sicilian *omertà*—"manliness"—which rules the public conscience and is sustained so often even in the face of death. It is a word which calls for further examination, and is best understood by the study of an extreme case of *omertà* in action.

Around 1960 one of two brothers living together in a Sicilian farmhouse disappeared. The men were known to have been on the worst possible terms for years, and the younger and stronger one frequently knocked his older brother about and even threatened to kill him. Finally the older brother vanished and the police got to hear about it, searched the farmhouse, and found inefficiently cleaned-up bloodstains on the floor. It is a popular misconception that a case for murder cannot be made out if no body can be found. In this case it was decided by the examining magistrate that a *corpus delicti* existed, constituted by the threats of murder known to have been made, the man's disappearance, the bloodstains, and the suspect's immediate assumption of his brother's property. The younger brother was accordingly tried for murder, found guilty, and sentenced to imprisonment for life.

A year or two later a *carabiniere* who knew the older brother suddenly found himself face to face with the "murdered" man. He was working quietly as a laborer on a farm in the mountains, only two miles away. It emerged that as part of his plan to be revenged on his brother, the man had changed his name, although most of his fellow laborers and some of the neighbors knew who he was, all the same. This was *omertà* with a vengeance. It simply did not occur to these people to go to the police, despite the terrific injustice that had been done. It was "manly" to solve one's own problems in one's own way and leave others to do the same, and one "lost respect" by poking one's nose into other people's affairs.

The Sicilian conscience is further bedeviled by an unfortunate linguistic confusion arising out of the similarity between the words *omertà* and *umiltà*—humility, the Christian virtue so much extolled in the Church. Many illiterate Sicilians have combined the two words to produce a hybrid of mixed pagan and Christian significance. The virtuous man is in Mafia fashion "manly" and silent, and as a Christian humble.

Far from protecting the underdog, the Mafia today has taken the place of the oppressors of old, but it still benefits from a moral climate formed in past centuries. The Sicilian is a trifle cynical and quite self-sufficient. He fights his own battles, keeps his mouth shut, and has little interest in the doings of humanity outside the circle of his family, extended perhaps to include his second cousins. "Manliness," once a barricade raised against injustice, now serves to keep justice out.

In the past, it was the Mafia—the product of weak government that had developed its own vested interest in governmental weakness—that whipped up the frantic *jacqueries* of 1820, 1840 and 1866. The savageries of these outbursts of peasant hatred are quite inexplicable to anyone unaware of the long years of contempt that had preceded them. As in Spain, the targets of popular fury were always the same: the landlord, the Church, the police. There is no better description of the kind of thing that could happen than that given by Giovanni Verga, in his story "Liberty," which is largely factual and based on the rising at Bronté put down by Nino Bixio, lieutenant of Garibaldi—the man who was to have given the land to the peasants.

> Like the sea in storm, the crowd foamed and swayed in front of the club of the gentry, and outside the Town Hall, and on the steps of the church—a sea of white stocking caps, axes and sickles glittering. Then they burst into the little street.
> "Your turn first, baron! You who have had folks cudgeled by your estate guards!" At the head of all the people a witch, with her old hair sticking up, armed with nothing but her nails. "Your turn, priest of the devil, for you've sucked the soul out of us!" . . . "Your turn, police sergeant, you who never took the law on anybody except poor folks who'd got nothing!" "Your

turn, estate guards, who sold your own flesh and your neighbor's flesh for tenpence a day!"

Now they were drunk with the killing. Sickles, hands, rags, stones, everything red with blood. The gentry! Kill them all! Kill them all! Down with the gentry!

"Don't kill me," pleads the priest; "I'm in mortal sin!" Neighbor Lucia being the mortal sin; neighbor Lucia, whose father has sold her to the priest when she was fourteen years old, at the time of the famine winter. But the priest is hacked to pieces on the cobblestones of the street. Then it is the turn of the apothecary, the lawyer, and the lawyer's eleven-year-old son. The estate guards fire on the crowd from the castle, but the castle is stormed and the defenders massacred, the baron's young sons trampled to death, the baroness and her baby thrown from her balcony to the street.

And then suddenly the slaughter is over. They are free of the gentry and rage is dead. Now they have their liberty, but nobody knows what to do with it. And in any case there is no time to learn, for the Army, with its firing squads, is on the way. Quietly and sadly, arms folded, they sit waiting behind closed doors.

In those days the Mafia was still with the people; then, gradually, as it gathered its power it began to draw apart. The Mafia was paid for its part in Garibaldi's triumph, it organized the plebiscite (at Lampedusa's Donnafugata—Voters, 515; Voting 512; Yes, 512; No, zero), its chieftains, like his illiterate Sedaras, married their daughters to penniless princes. From that time on the Mafia began to elbow the feudal aristocracy aside. By 1945 the process was complete. Don Calogero Vizzini was the feudal overlord of all Sicily as well as head of the Mafia. And thereby he had become the worst single thorn in the peasants' side since the bad old days of the Bourbons.

Don Fabrizio, the ruminative and unworldly princeling of Lampedusa's novel, philosophical in his acceptance of Garibaldi and the Mafia, felt queasy at the first sight of the infant democracy newly delivered at Donnafugata. "Something had died, God only knew in what back alley, in what corner of the popular conscience." People always had done, and always would do what they were told, and he found it in some way demeaning that anyone should find it necessary to construct this elaborate edifice of pretense dedicated to the lie that free will and freedom of choice actually existed.

However sickening to Don Fabrizio's stomach the newly imported democracy might have been, for the Mafia it was an invention as promising as the new steam engine. In the old days the Viceroy had given the orders—at most, and as a matter of courtesy taking the advice of his council of nobles. Now it was to be the turn of anyone who could fight his way to the controls of this wonderful new machine. In 1881 communal elections were held at Villalba—the town that was to become Don Calogero Vizzini's capital—and the Marchese of Villalba, supported by the Mafia, took his precautions ten days in advance. The 214 citizens possessing the qualifications entitling them to vote were locked up in a granary, from which they were released, eight at a time, and escorted by the Marchese's armed guards to the polls. The Marchese was elected.

Later the Mafia invented and perfected new methods of democratic suasion. By the time the government of Giolitti reached power, the Mafia had become the only electoral force that counted in Sicily and the government was realistic in its acceptance of the fact. Alongi, who published a study of the Mafia in 1902, describes the arrangements for voting he had witnessed a year or two previously. "Some short distance from the polling station the road was barred by a group of sinister figures. Here each voter as he approached was seized, thoroughly bastinadoed, and forced to drink a huge glass of wine. There followed a thorough search of his person, after which the government candidate's voting slip was put into his hand and he was led or dragged to the ballot box, where the president took the slip from him and put it in."

Later still, this physical suppression of the element of choice gradually came to be considered unnecessary; it was found that the same result could be obtained by making the voter understand what he stood to lose by voting for the wrong side. As it was never explained to the voter what program the candidates stood for, and he was assumed to be quite ignorant of the function of Parliament, the contending parties might be represented by symbols such as the mule and the ox, and the agricultural voters warned that it was either a case of voting for the mule or looking elsewhere for work in future. The system recalls the last election held under French tutelage in parts of then colonial West Africa, where bloody disputes took place between villages over the relative merits in terms of strength, courage and sagacity of the lion and the elephant, which were the symbols adopted by two of the parties soliciting their votes.

This somewhat special interpretation of the democratic process persisted in Sicily even after the end of the Second World War. In 1945 when the Mafia and most of Sicily's aristocracy were hoping that Sicily would secede from Italy to become an American state, or at worst a British colony, a Separatist congress was convened at which Don Calogero Vizzini appeared unexpectedly and without formal invitation. When asked whom he represented, he replied with proud simplicity: "I have only to whistle, and every man in the province of Caltanisetta will vote Separatist."

When a year or two after that the Mafia threw the idea of Separatism overboard and became, by order of Don Calò, Christian Democrat, there was one serious breach in the Honored Society's political unity in the person of the awe-inspiring Don Vanni Sacco, head of the Mafia of Camporeale. To the remonstrations of Don Calò, when he refused to accept a badge sent him in the form of a cross on a shield—the Party emblem—Vanni Sacco replied: "I've been a liberal all my life, and my father before me. After all, politics, as I see it, is a stick, and I've got used to the feel of this one." It took lunch with the Archbishop of Monreale, Monsignor Fillipi, and the Archbishop's consent to Vanni Sacco's request that his daughter, Giovanna, should be granted the honor of christening the cathedral's new bell, before Don Vanni would agree to change his politics.

At the turn of the century, with the political machine finally and firmly under control, and the manicured hands of that distinguished ruffian Don Vito Cascio Ferro on its levers, the Mafia could go ahead and trim up the details of the "state within a state" that existed until the coming of Mussolini, and was to re-emerge in 1945 under the generalship of Don Calogero Vizzini of Villalba.

It was Don Vito who developed with a certain artistry the system of the *pizzu*, as he called it—an onomatopoeic and picturesque word from the Sicilian dialect which translates rather flatly into English as "racket." *Pizzu* means the beak of a small bird, such as a canary or a lark, and when Don Vito with his inborn habit of understatement spoke of levying a Mafia toll, he called it in Sicilian *fari vagnari a pizzu*—"wetting the beak." By the time Prefect Mori had succeeded in putting Don Vito away on his faked-up charge, beak wetting was included in almost every conceivable activity in Sicily.

A great gathering of vulturine chieftains had collected to wet their beaks at the expense of the farmers, whose produce they bought dirt cheap on the spot and carried to the market in the Mafia's own beautifully decorated carts—or later, trucks. In the market only those whose place had been "guaranteed" by the Mafia were allowed to buy or sell at prices the Mafia fixed. The Mafia wetted its beak in the meat, fish, beer and fruit businesses. It moved into the sulphur mines, controlled the output of rock salt, took over building contracts, "organized labor," cornered the plots in Sicily's cemeteries, put tobacco smuggling on a new and more profitable basis through its domination of the Sicilian fishing fleets, and went in for tomb robbing in the ruins of the Greek settlement of Selinunte—the results of its archaeological excavations being offered at bargain prices to foreign tourists. Looking around for further sources of revenue, the Mafia decided to recommend the owners of country houses and estates, however, small, to employ guardians for their property, and after a few stubborn landowners had declined to supply sinecures for ex-convicts and had seen their property burned down, the practice became universal. There were advantages, too, to be gained by stringing along. The Mafia gave monopolies to shopkeepers in different trades and then invited them to put up their prices—at the same time, of course, increasing their Mafia contribution. Some of the Mafia beak wettings were picturesque in a sort of depraved, Oriental way. Beggars, for example, would be granted exclusive rights to a certain pitch, thus guaranteeing a display of distorted limbs freedom from competition by simulated idiocy.

The most evident of the Mafia's criminal functions—and one that had been noted by the Bourbon attorney general back in the twenties of the last century—now became the normally accepted thing. The Mafia virtually replaced the police force, offering a form of arrangement with crime as a substitute for its suppression. When a theft, for instance, took place, whether of a mule, a jeweled pendant, or a motorcar, a Mafia intermediary was soon on the scene, offering reasonable terms for the recovery of the stolen object. In this way the matter was usually settled rapidly, and to the satisfaction of all concerned. The victim got his property back without delay. The thief received a relatively small sum, but at least escaped the risk of police interference, since no one would have dared to call in the police once the Mafia had interested itself. The Mafia intermediary, of course, wetted his beak at the expense of both parties. The situation was and is an everyday one in Sicily. The police charge nothing to restore stolen property but are only successful in one case out of ten. The Mafia is expensive, and may impose a commission charge of 33⅓ percent. However, the Mafia is successful 90 percent of the time.

But it was not only the farmer and the merchant who felt the weight of the Mafia's New Order. The rich man, drawing his income perhaps from investments, could not be allowed to escape the net, and he became increasingly the target of letters of extortion. Such letters are commonplace in Sicily, but most of them are composed by novice delinquents who give themselves away by their brusqueness, their semiliteracy, and their habitual decoration with drawings of skulls and crossbones and dripping daggers. Letters of this kind go into the wastepaper basket, or may even be handed over to the police. The genuine Mafia letter writer is unmistakable in his style, which is likely to have a touch of the nineteenth century about it, with outmoded epistolatory flourishes and protestations. It may even express regret for the inconvenience caused. As no second requests are sent, it is usual for payment to be made promptly.

Some of the rackets sound a trifle fantastic, such as the tax imposed on lovers in Don Vito's day when they went to carry on their courtship in the Spanish fashion with a girl who sat behind a barred window, and had to pay a Mafia concessionaire "the price of a candle" for his protection.

More fantastic was the racket, or rather the interlacing series of rackets, built up around religious devotion. The Mafia—always ready to ally itself with the Church as a matter of expediency, in the manner of Don Calogero Vizzini—moved cautiously at first. By the middle of the last century it controlled the confraternities devoted to the cults of the various patron saints, and more important, it directed the standing committees of the cults. It was the standing committees that raised the funds required for the saint's annual feast day: for the processions, the illuminations, and the firework displays. Later a Mafia trust interested itself in the manufacture of devotional candles, and obtained a virtual monopoly. In nearly all Sicilian churches the seats are private property, and it was the Mafia that hired the seats. The Mafia took over the manufacture of religious objects of all kinds and, being on the whole free of sentimental prejudices, attacked the problems of manufacture and distribution in an entirely dispassionate manner. With the advance of the twentieth century and the streamlining of production, its factories produced statues of saints and Madonnas and religious medallions by the million. It employed the most persuasive traveling salesmen, appointed the most go-ahead retail firms as exclusive stockists, awarded bonuses and special quantity discounts, and supplied tasteful window displays to the shops in the bigger cities. Many of the faithful liked to have their religious medallions blessed by a bishop, and the Mafia had no objection to arranging that—and blessed they were, in basketfuls and by the thousand.

Back in the last century the Mafia had turned its attention to the lucrative business of manufacturing relics. The process was a simple one, requiring only the cooperation of the sacred object's custodian—in most cases a village priest. The relic was usually some portion of the body of a saint or a lock of his hair, or occasionally a more fanciful object of devotion such as a miniature urn full of the ashes of Abraham, or a bone from one of the fishes multiplied by Christ in the miracle of the loaves and fishes. All that was necessary to create a second relic having a large portion of the virtue of the original was to bring the new object into contact with it. Although the authorities of the Church frown upon the practice, relics were and are mass-produced by the thousand in this way. The manufacturing process is simplified by the existence of a tremendous number and diversity of saintly remnants upon which local cults are centered. In the course of a recent study of Mafia penetration of devotional practices, the Italian publication *Le Ore* carried out, with remarkable results, a brief numerical survey of the most important of such relics. The paper discovered the existence of seventeen arms attributed to St. Andrew, thirteen to St. Stephen, twelve to St. Philip, and ten each to St. Vincent and St. Tecla. Sixty fingers belonging to St. John the Baptist were in circulation, and forty heads were revered as that of St. Julian.

The Mafia seems to have decided that there were profitable

pickings to be made in this direction shortly after 1870 when, as a measure of reform, the Italian government decided to close down a number of religious institutions and the relics they contained were dispersed. Most of these were bought up by the Mafia. A number of extra copies of each were made up from materials furnished by an abandoned cemetery, and duplicates of the original seals of authenticity attached by the Congregation of Rites of the Vatican were assiduously faked. A vigorous overseas market for such spurious articles of devotion—particularly in the Americas—quickly developed. *Le Ore* discovered that in 1962 alone minor sales to the United States made by the organization they had investigated included twenty suits of armor of Joan of Arc, twenty monastic gowns worn by St. Francis of Assisi, fifty rosaries alleged to have belonged to Bernadette, and—as a triumphant culmination of Mafia salesmanship—the wand carried by Moses when he led the Children of Israel into the Promised Land.

Where there was no saint, no holy relic, and consequently no flocking of pilgrims to be fleeced, the Mafia did its best with artificial substitutes. A well-publicized "miracle," such as the apparition of the Madonna to a child, filled the specially chartered buses, the shops, and the hotels, and produced an upswing—however short-lived—in the sales curve for religious merchandise. Thus it was with Padre Pio, the "stigmatized" monk of San Giovanni Rotondo, whose cult was thought important enough to justify the transfer of a Mafia commando to the Italian mainland itself.

The appearance of a monk whose followers claimed that his hands miraculously reproduced Christ's wounds from the cross's nails was enough to provoke a delirium of commercial speculation. Within a few years, the remote hamlet near Foggia had turned into a sort of embryo Lourdes with half a dozen prosperous hotels, innumerable boardinghouses, and a hospital with a helicopter landing stage on its roof, to which rich patients were brought to be exposed to the saintly influence. Books describing Padre Pio's miracles were sold by the hundred thousand, and records by the million of the father saying mass or at prayer. The photographs of the monk displaying his wounds would not have convinced the hardened skeptic, as the negative had obviously been subjected to crude retouching and the prints daubed all over with a red dye, but they were happily bought by the pilgrims who poured into

San Giovanni Rotondo. Such was the clamor to be confessed by Padre Pio (95 percent of the applicants were women) that confessions had to be booked, and the waiting list grew so long that pilgrims had to spend days and even weeks in the town's expensive hotels awaiting their turn. By arrangement with the Mafia, however, and on payment of a substantial sum, the queue could be jumped. Mafia agents waited, too, at the bus terminals, ready to carry off new arrivals to be confessed on the spot for sums varying between two and five thousand lire by false Padre Pios who awaited their prey in hastily faked-up back street rooms. Most impudent of all was the sale of revolting relics of the monk's "stigmata"—hundreds of yards of blood-soaked bandages displayed on market stalls outside the convent. Even when in 1960 the newspapers published analyses showing the blood to be that of chickens, the sales did not slacken.

It is this scene of the Mafia presiding over charlatans selling cock's blood and amulets against the evil eye that reminds us how fully the wheel has turned. The Mafia that had come into being as the peasants' refuge against the worst abuses of the Middle Ages now gleefully resuscitated all the bagful of medieval tricks to exploit the peasants' ignorance. The Mafia that had fought feudalism, that had lain in wait on the moonless night for the baron no officer of the law could touch, now elected and manipulated politicians who would guarantee to fight for the survival of the feudal order.

4
How the Mafia Came to America

FREDERIC SONDERN, JR.

The Mafia discovered America in the 1880's. The few mafiosi among the Sicilians who joined the great Italian emigration at that time soon found splendid opportunities for their traditional occupation. The new immigrants, bewildered by the strange land, its language and customs, naturally huddled together in the Little Italys of New York, Chicago, New Orleans and many other cities and towns across the country. For the inherent organizing talent of the mafiosi, they were easy prey. The members of the brotherhood had brought all of their talents and philosophy with them. Word of the bonanza of course quickly reached Sicily and more were on their way.

The Black Hand came into being. There has been much confusion about it. It was never a society in itself. Mafia extortion gangs simply used the imprint of a hand as a signature on their warnings, ransom notes and other demands. In Sicily for decades they had signed with a skull, a dagger or a hand. In America they discovered—and they have always been clever psychologists—that the hand was for some reason the most effective symbol. The first targets of the brotherhood were prosperous Italian farmers and merchants, who understood the Mafia's capabilities. A Long Island truck farmer would receive a notice to leave a hundred dollars in cash in a certain place, or else. The note was written in the unmistakable Mafia style of the Sicilian dialect and signed with

The Hand—the *Mano Nera*. If he failed to meet the deadline, a stenciled black hand would appear on a fence or on the side of the house. That was the final warning.

"Then my father would pay," an elderly Italo-American vegetable grower near New York City, who was brought over from Sicily as a child, explained to us. "He would say, 'Giuseppe, you see, it is the same as at home. The Mafia is always with us.' Then I would plead with him to go to the police. After all, we were in America. 'No, Mother of God, no,' he would shout. 'The police here cannot do even as much as the police at home. They do not know the Mafia. We get put out of business or killed and no one will know why. They do not understand the mafiosi and they never will.' " Italian merchants and manufacturers in the Italian districts of New York, Chicago, San Francisco felt the same way. They paid, and the mafiosi prospered.

The first American policeman to cross swords with the Mafia and to begin to understand the strange brotherhood was Chief David Hennessey of New Orleans. The year was 1890. . . . A group of mafiosi had taken over control of the New Orleans docks. The city and its harbor had become the center of the country's rapidly growing fruit trade from Latin America. No banana freighter could be unloaded until a fixed tribute was paid by the importer to the firm of Antonio and Carlo Matranga, originally of Palermo. No Negro or Italian longshoreman would move unless he had his orders from one of their appointed bosses. The importers were complacent, dock racketeering was common—as it is today— all along the seaboard, and there were no complaints.

Suddenly a series of particularly brutal murders shook the city. One Italian had his throat cut and was dumped into a canal. Another, almost decapitated, was found with what was left of his head stuffed into his own roaring fireplace. Shotguns, bombs and daggers—the traditional Mafia methods—were accounting for several murders a week. Chief Hennessey was an honest, intelligent, imaginative policeman of a kind most unusual in his day. His investigation, most of which he conducted by himself, was thorough. The more he found out, the angrier he became. He ran head on into the system which the mafiosi of New Orleans had created. Most of his own policemen, many of them Italian, were suddenly deaf, dumb and blind; so was the Italian colony. But

Hennessey was a stubborn man. He was warned time and again to lay off; financial proposals were made. He ignored both threats and bribes. Gradually he pieced together the details of the mechanism with which the formidable Matranga family ruled the New Orleans docks. The murders, he discovered, had been the result of a typical Mafia feud between the Matrangas and the Provenzano brothers who had tried to move in on their territory. It was hard going for the chief in those days . . . with no FBI or Treasury Department to help. Nevertheless, Hennessey put together an accurate picture of the mafiosi's operations and, finally, was ready to present it to a grand jury. The brotherhood decided that he had moved in too close and knew too much. A few days before he was to testify, as he was walking home from police headquarters one evening, a salvo of shotgun blasts cut him down. He was terribly wounded, but he managed as he staggered and fell to pull his service revolver from its holster. Heaving himself up in a last gesture of defiance, he emptied the gun. A detective who happened to be nearby and heard the shooting dashed up and found the chief sitting on the stoop of a house, gun still clutched in his fingers. . . . A few hours later, after a number of violent struggles in the hospital against the paralysis that prevented him from speaking, he was dead.

The New Orleans Police Department at the beginning was not too energetic about investigating Chief Hennessey's death, but the anger of the citizenry could not be ignored. One grand jury, after hearing the testimony of a number of the chief's more loyal assistants, returned a presentment that might have been written today. "The existence of a secret organization known as the Mafia has been established beyond doubt." The jury spelled out the details. It found, officially, that "the society" was composed of Italians and Sicilians who had left their country to avoid punishment for crimes they had committed there. Although the jury had never heard the word *omertà* and would not have known what it meant, they catalogued some of its rules clearly. ". . . strangely difficult, almost impossible to discover the perpetrators of these crimes or to secure witnesses. . . ."

Under increasing public pressure the police was compelled to go to work. Indictments were returned and nineteen Sicilians finally went to trial for the Hennessey murder as principals and conspirators. It should have been a simple case for the prosecution. Fear of reprisal by the Mafia had gradually been overcome by the intensity of public opinion and almost 60 witnesses were ready to testify against the defendants. Some had seen and could identify four who had been running from the scene of the killing. There was overwhelming corroborative evidence. The verdict, according to the New Orleans newspapers, was a foregone conclusion.

But the Mafia, as subsequent investigations showed, had also been at work. The mafiosi of 1890 were as determined as their offspring of 1957 at Apalachin to protect the brotherhood's anonymity. Money flowed into New Orleans to hire the best legal talent available. Thomas J. Semmes, a spectacular attorney who was considered one of the country's greatest criminal lawyers at the time, headed the defense. A battery of five others, all with Anglo-Saxon names, assisted him. . . . At least half of the jurymen were both intimidated and handsomely bribed. On the guilt of three of the defendants the jury could not decide, the rest were held innocent.

Mayor Joseph A. Shakespeare of New Orleans made a report to his City Council. . . . "A decent community cannot exist," the mayor wrote, "with such a society in its midst. The society must be destroyed or the community will perish. The Sicilians who come here must become American citizens and obey the law of the land, or else there is no place for them in our country."

The mayor was angry. He had admired his chief of police despite the political trouble which the often tactless Hennessey had caused him. The city was even angrier. As in Chicago in the 1920's under the rule of Al Capone, the people were afraid of the mafiosi; they were also ashamed of themselves. Although Shakespeare was a reform mayor, New Orleans at the time was probably one of the most corrupt cities in the country. But the brotherhood had gone too far. Two days after the verdict on the Sicilians had been brought in, New Orleans erupted into one of the most horrible mass lynchings in our history.

A protest meeting called by a group of the city's leading people, with the approval of Mayor Shakespeare and the editorial encouragement of the *Picayune* and the *Times-Democrat*, began peacefully enough but suddenly turned into a roaring, bloodthirsty mob of several thousand who marched on the jail and battered

down its gates. The mafiosi after the conclusion of their trial had
not been released, but had been taken back to the Parish Prison
to await completion of various legal formalities. Self-appointed
execution squads searched the building for the Italians as deputy
sheriffs discreetly disappeared. Two prisoners were dragged
screaming into the street in front of the prison, ropes materialized,
nooses were fashioned and men hoisted them onto lamp posts. A
group of armed citizens carefully riddled each with bullets as they
swung, kicking. Nine more mafiosi were discovered and lined up
in front of a prison wall. Another firing party with rifles, pistols
and shotguns methodically cut them to pieces.

The press in this country and newspapers abroad—including
the stately *London Times*—discovered the Mafia for the first time.
Some editors approved, some disapproved of the action of the New
Orleans mob. It immediately became an international incident. The
irascible James G. Blaine was our secretary of state. The Marquis
Rudini, the Italian foreign minister, was no more tactful. A series
of extremely vituperative messages was exchanged by Washington
and Rome. The marquis inferred that we were barbarians incapable
of enforcing our own laws and Mr. Blaine replied sharply that
although we were a relatively young country, we did not have
the criminal societies which seemed to flourish in Italy. The Italian
ambassador was withdrawn from Washington. President Harrison
decided that the trouble was not worth the bother and he authorized the payment of some $30,000 as an indemnity. The Italian
government was placated, King Umberto sent a flowery message,
relations between the countries returned to normal, and the
existence of the Mafia was forgotten for a time.

The Mafia, its ramifications and some of its activities were
discovered again just after the turn of the century by a tubby,
shrewd detective of the New York Police Department—Lieutenant Joseph Petrosino. Born in the coastal town of Salerno, near
Naples, the stocky little man had heard much about the Mafia
from his parents. As the brotherhood began to flourish in New
York—it came to be known then as the Black Hand—Petrosino
with his background and knowledge made it his specialty. A systematic man, he built up a file on the dock racketeers, brothel
owners, fish and meat market gangsters and other mafiosi of that
day. He was brilliant in the organization of the cases which he

developed and several hundred Italians, especially Sicilians, who had neglected their naturalization procedures were deported as undesirable aliens. It became almost an obsession with Petrosino. He felt very deeply that the Mafia's abuse of American freedoms and process of law was not only an outrage to himself as an American citizen but a disgrace to the parent country which he loved. In 1909 he talked Theodore Bingham, one of New York City's few great police commissioners, into an unusual operation. A secret service unit, officially known as Italian Squad of the Police Department, was to be created to combat the Black Hand extortions of the Mafia. The Board of Estimate was unimpressed and refused to appropriate money for the purpose. Bingham, however, was well informed, convinced and determined. Private funds were raised, as they were years later in Chicago to destroy Al Capone and his mafiosi. Petrosino was authorized by the commissioner to go on an unprecedented trip. The lieutenant was to contact Italian police chiefs—particularly in Sicily, Calabria and Naples—and set up arrangements with them for warning the New York City Police Department whenever an important criminal left for the United States. This was unheard-of at that time. It was years before the establishment of Interpol, the International Criminal Police Organization, which functions so efficiently today, and the law enforcement agencies of Europe and the United States very rarely even corresponded with each other. The State Department as well as foreign governments were inclined to frown on the international cooperation of policemen, which the diplomats regarded as an uncouth and embarrassing crew in any case. Commissioner Bingham dispatched Petrosino anyway.

The lieutenant, fully aware that he was attacking a very formidable enemy, was careful. He traveled under an assumed name and in Rome went directly to the minister of the interior. His excellency was sympathetic. Petrosino was equipped, surprisingly enough, with credentials from the ministry which made him practically an Italian policeman of high rank. A few weeks later he set out confidently for Palermo to begin his investigations. That was as far as he got. On the morning of March 13, 1909, while on his way to the Questura—the city's police headquarters—he paused in the Piazza Marina to watch the colorful scene and people. Two men came up behind him. Unhurriedly, they drew revolvers from under their jackets and fired four bullets point-blank into his back and head. Petrosino, like Hennessey, had gone too far into the affairs of the brotherhood, and somewhere along the line the news of his presence and the nature of his job became known. He was dead when he hit the pavement; his executioners mingled with the excitedly gathering crowd, walked away and were never found. Cables and letters again went between Rome, New York and Washington. The Italian government offered a lire reward for the arrest of the criminals, Commissioner Bingham in New York used harsh words—all with little result. The body of Lieutenant Petrosino was in due course shipped home. His widow was granted a pension, he was given an impressive funeral by the Police Department and tributes to his work came even from the White House.

Lieutenant Petrosino's knowledge of the Sicilian brotherhood, unique at that time, was buried with him. The New York Police Department's special squad of detectives, which he had organized, went out with Commissioner Bingham. The Italian vote made such activity embarrassing politically to the new city administration. Petrosino and his special squad might have done much over the next few decades against the almost incredible rise of the brotherhood in the United States and the foundation it built for the organized crime of today. Dozens of capi mafiosi of the future, who were to control bootlegging, gambling, prostitution and other racketeering in the roaring twenties, were growing up in various parts of the country. They were eventually to cause us untold damage, financially and particularly morally. But no one was to know for a long time still who they were and how they were connected.

In 1925 another wave of Mafia immigration began. Benito Mussolini had decided that Sicily was to be the political and intellectual center of his Fascist empire of the Mediterranean. Before this could be done however, the dictator realized, the brotherhood's rule of the island had to be broken. For the difficult job Mussolini picked the able and energetic questore of Milan, Colonel Cesare Mori—a professional policeman who had come to hate the Mafia and its works as much as Petrosino and Hennessey ever had. Mori was given extraordinary powers and over a thousand picked policemen. He descended on Sicily like a cyclone. His preparatory intelligence was fairly good. Whole families of mafiosi were arrested, given drumhead trials and deported to the penal colonies of the Lipari Islands and the island of Ustica.

For the time being, the activities of the Mafia in Sicily ceased almost entirely. Those who were sent to the islands pretended profound penitence and expressed enthusiastic support of Il Duce and the new Fascist way of life. Many were released as a result. Others escaped with the help of fishermen who knew that the Mafia would show its gratitude. Those who had not come to Mori's attention—and these included some of the most dangerous—simply stopped operations. The extortion rackets, robberies, smuggling, feuds and murders dipped sharply. In 1928 Prefect Mori reported to Mussolini that the Mafia had been so disrupted that it would never function again. Through an intensive psychological campaign, he said, he had convinced the Sicilian people that the brotherhood was a disgrace to them all. They had responded, even to the children in the schools. The Mafia was dead.

The prefect was mistaken. Some of the mafiosi either by choice or from lack of means lived more or less honestly for several years until the collapse of Mussolini's regime in World War II gave them their next opportunity. Many, however, managed to come to the United States by devious means without immigration formalities, as merchant seamen or across the Mexican and Canadian borders, to join friends and relatives already established in this country. (Several of the Apalachin delegates stemmed from this era.) They were easily absorbed by the brotherhood. By 1925 the Mafia in the United States was reaching new and undreamed-of heights of wealth and power as a result of Prohibition and the organizing genius of Al Capone in Chicago and Charlie "Lucky" Luciano in New York.

5
The Purge of the Greasers

FRED J. COOK

Joe (the Boss) Masseria had led a charmed life. Or, looking at it another way, the devil had long protected him. Joe the Boss ruled the New York Mafia, then usually called the Unione Siciliano, throughout most of the decade of the twenties. He had escaped murder so many times that the legend grew he could run faster and dodge quicker than any bullet could fly. The legend, like most legends, strayed from truth. Joe the Boss could dodge only the bullets of his enemies, not those of his friends.

Joe the Boss had climbed to power in 1920 by gunning down a rival, a bootlegger named Salvatore Mauro, in a pitched battle in the middle of Chrystie Street. During his early reign, he sometimes had to fend off challenges from upstarts suffering an excess of brashness and a deficiency of discretion. One of the most ambitious of these rivals was Umberto Valenti. In the spring of 1922, Valenti decided to strike directly at the authority of Joe the Boss, and he made his intentions clear by murdering Vincent Terranova, the younger brother of Ciro Terranova, the Artichoke King, who ruled the Bronx and was a close ally of Joe the Boss.

The murder of the brother of so prized a cohort could not be ignored, and Joe the Boss planned retribution in the very shadow of Police Headquarters. In those days, the mob had established what became known as "the curb exchange" in the streets outside headquarters. The curb exchange was the rumrunner's ver-

86

sion of the stock exchange. A bootlegger might become over-loaded, for example, with good bourbon just when his customers all developed an exclusive taste for Scotch. In such exigency, he would have to swap the liquor he had for the liquor he needed; he would have to make contact with other members of the fraternity to make his deal. So, with a brashness that seems incredible today, the top bootleg barons of the period had established the curb exchange along Kenmare, Broome, Grand, and Elizabeth Streets, practically encircling headquarters; and, when disputes broke out over who had gypped whom in a deal, they settled matters with gunfire not far from the windows of the Police Commissioner and Chief of Detectives. Joe the Boss had little doubt that his rival would show up at the curb exchange to transact necessary business, so he stationed himself and two henchmen in the doorway of 194 Grand Street, only a short distance from the southern end of headquarters.

Events worked out as Joe the Boss had foreseen—up to a point. Early in the evening of May 8, 1922, as workmen were hurrying home from their jobs, Umberto Valenti and a hired gun, Silva Tagliagamba, turned out of Mott Street into Grand and began walking toward the ambush of Joe the Boss. Masseria waited until Valenti and Tagliagamba were in front of 190 Grand, then he nodded his head and he and his two torpedoes popped out into the street, the guns in their hands going off like firecrackers. Valenti and Tagliagamba fired back, and the bullets zinging along the street wounded four passersby, two women and two men. Valenti and Tagliagamba fled.

With the racket almost splitting the eardrums of detectives in headquarters, the law made an appearance—and Masseria and his helpers also took to their heels. Joe the Boss, short and heavily built, churned around the corner of Mulberry Street into Broome, where his agents were transacting the day's business. The boys ducked into doorways when they saw The Boss charging by with two detectives on his heels. Joe the Boss lightened his load by tossing a .38 caliber revolver into the gutter. And while one of the pursuing detectives stopped to repossess it, Joe the Boss sped on. He dashed across Broome toward Kenmare Street, but here ran into Edward Tracey, a detective sergeant, on his way to headquarters. Tracey swerved his car directly into Masseria's path, jumped out and struck Joe the Boss over the head with a nightclub.

In the nearby headquarters, when detectives frisked Joe the Boss, they found a curious document—a gun permit signed by Justice Selah B. Strong in Supreme Court permitting him to carry a weapon anywhere he went in the state. Naturally, gun permits were not supposed to be issued to notorious criminals, but in the New York of those days and in most other parts of the country as well, a lot of strange things were happening.

There was, of course, a great scandal. But like many of that period, this quickly and conveniently died, achieving little beyond the disclosure that Joe the Boss could persuade the law to issue him a pistol permit. Other matters stemming from the ambush in the shadows of headquarters were not settled so fast.

Valenti's henchman, Tagliagamba, who had been wounded in the gun battle, held on until late June before he succumbed. The law went through the motions of charging Joe the Boss with murder, but it permitted him his liberty on bail, an indication of the law's generosity during this period to distinguished citizens of Joe the Boss's stature. Another indication was the fact that the case against Joe the Boss never came to trial. Postponement followed postponement, and Joe the Boss continued to do business as usual at his old stand.

Umberto Valenti became impatient. He had held his fire, hoping the electric chair might do his work for him; but when it became apparent the only chair Joe the Boss would ever sit in was his own upholstered one, Valenti decided he would help the law. For this high-minded mission, he picked four torpedoes who were supposed to know their business.

Joe the Boss lived with his wife and two children at 80 Second Avenue, just a few doors from the corner of Fifth Street. Shortly after noon on the hot summer day of August 9, 1922, he left his apartment, sporting a new straw hat, and turned north toward Fifth Street. Two of the torpedoes had been waiting in a black limousine parked down the street and two others in a coffee house across the way. These latter, the instant they saw Joe the Boss emerge from his home, dropped their coffee cups and ran out, one cutting behind him, the other racing ahead to cut him off.

The man in front was too eager; he opened fire too soon and Joe the Boss, alerted to his danger, sprinted into Heiney's Millinery

Shop at 82 Second Avenue. The gunman followed at his heels. Fritz Heiney, the proprietor, stood petrified at the scene that now took place before his eyes.

"The man with the revolver came close to the other fellow and aimed," he said. "Just as he fired the man jumped to one side. The bullet smashed the window of my store. Then the man fired again and the fellow he aimed at ducked his head forward. The third shot made a second hole in my window."

Out of bullets, the frustrated torpedo clicked his revolver futilely a couple more times at Joe the Boss's bobbing head, then dashed out of the shop and ran with his companion to the getaway car. The car swung the corner into Fifth Street, swarming at the time with members of the International Ladies' Garment Workers' Union coming from a meeting in Beethoven Hall, half a block away. Some of the unionists tried to stop the speeding car, but the thugs who had failed to eliminate Joe the Boss were equal to pumping bullets into this massed, unarmed humanity. Their shots felled five of the workers, and two others were knocked down by the speeding car. One man subsequently died of his wounds.

Detectives, arriving belatedly, found Joe the Boss at home, sitting on the side of his bed, his feet, aching from his latest marathon with death, soaking in a pan of hot water. On his head he still wore his new straw hat—with two bullet holes in its crown.

Far from eliminating Joe the Boss, the clumsiness of Valenti's stooges had boosted him to greater status in the underworld. Squat, chunky, hard-running Joe Masseria became a living legend—the man who could outrun and outdodge bullets. Such celebrity, however, would not settle the issue between him and Umberto Valenti. Only bullets would do that, and Joe the Boss decided the next bullets would be fired from his side of the fence.

To achieve this end, Joe the Boss reasoned, he must move swiftly and nothing could serve his purpose better than a peace conference. So he sent an emissary to Valenti, suggesting that they compose their differences. The deluded Valenti, evidently thinking Joe the Boss must be winded by his bullet-dodging feat, closed his eyes and consented.

The opposing factions met in a spaghetti house on East Twelfth Street near Second Avenue on August 11, 1922. Valenti came with one retainer; Masseria, with one. What Valenti didn't know was that Joe the Boss had two more thugs in hiding outside. After breaking the bread of peace and stuffing themselves with spaghetti, the conferees adjourned to the street and took a leisurely stroll along Twelfth, walking in the direction of Second Avenue. At the corner, they halted—and Masseria's two extra guns appeared. At a signal from Joe the Boss, all his boys suddenly whipped out their barkers.

The street-corner group, so amicable a few seconds before, split and ran in all directions, guns blazing furiously. Valenti, trying to emulate Joe the Boss's agile footwork, sped diagonally across the intersection toward a waiting taxicab. One of Masseria's gunmen followed him out into the intersection, stopped, and touched off a full clip of bullets. Valenti managed to reach the taxicab and open the door. Then he pitched over backwards from the impact of the final and fatal shot.

At such hazards had Joe the Boss pulled off his coup. Valenti had been eliminated, and only Joe the Boss ruled the New York Mafia.

Though two murder charges had been brought against Joe the Boss in three months, nothing happened to him. Witnesses, confronted with the sinister power of the Mafia, suddenly lost all recollection of events, and the law, for whatever mysterious reasons, never seemed very eager to prosecute anyway. So Joe the Boss went right on running the affairs of crime.

He did make certain alterations in technique. After the Valenti shoot-down, he exhibited more circumspection. He seemed to have learned well the first lesson of a criminal boss: never get yourself out front, never attract a lot of newspaper notoriety. That's dangerous. Let others man the front-line trenches and take the rap if things go wrong; stay in the background yourself and pull the strings. Such is the prescription for immunity, longevity, and ever more millions.

Operating on this theory, Joe the Boss let it be known that he had retired and was living on his accumulated hoard. He was, of course, doing nothing of the kind. A Mafioso hardly ever retires; he pursues his career of crime to the end. And Joe the Boss was no exception to the rule.

He learned, however, to keep well in the shadows. His name

no longer made newspaper headlines. Lieutenants and underbosses now carried out his missions. In the Bronx, he still had his alliance with Ciro Terranova. In Manhattan, Charles (Lucky) Luciano gradually rose in status and power until he became right-hand man and principal lieutenant. Across the river in Brooklyn, there was, originally, Frankie Yale to keep an eye on his interests; and after Frankie was toppled from the barony, there were other lieutenants who took over: first Anthony (Little Augie) Pisano and next, right behind him, an even more potent figure—Joe Adonis.

With affairs of crime so well organized, with his own pinnacle so secure against assault by the law, Joe (the Boss) Masseria ruled with hardly a hitch until 1930. Then war broke out, a bloody conflict that shook the underworld. It was a warfare waged on two levels: first, the open battle of two powerful gang chieftains for control of the New York Mafia; secondly, submerged within this visible conflict, the secret, conspiratorial thrust of the new breed—Luciano, Costello, Adonis—to rise, seize supreme power, and impose upon the lawless the rule of gang law and order first drafted at Atlantic City.

At this point Joe Valachi comes . . . into our tale. The prize informer of 1963 had viewed the 1930 battleground from the level of the troops, from the limited perspective of the button man carrying out killings on assignment. He knew nothing about the Atlantic City conclave of the previous year or the far-reaching decisions made there; all he knew was that the forces of Joe (the Boss) Masseria were at war with those of Salvatore Maranzano— and that he was a soldier in the army of Maranzano.

According to Valachi, the trouble started when Joe the Boss assigned one of his triggermen to gun down Tommy Reina, head of a family in the Maranzano group. This deed, carried out on February 26, 1930, was to set off a succession of explosions. Valachi might be expected to know as much as anyone about this initial act, for his wife is the former Mildred Reina, daughter of the slain gang chief. Yet the reasons for the Reina murder remain obscure unless it was, as Valachi intimates, that Joe the Boss felt himself so powerful he could take over another family at will. In any event, that is what Joe the Boss endeavored to do, installing one of his own henchmen, Joseph Pinzolo, as new boss of the family. The slain Reina's underboss, Thomas Gagliano, did not take kindly to this usurpation, and so an alliance was formed between the original Reina-Gagliano troop and the forces of Maranzano.

It was at first a secret pact. Maranzano and Gagliano wanted to gain as much advantage as they could by "sneaking." This, as Valachi explained, was a strategy of lying low, perfecting plans, and then suddenly "hitting" as many of the opposition leaders as possible before they knew what was going on or just what quarter the bullets were coming from. The desire to sneak a few murders, Valachi explained, was the principal reason he had been recruited for the Maranzano family. New faces were needed. "The idea was they figured the opposite mob wouldn't know us," he explained.

The first body sneaked was that of the unpopular Joseph Pinzolo in the late summer of 1930. According to Valachi, the murder was committed by Girolamo (Bobby Doyle) Santuccio. "I was told by Bobby Doyle himself," he testified, "that he got the break of his life. He went down to Pinzolo's office and he found him all alone and he killed him."

It was at about this point, according to Valachi, that the war of the underworld took on the broader aspects of a racial feud. Joe the Boss passed a death sentence on all Sicilians coming from the Castellammarese area. Just why he should suddenly have developed such a passionate blood-thirst for all Castellammarese is not clear, but Joseph Profaci, who was one of them and who was to become one of the gang powers of New York, assured Valachi that it was so. Castellammarese were to be eliminated whenever Joe the Boss's gunmen found them—in New York, Buffalo, Chicago, anywhere in the United States.

The Castellammarese, headed by Salvatore Maranzano, naturally reacted to this edict and decided to conduct a counterelimination program of their own. A key figure in their plans was a rollicking killer whom Valachi knew only as "Buster from Chicago." This Buster was *persona non grata* with Al Capone, a very unhealthy state in Chicago, and so he had come East, a gun for hire, and had been enlisted by Maranzano. "Buster looked like a college boy, a little over six feet, light complexion, weighed about 200 pounds," Valachi told the McClellan committee. "He also would carry a violin case." In the case, there was, of course, no violin— just a machine gun.

With Buster from Chicago bolstering the fire power of the

Castellammarese, the Maranzano forces set out to sneak the top command of the Masseria group. They hoped, naturally, to sneak Joe the Boss himself, but Joe the Boss was not circulating very freely in these parlous days. The Maranzano forces decided, therefore, that their best tactic would be to keep a close watch on two of his important henchmen, Alfred Mineo and Steve Ferrigno, the latter known to Valachi under the name of Fennuci. Fennuci had an apartment at 750 Pelham Parkway in the Bronx, and Valachi was assigned the task of setting up a plant in another apartment directly across a courtyard from Fennuci's. Here Valachi, Buster from Chicago, the Doc, Nick Capuzzi, and Joe Profaci waited and watched for nearly two months.

Then, one day in early November, 1930, just as Valachi was about to enter the apartment building, a car drew up outside and Fennuci and Joe the Boss himself climbed out. They all entered the elevator together, the newcomers instantly wary and suspicious of Valachi. "Punch yours," they told him. So he punched the sixth-floor button, got off and ran downstairs to his second-floor apartment, where he told his waiting killers that Joe the Boss was visiting Fennuci. Great was the excitement. Buster, a true sharpshooter, set up a watch at the window, eager for the chance to draw a bead on Joe the Boss. Valachi began to sweat. He didn't want the killing to take place from *his* apartment.

Fortunately for both Valachi and Joe the Boss, Masseria and his henchmen didn't appear in public again that night. The next morning, to Valachi's relief, the sharpshooting squad rented another apartment in the building with an equally excellent view of the courtyard. Reinforcements poured in, including "Bobby Doyle" Santuccio, the killer of Pinzolo; and Valachi left, deciding he had fulfilled his chore as spotter and wouldn't be needed in the action that was to come. But he learned all the details afterwards, he said, from Bobby Doyle, who was ecstatic at the way things started to pop almost the moment he arrived. "I got a break," he told Valachi. "I didn't have to be around too long."

Evidently, Valachi said, there had been a big meeting of Masseria's troop in Fennuci's apartment. Valachi estimated some twenty to twenty-four hoods had gathered there. About 2:45 on the afternoon of November 5, 1930, the meeting started to break up. The troop slipped out in pairs and the watching killers let them pass, waiting for Joe the Boss to appear. But they caught no sight of Joe the Boss. Finally, with the gathering virtually disbanded, Alfred Mineo and Fennuci stepped out into the daylight.

"When these two appeared, they didn't want to gamble any more," Valachi said, describing the reactions of the killer squad. "They said, 'Let us grab what we have. Maybe Joe got out during the night,' and they shot these two, which were two bosses. They were just as important as Masseria was."

This statement probably reflects the greatest gap in Valachi's knowledge as his view was from the bottom, looking up. He had no intimate knowledge, in most instances, of the dealing in the executive suite of crime; he knew only what filtered down, what he learned by rumor and report. Mineo and Fennuci may have been important cogs in the machinery of Masseria's organization; but they weren't anywhere near as important as Joe the Boss himself or as Joe the Boss's real right arm, Lucky Luciano.

With the slaying of Mineo and Fennuci, the sneaking largely ended. The Masseria group traced the furniture that had been delivered to Valachi's Pelham Parkway apartment; they found it had been purchased by his sister and they realized that Maranzano had been behind the killings. Despite the loss of two key henchmen, Masseria, according to Valachi, put out peace feelers. Perhaps he was trying to pull another Umberto Valenti coup, or perhaps he meant it. In any event, the maneuver didn't work. Maranzano was not Valenti, and, besides, he still had a score to settle.

One of Masseria's henchmen, Joseph Catania, alias Soldier Joe Baker, had been hijacking some of Maranzano's liquor trucks. This was a serious affront, and Maranzano decreed that Soldier Joe Baker had to go. The chore of arranging for his departure was assigned to Nick Capuzzi, Salvatore (Sally Shields) Shillitani, and Buster from Chicago, with Joe Valachi as their getaway-car driver.

Maranzano's spies had discovered that Soldier Joe regularly called at an apartment on Belmont Avenue in the Bronx. They rented a lookout post down the street, but it was almost a block away, too far for any kind of accurate shooting. Joe Valachi was disgusted. He told Maranzano that, if the boys kept hanging out around the neighborhood, someone was going to spot them and Masseria's torpedoes would come in and blast them out. Joe favored action while his side still had the initiative. Maranzano backed him.

Using a couple of spring leafs from a car, Joe pried open the door of the apartment Soldier Joe Baker was in the habit of visiting. He and his troop had timed the crash-in for about a half hour before Soldier Joe's regular calling time, but they hadn't been prepared for the sight that met their eyes when they jimmied the door.

"So, to my amazement," Joe Valachi testified, "I crashed the doorway, the apartment was empty and there were three painters in there. . . . These painters wanted to give us money. They thought we were sticking them up. We said: 'We don't want any money, just keep painting.' "

The painters obeyed instructions. The gunmen waited. In about half an hour, right on schedule, Soldier Joe Baker came walking along the street.

"As soon as he made the appearance," Valachi continued, "I left to get the car ready. In other words, to have the motor ready instead of going down there and running down and starting the car. I left about a minute before and I had the motor ready. Within about a minute's time, they were right behind me. . . ."

In that minute, Soldier Joe Baker had been dispatched, shot six times in the head and body. Though he was still alive when he reached Fordham Hospital, he sealed his lips and died without naming his slayers.

The liquidation of Soldier Joe, coming on top of the murders of Pinzolo, Mineo, and Fennuci, seemed to indicate to the underworld that Maranzano was winning the war for control of the New York rackets. He had now at his command an army of about 600 thugs and more were "coming over" regularly. He had also the financing for an extensive campaign. Tom Gagliano, the boss of the Reina family once Pinzolo had been put out of the way, had contributed $140,000. Steve Magaddino, then as now the rackets lord of Buffalo, contributed $5,000 a week, and another $5,000 weekly came in from Joe Aiello, a Chicago gangster allied with Bugs Moran in the battle against Al Capone.

The button men saw little of this money. Valachi testified that he and his companions in murder were getting only about $25 a week, just enough to live on. He got so cramped for spending

money, he said, that he had to do a little "moonlighting"—pulling
off a couple of burglary jobs to raise some additional revenue.
Throughout the mobs, the Masseria-Maranzano struggle was dis-
rupting life, for a mobster who had to stay in hiding most of the
time for his own skin's sake couldn't go about business as usual.
In this pass, according to Valachi, Joe the Boss made peace over-
tures. He was willing to abdicate as a family chieftain and to become just another soldier in the army if Maranzano would agree
to leave him alone. But Maranzano wouldn't deal.

Out in Chicago, Al Capone gave Joe the Boss a helping hand
and cut off one source of Maranzano revenue when his gunmen,
operating from two apartment machine-gun nests, caught Joe
Aiello in a crossfire and riddled him with bullets. Maranzano
could afford the loss of this distant confederate and his $5,000
a week, for he now had a conspiratorial trump card up his sleeve.

The continuous blasting . . . made little sense to two of Joe
the Boss's most powerful aides, Lucky Luciano and Vito Genovese.
It was obvious to them, in addition, that their boss was losing the
war he had touched off with the slaying of Tom Reina. There
was only one way to end it, to avert complete disaster, make peace,
and get back to business as usual—Joe the Boss would have to
go.

Secretly, according to Valachi—and other sources agree—
Luciano and Maranzano reached an understanding. Charlie Lucky
would arrange for the slaying of his own boss. This would re-estab-
lish peace in the brotherhood. It would also, of course, create a
vacuum at the top of the Masseria family, and Charlie Lucky, the
heir apparent, did not appear distraught at the prospect.

Joe the Boss, not being a mind reader, naturally had no clue
to Charlie Lucky's thoughts. He liked Charlie Lucky, relied on
him, depended on him. Charlie Lucky in recent years had been
handling most of Joe the Boss's detail for him and handling it well.
Besides, Charlie Lucky had an old-world flair for living that Joe
the Boss liked. Charlie Lucky was almost like a son to him.

So Joe the Boss was agreeable when Charlie Lucky made a
date to go out to Scarpato's Restaurant in Coney Island on the
afternoon of April 15, 1931. They would have a good dinner, play
cards, get away from it all. Joe the Boss liked the prospect.

Others liked it, too—and began to make plans. Judge Samuel

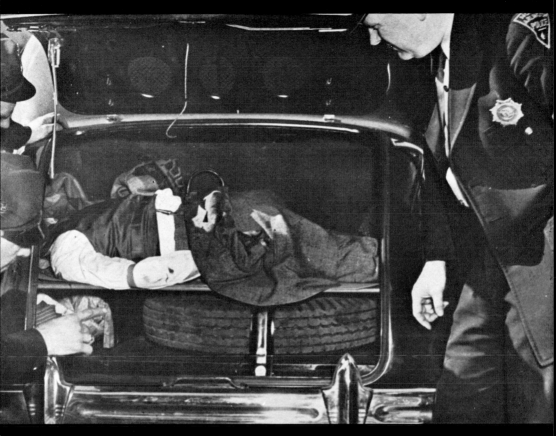

The contrast between real-life Mafia terrorism and pop sentimentality about its operations is illustrated by the trussed-up body of Dr. J. G. Littlefield of South Paris, Maine—typical of the dozens of victims of Mafia strong-arm methods.
Wide World Photos

Detailed, dramatic knowledge of Mafia activities was given U.S. government agencies and the American public by a one-time insider, Joseph Valachi. He is shown here as he testified before a Senate investigation committee in 1963. *N.Y. Daily News Photo*

Ernie Rupolo, wearing dark glasses, facing a judge during one of his many appearances in court. Rupolo was eventually brutally murdered by his Mafia superiors.
N.Y. Daily News Photo

A face out of the past: Joseph Masseria, one of the early Mafia figures who retained control until the purge of the "Greasers" made way for new generations of

99

Above: The legendary Al Capone as he appeared during the last years of his life, in "retirement" in Florida. *Right:* The victims of gang warfare between Capone and Bugs Moran for control of Chicago underworld traffic in liquor during the Prohibition era. The photo shows the results of the so-called "St. Valentine's Day Massacre" in 1929, when Capone gunmen invaded Moran's headquarters at 2122 N. Clark Street. They herded seven men into a rear garage, lined them up against a wall and riddled them with bullets. *Wide World Photos*

Frank Costello, his head bandaged after a mysterious shooting incident in the lobby of his apartment building in 1957. He refused to answer the questions of a Grand Jury on this matter on May 7 and received a jail sentence for contempt (see photo on next page). *Wide World Photos*

Frank Costello on his way to prison on May 9, 1957. He is being escorted by two New York City policemen on his way to detention on Rikers Island, to serve a 30-day sentence for contempt of court. The sentence was passed following the shooting attempt on Costello (see preceding page). *Wide World Photos*

Right: Charles ("Lucky") Luciano, flanked by two detectives, on his way to court on June 18, 1936. Luciano was sentenced to 30 to 50 years in prison on charges of compulsory prostitution. He was later deported to Italy (see photo on next page).

Wide World Photos

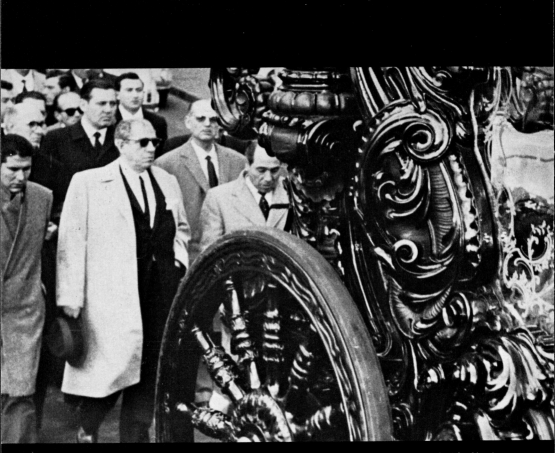

The funeral of Lucky Luciano. On January 29, 1962, Luciano was buried in Naples. The photo shows the elaborate hearse, carved in silver and black, and drawn by eight black horses, which carried his body to the cemetery. Directly following the hearse, in light overcoat and wearing dark glasses, is Bartolo Luciano, the dead man's brother. *Wide World Photos*

S. Leibowitz, of the Kings County Court in Brooklyn, was then a rising young lawyer, laying the foundations for his reputation as one of the outstanding criminal trial attorneys in the nation. He had defended some of the mobsters and was well known and well liked by them. On the morning of April 15, 1931, he was in court trying a case and his secretary was in his office at 66 Court Street when the door swung open and in walked Albert Anastasia, the man who in the not too distant future would be know as the Lord High Executioner of Murder, Inc.

"What time is it?" Anastasia asked Leibowitz's secretary.

She pointed to a big clock on the wall.

"There it is," she said. "Look for yourself."

"That says twelve o'clock," Albert A. reported, a bit doubt-fully. "Are you sure that's the right time?"

The girl glanced up at the clock, began to get annoyed.

"Sure," she said, "it's twelve o'clock. If you don't believe it, look out the window at the clock on Borough Hall."

Albert A. looked, pretended to be convinced.

"Is the law man in?" he asked, referring to Leibowitz.

"No, he's in court. He won't be back until one o'clock."

"I'll wait," said Albert A.

He helped himself to a chair and sat there patiently, establishing for himself an ironclad alibi should anyone ever want to question him about the events that were soon to take place in Scarpato's Restaurant in Coney Island.

Charlie Lucky and Joe the Boss were already seated at a table there. Joe Valachi's version of events departs considerably from all the official and unofficial reports of the time. Valachi seems to picture a considerable dinner party, attended by Ciro Terranova, Vito Genovese, Charlie Lucky, "a fellow named Cheech," and Joe Stretch. According to Valachi, Terranova was so unnerved on the way over, his hands trembled so he couldn't get the key into the ignition and he had to be thrown "off the wheel." This cost Terranova such a loss of face that he was soon afterwards deposed in favor of Trigger Mike Coppola.

Official and other reports of the time, however, seem to establish, that there were just two present at Joe the Boss's last dinner— Joe the Boss himself and Charlie Lucky. They had an excellent meal, relishing Scarpato's excellent clam sauce, the succulent lobster, and the Chianti wine. They took their time. When the dishes were cleared away, Charlie Lucky proposed a game of cards. Joe the Boss was agreeable. . . .

Lucky called for a deck from the house, and they played and talked for about forty-five minutes. It was now about 3:30 P.M. The restaurant had cleared. Just Joe the Boss and Charlie Lucky, his almost son, sat there at the table in Scarpato's, playing cards. It was at this point that Charlie Lucky politely excused himself and made a trip to the men's room.

He was hardly out of sight, when some crude characters wandered in from the street. They walked right up behind Joe the Boss, bemused by food and wine, and before he could turn his head, they whipped out guns and blasted away. Some twenty shots were sprayed around the premises. Six of them plowed into Joe the Boss's head and body, all from the back. He had no chance to turn and dodge. He pitched forward across the sparkling white tablecloth, his right arm extended as if it had been his play at cards, in his death-frozen grip the ace of diamonds.

Back in the men's room, Charlie Lucky heard the unholy racket.

"As soon as I finished drying my hands, I hurried out and walked back to see what it was about," he told investigating officers.

All he found, of course, was his dear, beloved patron dead. Those who had done the deed had left.

Joe the Boss, who had managed to outrun and outdodge the bullets of his enemies, hadn't been able to elude those of his friends. His failure in this final test wrought profound changes in the underworld. Charlie Lucky, his alter ego, succeeded to his power and perquisites. And Salvatore Maranzano ruled supreme as the boss of bosses. At least for the time being.

Salvatore Maranzano called a big meeting to tell the boys how it was going to be. According to Joe Valachi, Maranzano rented a big hall on Washington Avenue in the Bronx, and some 500 of the faithful attended. Maranzano began by describing the evils for which Masseria had been responsible—the unjustified shootings, the murder of Tom Reina, the war on the Castellammarese.

"Now, it is going to be different," he said. "We are going to have—first we have the boss of all bosses, which is myself."

Maranzano explained the organizational structure that hence-forth would govern the affairs of crime. Each family was to have its own boss. Next in rank would be an underboss, and below him a "caporegima," or commander of the troops. "Now, if a soldier wants to talk to a boss," Valachi continued, "he should not take the privilege for him to try to go direct to the boss. He must speak first to the caporegima, and the caporegima, if it is required and it is important enough, the caporegima will make an appointment for the soldier. . . . This is what I called second government."

According to Valachi, it was at this time that the Mafia struc-ture of New York was divided into the five families that have continued to rule it ever since. Maranzano headed his own group, which was soon split into two wings, one under Joe Profaci, the other under Joseph (Joe Bananas) Bonanno. The original Reina family was to be governed by Tom Gagliano, with Thomas (Three-Finger Brown) Lucchese as his underboss. Lucky Luciano sat atop the former Masseria family; under him, Vito Genovese. And in Brooklyn, according to Valachi, Philip and Vincent Man-gano were given control, with Albert Anastasia as their underboss. In this, there appears to be some confusion, for the Manganos did not acquire power until much later. At the time, there was just one crime czar in Brooklyn (curiously, a man whom Valachi never mentions), and he was Joe Adonis, as powerful a man as the under-world of his day was to produce and the one to whom Anastasia and his murder goons always owed their primary fealty.

Valachi's account of the early days of the reign of Maranzano continued in vivid detail. The boss of all the bosses, having ex-plained the gangland structure and enlisted his minions in the fam-ilies of their choice, decided he should have a coronation party. The result, according to Valachi, was a banquet that lasted five days. Every evening the mob gathered and held high revelry until three or four the next morning. This marathon celebration had a double motif: first, to hail Maranzano as the new boss of bosses; secondly, to raise money for the war-depleted treasury. Both pur-poses were achieved.

Valachi testified he "understood" that the five days netted $115,000. Maranzano, he said, "sent out, for instance, a thousand tickets to Al Capone, and Al Capone sent $6,000. He sent a thousand tickets to Buffalo, and they also sent $6,000. Charlie Lucky himself sent $6,000.

"Them were the big amounts I know. The rest, as they came in, the guests. Frank Scalise would be at the head of a small table. . . . As he would greet the guests as they came in, 'Have a drink'—you know, in Italian. He would go for his pocket, he would throw money on the table. They would follow suit. That was his duty. . . .

"I used to see piles of money on the table every night. Maranzano used to get it at night."

Originally, according to Valachi, the word had been spread that the button men were to share in these "contributions" as a reward for their loyalty in the recent war of the mobs, but Maranzano, with the insatiable greed of a gang chieftain, apparently gobbled all. "I never got a nickel of that, Senator," Valachi told Senator McClellan. "I used to go down, after that I used to go down to the office, I felt that, you know, some day I might be handed something, but I never did."

Valachi was so desperate for money that he talked Buster from Chicago into accompanying him on a burglary, though he knew that it was against Maranzano's rules for any of his troopers to engage in such free enterprise. Valachi reassured Buster by telling him the boss would never know about it, but Maranzano's pipelines of information were better than Valachi knew. The very next day, Bobby Doyle taxed him with having broken the rules by free-lancing in burglary and said the boss of bosses wanted a word with him. Instead of going to see Maranzano, the frightened Valachi took off for Buffalo to pay Steve Magaddino a visit. Bobby Doyle agreed not to let on to Maranzano that they had ever talked.

Magaddino played host to Valachi for about eight days. Then he had to "go to South America somewhere," but, before he left, at Valachi's request, he loaned Valachi $500. Valachi returned to New York; and, figuring that matters had had time to cool, he went directly to Maranzano's office at Park Avenue and 46th Street to make his peace.

"When I got back and I went up to the office, Mr. Maranzano was talking with Charlie Lucky and Vito Genovese," he testified. "As I walked in, they were in the middle of the floor, talking. He dropped them and walked right over to me and he kissed me. At that time they used to kiss, Senator."

It was, Valachi explained, an entirely friendly kiss.

"You know, I sent the check to Buffalo to Steve," Maranzano told his apprehensive henchman.

"You already know?" Valachi stammered.

"That's all right, don't worry about it," Maranzano told him.

"OK. Thanks," Valachi mumbled.

Relieved, Valachi sat down, and Maranzano went back to his business discussion with Charlie Lucky and Vito Genovese. The $500 that Maranzano paid for him was all he ever got out of the $115,000 kitty that had been collected to reward the soldiers. Valachi said that he never dared broach the matter of any greater reward to Maranzano; one just didn't do that with the boss of bosses. Besides, he figured, Maranzano might have more important matters on his mind and need the money. This conjecture, it developed, was absolutely right.

Not long after his return from Buffalo, Valachi got a summons from Maranzano to report at nine o'clock at night at the boss's home.

"When I got to his house," Valachi testified, "he was bandaging his son's foot, I remember.

"I walked in. He greeted me. I waited until he got through with his son.

"He said to me, 'You know'—now, Senator, I'm telling you. 'You know why I didn't give you any money? You must have been wondering.'

"I said, 'Yes.'

"He was referring to the banquet.

"'I didn't want to lose you. I didn't want you to get loose. But don't worry about the money.' He said, 'We have to go to the mattress again.'

"The 'mattress' means that we have to go back to war, that is what it means. . . .

"Naturally, I wasn't too happy to hear that. So he told me that we can't get along. He meant he can't get along with Charlie Lucky, Vito. He gave me a list. 'We have to get rid of these people.'

". . . On the list was, I will try to remember as I go along: Al Capone, Frank Costello, Charlie Lucky, Vito Genovese, Vincent Mangano, Joe Adonis, Dutch Schultz. These are all important names at the time."

In this, Valachi was not exaggerating. On that list were the names of men who were to rule the American underworld from that day to the present. The liquidation of any one of them would have made headlines across the nation, and the idea of knocking them all off seemed to indicate that Maranzano was toying with a fatal delusion. Valachi was worried, but not alone by the eminence of the names on Maranzano's execution list. An order had been passed around only a few days before that Maranzano's boys weren't to go up to his 46th Street office lugging their lethal hardware under their coats because there was a rumor the police might raid the place. Valachi didn't like to be left so naked and helpless. "I'm afraid they are trying to prepare us to be without guns," he had said to his friends at the time. "I just don't like it."

He liked it less when Maranzano told him that he had a meeting scheduled for the next day, a last conference, with Charlie Lucky and Vito Genovese. Valachi protested.

"Can I talk to you?" he said. "Look. After all, if I lose you, I am out in the street. I got all reasons to worry. Must you go to this appointment? Can't you let Angelo Caruso go? If this is your last meeting——"

"No, I got to go," Maranzano said decisively.

The meeting with Charlie Lucky and Vito Genovese was scheduled for two o'clock the following afternoon, September 10, 1931—a red-letter day in the history of the American underworld. Maranzano instructed Valachi to telephone the office at 1:45 P.M. to see if his services were going to be needed.

Not liking matters a bit, Valachi nevertheless telephoned Maranzano's office at the appointed time "and Charlie Buffalo answered the phone. He said everything was all right. He said I need not go down." So Valachi and his friend, "the Gap," decided to forget impending troubles and went to Brooklyn to visit a couple of girls they knew.

They had hardly departed on this pleasurable pursuit before matters ceased being "all right" in Rooms 925 and 926, Maranzano's suite of offices at 230 Park Avenue. Four men, all Jewish, walked through the entrance door. There was quite a crowd in the outer room. Some of Maranzano's boys, including Bobby Doyle, were on hand, and there were a number of other persons waiting to see the boss on business matters. The newcomers identified themselves as detectives. They had come, they explained, to see Maranzano.

The boss of bosses, having been primed to expect such a visit, came out of his inner office, welcomed the strangers and escorted them in. Evidently, from later accounts, the door had hardly closed before Maranzano sensed that something was fatally wrong. He dived for a gun he kept in his desk drawer, but the "detectives," having the drop on him, began blasting away and set upon him with knives. In a few seconds, it was all over. The "boss of bosses" was dead, with four bullet wounds in his body and six stab wounds in his abdomen.

In the outer office, the crowd scattered. The "detectives" came running out and headed for the stairway. As they ran, they encountered face-to-face one of the most ferocious killers-for-hire of the day, Vincent (Mad Dog) Coll. The Mad Dog was on his way in to take care of a commission from Maranzano, but he had arrived just too late. His employer was dead, and the "detectives" who had done the deed, in the fraternity of murder, simply waved to the Mad Dog to get lost—the cops were on the way.

Bit by bit, in after years, Joe Valachi pieced together what had happened. Maranzano's murder was a perfect example of an underworld double double cross. The "boss of bosses" had hired Vincent Coll to attend the scheduled 2 P.M. meeting and liquidate Charlie Lucky and Vito Genovese. But Charlie Lucky was faster with the double cross than anybody. He had contacted his long-time confederates, Bugsy Siegel and Meyer Lansky, and they had put at his disposal Sam (Red) Levine and three other efficiency experts from their Bug and Meyer mob. These were the detectives who had dispatched Maranzano.

The strategic weakness of Maranzano's position was that he had been at a fixed post. He had been waiting in his offices for two guests who had no intention of showing up—and so he was a sitting pigeon for the killers when they arrived a few minutes early, beating Mad Dog Coll to the murder draw. The coup had been plotted with the ruthless efficiency that was the hallmark of one of the best executive brains the American underworld has produced—that of Charles (Lucky) Luciano. Luciano had determined to change the face of the American underworld all in one day, and he did it, not just by the murder of Maranzano, but by a cross-continent carnival of execution that was to make September 10, 1931, memorable in the annals of crime.

On that April day that saw the elimination of Joe the Boss, Gerardo Scarpato, proprietor of the Coney Island restaurant chosen as the execution site, had been stricken with terror. "Take my fingerprints," he pleaded with police when they questioned him. "Take 'em for your books. I may be next."

He was not next, but he was right. On September 10, 1931, Scarpato's body was found in a burlap bag in a parked car in the Prospect Park section of Brooklyn. He had been knocked unconscious by a blow on the head, and then trussed up in such fashion, with his knees drawn up under his chin, that he had strangled himself when he tried to straighten his legs.

This ghoulish touch was only one of many that marked purge day in the Unione. Within a few short hours, the old-line crime bosses who had been born and reared in Sicily and were mostly illiterate—the "Mustache Petes" or "the greasers," as they were sometimes called—were liquidated by the new breed of Americanized, business-oriented gangsters of the Luciano-Costello-Adonis school. Beginning on September 11th and lasting through the next day, some thirty to forty executions were performed across the nation—a purge unprecedented in scope, precise in timing, and as bloody, abrupt, and final as any ever masterminded by a Stalin or a Hitler.

The result left Lucky Luciano enthroned atop the New York underworld, with no formidable rival in sight, and made him, by the same stroke, the dominant voice in Mafia councils across the nation. . . .

. . . The new underworld began to run smoothly along the lines that Luciano had established for it. Luciano himself and Vito Genovese, then his principal henchman, were not to remain long at the helm. In 1934, Genovese committed the indiscretion of arranging the murder of Ferdinand (The Shadow) Boccia—and of leaving witnesses who might tell about it. The law began to build a case against him, and Don Vitone, as he was sometimes known in the fraternity, departed for the healthier climate of his native Italy, where soon, incredibly enough, he was to attach himself to the court circle of Mussolini, the dictator who had vowed the death of the Mafia. Luciano encountered similar, and for a time even more devastating, misfortunes at the hands of the law. In 1935 . . . Thomas E. Dewey, then a young and crusading prosecutor, decided to go after Lucky Luciano, the overlord of crime.

Luciano was then living fastidiously as Charles Ross of the Waldorf, but Dewey became convinced that his income derived from sources not fastidious at all. He proclaimed that Luciano was not only the city's king of crime, he was also its overlord of vice, living on the proceeds of a $10 million-a-year prostitution ring, with more than 200 madams and 1,000 working girls paying him tribute. Dewey, with his awesome reputation as the young paladin of the courts, got some of the girls and madams to testify, and in 1936 Luciano was convicted and sentenced to Clinton State Prison at Dannemora for 30 to 50 years.

In the old days, such deactivation of the top command of the New York rackets would have precipitated the kind of crude struggle that so often had wounded or killed innocent bystanders along with the gangsters. But not this time. Luciano's new system functioned so smoothly that the transition in command caused hardly a ripple. Frank Costello, whose role as sage counselor of the mob had been demonstrated by his sponsorship of the Atlantic City conclave in 1929, took over and swiftly established his own reputation as Prime Minister of the underworld.

6

After Luciano

RALPH SALERNO and JOHN TOMPKINS

World War II came as a godsend to the Mafia. For four solid years, law enforcement on every level slowed almost to a standstill, while the opportunities for crime burgeoned. The FBI and most other Federal agencies turned their attention to internal security, counterespionage and antisabotage activities. Local police forces were plagued by the draft and manpower shortages. The Syndicate had never had it so good.

Gambling became a big-time business.

The war meant a huge rise in personal income as the country moved out of the tag end of the depression and into full employment. Women as well as men went to work, with plenty of overtime earnings. At the same time rationing restricted the things that people could buy with their newly inflated incomes. There were no new cars being made and tires and gasoline were rationed, so normal recreation was cut down at the same time. Gambling became, almost overnight, an easy and pleasant way to spend money.

With Las Vegas the center of present-day gambling in this country, it is easy to forget that casino gambling was available during the war where the customers were, which is to say pretty much all over the country, from Ben Marden's Riviera, across the river from New York City, to the Club Royale in Detroit, the Beverly Club in New Orleans, to Florida, Maryland, and California. Organized gambling was a national pattern. And when the Kefauver Committee made this revelation in the early fifties, showing widespread corruption of politicians and sheriffs, gambling was moved to locations where it was legal all the time. The airlines helped to make Vegas what it is today, but Senator Kefauver really created it by forcing the mob to move.

Narcotics boomed.

Demand was high due to the shortage of other diversions, but the war interfered with the normal importing channels and drove the cost of narcotics up. The opportunity and the problem brought organized crime into the picture on a large scale, taking over the narcotics business from the older, less well-organized groups that had been running it. The Syndicate was able to circumvent the wartime interruption of transportation handily: it simply reopened the underground routes that had been used a decade earlier for smuggling liquor into the country.

Arrangements were made with ship captains and sailors operating from North Africa, the Near East, and, as they were freed from Axis control, Italy and France. Mexican poppies were cultivated as a nearby source of heroin free from the danger of German submarines.

Illegal alcohol returned.

Legal liquor production was cut by the need for industrial alcohol. To stretch out the available civilian supply, a smaller than usual bottle, containing ⅘ths of a quart, was introduced. The shortage, and the tremendous demand for liquor by civilians and servicemen, produced a renaissance of the illegal alcohol industry. Organized crime had a competitive advantage over legitimate distillers in that it could get the necessary sugar from black market connections.

The black market flourished.

In a parallel with Prohibition, all those things that were rationed or in short supply, from men's shirts to steak to gasoline, offered opportunities for fat profits. Using the direct approach, the Confederation began to enter businesses that promised black market profits—sugar, syrup and molasses companies, meat packing and marketing firms, clothing manufacture and others. In some cases existing businesses were penetrated and in others new enterprises were started.

A lot of money was made in the sale of ration stamps for meat and gasoline. Organized crime always dealt in genuine stamps. These were bought from bribed civil service employees. If caught in possession the law called for only a short sentence and a small fine. Amateurs were sometimes tempted to counterfeit ration stamps, but the penalty for that was a fifteen-year prison sentence.

Many members of organized crime served in the Armed Forces during World War II. Police officers occasionally meet old buddies who are now on the other side of the fence. During the Gallo-Profaci war, Vincent Kelly, a New York City detective, ran into Tony Abbatemarco, one of the Gallo gang; sitting out the local war for a moment, they recalled their adventures together while serving with the Third Marine Division on Guam. Most of the Bosses of organized crime, however, were either too old to serve, had physical defects, or were deferred as the managers of essential businesses.

There was also a case of what might be considered collaboration with the enemy, though·it was certainly opportunism rather than disloyalty. Carlo Tresca, an anarchist of the 1920s and later a dedicated anti-fascist publisher of an Italian language newspaper in New York, was shot to death on the street in 1943. There were later attempts to blame the killing on Soviet agents, but the police believe that the murderer was Carmine ("The Cigar") Galante, Underboss of the Bonanno family of Cosa Nostra, who is now in prison for another crime.

We don't know why an American gangster might want to do Mussolini a favor, but several members of Cosa Nostra did enjoy the dictator's hospitality before and during World War II. Vito Genovese and Michele Miranda, both indicted for murder, fled to Italy in 1937 rather than stand trial. Once there, Genovese ingratiated himself with the government and was cited by Mussolini for his generosity in donations for the construction of public buildings. . . .

While the war years were marked by little official action against organized crime, there was some activity on the local level in the form of citizen crime commissions. In 1942, the Chicago Crime Commission was brought back to life when former FBI agent Virgil Peterson was named its executive director. Later, the Metropolitan Crime Commission of Greater Miami was formed and Daniel Sullivan, another former FBI man, was appointed to run it. Both men were well informed on Syndicate methods and operations, but they were unable to bring pressure on local government and police officials. They were frequently called "scaremongers" who made noises about crime to justify their jobs.

Early in the 1950s the Kefauver Committee called on both crime commissions for help—after it found that official records and documentation on organized crime did not exist in the police files of either Chicago or Miami.

The decade of the fifties opened on a familiar note: a procession of city and state officials came to Washington to ask that something be done about organized crime. It was reminiscent of similar groups that had made the same trip, for the same reason, twenty years earlier. And it got similar results.

The U.S. Conference of Mayors and the National Association of Attorneys General clamored for help. "Organized crime," they complained, "is capitalizing on the jurisdictional as well as geographical limitations of Federal, state, and municipal law-enforcement agencies to such an alarming extent that successful detection and prosecution are being evaded." President Truman's Attorney General, J. Howard McGrath, heard the cry and responded by calling a Conference on Organized Crime in February 1950. There was much discussion at the Conference, and a list of proposals was drawn up similar to those produced by every investigation of syndicated crime. The only result of the Conference, however, was the general agreement that the government should not encroach on the responsibilities and authority of local officials.

Three months later a Senator from Tennessee named Estes Kefauver launched a seventeen-month-long investigation of organized crime with hearings televised from fourteen cities all over the country. With access to income tax files granted by Presidential Executive Order, the Kefauver Committee was able to ask many penetrating questions that its small staff might not otherwise have been able to formulate. The investigation was restricted to matters involving interstate commerce, and many things that came to its attention were violations of state law, but it often used the presumption of tax evasion to broaden its scope.

The Kefauver hearings had profound impact on the public. They came when nationwide television was in its infancy and the networks seized on the hearings and filled many hours of air time. Many of the 600-odd witnesses took the Fifth Amendment. . . .

[By] 1956 . . . the Syndicate had become so used to endless Congressional palaver that it paid no attention to the proceedings of a Senate Subcommittee on Improvements in the Federal Criminal Code which held hearings around the country in 1955. Chaired by Price Daniel of Texas, the Committee was looking into the

Federal laws on the narcotics traffic. Before the Confederation appreciated the threat, and tried to move against it, the new law was in force and mandatory minimum sentences of five years for the first offense and ten for the second were on the books. Suddenly, it became obvious that the previous practice of fixing the judge to get a light or suspended sentence would no longer work—the judge was bound by the law to hand out no less than the minimum sentence, and if he was unsympathetic it could be much longer. John ("Big John") Ormento drew forty years under the new law. When the men of the Confederation had the time to study the 1956 act—it was one of the subjects discussed at Apalachin the following year—it became obvious that the risk of narcotics was no longer worth the reward involved.

At that point, when the scales of value tipped against them, the Confederation began its slow and halting withdrawal from narcotics, a business that had become its quickest moneymaker since the repeal of prohibition. It has not yet completely severed its connections, for some of the younger men still find the enormous profits and quick turnover of investment appealing enough to take the chance of arrest. And, of course, there are those who hope for a change in the law.

The mandatory sentences have drawn considerable fire from judges and others who think that discretion in sentencing should be restored. Their arguments mainly concern the excessive punishment that now falls on amateur smugglers and narcotics users. It remains to be seen if organized crime can use its influence to upset the whole idea of mandatory sentencing.

Early in 1957, still another Congressional committee began a probe. The Senate Select Committee on Improper Activities in the Labor or Management Field was composed of some shrewd and ambitious men: John F. Kennedy of Massachusetts (his brother Robert F. Kennedy was Chief Counsel of the Committee), Joseph R. McCarthy of Wisconsin, Barry Goldwater of Arizona, and the chairman, John L. McClellan of Arkansas. Where the Kefauver Committee had concentrated on gambling, the McClellan Committee found that labor racketeering was as easy a road to headlines, but even harder to do something about.

The Committee's investigation into the activities of Teamster Union President Dave Beck led to his going to jail for income-tax evasion. His successor as head of the Teamsters, James R. Hoffa, became a principal target of the McClellan Committee, but Hoffa managed to stay out of prison until 1967.

After its first year of work, the Committee reported that it had found "union funds in excess of $10,000,000 were either stolen, embezzled, or misused by union officials over a period of fifteen years." The investigation turned up evidence of gangster infiltration into seven unions with total membership of two million and domination of some fifty companies in the juke box, vending machine and garbage collection industries. It found that organizational picketing was used as a weapon of extortion against management and that companies employed labor spies and consultants to defeat legitimate union activity.

As the McClellan Committee picked its way through the complexities of labor union finances and probed the hidden ties between crooked union officials and executives willing to pay for sweetheart contracts, it hardly noticed a series of violent, and seemingly unconnected incidents that took place in New York. Early in May 1957 Frank Costello's head was creased by a bullet intended to kill him. Two months later Frank Scalise, an Underboss of a Cosa Nostra family, was shot down at noon on a Bronx street. In October of that year, Albert Anastasia, who had moved to the top in the 1930s and '40s as a leader of the hit squad known as Murder, Incorporated, was shot to death while sitting in the barbershop of a midtown Manhattan hotel.

These incidents were not simple outbreaks of mob violence or gangland revenge. They were political assassinations similar to those that precede a Latin American coup. Costello, Scalise, and Anastasia were marked for death as part of the takeover of their respective families by ambitious subordinates.

It was started by Vito Genovese. Until he fled to Italy in the thirties, Genovese was Underboss of the Lucky Luciano family of Cosa Nostra. After World War II, however, Luciano was deported and Genovese returned from exile to find that Frank Costello had taken over as de facto Boss. Genovese buried his resentment for ten years, but never gave up the idea that he would eventually be Boss. He spent that time carefully cultivating and cementing the loyalties of his old friends and as many newer members as possible. Finally, in 1957, he decided that the time had come to eliminate Costello and seize control. He had two things to worry about:

Family members loyal to Costello who might try to revenge his death.

The power of Albert Anastasia, a rival family Boss, and old friend of Costello.

Genovese figured that his own group of followers was strong enough to repel any counterattack. So, the main problem was to neutralize the Anastasia threat. He did this by sounding out Carlo Gambino, an Anastasia aide, about the possibility of him killing his boss. . . .

. . . The killing of Anastasia and Scalise could easily be rationalized because they had begun to corrupt the organization by selling memberships to outsiders. Costello, however, simply stood in the way of Genovese's ambition. But, as long as he chose not to fight for control, it did not matter that the gunman had missed his mark.

It was partly to discuss these shootings that a national meeting of the Confederation was called even as the McClellan hearings were going on. The location was a private estate in a small town in the mountains of central New York, a few miles north of the Pennsylvania line. Secluded Apalachin, New York, should have been a good place to meet, but the planners forgot how obvious the evidence of a large meeting would be in such a small town. And what was worse, the host, Joseph M. Barbara, who operated a soft drink bottling plant in the area, had been under suspicion and more or less casual surveillance by a sergeant of the New York State Police for more than a dozen years. Aware that Barbara carried a gun and had twice been arrested in Pennsylvania murder cases in the early 1930s, Sergeant Edgar D. Crosswell was looking into a routine bad check case in November, 1957, when he ran across a bloc of reservations being made in Barbara's name at a local motel. Recalling a meeting with a handful of well-known members that Barbara had hosted the year before in a Binghamton hotel, Sergeant Crosswell decided to do a little more checking. He found evidence of a much larger group gathering at Apalachin.

The next morning, Crosswell and another trooper and two agents of the Treasury Department's Alcohol & Tobacco Tax Unit—who had suspected Barbara of being a bootlegger ever since his wartime conviction for illegal sugar—converged on the estate. They were amazed to find it jammed with dozens of limousines. As they entered the driveway a fish market truck was coming out, but seeing the police cars, its driver made a quick U-turn and raced back to the house. The fish peddler gave the alarm and within minutes dozens of well-dressed men ran out of the house and across the fields in all directions.

Using road blocks, Sergeant Crosswell and reinforcements collected and identified sixty-three men who happened to be visiting Mr. Barbara that day. More than forty others, including the Chicago delegation, had kept their cool and simply stayed inside the house knowing they had nothing to fear from the police. Crosswell had no search warrant and no authority to arrest anyone since none of them had committed a crime by visiting Apalachin. But under the state motor vehicle laws he could, and did, ask the visitors to identify themselves once they were off the private property and on a road. Fifty of those questioned had arrest records and twenty-three had served time. Most were from the New York area, but some came from as far away as California, Colorado, and Texas. Nearly a third of the men identified owned bars or restaurants and nearly as many were garment manufacturers or truckers. Eleven were involved in the olive oil and cheese business and nine each were in vending machines and construction. Other businesses represented were: automobile sales, coal, laundry service, entertainment, trucking, taxis, bakeries, race tracks, funeral homes.

With nothing to do while they waited for the police to go away, the forty-odd men who had stayed inside the Barbara house discussed the questions for which the whole affair had been called:

1. The shooting of Costello and the killing of Scalise and Anastasia represented changes at the top of two important groups and they had to be explained and ratified by the National Commission.

2. The meaning of the Narcotics Control Act of 1956 and how it should be dealt with.

3. The threatened loss of a non-union garment industry labor preserve that had been built up in eastern Pennsylvania was of particular concern to the Pennsylvania and New York area delegations. These shops, either entirely non-union or safely organized under sweetheart contracts with several Anthracite Workers locals, were now the target of an aggressive union organizing campaign.

To be sure, since there was no longer a quorum of National Commission members, or their alternates, no binding decisions were reached that day at Apalachin. They had to wait until several smaller sit downs took place a short time later.

If it did nothing else, the Apalachin fiasco convinced the Mafia that large meetings were dangerous no matter where they were held, and that it was better, if less efficient, to hold a number of small meetings with liaison between them when questions of national policy were to be taken up.

Sergeant Crosswell's handling of the Apalachin affair was simply to put the names he had collected into a report to his superiors. But the flap did not end there. The newspapers immediately took up the cry, calling Apalachin a "convention of crime" and prodding county prosecutors and district attorneys all over the country into investigating the men in their area who had attended the meeting. Predictably, little came of these charades, but the ripples of Apalachin went much further. For at least a year after the meeting, those identified as having attended were hounded almost continually by one investigating group after another. And none of these probes really got anywhere.

In New York the State Commissioner of Investigations began looking into Apalachin almost immediately, soon followed by a watchdog committee of the New York State Legislature. In the spring of 1958, the newly appointed New York State Investigation Commission called all the resident Apalachin visitors in for interviews. By early summer the McClellan Committee had gotten into the act and Chief Counsel Robert F. Kennedy questioned Sergeant Crosswell and elicited the Fifth Amendment from a procession of men who had been at Apalachin.

Meanwhile, Attorney General Rogers formed a Special Group on Organized Crime in the United States specifically to look into the Apalachin meeting. Headed by Milton Wessel, the unit set up regional offices to gather intelligence and conduct grand jury proceedings on the Apalachin conferees. In his investigations, Wessel used Federal Narcotics Bureau agents and got the cooperation of the New York State Police and officers in various cities who had interviewed the men from Apalachin. He asked for FBI men to be assigned to the Special Group, but [J. Edgar] Hoover refused the request. Characterizing the program as a "fishing expedition," the FBI Director told Congressmen: "Obviously we have neither the manpower nor the time to waste on such speculative ventures."

Wessel's Special Group managed to get twenty of the

Apalachin delegates convicted for conspiracy to obstruct justice: under the charge that they had agreed not to tell the true purpose of the meeting. While this was a somewhat novel approach, Wessel proceeded with it after getting opinions from leading jurists that it was valid. He was naturally surprised when the convictions were reversed in an appellate court because, said one judge, there had been no proof that a specific crime had been committed.

In retrospect, many legal experts feel that Wessel might have made the convictions stick if he could have produced a witness who would swear that there was a Cosa Nostra, that it had a code designed to frustrate justice, that he was a member of it and that he knew the defendants to be members. Of course, a man fitting this description did appear several years later in the person of Joseph Valachi, but no prosecutors tried to use him to make conspiracy cases.

Wessel's experience did have some effect, though the comments and recommendations he made for improving the Organized Crime and Racketeering (OCR) section of the Justice Department got the usual Washington treatment. The very fact that his Special Group had been created to deal with Apalachin made the weaknesses of OCR obvious. The OCR was a weak coordinating body, with no field organization, little authority, and a limited staff and budget. Wessel also suggested the creation of a Federal criminal intelligence unit to bring together prosecutors and investigators with those best qualified to help them. This was recommended to Congress by Attorney General Rogers, but ignored.

The New York State Investigation Commission came to a similar conclusion when it checked thoroughly into the backgrounds of the New York delegates to Apalachin and found in two years of searching that it had to look at files in more than 3600 different offices that held an estimated 60,000,000 forms. From small town sheriff's files to prison records to county courthouse papers to state liquor commission applications on through a jungle of Federal agency branches from the Securities and Exchange Commission to the Federal Housing Authority. One Apalachin visitor, who was not exceptional, turned up in the records of nearly two hundred different police departments around the state.

Much of the information that SIC raked over was duplicate, but here and there were scraps of new material—a photograph, a note on a paper napkin, a handwritten letter, a telephone number—that is the raw stuff of intelligence. To create intelligence data out of a mass of facts an analyst must fit hundreds of different bits of information together into a mosaic. If he is skillful the picture will be more useful and informative than the mere sum of its pieces. But the sheer mass of information that New York's Apalachin investigation turned up made it obvious to New York's SIC Chief Counsel, Eliot H. Lumbard, that some form of electronic data processing was the only answer.

In 1961 Lumbard was appointed Special Assistant Counsel to the Governor for Law Enforcement. While involving himself in such programs as raising the standards of police training and making state facilities available to local law-enforcement people, he plumped hard for a computerized criminal information system, and a major feasibility study was launched. It might well have gotten pigeonholed except for Lumbard's pushing, and the effect of the Valachi hearings. But in 1964, something called the New York State Identification and Intelligence System, popularly called NYSIIS (rhymes with crisis), was established as a state agency. It was billed as an automated system for sharing criminal information—arrest records, personal data, aliases and disguises, friends and associates, probation, prison and parole information, photographs and fingerprints, handwriting samples, travels, and habits—between various state and local law-enforcement agencies.

Actually, NYSIIS was and is aimed at organized crime. The problems of the Apalachin investigation were what inspired it, but those connected with the effort prefer to talk about its usefulness against stickup men and automobile thieves. Obviously, they fear attack by politicians and others hostile to the police who worry about invasions of privacy that might come from the increasing use of computer data banks. NYSIIS is a real threat to the Confederation. If it succeeds, and the idea spreads across the country, the Confederation one day might face a national crime information data bank that could really do it harm.

Syndicate strategy against NYSIIS and other attempts to computerize police intelligence will be to support groups who oppose data banks and to try and blur the distinction between (a) government or business prying into the lives of private citizens and (b) systems designed to fight crime. The old American horror of a national police can also be invoked to keep criminal information fragmentized as it always has been.

To forestall future objections, NYSIIS has designed an elaborate system of electronic safeguards for the information it proposes to store and handle. Classification procedures will be used to govern who has access to the computers and what level of information he may draw out of them. Considerable physical security is provided for as well as communication safeguards such as telephone scramblers and teleprinter codes. Breaking through this security will be a top priority project of organized crime.

Coincidentally with the beginning of the NYSIIS project, Lumbard suggested what became the semi-annual Oyster Bay Conference on Combatting Organized Crime. Meeting by invitation at a secluded Long Island estate, the conference has pointedly been referred to as a legal Apalachin. It brought together about forty experts from all over the country. Mostly lawmen, there are also a number of systems engineers, military intelligence men, professors of criminology and representatives from citizens' groups. As it turned out later, the Oyster Bay Conferences produced many of the consultants and much of the information that appeared in 1967 as the organized crime report of the President's Commission on Law Enforcement and Administration of Justice.

Oyster Bay meetings are not in themselves a direct threat to organized crime, but it is somewhat disquieting to the Confederation that the nation's top law-enforcement brains have begun to exchange ideas on a regular basis. The first job that the first Oyster Bay meeting took on in May 1965 was defining organized crime. It may have seemed foolish that forty experts had to discuss the point for an entire day, but the fact that they finally agreed on a definition, and that it is a good one, was more disturbing than amusing to intelligent Confederation men.

Wessel's long probe into the affairs of the Apalachin crowd as well as the job that the New York State Investigation Commission did, convinced many Confederation men that it might be wise to begin reporting more of their income to the Internal Revenue Service. Neither investigation had involved the IRS, it was simply that formerly anonymous men had gotten so much publicity that the tax people were almost forced to get interested in them. Thus, one prominent Syndicate leader reported a taxable income of $1093.33 before Apalachin, and $68,369.12 after becoming better known. This figure was not all of his real income. It was just enough to keep the IRS happy.

The idea that organized criminals pay anything near their real tax liabilities does not stand up under the most cursory examination. After all, if a man paid his full tax there would be little point to engaging in many illegal operations. He might just as well really go legitimate. The Syndicate exodus from Las Vegas that began late in 1967 is a good example. For a decade, they had made a good thing out of casino gambling. It was attractive because a slice of each day's cash profits was diverted—or "skimmed"—off before the figures were tallied for tax purposes. The owners enjoyed large untaxed profits in addition to their taxed income. When Internal Revenue began to zero in on skimming, though, the whole Las Vegas scene lost its charm as an investment and the Syndicate interests started to move on to other pastures.

The Internal Revenue Service likes to give the impression that it has always been the nemesis of racketeers. But the fact is that for nearly thirty years, from the early 1930s until 1961, it preferred going after ordinary citizens who were cheating on their tax returns. One reason for this was much the same attitude that has kept organized crime free of harassment under the antitrust laws: the IRS men liked to say "We are tax collectors, not policemen."

But there is another reason why the tax laws fall more heavily on ordinary citizens than they do members of the Confederation. The Internal Revenue Service likes to tell Congress at appropriation time that it has increased its tax collections without increasing the cost of each dollar collected. To do this, the Service must avoid too many unduly expensive legal actions where the return might be less than the cost of prosecution. Realizing this fact, the Confederation makes it as difficult and expensive as possible for the IRS when one of their number is hauled into court. The result is that they have often gotten away with tax evasion on a grand scale. A few years ago, a well-known Cosa Nostra Underboss, whose real income ran into the middle six figures, was revealed to have been submitting an annual tax return on which he put down $15,000 of income "from various sources." He took no itemized deductions and paid the computed tax of some $2260 in full. He also refused further information, and if the IRS had asked (which it didn't) he would have taken the Fifth Amendment. Naturally, all of the man's income was in cash. He owned a successful restaurant through a front man and was the silent partner in several other businesses. He was also active in gambling and loansharking and earlier had made considerable money in narcotics. He lived very well, but had few possessions that anyone could prove were really his. He drove a car that was registered to an aged aunt. He lived in a luxurious apartment lent to him by a friend. His solid gold wristwatch had been a gift from a girl. It would have taken a small army of Internal Revenue agents to uncover his real income, and a platoon of lawyers to prove it in court. The man is now dead, but the IRS did not drive him to his grave. They never bothered him.

Still, the tax collectors are not entirely impotent—when they are pushed into being policemen.

The drive on organized crime launched by the Kennedy Administration started the IRS on its first campaign against gangster tax evaders in a generation. From 1961 through mid-1965, the Service has bragged, over 60 percent of the convictions of organized crime figures resulted from IRS investigations. Of course, many of the sentences handed out were minor, and the money recovered was usually a small fraction of the taxes evaded, but it was a threat.

This threat has since diminished, however. For this, the Mafia can thank Senator Edward V. Long of Missouri who spent 1965 leading an investigation into invasions of privacy that pilloried the IRS for using wiretapping and bugging and other electronic paraphernalia in its intelligence operations. Some officials began to question whether special emphasis upon organized crime in tax enforcement was appropriate or fair. And it is evident that the Service got the message.

On the surface the Apalachin affair seemed to have no effect on the Federal Bureau of Investigation. There are, in fact, two FBIs and we should be at pains to distinguish between them. One is the splendid organization itself; the other is its long-time [late] director. As late as 1959, FBI Director Hoover still denied the existence of any national criminal Syndicate. He stressed instead Communist subversion as the major threat to the nation. About once a year, agents were asked to submit memoranda, setting forth any information they might have picked up on major racketeers and the like. To be fair, there were questions of jurisdiction. But the FBI, lacking direct jurisdiction over some of the possible Confederation activities, also appeared to lack interest.

The Bureau began looking into organized crime a bit more intensively at about the time of the Apalachin meeting. In New

York, for example, the Bureau had no staff assigned to the problem before Apalachin. Afterward, seventy-five men were taken from other assignments in the metropolitan region and detailed to do a thorough background investigation into every person who had been present in upstate New York. (The matter of jurisdiction was set aside for the moment.) Elsewhere across the country, other FBI men were assigned to check into delegates who had come to the summit from Chicago, Tampa, Kansas City, Dallas, and California.

A week or so after Apalachin, a comprehensive report on a major criminal organization which used the words Mafia and Mafiosi—terms that J. Edgar Hoover later derided—was submitted to the top command of the FBI. (This information was supplied in large part by agents of Italian background, by the way.) Circulation was limited to a few key men.

As the vastly multiplied corps of agents did their field work, they became convinced that there was a national crime Syndicate. Their reports reflected this view. In so doing, they clashed with the established position of the director and were guilty of a form of heresy. The agents who believed the evidence they turned up were not burnt at the stake but those who persisted in making waves about organized crime—FBI headquarters referred to this as "the New York attitude"—made little career progress until the advent of a new Attorney General three years later.

When that investigation of the Apalachin meeting was concluded and reports submitted, the agents were returned to their regular duties. By 1960, just before the Kennedy Administration, there were only five men in the New York office continuing the major racketeering probe.

After Robert Kennedy was installed as Attorney General, he established a high priority which raised the number of men in metropolitan New York to eighty-five.

The New Frontiersmen have been attacked for more style than substance, more ambitious pronouncements than accomplishments, for having created an atmosphere of youthful excitement and then being unable to get ideas through into action. In one specialized area, the Kennedy Administration was quite effective. Under the new Attorney General, the Federal law-enforcement establishment did more against organized crime than had ever been done before—or has been done since. At the same time, this effort received little publicity, probably because it was a hard and dirty little war and there were many more glamorous episodes of the New Frontier to seize the headlines.

The late Robert Kennedy became interested in organized crime as Chief Counsel to the McClellan Committee. He was a man who hated to lose any fight, and was obviously galled by the seeming inability of the nation to do much about the labor racketeering, the criminal domination of business, and the pervasive influence of organized crime that the investigation uncovered.

As Attorney General, Robert Kennedy knocked heads together in the Federal establishment, making it clear that everyone was to contribute to the effort against organized crime, and that he would not tolerate any department merely going through the motions. In a short time there was real cooperation. In fairness to earlier, and later, Attorneys General, Kennedy had the unique advantage of being the President's brother. He did not have to worry as much as other appointed officials about political attacks from the rear or bureaucratic undercutting. Because he dealt from strength he showed that close cooperation between the fragmentized law-enforcement agencies of the government was possible without any new laws or regulations. The only reason it had never been done before was because of the resistance of department and agency heads to surrendering any of their power or prerogatives to a common effort.

At the same time, a package of new laws, known as the Travel Bills, gave the FBI increased jurisdiction in the sector of organized crime and helped the Kennedy drive by undermining Director Hoover's favorite reason for not getting the Bureau involved in any activity that did not interest him. The new laws made interstate travel in connection with gambling and extortion a Federal offense. Loansharking was left out, though it had been recommended for inclusion in the laws. The only way that the Bureau could enter such a case is when force and fear in collection of loan payments made it extortion. In 1968 FBI jurisdiction over loansharking was indirectly, perhaps unintentionally, widened. As part of the "Truth in Lending Bill" intended for consumer protection, it became a violation of Federal law, not to clearly state annual interest charges in business transactions.

Even more important than the Travel Bills, though, was the crusading spirit that was brought to the feeble Organized Crime

Section of the Justice Department. The legal staff was more than doubled the first year and quadrupled by 1963, not with civil service sinecure-seekers or opportunists looking for experience, but with a group of sharp and eager young lawyers. Such zeal had not been seen in Washington since the early days of the New Deal. They became the spearhead of the Kennedy drive against organized crime. Fanning out from Washington they developed prosecutions in cities all over the country. They were able to by-pass long time political relations that the Syndicate had spent a generation cementing.

The group had several distinct advantages which made them more effective than local Federal prosecutors. They were not involved in local politics, so that local sensitivities couldn't stop them. Moreover, they did not take the usual attitudes—resignation or disbelief—toward organized crime. And when the Justice Department's actions made it obvious that a new broom was sweeping, this had the effect of encouraging sympathetic local police to action.

Robert Kennedy demonstrated his personal interest in the drive by making frequent visits to cities where organized crime was known to exist. He would hold conferences with Federal agents and their supervisors on the progress and problems of the effort. This had not been done before and—fortunately from the Confederation's viewpoint—has not been done since. Even the FBI was caught up in the new spirit of the Justice Department.

New York agents who had been talking about organized crime since Apalachin suddenly found themselves no longer pariahs, but key men who were moved back to Washington and to other cities to indoctrinate other agents on the activities and scope of Cosa Nostra. With the advent of this new order, the Bureau speedily made up for lost time and within a couple of years had more Syndicate intelligence in its files than any other law-enforcement group except the Bureau of Narcotics, which had been working in the area since 1930.

While all of this activity was going on, the Confederation was also occupied recovering the ground lost at Apalachin. The many, often overlapping investigations that went on seemed to confuse as many experts and citizens as they educated. Everyone was so busy arguing the semantics of the Mafia, the Syndicate, the Organization, the Cammora, and L'Unione Siciliano and how they all fitted, or didn't fit, into Italian history and the black hand in this country at the turn of the century, that they did not notice that certain non-Italian partners of Cosa Nostra with names like Lansky, and Dalitz were moving into the spotlight and carrying on for the organization without much difficulty. Investigators, with just enough knowledge to be dangerous to themselves, figured that since no one not of Italian blood could be a formal member of the Mafia, these dapper gentlemen must be independent operators.

One of their important activities during this period was finding a replacement for Cuba as an off-shore gambling haven after Dr. Castro puritanically closed the clubs. The Bahamas turned out to be the best substitute, though recent changes in the political balance of power in the islands created a threat. Haiti seemed a likely spot, but it became politically hazardous even sooner.

At about the same time England began to develop as a land of opportunity. The law was changed to allow gambling clubs and street-front turf accountants or bookmakers. The British could make their own roulette wheels and other traditional equipment. But there were no domestic manufacturers of slot machines. The Syndicate moved to fill the need. Quietly, one-armed bandits were taken out of storage in upstate New York, the Middle West, and Louisiana and shipped to London. Though there was a law against the interstate shipment of gambling devices (the Johnson Act), prosecutions proved difficult. At least one shipment of machines was seized on a Brooklyn pier for violation of export regulations: they were improperly labeled as farm machinery. Within a few years the men who had supplied London with slot machines were buying into local gambling casinos and extending their influence in other directions.

In the fall of 1963, the McClellan Committee hit the headlines again with that most dangerous attack on the Confederation, the public confessions of Joseph Valachi. A member since 1930, the gravel-voiced Valachi spent a week on the witness stand outlining for a nationwide TV audience the story of his life from the first burglary in 1921 until 1962 when he killed a man in the yard of Atlanta prison because he mistook the man for another Cosa Nostra member he thought had been ordered to kill him. Valachi detailed a rambling story of Byzantine intrigues, routine business deals, and matter-of-fact murders. He identified hundreds of Cosa Nostra members and described the organization in detail.

In all of the months of questioning and checking and piecing together the information that Valachi gave, none of the law-enforcement men ever caught him in a lie. At the same time, he protected a few friends and acquaintances from the past by refusing to identify them or implicate them in specific crimes. He confirmed and added depth and dimension to the knowledge or fragments of information the police already had.

Damaging as Valachi's testimony was, however, the Syndicate was able to attack it more easily and effectively than it had the Apalachin affair. The response to Valachi was a two-pronged public relations campaign: one side directed toward the general public and the other to the membership.

To the outsiders, Valachi was denounced as a minor figure with delusions. It was also said that he revealed nothing new and that all of his lurid tales had already been described in books about Al Capone, in reports of the Bureau of Narcotics, in the Murder, Incorporated, case, and by the Kefauver Committee. It was pointed out that no one went to jail as the result of any direct testimony that he gave.

To reach the members, the grapevine went into high gear with stories designed to blacken Valachi's character. It was jokingly repeated that one of Valachi's nicknames—"Cago"—was an Italian word for excrement. Stories were circulated accusing him of incest. Old-timers in the Mafia began saying: "I didn't trust him twenty years ago." And at the top levels of the hierarchy, men who could understand his informing about particular murders, robberies and narcotics deals, asked each other: "Why did he have to tell about the organization, the oath and the ritual?"

The downgrading of Valachi's importance and credibility got considerable support in some circles. Suspicious of the motives of the police, the FBI and the Bureau of Narcotics, some editorialists saw the Valachi hearings as a sort of show trial staged to marshal public support for new laws that would infringe on civil liberties, such as federal bills to legalize wiretapping and/or New York State's "stop and frisk" law and "no knock" law.

In police intelligence work, as in military and CIA operations, failures are obvious but successes cannot be advertised. The Valachi confessions are ranked next to Apalachin as the greatest single blow ever delivered to organized crime in the United States. This evaluation came from the lips of those most affected by it: members of the criminal network whose comments were overhead through bugs and wiretaps.

Many of the incidents Valachi described had, indeed, been known to the police, but he was able to fill in the gaps and connect one incident to another. This was the real danger of Valachi to Cosa Nostra. He drew a schematic picture of the organization, described it and told how it worked. The police, for example, had long realized that certain underworld figures were often seen with each other, but they did not realize that these were formal not casual associations, relationships of rank in a system governed by rules and regulations. The pattern that Valachi furnished made it possible for police intelligence men to begin to see the dimensions of syndicated crime and stop looking at it as a series of unconnected cases.

To be sure, Valachi did not change the outlook of all law-enforcement men. The Confederation can still count on the fact that many police, for political and other reasons, persist in looking at crime in the same old way. The hearings themselves were a demonstration of this. Valachi's testimony was corroborated by men from the Department of Justice, the Bureau of Narcotics and by police intelligence officers from New York City, Connecticut, New Jersey, Rhode Island, California, Chicago, Detroit, Buffalo, Tampa, and Orange County, Florida. But the McClellan Committee had also invited Philadelphia and Miami to send officers to the hearings. Both cities declined the invitation.

Joseph Valachi became a defector from the organization during the year between his murder of another prisoner and his appearance in Washington. The feeling that he had unjustly been condemned to death by his Boss, Vito Genovese, started Valachi down that road—and this fortuitous circumstance was taken advantage of expertly. Valachi was in solitary confinement in Atlanta Federal Penitentiary when he heard that a Federal Narcotics Bureau agent was visiting the prison. He got word to the agent that he wanted to get out of Atlanta bad enough to cooperate with the law. The Bureau got Valachi moved to the Westchester County Jail near New York City in July 1962, where he lived in the hospital ward under the name Joseph De Marco. As it turned out, Valachi was not nearly so cooperative with the Narcotics agents as he had promised to be. The FBI entered the picture at that point in the person of Special Agent James P. Flynn, who had specialized in organized crime since the Apalachin meeting.

Flynn (now a roving inspector for the Bureau) inspires confidence in everyone he deals with. Local police, who often resent the superior attitude and glory seeking tactics of some FBI men, like Flynn because he always plays square with them. He is soft-spoken, calm, and inclined to understatement. At the same time, Flynn is solidly built, muscular, and interested in sports: a man's man. The same qualities that made him successful in the FBI made him successful with Joseph Valachi.

In his first meetings at Westchester County Jail Flynn didn't try pumping Valachi at all. He worked on being helpful and friendly and establishing a rapport with him. He told Valachi that he was in bad shape physically and emotionally, and that he would try to help him get into better condition. Flynn brought him a hand squeezer and a chest expander and other simple exercise gadgets and outlined a program of training for Valachi to follow. He relieved his anxiety by deliberately not pressing him to talk about his friends, but spending time on things that Valachi liked to talk about.

Flynn and Valachi spent hours handicapping horses out of the racing news to see who could pick the most winners. Valachi, who had owned and raced horses, knew more, and invariably won this game. It was part of Flynn's technique to build a sense of superiority in Valachi—and a willingness to give his new friend the benefit of his greater knowledge. The same psychology entered into many other areas of their relationship. Flynn would bring in Italian delicacies like Genoa salami or Provolone cheese, and then bow to Valachi's superior knowledge by listening to long descriptions of varieties Flynn acknowledged he had never heard about.

The first discussions about Cosa Nostra began as unobtrusive parts of conversations on other subjects. Valachi would say, for example, that there was a good restaurant down on 116th Street. Flynn would say he knew the place and suggest that a lot of guys Valachi knew hung out there. He would start to recall a few names. Valachi would butt in to correct Flynn and supply the names of the men he knew.

Similarly, a casual reference by Flynn to "the Harlem mob" launched Valachi into a long demonstration of his superior knowledge of the underworld. He explained that Chink Leo, Carmine Tramunti, and Joe Pagano, whom Flynn had linked together in one gang, were actually members of three different Cosa Nostra families.

In short, Flynn did not treat Valachi as an informer but as a defector. He talked to him, argued with him, reminisced, listened. Sometimes he saw that Valachi was withdrawn, and he would drop the subject of Cosa Nostra for that day. Sometimes he would pretend to get angry and call Valachi a lying son of a bitch to try to provoke him into revealing more to justify himself. Valachi was "handled" in much the same fashion that the Soviets used to induce Swedish Colonel Stig Wennerström to become a secret defector.

Valachi never intended to become a full-fledged defector. In the beginning he planned to tell only enough to get revenge against Vito Genovese by implicating him in various unsolved crimes. But as the information began to build into a picture, and as Valachi relived his life in the organization, long-buried resentments against the Bosses' exploitation of him came to the surface and were encouraged. In February 1963 Valachi was moved from Westchester Jail to Fort Monmouth, New Jersey, a U.S. Army post. He stayed there until August when he was transferred to the Washington, D.C., Jail in preparation for his appearance before the McClellan Committee. By that time he was willing to testify against the organization itself.

On the witness stand Valachi was asked by Senator McClellan why he had decided to cooperate at the risk of his life:

> MR. VALACHI. The main answer to that is very simple. No. 1, it is to destroy them.
> THE CHAIRMAN. To what?
> MR. VALACHI. To destroy them.
> THE CHAIRMAN. Destroy who?
> MR. VALACHI. The Cosa Nostra leaders, or the bosses. The whole—how would you explain it—that exists.
> THE CHAIRMAN. You want to destroy the whole syndicate or the whole organization?
> MR. VALACHI. That is right; yes, sir.
> THE CHAIRMAN. Why do you feel like it should be destroyed?
> MR. VALACHI. Well, through the years, first of all I was concerned, and second, they have been very bad to the soldiers and they have been thinking for themselves, all through the years. It is all put together, and I put together so many things that it all comes to that, to destroy them.

Valachi was a danger to the Syndicate on several levels. Most obvious was the impact of the hearings on television. Unlike the Moreland Commission and Kefauver hearings, the audience was treated to the spectacle of a man who was not taking the Fifth Amendment, but who implicated himself and many others in a whole series of crimes. If some of the material was old stuff to those who remembered Murder, Incorporated, it was new and shocking to millions of younger viewers. If it had no other impact, the Valachi testimony reminded many that there was something more to crime than narcotics peddling and muggings in the street.

On a second level, Valachi undermined Confederation discipline by violating the code of silence, and not getting killed for it. A life of solitary confinement may not be a very attractive alternative to keeping your mouth shut, but the code is unequivocal: Valachi should have been killed, and he wasn't. And if he had not already drawn a life sentence for killing the man in Atlanta, he might well be living under an assumed name on a government subsidy in Brazil or Scotland or South Africa. Valachi alive is so dangerous an example that there is a $100,000 price on his head, but no one has figured out a way to collect it so far.

Most dangerous of all to the organization is that police intelligence men now realize that the way Valachi was handled—and the things that troubled him and made him vulnerable to defection—can be used against other members. For the first time it became apparent that the organization was a despotism that was not always benevolent and that its subjects were not all satisfied. Valachi even went to the extent of pointing out certain unhappy members who might be turned into covert informers, and some of them have been "corrupted" by the law. Since Valachi, public relations and psychological warfare have been used against the Cosa Nostra.

On the other side of the fence, the Valachi affair gave a shot in the arm to law-enforcement intelligence men who had been sneered at for years as alarmists. And while Valachi's direct testimony did not send anyone to jail, it had the same effect indirectly. Late in 1966, the New York City Police Department conducted a survey which showed that more members of the Mafia had been sent to jail in the New York-New Jersey-Connecticut metropolitan area during the three years since Valachi talked than in the previous thirty years.

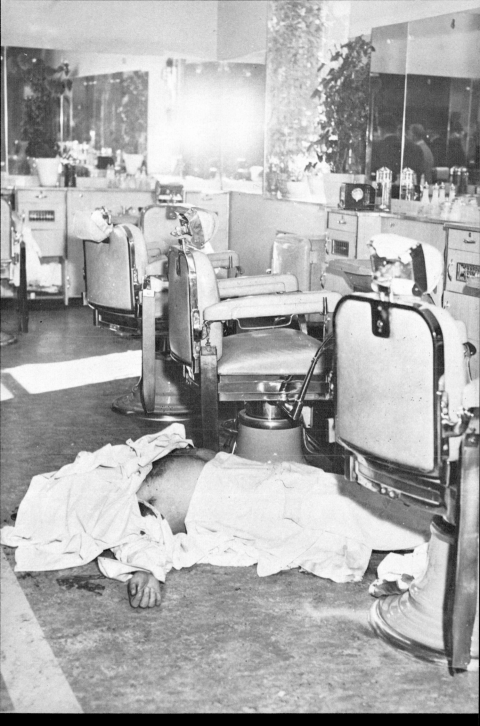

Albert Anastasia was gunned down as he sat in a barber's chair in a New York hotel on October 25, 1957. The killers were masked, invaded the barber shop, and escaped without being recognized. *N.Y. Daily News Photo*

Anthony ("Tough Tony") Anastasia, showing the strain of identifying the body of his brother Albert, who was shot in a barber's chair (see preceding page). "Tough Tony" is shown here after leaving the New York hotel where his brother was slain.
Wide World Photos

Below: Victor Genovese, preparing testimony concerning alleged narcotics traffic. *Right:* Genovese entering Federal Courthouse in New York City on February 11, 1960, to surrender and start serving a 15-year federal prison term on a narcotics conspiracy conviction.

Wide World Photos

The Death of "Bugsy" Siegel. The body of Benjamin Siegel in his house in Beverly Hills, California, where he was murdered on June 20, 1947. *Wide World Photos*

Right: This meek-looking man has his hands folded, because they are manacled. He is Carlo Gambino, one-time "Boss of Bosses" in New York's organized crime. Accompanied by a federal agent, Gambino is shown after his arrest in March, 1970.
Wide World Photos

"Mrs. Trigger Mike," the wife of Michael Coppola, is shown here in a rare photograph as she accompanies her husband to the District Attorney's office on July 31, 1947, about one month after the fatal shooting of "Bugsy" Siegel (see preceding page). Doris Coppola is shown wearing dark glasses, while her husband seeks to use an umbrella to hide them from photographers.

Wide World Photos

Right: Frank Sinatra, the singer whose testimony on organized crime was requested on several occasions, is shown here being escorted into the Royal Festival Hall, London, in 1970.

London Daily Express

Frank Sinatra (see preceding page) is shown here at a Hollywood dinner soliciting support for Governor Ronald Reagan of California on October 4, 1970. Governor Reagan (left) is seen chatting with singer Dean Martin, while Mr. Sinatra is on the right of the photograph. *Pictorial Parade—Alan Kent*

Men of Power

MAFIA, U.S.A., like the country in which it settled, has been molded by its own heroes, villains, geniuses and would-be dictators. The following section profiles four of the strong and ambitious men who played important roles in creating the Mafia of today: Lucky Luciano, who led the 1931 revolt against the Mustache Petes; Vito Genovese, who came to dominate the Mafia after World War II; Carlo Gambino, the most influential of the Mafia bosses now in power; and Joseph Colombo, Sr., who tried to give the Mafia a new look before he was gravely wounded in 1971.

Luciano, who died in 1962, radically changed the structure of the Mafia by eliminating one-man rule (under a "Boss of Bosses") in favor of collective leadership through a national *Commissione*. He also guided the Mafia into new ventures such as prostitution, numbers operations and labor racketeering. Luciano's story is told by Frederic Sondern, Jr., the late journalist and organized-crime expert.

Shortly after Luciano was sent to prison by Thomas Dewey in 1936, his underboss, Vito Genovese, fled the country to escape a murder charge. This left Frank Costello, Luciano's number three man, as the dominant figure in the Mafia. Costello preferred political influence to muscle and used his power with politicians to increase the fortunes of the Mafia. After World War II, Genovese returned, beat the murder rap hanging over him and, through Byzantine machinations that included an assassination attempt, pushed Costello out of the seat of power. Genovese was a tough Mafioso of the old school who revived the more brutal instincts of the Mafia that Costello had partially suppressed. His life is chronicled by Frank Prial, a reporter for the *New York Times*.

Genovese's rise to power also affected the fortunes of Carlo Gambino. After Albert Anastasia, a Costello supporter, was assassinated in 1957, Anastasia's family was given to Gambino who allegedly had conspired with Genovese to have Anastasia eliminated. The years of Gambino's reign as a Mafia boss have seen the death, exile or imprisonment of most of the men who took control of the Mafia after the 1931 purge. Gambino alone has survived and has made his family the biggest and richest in the country. He is, therefore, the most influential Mafia boss in the United States. How he exercises this influence is described in the third article in this section.

When Joseph Colombo, Sr., in 1963, warned Gambino and other members of the *Commissione* of a planned attempt on their lives, he quickly rose from a lowly *capo* to the youngest Mafia family boss in the country. Colombo had some radical ideas about how a Mafia boss should act, and many observers both inside and outside the organization considered Colombo representative of the new-style Mafioso and watched with interest to see what would happen. But Colombo's hubris and his desire for publicity and power alienated the old-timers, including, eventually, even his mentor, Carlo Gambino. Colombo's fate and the life that preceded it are described in the last chapter of this section.

7
Lucky Luciano
— Boss for All Seasons

FREDERIC SONDERN, JR.

On a cold February evening in 1946, the S.S. *Laura Keene*, a tired Liberty ship, was making ready to sail from New York for Italy. It was a historic evening for the Mafia, one which no one who witnessed it will ever forget. Charlie Lucky Luciano, former overlord of New York City's rackets and organized vice, was being deported by the United States government. No departure of royalty could have been more impressive. In front of the entrance to the pier in Brooklyn at which the *Laura Keene* was berthed stood a double row of burly longshoremen shoulder to shoulder with bailing hooks hanging like policemen's sidearms from their belts; they were the guard of honor. When Charlie Lucky arrived he was surrounded by a phalanx of agents of the Bureau of Immigration and Naturalization who had brought him over from Ellis Island, where he had been held for several days. It seemed that the heavy federal bodyguard was there more to protect him from the press than to prevent his escape. The big longshoremen scanned the official party, permitted it to pass. There were shouts of "You'll be back, Lucky"—"You keep punchin', boss." Then the ranks closed again to prevent newsmen from following.

What happened during the next few hours before the ship sailed still seems incredible. Big cars kept arriving with members of the top echelon of the Mafia. Their bodyguards lugged out great baskets of wine and delicacies which grinning stevedores wheeled carefully onto the pier. Frank Costello and Albert Anastasia came to pay their respects to Don Salvatore and wish their old *compadre* well. There were others of almost equal underworld rank including prominent Mafia satellites such as Meyer Lansky, the great gambling organizer, and Joseph (Socks) Lanza, boss of the Fulton Fish Market and the Lower East Side docks. Tammany Hall was also prominently represented. The party aboard—with champagne, caviar and lobster, as reported by a federal agent—was very gay, while the longshoremen and their bailing hooks, city police and dock patrolmen kept newsmen and all others at bay. Finally the *Laura Keene* blew her whistle, an impressive group of cheerful gangsters gathered on the pier to wave and shout a last good-by and Don Salvatore was on his way to Italy, a new life and, supposedly, oblivion.

The early career of the extraordinary gangster who was Lucky Luciano has been told many times with varying degrees of accuracy. . . . He was the personification of the brotherhood of evil, in American dress, with all of its ruthlessness, savage cruelty, sentimentality and peculiarly twisted ideology.

Salvatore Lucania was born in 1897 in the little Sicilian town of Lercara Friddi near Palermo. His father, Antonio, was a hardworking, thrifty laborer in the sulphur pits close by. When Salvatore was nine, Antonio Lucania had saved enough to realize his ambition of years—America. By the time he was ten, young Salvatore was on the streets in the toughest section of New York City, the Lower East Side around Brooklyn Bridge. The teeming tenement district where hundreds of thousands of recent immigrants huddled in poverty and squalor was the city's center of vice and crime. Both of the boy's parents worked long hours and had little time for him, he disliked school intensely, was often a truant and a criminal career began. At 15 he was already a petty thief, an expert gang fighter with knife and stone and chief runner for an important narcotic peddler. He was caught delivering a parcel of heroin and served six months of a year's sentence in jail. This made him eligible for underworld promotion. He applied to the Five Point Gang, which terrorized Little Italy around Mulberry Street, for admission. They had been watching him. Young Lucania was small for his age, with delicate hands and feet, but he was very quick, shrewd, hard and always seemed to use his head. His application was accepted.

From here on, others far more important began to watch Salvatore Lucania. One in particular, Mafia boss Giuseppe Masseria, saw the young man's possibilities and qualifications. . . . Salvatore had convincingly demonstrated on many occasions the cardinal virtues of the true mafioso: he had an iron self-control. No matter what the provocation or the emergency, the hoarse voice never rose in pitch; the cold, seemingly unblinking eyes showed no emotion whatever. The sensitive hands might flutter slightly, but that was all. Always penetratingly alert to the emotional reactions of others, he was an underworld diplomat of the first order who believed in using brains and mediation first, guns only when absolutely necessary. Even as a junior member of the Five Pointers he had been able to calm down the explosive young hoodlums, and the older ones as well, who liked a fight for the battle's sake, and without seeming to, had begun to guide them into disciplined and lucrative racketeering.

By the early 1920's, Salvatore Lucania had emerged as Giuseppe Masseria's chief of staff and, at a remarkably early age, a power to be reckoned with in the grand council of the brotherhood in New York. A few bloody years followed, as in Chicago, while the bootlegging empire of the eastern seaboard was being organized. After at least a hundred murders and untold mayhem of various kinds, Giuseppe Masseria was established as the area's principal capo mafioso and Lucania as his crown prince. It was a powerful team. The squat, crude, older man with little pig's eyes, who could consume three heaping platters of spaghetti at one sitting, had great seniority in the brotherhood and a fearsome reputation for ruthless and efficient killing that went back to 1905. Young Salvatore became his brains, his memory and his constant companion—but always, as far as the police and public were concerned, in the shadows. Very few, even in the underworld's upper reaches, knew of the great influence that he was beginning to exert on the New York mafiosi's thinking and operations. Like Al Capone, he was a businessman of crime and a superb executive. He had the same sense of tidy organization and orderly chain of command. But unlike the noisy Neapolitan, the basically austere Sicilian preferred anonymity—not only for business reasons but from personal preference.

With the weight of Don Giuseppe Masseria's influence behind him and his own uninhibited imagination, he—again like Capone in Chicago—started a gradual expansion of the brotherhood's activities from bootlegging into other fields which he also sensed would remain after the inevitable end of Prohibition. . . . One day in April 1931, therefore, Charlie Lucky invited him [Masseria] to lunch at Scarpato's, an excellent Italian restaurant in Coney Island. The capo liked plenty of food and wine; it was late before they finished and the dining room was almost empty. Charlie Lucky went to wash his hands. He was unquestionably and provably in the men's room when three men materialized behind the tiddly don's chair, methodically emptied their revolvers into him and as rapidly disappeared. By the time Lucania dashed out, as he told the police a few minutes later, the killers were gone and his beloved old patron was very dead. None of the restaurant's staff could give even the vaguest description of the men. All they did know, and very definitely, was that Mr. Lucania had been in the washroom. It was the perfect example of a Mafia execution carried out in the traditional manner. By ancient custom a ranking mafioso when condemned by his own brotherhood must be killed, if at all possible, humanely and unexpectedly, and preferably after plenty of food and wine. It has always been so, and still is.

Salvatore Lucania by succession was now a capo mafioso of the first class. His extraordinary rise to racketeering and political power during the next years was less spectacular than that of Capone in Chicago had been, but it was more careful and thorough. With the flexibility of a new generation of mafiosi which had grown out of American influences on the brotherhood's original exclusiveness, Charles Luciano, as he now began to call himself, realized that he had to work out a system of peaceful coexistence with the non-Italian gangs of New York; until they could be subjugated or suppressed, that is. Various reporters who have written about the brotherhood believe that the Mafia as such came to an end during this period; that its membership became simply a part of a nationwide syndicate of criminals of all races and kinds. This seems, on the basis of much evidence, an incorrect assumption.

The story of organized crime in the United States from Luciano through the Apalachin meeting up to this writing indicates that the brotherhood has not deviated from its essential principles by a degree. Capone and Luciano changed its methods, modernized them, but basically Salvatore Lucania was just as much of a mafioso as Giuseppe Masseria of the previous generation.

Before long Charlie Luciano had working arrangements not only with his fellow mafiosi, but also with such un-Sicilian associates as Louis (Lepke) Buchalter, dictator of the garment center rackets; Meyer Lansky of New York gambling; Longy Zwillman of various New Jersey gangs and very powerful; the Scalici brothers of the Brooklyn docks (they were Sicilians) and others. It was the first of the big racket syndicates perfected by Luciano in the post-Capone period. Its members quickly realized the advantages of this sort of arrangement and subscribed to it. In New York the destructive internecine warfare stopped abruptly. The idea of large-scale underworld communications and consultations, with their economic dividends—developed by Al Capone and worked into a permanent pattern by Salvatore Lucania—spread through the country's racket combines from coast to coast. Meetings of gang leaders not only of states but from whole sections of the nation became increasingly frequent; so did long distance telephone calls, as recent investigations have shown.

Many writers have lumped these groups together and called them The National Syndicate or just The Syndicate. Actually, what Capone and Lucania inspired by their examples is a number of syndicates, all continually in touch with each other. On careful examination, one finds that almost every one of them is either dominated or strongly influenced by a group of mafiosi. Senator Estes Kefauver after many months of investigation wrote that "the Mafia is the cement that binds organized crime." And the man who perfected this peculiar kind of cement was Lucania.

Salvatore Lucania made another important contribution to the top bracket of the brotherhood and its associates. He radically changed their dress and their manners. He became the underworld's exemplary Beau Brummel, in a quiet way. His suits were conservative and well tailored; his shirts, ties, shoes and accessories were expensive but not ostentatious. The wide-brimmed fedoras and odd overcoats which had been the mafioso's uniform for so long had already begun to disappear, and the quietly elegant Mr. Luciano carried the trend further. Everybody who worked for him, as he is reported to have once said to his immediate staff, "has to look legit." This precept has been maintained by the brotherhood ever since. He influenced the brotherhood's manners in the same way. Under his chairmanship a meeting of the heads of various cartels at the Waldorf Astoria—where, as Mr. Charles Ross, he lived for a number of years in an apartment suite—became a far more austere gathering than a convention of industrial executives in the same hotel might have been.

The detailed story of the rise and fall of Charlie Lucky Luciano . . . has been told so often that only the barest chronology of it seems necessary here.

By 1935, "Mr. Charles Ross" in his elaborate headquarters in the Waldorf Astoria was . . . the most powerful mafioso which the brotherhood has ever produced. He was master of the most lucrative of the New York rackets. No gambling operation, no important dock or garment extortion could be organized without his permission and a provision for his cut. He had ironclad protection from Tammany Hall which extended from New York City to Albany. Frequently, members of the New York judiciary and sachems from the Hall would attend his morning levees, which, as the hotel staff later testified, had a regal air. Don Salvatore had reached the pinnacle. He might have stayed there for quite a while had he not made, despite all his caution and perspicacity, two very serious mistakes. . . .

As a youngster on the Lower East Side he had been, besides thief and narcotics runner, a messenger and solicitor for a number of brothels. He had learned the business from the ground up, its economics and personnel problems. As he rose to the New York overlordship, he realized that organized prostitution could earn almost as much as narcotics or extortion. With three stalwart mafiosi as field generals, he put together the largest combine of brothels in the history of this or probably any other country. At the height of its operation, more than 200 madams and well over 1,000 girls were paying tribute to Charlie Lucky's organization from a business which grossed approximately $10,000,000 a year. Charlie Lucky, however, was too greedy. The madams had to pay too much for protection, and the girls had little take-home money.

The strong-arm methods of Davey Betillo—Charlie Lucky's executive officer for this division—which produced brutal beatings and slashings for the slightest defection or failure to pay was finally more than the girls could take, and rebellion began to simmer. "Mr. Ross" in his luxurious eyrie at the Waldorf, surrounded by obsequious assistants, did not sense the growing unrest and its menace. "Whores is whores," he said on one occasion over a tapped telephone. "They can always be handled. They ain't got no guts." This was his first mistake.

Charlie Lucky liked the company of prostitutes and constantly had them in his entourage. That was his second mistake. He regarded all of them as "dumb broads" and thought nothing of making telephone calls and conducting business with his assistants in their presence. Unfortunately for him, several women like Nancy Presser, Cokey Flo Brown and Mildred Harris were neither stupid nor without courage. He had abused them all, finally, with contempt. Their peculiar prostitute's pride was offended. They all had excellent memories.

In 1935 New York City went through one of its infrequent revulsions against chronically inefficient and dishonest government. A special grand jury brushed aside the regular district attorney and demanded a special prosecutor. Thomas E. Dewey was appointed. He soon found that Charlie Lucky Luciano was his main objective; that almost all of New York's organized crime stemmed from the sleek, apparently untouchable Mr. Ross of the Waldorf. Dewey's brilliant investigation and prosecution of the great capo mafioso is history. Charles Lucania was indicted for the crime of compulsory prostitution, tried in General Sessions Court and found guilty on sixty-two counts. The prostitutes that Charlie Lucky had regarded as such harmless trash were superbly convincing witnesses. Dewey could also have prosecuted for narcotics trading and extortion on a huge scale, but the white slavery charge was the easiest to prove, aroused the greatest public indignation and would bring the most severe penalty. Before pronouncing sentence Judge McCook fastened the cool, immaculate don with his eyes. "You are," he said quietly but with venom, "one of the most vicious criminals that has ever been brought before this court. It is the sentence of this court . . . 30 to 50 years. . . ." The judge thought that he was handing down the equivalent of a sentence

for life. He did not reckon with the don's ingenuity, lawyers, connections—or his position as a Mafia boss.

Charlie Lucky disappeared from public view in the State Penitentiary at Dannemora, a maximum security prison known to New
York felons as "Siberia." It is an interesting fact that a big-time
racketeer maintains his prestige and certain privileges even behind
the walls. Many chores are done for him by fellow convicts, he
becomes an arbiter of disputes, his advice far more sought than
that of the chaplain. "He practically ran the place," a guard who
saw much of Charlie Lucky told us once. "He used to stand there
in the yard like he was the warden. Men waited in line to talk
to him. Charlie Lucky would listen, say something and then wave
his hand. The guy would actually *back* away. It was something
to watch. The real mob boys when they were about to be dis-
charged would always have a last talk with the Boss, as they all
called him. He was sort of philosophical about the whole thing.
He thought he was going to be there for a long time and tried
to make the best of it." The coming of World War II did not
excite Charlie Lucky. He had no idea of what it was going to
do for him or that it was going to make him, at least for a while,
an asset to the United States government.

The value of Don Salvatore's war effort has been the subject
of much controversy. Some writers have claimed that it was outstanding, others that it was negligible. The truth seems to lie in
between.

In 1942 an unusual group of men gathered in the headquarters
of the Bureau of Naval Intelligence for the 3rd Naval District,
which covered New York, New Jersey and the largest and most
important eastern seaports. Among them were former prosecutors,
FBI and Treasury agents, city detectives—all handpicked for the
almost superhuman job of protecting the miles of docks which
were the anchor of our lifeline to Europe, and of stifling the
sources of information which Hitler's intelligence services had set
up in the New York area. Sabotage on the piers was increasing.
The huge French liner *Normandie*, which was being converted
into a troopship capable of carrying an entire division, burned and
sank at her Manhattan berth. Accurate information on sailing dates
and cargoes of ships leaving New York was reaching the cordon
of German submarines which then virtually controlled the eastern

seaboard and sank our and British shipping almost at will. At a
meeting of the harassed Naval Intelligence staff at 90 Church Street
one day, someone advanced the idea of enlisting the tightly organized New York-New Jersey dock underworld in the struggle.
The Annapolis men present thought it unorthodox and dangerous.
The professional police officers saw the possibilities at once. No
force could patrol the vulnerable piers and ships as effectively as
the tough, alert longshoremen, truckers and watchmen who knew
every inch of them. The waterfront prostitutes and their pimps
could be a counter-intelligence corps, if properly organized, of
the first order. An unusually shrewd and courageous officer, the
late Lieutenant Commander Charles Haffenden, USNR, appointed
himself coordinator of the whole extraordinary operation.

It was not easy to pick an underworld autocrat of the caliber
that the Navy needed. He had to be a patriotic, reliable crook.
Haffenden and his staff finally chose Joseph (Socks) Lanza, an
immensely energetic organizer whose predominantly Italian gangs
controlled the huge Fulton Fish Market and the docks on Manhattan's Lower East Side. Lanza, who was under indictment at
the time for extortion, accepted and proceeded to do an excellent
job. Longshoremen, under orders from Lanza, became among the
Navy's most vigilant patrolmen and agents. The fishermen who
supplied the market and knew the offshore waters as only they
can, formed a first-class observer corps. The organization was so
successful that Haffenden wanted to expand it to the critical piers
of Brooklyn, the West Side of Manhattan and Jersey across the
Hudson. Here, however, the planners at 90 Church Street ran into
a wall of underworld suspicion and resistance. Even Lanza, with
all his power and connections, was unable to breach it. The racketeers in control, many of them mafiosi, regarded the Navy—war
or no war, and despite the fact that they hated Mussolini—as part
of government and law, and therefore anathema. Lanza had a suggestion. There was only one man who had sufficient authority to
solve the problem—and that was Charlie Lucky Luciano. The
more conservative elements at 90 Church Street had misgivings,
to say the least. The idea of the United States Navy approaching
the exwhoremaster-general of New York—in prison at that—
seemed too fantastic. It was done nevertheless.

Most of the details of what happened from here on are still

classified information in unapproachable Pentagon files. An angry
Senator Estes Kefauver, with all the authority of a congressional
investigating committee behind him, tried to get at the facts in
1951. He had little success. The Navy, members of District Attorney Hogan's office and everybody else who really knew anything were and remain vague for a good reason. It was a very
embarrassing business.

The main features of the story are clear enough. At the
Navy's request, Charlie Lucky was suddenly transferred from
Dannemora, in the farthest corner of New York State, to the
equally secure but more accessible Great Meadows Penitentiary
just north of Albany. Every few weeks a small group of naval
officers in civilian clothes headed by his old lawyer, Moses
Polakoff, would go to visit him. These conferences were arranged
with utmost caution and secrecy. Various writers have published
quotes from the conversations—all entirely spurious. But there
is no doubt that Charlie Lucky unlocked doors for 90 Church
Street. . . . There was surprisingly little sabotage or any other
trouble on the docks of the 3d Naval District during the remainder
of the war. Various Nazi intelligence officers interrogated in Ger-
many after the war, incidentally, commented on the extreme difficulty which their agents had in doing any damage in New York at
all. They had thought that the teeming port would be an easy sabotage target, with plenty of American *Bund* members to place incen-
diaries and delayed-action bombs. It wasn't. According to the
German chiefs, some of whom we interrogated, their men were
discouraged by the vigilance of a very tough and violent, as they
put it with amazement, group of Italians.

Don Salvatore's contribution to our invasion of Sicily, on the
other hand, was probably negligible. The details, again, are buried
in the Navy's "red files." But it is a safe assumption that he would
not have been trusted with even the slightest intimation of our
war plans. The Sicilian Mafia, as it happened, was of solid assistance
to our forces. They supplied reliable fishermen as scouts, skilled
and secure villains of every kind, "safe houses" from which advance agents could work. But the capi mafiosi of New York had
nothing to do with it.

In 1945, counselors Polakoff and Wolf brought the case of
Charles Lucania before the New York State Parole Board. It was

a long and difficult hearing. The witnesses—racketeers, law officers, lawyers and Charlie Lucky himself alike—were all amazingly mute when it came to details. Finally, however, the board came to several conclusions. Charles Lucania had definitely made a contribution to the war effort. It was customary in New York to deport a criminal alien after he had served a substantial part of his sentence, and that under the circumstances nine years should be regarded as such. And finally, the board thought, Charlie Lucky exiled to Italy for life could do no further damage to the United States. Governor Dewey, although as district attorney he had convicted Charlie Lucky in the first place and should have known his character as well as anyone, concurred. The governor granted parole and the federal authorities ordered deportation. Charlie Lucky, like many mafiosi, had never bothered to become an American citizen.

In thinking that Don Salvatore could do no more damage, however, the Parole Board and the governor were very much mistaken. In Italy, the don behaved himself very quietly at first. He was properly deferential to the Italian police who ostentatiously ordered him at once to his birthplace at Lercara Friddi, where he was welcomed as a returning hero. There are reports in the files of the Rome Questura of the exuberant celebration which drew mafiosi from all over Sicily to drink to the health and success of the don. Luciano stayed in the dusty little town for only a few weeks, however; he had no intention of becoming a Sicilian country squire. Government palms were crossed with dollars and before long Don Salvatore installed himself with the full approval of the Questura in a modern apartment on the banks of the Tiber in Rome.

Barely a year after Charles Luciano was deported from New York, a Salvatore Lucania arrived by air in Havana, Cuba. His Italian passport and Cuban visa were in perfect order. Preparatory to finding a suitable house, he rented the penthouse suite of one of Havana's finest new hotels, paid several months' rent and proceeded to make a series of telephone calls to New York and other cities in the United States. An impressive list of capi mafiosi headed by Joe Adonis (he had not yet been deported to Italy) and satellites such as Meyer Lansky began to appear in the Cuban capital. At the same time Charlie Lucky, with his usual foresight and skill, was entrenching himself in Cuban politics. Legislators, judges, police chiefs came to Signor Lucania's elaborate and carefully organized parties; they and their wives received expensive presents from an always open hand. It looked as though Signor Lucania was on the way to becoming a power in Cuba.

Unfortunately for Charlie Lucky, the Bureau of Narcotics in Washington was watching every move. Two narcotic agents had been dispatched to Havana and several employees of the Hotel Nacional were temporarily on the Treasury Department's payroll—an elevator man and a telephone operator among others. The Bureau had good sources of information in Rome which had reported Charlie Lucky's departure for Cuba. They had reason to believe that before leaving Italy he had set up an extensive organization in that country to smuggle narcotics into Cuba which he would then send to the United States.

When the Bureau of Narcotics informed the Cuban government through the State Department that they would appreciate his being sent back to Italy, there was considerable indignation. The Havana authorities demurred. It finally took the combined pressure of the State and Treasury departments to persuade them that Charlie Lucky would be a constant source of embarrassment between the two governments. But it was not until Washington threatened to cut off the shipment of all legitimate medical narcotics that the Cuban government at last reluctantly took action. When a polite squad of detectives of the Cuban Federal Police arrested him Luciano showed, as usual, no emotion at all. "Be seeing ya," he said curtly to his two bodyguards, who had been eating with him, and departed ringed by policemen. A few weeks later he was on a ship back to Italy.

The failure of the Cuban venture was a heavy blow to Don Salvatore and the other members of the brotherhood who had been in on it with him. Substantial money had been invested. Besides, from the purely personal point of view, Havana might have been such a pleasant and understanding headquarters. But the mafiosi are flexible.

The don undoubtedly knew that he faced a rough few months. But he was quite cheerful when he came down the gangplank of the wheezing old freighter which had very slowly brought him across the ocean, to be received by the chief of the Genoa police—personally—and taken to a cell in the city's Questura to be questioned and held until the authorities in Rome decided what should be done with him. Rome again decided that he should be exiled to his birthplace in Sicily. This time Don Salvatore stayed only a few days in Lercara Friddi before returning to the capital, his pleasant apartment and his attractive mistress, Igea Lissoni. But the friends in the Ministry of the Interior and the Questura were nervous. An order of exclusion against the don was imminent, which would bar him from Rome. Charlie Lucky anticipated the move. He had plans, and Rome was not the place for their fruition. Neither was Palermo. In Rome, even if he could buy his way out of the order, he would be under constant surveillance. In Palermo there would be too many mafiosi to pester him and interfere with their equivalent of small town politics. He settled for Naples, the thriving, utterly corrupt big seaport where all branches of the police would be easy to handle and where several ships a week would make communications with the United States fast and regular. In and around Naples were several dozen Italo-American gangsters who had been convicted of serious crimes in the United States and eventually, like Charlie Lucky, deported as "undesirable aliens." Most of them were of Sicilian origin, reliable mafiosi, and were an efficient pretorian guard for the Boss. Don Salvatore transferred his headquarters to the excellent Hotel Turistico in Naples, where an admiring and eagerly subservient staff soon became his personal retinue. It was a secure fortress, as policemen and newspapermen were to discover.

Don Salvatore was again in business. None of his old executive ability or efficiency had been impaired. He had plenty of capital, in hard American cash. Money reached him regularly by courier from his "administrators"—he let the phrase slip once during a police interrogation—in the United States. It is a strict rule of the brotherhood that a mafioso in prison or exile gets dividends from the projects which he organized or helped to organize. The Guardia di Finanza, the Italian treasury police, have only once been able to prove this link. A courier was traced and it was found that Don Salvatore had received almost $50,000 in one batch. He was fined $4,000, which he paid cheerfully, and let off with a warning.

The Italian underworld soon began to feel the impact of Don Salvatore's superior imagination and organizational genius. The "American Colony," as the Italian police calls our deportees, jumped into action. A skillful generalissimo, Charlie Lucky soon had them posted in strategic places. In Rome, Milan, Palermo and other centers, his carefully selected deputies—formerly of New York, Chicago, Detroit—became local powers. In Genoa, for example, a former Brooklyn gangster took over the highly profitable smuggling operations in that port. He organized a flotilla of fishing boats which met the coasters that crossed the Mediterranean from the free port of Tangiers loaded with American cigarettes and other black market staples. Many Italians had acquired a taste for American cigarettes from our GI's during the war, but the duty imposed by the Italian government made them prohibitively expensive in the legal market. Don Salvatore's excellent Genoa organization and others which he established subsequently began to supply a large selection of our brands to dealers all over Italy at a price that the Italians were willing to pay. The don took a comfortable but not exorbitant cut. This lesson he had learned.

The strange, sullen mafioso with the mentality of a Sicilian and the organizational ability of an American had reached a new phase of his career and so had, with him, the whole brotherhood. For the first time the Mafia had an international organizer of the first order. Don Salvatore's frequent tours of Italy were underworld affairs of state. He was finally barred from Rome as a "crime threat," but he made regular trips to Milan for the horse races, to Capri and Palermo to take the sun. Whenever the don arrived at his fashionable hotel in Milan or the famous Quisissana on Capri —flanked by Igea Lissoni and an impressive group of bodyguards—his local representatives would gather to pay their respects. As at the Waldorf and later, in prison, he would grant audiences, listen to his henchmen's problems, pronounce judgment and dismiss them with the air of the emperor that he was. At the races . . . he was always surrounded by a group of subordinates who murmured dutifully at his bets, which were never less than $100 a horse. Once, after a losing streak that cost him several thousand dollars, Charlie Lucky characteristically decided to make a fix. He bribed various jockeys. They took his money but failed to throw the races that he was gambling on. He thereupon sent some of his boys to extract the bribe money plus damages from the brash riders who apparently did not realize with whom they were dealing. They paid up. . . .

Don Salvatore soon had his fingers in various businesses of the usual kind. A Mr. Kenneth Rogers of New York, for example, had started a laundromat business in Austria. It was successful and he wanted to expand it into Italy. He had barely begun his applications for the necessary franchises and licenses in Rome when he was approached one evening at his hotel by two svelte but hard-eyed gentlemen with Brooklyn accents. They were very polite. They simply wanted to bring to Mr. Rogers' attention the fact that any laundromat operation south of Rome would have to have Mr. Lucania's approval. There might be difficulties otherwise. Mr. Lucania would, of course, expect to share in the profits of the venture in exchange for his services and protection. Mr. Rogers decided to give up the whole scheme.

But all business ventures were very small in comparison to the tremendous possibilities which Don Salvatore found in the field of narcotics. It was all made to order for him. The manufacture of heroin for medicinal purposes by pharmaceutical concerns was perfectly legal in Italy and its licensing carelessly administered. (Some Italian medical authorities still claim that properly administered heroin can be beneficial for various ailments; it has long been banned from the American pharmacopoeia as of no value and simply dangerous as the worst of the habit-forming drugs.) The combination of this safe and simple source in Italy with his connections in New York promised the capo mafioso with his lines of communication and expert couriers an important business. Don Salvatore went about the elaborate setup of his organization of it with great care. He did not intend to have his fingers burned again. The reliable Giuseppe Pici, formerly known in the American underworld as Joe Peachy, also a deportee, was made chief of staff for Sicily. Ralph Liguori, an exile as well, became his opposite number in Naples. The don himself from there on never handled so much as a grain of narcotics himself and had no direct connection with anyone who did. It was . . . quite an operation. A courier from one of the brotherhood's New York groups went to Palermo—always to see relatives. He, in the course of his visit, discussed price and delivery date of so many kilos of heroin with the executive on duty, usually a relative. If the price was right and delivery could be made, the courier went on to Naples to get final permission from the capo. If Don Salvatore, in a few moments of apparently chance meeting on the beach or in a well guarded café, gave consent, the messenger proceeded to Milan or elsewhere to contact the name which he had been given. There were no telephone calls; nothing was ever written down. As a rule, the job of the emissary would be finished when he reached Milan. He would pay an advance, and then a whole new system of controls would go into action. Another courier would take the heroin from the factory in Milan to Naples or Genoa and give it to one of the seamen-smugglers which Don Salvatore's group had carefully organized. After the narcotics had been delivered in New York, still another messenger—coming over with another order—would bring the cash agreed upon. No formal contracts were required; Don Salvatore's power in the United States was still such that any welching would have quickly brought severe punishment to the offender.

On January 26, 1962, Luciano was called to Rome by Italian police who had been given new information by American authorities linking him to the narcotics traffic. After pleading innocence for several hours, he was allowed to take a break and go to Rome airport to meet a movie producer arriving to discuss filming his life story. As he and the producer left the terminal, he suddenly collapsed. Within a few seconds Lucky Luciano was dead from a heart attack.

8
Vito Genovese —Power to Spare

FRANK J. PRIAL

"He was a good father who raised his children to be honest, well-behaved and religious."

Thus did an obscure police captain in Atlantic Highlands, New Jersey, describe one of his community's prominent citizens back in 1963. The policeman may have been less than candid. After all, the man he praised was then serving 15 years in a federal prison on a narcotics conviction.

But if he held back a bit, the policeman might be forgiven. For the man he described so positively was Vito Genovese, in his time the most feared Mafia boss in the country.

In any small town—and Atlantic Highlands is a small town—the cops have a pretty good idea what's going on. Thus, it's highly probable that Police Captain James Egidio knew far more about Vito Genovese than he cared to let on to an unknown wire-service reporter.

It's probable, for instance, that Captain Egidio knew Genovese had been charged, but never convicted, of three homicides. It's probable that he knew literally scores of men had died or disappeared because they had incurred Genovese's wrath or suspicion.

It's possible, too, that Captain Egidio may have had some inkling of Genovese's vast power. After all, there had been New Jersey politicians at the famous 1949 Copacabana party thrown by Genovese to show that even the awesome Frank Costello paid him homage.

And certainly Captain Egidio was fully aware of the testimony a few years earlier of Genovese's second wife, Anna. In seeking a divorce and alimony, Mrs. Genovese claimed that her husband had an income of some $30,000 a week, tax free, just from one phase of his operations, the Italian lottery.

What's more, the policeman must have known of the magnificent mansion Genovese maintained overlooking the Atlantic in the days before his divorce.

All these things must have rushed through Captain Egidio's mind when he was asked what he thought about Vito Genovese. Little wonder he contented himself with saying: "He was a good father who raised his children to be honest, well-behaved and religious."

Vito Genovese was born in Rosiglino, Italy, a dreary, poverty-stricken town not far from Naples, on November 27, 1897. He came to New York in steerage in the summer of 1913 and settled on Mulberry Street, then as now the heart of Little Italy in New York. His father, according to one report, had arrived here a year earlier, stayed briefly on the Lower East Side, then moved to rural Queens where he started a small contracting business.

The young Vito was not interested in Queens. He quickly learned to fend for himself in Mulberry Bend, stealing fruit and extorting money from pushcart peddlers and small store owners. There is a legend—a Horatio Alger story in reverse—about the young Genovese first showing the makings of a future gangland chieftain. When an angry vendor grabbed the young thief, so the story goes, Genovese shouted: "Don't touch me. Call the cops, but don't touch me. I'll kill you if you do."

There is no authorized biography, of course, so Genovese's early days are known only through the stories of other hoodlums and a general idea of what life in Little Italy was like. He put in the required apprenticeship to older criminals and undoubtedly rose to the top by being more industrious and more savage than his contemporaries. And, of course, he was smarter. He had to be to survive the unending internecine Mafia wars.

Genovese's first brush with the law was in January, 1917. He got 60 days for carrying a gun and, according to one story, was released only two days before his mother arrived from Italy.

The Mafia was already well established in this country by the time Vito Genovese and his friend Salvatore Lucania—also known as Charles Luciano, Charlie Lucky, and, finally, Lucky Luciano—arrived on the scene. There had been Irish gangs in the city since before the Civil War, and, in the days before World War I, it was said that while Jews made up less than 20 percent of the city's population, Jewish gangsters were responsible for more than half of the city's crime.

Prohibition was the cue for the entrance of the big-time Italian gangster. Scarface Al Capone and his Chicago associates and rivals held the public eye in the 1920s, but according to Joseph Valachi the decade ended with one Giuseppe Masseria reigning as the most powerful man in the Italian gangs. Among the men allied with Masseria, who was known as Joe the Boss, were criminals who would long outlast Capone and who would make his misdeeds appear trifling by comparison. They included Luciano, Genovese, Willie Moretti, Joe Adonis, and Frank Costello. When Masseria began to lose his war with his rival, Salavatore Maranzano, in 1931, Luciano and Genovese contacted Maranzano with an offer to kill Masseria. The deal was made and Joe the Boss was gunned down in a Coney Island restaurant on April 15, 1931.

Maranzano then set up a new table of organization for the Italian gangsters in the city, creating five "families." Luciano was named to head one of them. His underboss: Vito Genovese. It was to be a short-term arrangement, however; Luciano and Genovese discovered that Maranzano had contracted with an "outsider," the Irish gunman Vincent (Mad Dog) Coll, to kill them.

They acted quickly. Luciano hired a group of Jewish thugs, members of Meyer Lansky's mob. Dressed as policemen, they entered Maranzano's office on September 10, 1931, and killed him. That same day, all of Maranzano's top men were killed elsewhere in the city and the suburbs, leaving Luciano in complete control of the Italian gangs here. According to Valachi, Genovese became the underboss and Frank Costello third in command.

Luciano's ascent to the top of the Mafia heap made for relative peace in the mob ranks for a while. It was during this period that Genovese married for the second time. He had been married around 1924 and his first wife died of tuberculosis in 1929. Now, about a year later, he met and fell in love with a distant cousin named Anna Petillo. The only problem was that Anna had a husband, one Gerardo Vernotico. On March 18, 1932, Vernotico's body was found on the roof of a building not far from the Genovese Trading Company at 184 Thompson Street in Greenwich Village, one of Vito's legitimate enterprises. The hapless Vernotico had been shot, stabbed and strangled. Twelve days later, his 22-year-old widow and Vito Genovese, at 34 already a millionaire, were married in a civil ceremony at City Hall.

There was no honeymoon. At least not right away. The Democratic National Convention was coming up in Chicago, and Luciano, Genovese and Costello were to attend. They stayed at the Drake Hotel, actually sharing rooms with the incumbent leaders of Tammany Hall. Not until the following year, 1933, did Vito and Anna sail for Italy on their delayed wedding trip.

Actually, it was something more than a honeymoon. Valachi said years later that Genovese told him he took $750,000 on that trip, much of which went to buy favor among the leaders of the Fascist party. These contacts were to serve Genovese well during his voluntary exile in Italy some years later. Whether he anticipated that he would have to flee the United States is not known, but his planning, from a mobster's point of view, was phenomenal.

Back in New York, a young prosecutor named Thomas Dewey had arrived on the scene and he proceeded to put mobsters behind bars with dispatch and vigor. In 1936 Mr. Dewey stunned the nation by locking up Charlie Lucky himself—along with a horde of confederates—on prostitution charges. Dewey had no sooner slammed the prison gates on Luciano than he promptly announced that Genovese was his next target. It was at this point that Don Vitone, as Genovese had come to be known, decided to take an even longer sabbatical in the land of his birth. Entrusting his many criminal activities to his wife and to Frank Costello, who now became titular head of the Luciano family, Genovese once again sailed for Italy.

There he quickly made himself a confidante of the dictator, Benito Mussolini, hosting dinners for him and being honored in turn by the Fascist leader. According to some reports, Genovese and Count Ciano, Mussolini's son-in-law, became fast friends. According to Anna Genovese's testimony in her 1952 divorce suit, her husband contributed $250,000 to the construction of a Fascist party headquarters. She also testified that his lavish spending in Italy had been financed by the rackets he still controlled in the States. She said she had made frequent trips to Italy before the war broke out to bring him the cash he required.

Genovese's shrewd foresight, his limitless funds and his friends in high Fascist places made it simple for him to become a kingpin, first in the Italian black market during the war and later in the theft and resale of U.S. military supplies. In 1944 Army investigators in Italy first began picking up black marketeers who said they worked for Don Vitone Genovese. Later that year they arrested Genovese himself. They found him living in magnificent luxury in a Naples apartment, armed with government passes enabling him to travel anywhere and see almost anybody.

A member of the Army's Criminal Investigation Division, Sergeant Orange C. Dickey, was in charge of the Genovese case. Somehow he learned that Genovese was still wanted in New York for the 1934 murder of one Ferdinand Boccia. Dickey resolved to have Genovese returned to the States for trial.

The Boccia shooting was a classic gangland incident. According to one version, Boccia had been the manager of one of Genovese's gambling places in Brooklyn. One day in 1934 Boccia told Genovese that he had lined up a "mark," a wealthy businessman who could be fleeced for a small fortune. Genovese told him to go ahead. Several weeks later, Boccia dutifully turned over to Genovese some $100,000 that he had extracted from the unsuspecting mark. By mob rules, he was entitled to one-third, which Genovese promised to pay. Instead, Genovese decided to kill Boccia and keep all the money for himself. Two underlings were given the contract, Ernie Rupolo and Willie Gallo. Actually, Rupolo was given two contracts. He was told to kill Gallo, too, as soon as Boccia had been finished off.

Boccia was killed as planned. Then Gallo was shot three times in the head, but lived. Realizing he had been double-crossed, he told the police everything. Rupolo and Genovese were arrested. Rupolo went to prison, but Gallo reneged on implicating Genovese, and Don Vitone went free. Later Rupolo said there had been a witness to the Boccia shooting who could implicate Genovese, a gangster named Peter La Tempa. On the strength of La Tempa's testimony, Genovese was reindicted, and it was on this indictment that Sergeant Dickey sought to return him to the United States.

Every kind of pressure was brought to bear on the Army sergeant, including an offer of $250,000 cash from Genovese, but Dickey persisted. So Genovese's organization took another tack. La Tempa was in protective custody in a Brooklyn jail, but, somehow, someone got to the pills he took regularly for a stomach disorder. He was found dead in his cell of poison, and Genovese, by then back in New York and on trial for murder, was free once again. Years later, as was seen in Chapter 2 of this book, Rupolo's body was found floating in Jamaica Bay.

Free of the old murder charge, Genovese set about rebuilding the organization he had been forced to run by proxy during the years in Italy. Costello had taken charge and done well, but he was not Genovese and he did not operate like Genovese. It's likely that Don Vitone decided at this point that someday Costello would have to go. He would work slowly, however, waiting until the right moment to spring.

Meanwhile, he enjoyed the life of a Mafia chief, highrolling in the night clubs of New York and loading his mansion in Atlantic Highlands with Italian marble fireplaces, swan-shaped beds and dozens of $350 suits. The flatware and dishes were made from 24-carat gold and platinum, and his wife Anna could drape herself in any of a collection of mink, ermine, persian lamb or broadtail coats.

But platinum and ermine do not always a happy marriage make. There had been some talk about Vito's insatiable appetite for new girls. Once, at a party, Anna's objections led to her having two teeth dislodged by Vito's fist. But she kept it up, and so, apparently, did he. Eventually she tired of his philandering and also got a little scared by his threatening to kill her. Obviously they were not idle threats, as Anna well knew. So she moved out and sued for divorce. The trial in nearby Freehold, New Jersey, the Monmouth County seat, caused a sensation. Apparently unafraid of Mafia retaliation, Anna testified at length about Vito's vast income from his illegal activities. She said he had a hidden majority interest in four Manhattan night clubs and a dog track in Virginia and almost complete control of the Italian lottery. She said her errant husband took in something like $40,000 a week, tax-free.

Vito blandly denied it all. The only income he had, he said, came from his scrap-paper business in Manhattan. Even so, the court ordered him to pay his wife $300 a week and $1,500 court costs. Almost immediately, Vito Genovese sold his mansion and moved into a bungalow that cost him $100 a month rent. He told neighbors he was forced to move to be able to pay the alimony—this at a time when Federal Investigators estimated him to be worth some $30 million.

But the court trial had other repercussions. Several investigations were initiated, and in one instance in Mercer County, New Jersey, a grand jury called Anna in to learn something more about her ex-husband. It was a waste of time.

Shortly after the divorce trial, a man named Stephen Franse was found strangled in his car parked on East Thirty-Seventh Street in Manhattan. Franse had been a partner of Anna Genovese in the 82 Club, a Greenwich Village night club. It was, Mafiosi said, Vito's warning to Anna to keep quiet. She took the advice. In answer to the Mercer County Grand Jury's queries, she said she knew nothing and that if she ever did, she had forgotten it.

Meanwhile, Genovese had not let domestic strife interfere with his plans for eventually taking over from Costello. The first part of his long-range plan was the murder of Willie Moretti. Frank Costello and Moretti had grown up in East Harlem and had been friends all their lives. Moretti moved to New Jersey in the 1930s and had become rackets boss in that state while corrupt state and local officials looked the other way. He also contracted syphilis, and by 1950 it had reached his brain. He was lucid much of the time, but there were other periods when he would ramble on about Mafia activities, much to the consternation of his associates. Costello kept him under medical care during those times.

Genovese began to suggest in conversations with the Luciano family soldiers that Costello was wrong to protect Moretti. He suggested that Willie should be done away with for his own good. "If tomorrow I go wrong," he is supposed to have said, "I would want to be hit so as not to bring harm to this thing of ours." Eventually, the *Commissione* of family bosses agreed, and Moretti's death sentence was official. The contract was open; anyone could carry it out.

On October 4, 1951, Moretti was meeting with several other men at Joe's Restaurant in Cliffside Park, New Jersey. The owner and his waitress were in the kitchen when they heard shots. They found the place deserted except for Moretti's body on the floor with two bullets in the head.

Later, Joe Valachi was to say it was "a hell of a funeral. It was, sort of, as we put it, a mercy killing."

Now Genovese determined to go after Costello himself. The urbane racketeer dined at L'Aiglon, a fashionable Manhattan restaurant, on May 2, 1957, then returned to his Central Park West apartment. He was walking through the lobby when he heard a voice say, "This is for you, Frank." As he turned, a single shot creased his skull.

Costello was covered with blood, but he made it to nearby Roosevelt Hospital and soon recovered. The bungled shooting— Valachi later said the hit man was an ex-prizefighter named Vincente Gigante—sent shock waves throughout the underworld. Everyone prepared for a gang war.

Genovese took 40 men and barricaded himself in a house in New Jersey. He called all the Luciano lieutenants to join him as a sign of fealty. All but one did, and he later met a predictably sudden and violent death. But there was no war. Costello, after saying publicly he had no idea who had shot him, let it be known that he was retiring as a Mafia family boss.

The fact is, Costello was different from Genovese. He was a throwback to the older, less complicated, more savage breed of capo Mafioso. Costello apparently was content to tend to his own rackets and legitimate businesses, leaving control of the mobs to Genovese—or to whomever could wrest it away from Genovese.

One man still stood between Genovese and complete control: Albert Anastasia, possibly the most ruthless of all the Mafia leaders, a man who killed other men almost for sport. He had been a top gun in Murder, Incorporated, and apparently ordered the execution of Arnold Shuster, the youth who fingered bank robber Willie Sutton, simply because as he said, "I can't stand squealers."

Anastasia apparently wanted to bring Costello back out of retirement. Genovese, in his characteristically byzantine manner, contacted an ambitious lieutenant in Anastasia's own family, Carlo Gambino. He convinced Gambino he would have a great future if Anastasia was out of the way. Gambino in turn gave the contract to Joseph Profaci, a Brooklyn Mafia boss, who in turn parceled it out to two of his men.

On October 25, 1957, Anastasia was reclining in the barbershop at the Park Sheraton Hotel, his face covered with hot towels. His bodyguard was away for a few minutes when two gunmen walked in and shot Anastasia dead.

Genovese was now in a position to take over all the Mafia families in the area. His ascension to power was approved at the famous Apalachin, New York, conference of national Mafia figures, the meeting that was broken up by alert State Police.

One of the items on the agenda that day was said to have been an order from the Mafia's top men to get out of the narcotics business because it exposed too many underling Mafiosi to arrest by government agents. But Genovese's greed, or possibly his arrogance, got the best of him and he bankrolled a huge narcotics smuggling operation. Federal agents found out about it, and eventually Genovese and 14 codefendants went to prison on narcotics charges. Vito Genovese entered prison in 1958, and it was in the federal penitentiary in Atlanta that Genovese's path and that of Joe Valachi were to cross for the last time—with enormous repercussions for all organized crime.

Valachi had been an obscure soldier in Genovese's Mafia family, but he had watched and listened. In prison he roomed with Genovese and saw how he continued to run his vast operations from his cell. He also learned that Genovese suspected him of talking to federal agents and wanted him killed. Valachi grew more and more paranoid and eventually killed another prisoner whom he mistook for one assigned to kill him. In a desperate attempt to save his life, he agreed to tell everything he knew about the Mafia.

Genovese's high-handed exercise of authority at Atlanta, which included his giving Valachi the "kiss of death" and ordering his murder, led to Valachi's starring role before a Senate committee on the operations of big-time crime. It also led to Genovese's transfer to the federal penitentiary at Fort Leavenworth, Kansas, where he contracted his final illness.

He was later transferred to the Medical Center for Federal Prisoners at Springfield, Missouri, and died there of a heart ailment on February 14, 1969.

9
Carlo Gambino
—Mafia Patriarch

NICHOLAS GAGE

Carlo Gambino is the godfather of the Mafia. With men like Genovese and Luciano dead, Carlo Gambino, who is in his seventies, is the Old Man and the boss of the most powerful Mafia family in the country. So when Gambino speaks, everybody listens, and he doesn't have to raise his voice.

Gambino, who was born in Palermo, Sicily, in 1902, is known as a quiet, cautious, soft-spoken man with a courtly manner. He has a beaklike nose in a puckish face, thinning gray hair and a generally benign expression and he walks with a slight stoop. He looks like everyone's ideal of a kindly old uncle. His friendly manner doesn't waver even when he is trying to extort money. A Manhattan restaurateur several years ago received an offer from Gambino, who has great influence in the labor unions. Gambino offered him labor peace for a price. The restaurant owner remembers him as "unusually sympathetic, like doctors in movies." In spite of Gambino's sympathy, the restaurateur told him he preferred to close his restaurant instead. The Mafia boss, he says, then tried to appeal to his civic conscience. "Where would this city be if every businessman threw in the towel because of a little unpleasantness?" he quotes Gambino as saying.

Gambino may not be as flashy or as well known as other top mobsters, but his low profile has stood him in good stead. He has not seen the inside of a prison since 1937, he has stayed on

172

top throughout all inter-Mafia disputes, and his family is reportedly not only the largest in the country but the most profitable as well. There is none of the kind of factionalism that tore the Profaci family apart and that frequently leads to jealousies and bloodshed within families. In the Gambino family nobody's inclined to rock the boat. "Gambino runs a smooth, efficient operation and everybody makes money," said one lawman who has followed the affairs of the family for six years.

The Gambino network includes about 1,000 men, half Mafia members and the other half associates. Gambino's rackets stretch from western Connecticut to the outskirts of Philadelphia, and he also has a highly profitable unit in New Orleans with the consent of the Mafia boss there, Carlos Marcello. The Gambino group specializes in such moneymaking rackets as gambling, loansharking, hijacking, narcotics and labor racketeering. Gambino's power is strong in unions affiliated with night clubs, restaurants, construction and the waterfront.

Gambino carries such clout with the labor unions that he decided to go into the labor-relations business and from 1955 to 1965 he was one-third owner of a labor-relations concern called SGS Associates. Its clients included Wellington Associates, the real-estate concern that owns the Chrysler Building and other prestigious properties; Howard Clothes; and the Concord Hotel in the Catskills. The company was dissolved after Gambino's connection with it came to light.

Gambino's top men, according to a list given by the Justice Department to the Senate Subcommittee on Criminal Laws and Procedures, include Aniello Dellacroce, the underboss; Joseph Riccobono, the *consigliere;* and 27 captains.

Dellacroce, who frequently goes by the name of Mr. O'Neill, is quiet and efficient like Gambino, but unlike his boss he has a reputation as a womanizer. Gambino is willing to indulge this weakness in his underboss because Dellacroce, who is 12 years younger than Gambino, is wise enough to stay away from wives or daughters of Mafia members. (A former Gambino soldier who was not so judicious was lured by several colleagues to a deserted section of Connecticut one day where he was stabbed to death and fed into a commercial garbage-disposal unit. Tampering with the woman of a fellow Mafioso has carried the death penalty since the earliest days of the Mafia, as has breaking the sacred law of *omertà*—silence.)

The 27 captains in the Gambino family include Carlo's two brothers, Joseph and Paul Gambino, and Paul's brother-in-law, Paul Castellano. The Justice Department list also named Anthony Scotto, president of Local 1814 of the International Longshoremen's Association, as a Gambino family captain. Scotto said there was "no truth" to the charge.

Lawmen and mobsters agree that Gambino personally is a very wealthy man. Two of the ways he amassed his large fortune were outlined by Joseph Valachi before a Senate investigating committee in 1962:

> "Some years ago Gambino tied up the alcohol market by buying up almost all the alcohol in the New York area. He dried up the town. And where he paid about four bills a tin, after he dried up the market he was able to get any price he wanted, up to fifty a tin.
>
> "Another thing Carlo pulled that made him rich. Him and his brother Paul and Sam Accardi (a New Jersey gangster who has since been deported) made over a million from ration stamps during the war. The stamps came out of the O.P.A.'s offices. First Carlo's boys would steal them. Then, when the government started hiding them in banks, Carlo made contact and the O.P.A. men sold him the stamps. He really got rich on that."

Because of his vast fortune and the size of his rackets, Gambino has been referred to by some journalists as the Mafia "Boss of Bosses." This position, however, was eliminated by Lucky Luciano in 1931 (after he had Boss of Bosses Salvatore Maranzano bumped off along with about 40 other old-timers). Luciano replaced the position with a national commission made up of the most important of the Mafia family bosses in the country. Needless to say, Carlo Gambino has a chair on the *Commissione*, and it would not be far off to describe him as "first among equals."

Because of his power, Gambino is a very important ally. It was Carlo's backing, for example, that made Joseph Colombo, until then a "bust-out guy" (petty gambler) in the Profaci family, the new boss of the family in 1964 to the dismay of other Mafiosi.

But Gambino owed Colombo a favor. When Joe Bonanno, boss of one of New York's five Mafia families, got ambitious and wanted to bump off three members of the *Commissione*, the contract for the killings was passed on to Colombo. Knowing his big chance when he saw it, Colombo went straight to Gambino and, instead of shooting him, spilled the entire story. His reward was the leadership of the Profaci family. Many Mafiosi were appalled to see Joe Colombo in such a high position, but with Carlo Gambino as his mentor, they were not about to complain very loudly.

When Gambino changed his mind about Joe Colombo, however, Colombo's throne at the head of his family suddenly got very shaky. Colombo succeeded in alienating his benefactor's affections when he got too carried away with running the Italian-American Civil Rights League which he founded in 1970. Colombo had the league picket FBI offices in New York for months on end, which Gambino felt was only making the FBI agents more determined to crack down on Mafia rackets.

Older Mafia leaders thought Colombo should use the League to pressure the Italian government into releasing some of the Sicilian Mafiosi who had been exiled to barren Mediterranean islands. Carlo Gambino himself made the suggestion to Colombo, but Colombo, born and raised in New York, was not interested in the welfare of the Sicilian Mafiosi.

Gambino remained on Colombo's side longer than most of the top Mafiosi, but eventually Colombo's flamboyance and his weakness for publicity became too much for the conservative Gambino. By June of 1971 it was clear to everyone but Joseph Colombo which way the wind was blowing. In early June, Joseph De Cicco, named as a member of Carlo Gambino's family, suddenly resigned as chief organizer of the league, saying that his health wasn't up to it. Then word went around to Gambino's territory, particularly on the New York waterfront: The second annual Unity Day rally of the League, at Columbus Circle, scheduled for June 28, 1971, was to be avoided.

Shortly before noon on Unity Day, Joseph Colombo was shot in the head as he prepared to speak to the gathering crowds. He was shot by a black named Jerome A. Johnson who was instantly shot to death himself. Colombo survived, but was left unable to walk, speak or care for himself. No arrests were made in the shooting of Johnson.

The police promptly brought Gambino in for questioning. Gambino told them that although he did not support Colombo's League, he was very disturbed by Colombo's shooting. He told federal agents the same thing two weeks later.

Gambino had been equally uninformative 14 years earlier when police called him in to talk about the unfortunate and sudden death of Albert Anastasia, at which time Gambino was the underboss in Anastasia's family. After Anastasia's demise in the barbershop in 1957, Gambino suddenly advanced from underboss to boss of his family.

Although no action was ever taken against Gambino in the Anastasia murder, Joseph Valachi later said that Gambino planned the murder at the instigation of Vito Genovese, who wanted Anastasia out of the way because he considered him a stumbling block in his grab for power in the Mafia. "Without Vito backing him, Carlo never would have went for it," Valachi said. "But he had a good excuse. . . . Albert was losing heavy at the track, he was there every day, and he was abusing people worse than ever on account of that."

The actual killers of Anastasia were members of the Joseph Gallo gang acting on orders from Gambino and Genovese, according to both Valachi and another underworld informant (though not a member of the Mafia) named Sidney Slater. Slater said that he ran into Joseph Gallo and four of his associates in a bar after the Anastasia killing and that Gallo told him, "From now on, Sidney, you can just call the five of us the barbershop quintet."

Police never managed to tie anyone to the Anastasia killing. And if Joseph Gallo was acting on Gambino's orders and shot Anastasia, it didn't do him any good in the end. Like his rival Joe Colombo, Joey Gallo also finally alienated Carlo Gambino before he was murdered in Umberto's Clam House on April 7, 1972.

After he won the leadership of the Anastasia family, Gambino at first had a little trouble establishing his authority. His takeover was contested by Aniello Dellacroce, who is now his second in command. Gambino showed his mettle as a boss by the way he handled the opposition. First, one of Dellacroce's closest allies, a man named Armand Rava, disappeared. Word went around that Rava was dead. Then feelers went out: Was Dellacroce willing to meet for a peace conference? A few days later Dellacroce emerged as a key man in the Gambino camp and all resistance to Gambino's leadership faded away.

During his years in power, Gambino has seen most of the famous Mafia leaders who seized power in Lucky Luciano's coup pass from the scene. Each passing has left Gambino more powerful and more respected. Throughout the years his Mafia family has quietly grown to be the strongest in the country.

Characteristically, Gambino lives well but quietly and does not make a display of his wealth. He maintains a home at 2230 Ocean Parkway, Brooklyn, and a waterfront estate at 34 Club Drive, Massapequa, Long Island. During their marriage, Gambino's wife Kathryn preferred the Brooklyn apartment, and after she died in 1971 Gambino, who was devoted to her, continued to spend most of his time there.

Unlike Frank Costello, Lucky Luciano, Joe Colombo and other Mafia leaders, Gambino avoids the company of politicians, entertainers or anybody else who might bring him public attention. When his wife died, Carlo sent out word to all his influential friends not to risk coming to the funeral or sending flowers or telegrams that could be traced.

Carlo and Kathryn's three sons and one daughter are all grown up. One son, Thomas, is married to the daughter of the late Gaetano (Three-Finger Brown) Lucchese, who was head of another New York family until his death in 1967.

Carlo Gambino was 19 when he arrived in the United States from Palermo, Italy, in 1921 as a stowaway. He soon became a promising soldier in the Brooklyn Mafia family then led by Vincent and Philip Mangano. In all the years since then Gambino has managed to avoid any lengthy stretches behind bars through a combination of wiles and incredible luck. His only significant stretch in jail was in 1937, when he served 22 months for operating a million-gallon still in Philadelphia. A year earlier he was indicted on charges of leading a bootleg ring that operated from Long Island to Pennsylvania. His indictment looked like a sure thing until, just before his trial, the Supreme Court ruled that wiretap evidence was inadmissible in court. His case was based mostly on information obtained through wiretaps, so the charges against him were dismissed.

In recent years a convenient heart condition has made it possible for Gambino to avoid being questioned by anyone, from the district attorney of New York to the Senate Rackets Committee. In March of 1970 he was indicted on charges of conspiring to hijack an armored car carrying $3 million to $5 million for the Chase Manhattan Bank, but it is doubtful that he will ever be brought to trial because of his health.

Over the years the United States has tried to deport Gambino to his native Sicily on the grounds of his illegal entry as a stowaway. He battled every attempt to deport him, but in 1970 the Supreme Court upheld a 1967 order. Gambino had to go.

After defeating several more legal maneuvers by Gambino, the United States in 1971 got set to carry out the deportation order. But first, according to law, a doctor had to examine him to determine if he was physically able to travel. Shortly before the scheduled examination Gambino was rushed to a hospital. His family said he had suffered a massive heart attack. The timing of the attack seemed remarkably convenient, but when the government had doctors examine him they announced that the heart attack was genuine and serious as well. In fact, the government doctors concluded, it was likely that Gambino would never be strong enough to be deported. So Gambino serenely remains the Grand Old Man of the Mafia. "Unfortunately," said a federal agent, "it looks like Carlo is going to be with us till the end."

10
Joseph Colombo
—Impulsive Innovator

TIME MAGAZINE

It was to be a *celebrazione*, a party, an old-fashioned T-shirt, hot-dog and straw-hat festival of ethnic pride. Manhattan's Columbus Circle was roofed with plastic streamers in red, white and green, the colors of the old country. The guy wires hummed in the breeze as an organ on the bandstand piped out random tunes for the early arrivals. Vendors set up rows of gaily colored booths to sell buttons (WE'RE NO. 1), pennants (ITALIAN POWER!) and other paraphernalia of prideful protest. Now, in the already shimmering morning heat, the buses came rolling in from Corona in Queens, Bensonhurst in Brooklyn, Greenwich Village and all the Little Italys of the city. The occasion was the Italian-American Civil Rights League's second annual Unity Day, and it was meant to be fun for everyone.

No one was looking to enjoy himself more than Joseph Colombo, Sr., the league's burly founder, unofficial leader and chief promoter. The head of one of New York's five Mafia families of organized crime, Colombo had discovered a double life through the league. Started casually, in one year it grew into a genuine vehicle of expression for thousands of Americans of Italian descent who had nothing to do with the Mafia or crime. Harnessing their honest sentiments, Colombo had helped Italian Americans to achieve new pride—and managed to do a few things for the narrower cause as well, like embarrassing the Justice Department and

179

The Godfather film makers into dropping the words Mafia and Cosa Nostra from their vocabulary.

Thus, on his day, Colombo moved easily through the crowd, shaking hands, joking, posing for photographers. Suddenly shots rang out, barely audible above the noise of the happy crowd. Colombo crumpled to the ground, bleeding heavily from the head and neck.

Almost immediately, another volley sounded and his assailant, a black posing as a photographer who only seconds before had been filming Colombo, pitched forward face down, dead. Later identified as Jerome Johnson, 24, he had been silenced by a still unidentified league captain, Colombo bodyguard, or someone posing as part of Joe's retinue. Johnson's killer escaped as professionally as he had carried out his mission, shooting Johnson three times even as police clustered around.

Hysterical spectators either rushed to see what was happening or fled in fear of more gunfire. There were confused shouts of "They got Joe! Joe's dead!" As word that the assailant was black rippled through the crowd, shock gave way to anger. Several blacks were roughed up. One, a musician who had been hired to entertain later in the day, was beaten by five or six men as onlookers shouted, "Kill him! Kill him!"

With blood streaming from the bullet wounds, Colombo was rushed to nearby Roosevelt Hospital. In a five-hour operation, surgeons removed the most damaging bullet, which had lodged in Colombo's cerebellum. . . . A less robust man might have never made it to the operating table. Said one doctor: "He's tough as hell."

Soon after the shooting, telephoned threats were received that a man was going to "machine-gun the whole family." Colombo's wife Lucille and sons, Anthony, Joseph, Jr., and Vincent, 21, quickly converted a second-floor waiting room into a battle center. Within hours, Roosevelt Hospital took on the look of a grim, almost surrealistic parody of a Godfatheresque scene from Mario Puzo's bestselling novel.

In the book, Godfather Vito Corleone is shot down in the street by members of a rival Mafia family but survives, hovering near death. To guard against a feared second attack, his family stations private detectives and trusted *caporegimes* (lieutenants) throughout the hospital where he is recuperating. If anything,

Colombo security within Roosevelt Hospital was even tighter, despite the presence of uniformed and plainclothes New York City policemen.

At the hospital's entrances, small groups of outsize, burly men, wearing tiny green-and-red Italian-American League pins, nervously watched the streets, quickly sizing up each approaching pedestrian. "You watch this stairway," one bull-necked "captain" instructed a younger man. "If somebody goes into the hallway, you follow him. If he gets in the elevator, you get in with him. And if he gets off at the floor, you tell him he can't go no further."

Inside the hospital, *caporegimes* and "button men," or soldiers, the lowest-ranking Mafia family members, prowled the corridors near Colombo's room. No one was allowed near the room without the O.K. of Vincent ("Vinnie") Vingo, a Colombo family loan shark with a fearsome reputation for violence. Entertainer Sammy Davis, Jr., his wife, and Rabbi Meir Kahane, who had concluded an alliance between his militant Jewish Defense League and Colombo's league, were among the few nonfamily members to pass Vingo's muster. Davis, who emerged from the hospital grim and tight-lipped after visiting with the Colombo family, refused to comment on the shooting, saying only that Colombo has "our prayers."

The brotherhood that is the Mafia has always operated in secrecy. Sworn to an *omertà*—the oath of silence—in a ceremony of blood and fire, the old-line Mafiosi cultivated their anonymity as the first line of defense against arrest and prosecution. Despite the publicity caused by Prohibition gangland wars, the Mafia was still able to maintain a cloak of secrecy around its activities. Behind this shield, Mafia leaders gained control of gambling and narcotics, some labor unions and legitimate businesses. When the first systematic crackdowns by law-enforcement agencies started in the early 1960s, the bosses deemed their facelessness more important than ever.

Until Joe Colombo burst into headlines . . . the pattern of silence had never been broken. In an America now angrily aware of the Cosa Nostra, Colombo wanted to return to the *omertà* of turn-of-the-century Little Italys, where *Mafia* was a whispered word and bosses were not badgered by grand juries, tax investigators and wiretaps. To accomplish his goal, Colombo tapped deep-seated, legitimate grievances among Italian Americans and—shocking editorial writers and Mob *capos* alike—jumped into press conferences and picket lines. He sought to make Cosa Nostra private once more by turning any derision of Italian Americans—Mafiosi or not—into a cause for public censure. It was a radical notion that more traditional Mafia leaders could not have imagined and, in the end, could not countenance.

Ironically, Colombo's deviation from old-line Mafia methods resulted from his adherence to the traditional code of family loyalty. When his son Joseph, Jr., was arrested in April 1970 on a charge of melting coins into silver ingots, Colombo acted at once. He took the usual steps of putting up bail and hiring a top lawyer to look for irregularities and loopholes. Then he did something new. He began picketing the FBI, claiming that he and his family were being harassed. After several months of daily demonstrations, the Italian-American Civil Rights League was formed.

The league's first major action was to sponsor Italian-American Unity Day in 1970. The rally conspicuously closed stores in neighborhoods controlled by the Mafia: New York's waterfront was virtually shut down when many longshoremen took the day off for the ethnic celebration, and almost every politician in the city joined the 50,000 celebrants in Columbus Circle. Nelson Rockefeller was offered honorary league membership and accepted.

Not only did the league persuade the Justice Department and some moviemakers to ban the term Mafia, but its campaign against corporations that used Italian stereotypes in their advertising led to cancellation of television commercials, including a prizewinning Alka-Seltzer ad, "Spicy Meatballs." The Ford Motor Co. assured the league that in television series it sponsored the FBI would not track down criminals belonging to something called the Mafia. Plans for a $3.5 million hospital were announced: the league set up a children's summer camp. A year after the first pickets marched in front of FBI headquarters, Colombo was honored as league man-of-the-year. Thirteen hundred people came to the dinner marking his "undying devotion to the Italian-American people and all humanitarian causes."

There were articles in magazines . . . and newspapers on Colombo: a lengthy story in . . . *New York* analyzed Colombo's role as a catalyst for ethnic pride and an influence in New York City politics. To some observers, Colombo appeared to change as a result of the heady publicity: he started to view himself as a civil rights leader just as misunderstood by cops in New York as black leaders were by rural sheriffs in the South. Each of his successes— and some were formidable, even laudable—underscored his determination. But those same successes were writing his own contract.

Beyond Johnson lie several fascinating theories about the motives for the assassination attempt. . . .

Colombo's career as a gangster . . . could provide a plausible motive—revenge. One product of his years as a member of the assassination team of Joseph Profaci, head of a New York family, is a list of victims' relatives—young men orphaned by contract, brothers bound to avenge a family murder—who would like to see Colombo killed. His rise in the Mob hierarchy earned him the bitter enmity of former comrades, notably Joseph ("Crazy Joe") Gallo, onetime Profaci triggerman whom Colombo opposed during a bloody gang war in the early '60s.

But the most likely explanation for the Columbus Circle attack is as old as the Mafia itself and as new as Joe Colombo's vision of his role of Mafia chieftain. The New York families, or tribes, of the Cosa Nostra are on the edge of a classic power struggle, precipitated by Colombo's refusal to rule as Mafia bosses have always ruled—quietly and privately, in the tradition of the Sicilian dons. The Mafia that he insists is nonexistent almost surely tried to kill Joe Colombo. . . .

Colombo's new celebrity status attracted attention to men who decidedly opposed public scrutiny—the bosses of the other New York families. A great deal of the scrutiny came from law-enforcement agencies. Mafia bosses, who had built careful layers of insulation around themselves—never dealing directly with button men, trusting only a few close lieutenants—found their protective covering being stripped away. Grand jury subpoenas were issued to men convinced they were safe from such summonses. The high-rolling life-style they enjoyed was sharply straitened by Internal Revenue Service agents, who carefully checked any discrepancies between reported income and visible spending. Most of the scrutiny was the result of a growing public clamor for a curb on Mob activity—not Joe Colombo's public posturing. But

Mafia chieftains blamed him nonetheless, and at least one prominent
Mafioso believed that Colombo and the league had netted him a
grand jury subpoena.

Moreover the five New York families have just emerged from
a decade that left their tight paramilitary structure shaken and dis-
organized. The bitterness of past Mafia wars still lingered, especially
between Colombo and Joseph Gallo, the volatile former Profaci
triggerman whose defection sparked the 1961 war. He once kept a
wildcat in his basement and, for luck, a dwarf on his payroll. Released in March, 1971, after serving nine years for extortion, he
returned to New York with a grudge against Colombo and hereti-
cal ideas about recruiting blacks into Mafia ranks. These made him
the subject of speculation regarding the shooting.

Of the five dons in power a decade ago, only one—Carlo
Gambino—retains his position today. In the four other slots, the
old bosses have not been officially replaced or the men who succeeded them—including Colombo—were not considered their
equals. A measure of the scorn in which Colombo was held is revealed in the wiretap transcripts of a conversation between New
Jersey Boss "Sam the Plumber" De Cavalcante and his underboss,
Frank Majuri:

De Cavalcante: Joe Colombo. Where's a guy like that belong
in the Commission? What experience has he got?

Majuri: This is ridiculous.

The all-powerful Commission, which dominated Mob affairs
across the country for decades, has likewise fallen into disarray.
After the disastrous Apalachin meeting in 1957, where 58 mobsters
were arrested, the Commission abandoned full-scale gatherings. For
a while, its members met in twos and threes to conduct Cosa Nostra
business—sometimes on Sunday morning when, they assumed, FBI
agents would be in church. When these arrangements failed, the
dons were left to communicate with one another from outdoor
phone booths—a far cry from the grand council meetings in luxury
hotels. The vacuum in leadership and logistical planning opened
the way for the sole cagey survivor of the old days—Carlo
Gambino, head of the largest family in the U.S.

While some observers considered Colombo the prototype of
the new Mafia leader, the public relations-oriented businessman
needed to run the growing list of legitimate Mafia-controlled enter-

prises, to Gambino he was a recklessly visible member of a society that still needed invisibility in order to function properly. There is speculation that Gambino and other Colombo associates were unhappy over their failure to share in the estimated $2,000,000 the league raised since its founding. Gambino became convinced, as were law-enforcement officials, that Colombo was using the league for his own benefit.

As Colombo worked on preparations for what was to have been the triumph of the second Italian-American Unity Day, opposition was solidifying within the Mob. Tommy Eboli . . . of Vito Genovese's New York family let his disgust with Colombo be known in Mob circles. [Eboli was himself gunned down on July 16, 1972.] Gallo's soldiers went among Brooklyn merchants, telling them not to close for Unity Day, tossing league buttons into trash cans, burning Colombo's signs and asserting that Colombo was using poor Italian people's dues to help him fight the FBI. Longshoremen, who had swelled the previous year's crowds, withheld their support this year, partly accounting for the fact that only 8,000 showed, a drop of more than 40,000 from last year's rally.

Joe Colombo's civic career is a recent development. Until he organized the Italian-American Civil Rights League, he was a much more private person, intent on following his father's profession. Anthony Colombo was a successful Brooklyn mobster until he was garroted one night in 1938 in the back seat of his car along with his girl friend. The killing forced young Joe to quit high school and go to work in a printing plant to support his mother and younger sister. He enlisted in the Coast Guard in World War II, but he got into so much trouble that he was treated for psychoneurosis in a hospital and given a medical discharge. He collected a disability allowance of $11.50 a month.

Returning to Brooklyn, Colombo drifted into a life of petty crime under the shadow of the Mafia. By Mafioso standards, Colombo was not much of a success. He failed to compile the kind of record that would mark him for bigger things. For a while he served as a muscleman on the piers; later he organized rigged dice games. He was given a promotion of sorts when he was appointed to a five-man assassination squad under the direction of Mafia Boss Joe Profaci. Also on the team were the Gallo brothers: Larry and Crazy Joe.

According to police, the [Gallo] group performed efficiently, disposing of some 15 troublesome victims until 1959 when the Gallo's rebelled against Profaci.

Remaining loyal to Profaci but keeping as quiet as possible, Colombo escaped from the wars unscathed—but only just. On July 4, 1963, the Gallos planned to ambush him on his way home from the country club where he regularly played golf. Somehow, he got word and took another route.

Eventually, Colombo engineered a truce between the warring Mafia factions. At the same time he added to his power in another way. Two of the Mafia bosses, Joe Bonanno and Joe Magliocco, decided to let a contract for the extinction of three of their rivals: Carlo Gambino and Thomas Lucchese of New York City, and Stefano Magaddino of Buffalo. Who should be picked for the job but enterprising Joe Colombo? In this case, however, Joe thought the victims would be worth more to him than the contract. So he tipped them off, Bonanno made his hasty, celebrated disappearance and the "Bananas War" got under way. Some seven mobsters were slain, but once again Colombo escaped with profit.

In 1963 he was given command of the Profaci family. At 40 he was the youngest of the Mafia chieftains. Until then, his virtue had been his caution. Except for law-enforcement agencies, hardly anyone knew who he was. Though he had been arrested a dozen times on minor charges, he had been convicted only three times. He was fined twice for gambling, and he was jailed for 30 days in 1966 because he refused to tell a grand jury what he knew about mob infiltration of legitimate business. His bigger operations were largely untouched by the law or publicity: gambling in Brooklyn and Nassau County, loan-sharking in Manhattan, hijacking at Kennedy Airport.

He lives inconspicuously: the Mafia equivalent of the man in the gray flannel suit. A conservative if stylish dresser, he looks the part of the conventional real estate salesman that he claimed to be. His split-level home in Brooklyn, where he lives with his wife, his two unmarried sons and a daughter, is scarcely distinguishable from other houses in the neighborhood. Hidden away in Orange County, N.Y., is a more appropriate setting for a Mafia boss: an extensive estate, complete with tennis courts, a swimming pool and a horse-racing track. . . . . .

Colombo has been able to account for an income of about $18,000 a year through real estate dealings: associates report that he rarely has any difficulty collecting his commissions. On a Dick Cavett television show, Colombo explained that he also owns a piece of a florist shop and of a funeral home. When the studio audience laughed at the mortuary connection, Colombo bridled. He was not trying to be funny, he said, and he did not find the matter at all amusing.

When U.S. Attorney General John Mitchell stepped up the war on organized crime, Colombo lost his cool. He became angered when the FBI trailed him, questioned his friends and family and arrested Joseph, Jr. (he was later acquitted). In that anger the Italian-American Civil Rights League was born.

When Colombo pressed on, the pressure—and the signals—increased. In May, 1971, league officials were assaulted in Brooklyn, and Colombo was shoved and slapped when he tried to break up the fight. On June 11, Gambino lieutenants sent word for Colombo to ease up on Unity Day preparations, but he refused. A week later, Colombo was beaten once more. A golf partner reported that when a golf-cart tire blew out with a bang, "Colombo dove for the ground and crawled under the cart." Two weeks before the Unity Day Rally, some gangsters suspected that Colombo was a murder target.

For nearly a week, police investigators could establish no direct connection between Jerome Johnson and the Mafia. But they settled on the theory that Johnson had been chosen precisely because such a connection was difficult to prove. Johnson, police asserted, was a hired killer who had been silenced by a second triggerman at the rally. Colombo associates meanwhile continued to insist that the murder attempt was an isolated attack. "It seems like shooting civil rights leaders is 'in' in recent years," explained a league official.

Pride in the Family

THE MAFIA HAS CAUGHT THE PUBLIC IMAGINATION more than any other segment of the underworld. One reason it fascinates outsiders is that it is an organization with long and brutal traditions, very precise rules of conduct and complicated "business" procedures.

The following section examines the Mafia as an organization—how it is structured, how it works and what is demanded of a Mafia member. The first chapter describes the power structure of a typical Mafia "family," the duties that various members are expected to carry out in the operation of a racket and the rules of conduct governing the relationships between different Mafia families. It is written by Donald R. Cressey, a professor of sociology at the University of California in Santa Barbara who served as organized-crime consultant to the President's Commission on Law Enforcement and Administration of Justice.

In the second chapter Ralph Salerno and John Tompkins tell how men are recruited into the Mafia and trained to be worthy of full membership. He describes the precise rules that govern their conduct once they become Mafia members, rules that deal with everything from what a Mafioso tells his wife to how he acts toward another member. Salerno also reveals the reasons for the rules and the punishments for breaking them.

As he demonstrates, the Mafia has clear-cut rules for the behavior of members toward women. For example, one of the infractions punishable by death is the seduction of the wife or daughter of a fellow member. The reason, Salerno explains, is to protect the organization from the long and bloody vendettas over matters of honor that plagued the Mafia in Sicily. As Salerno says, the punishment must be severe because so many Mafiosi "are in a constant state of courtship," although their business practices don't leave too much time for romance.

11
The Power Structure

DONALD CRESSEY

The highest ruling body of the Mafia is the "Commission," sometimes called the "High Commission," the "Grand Council," the "Administration," "*Consiglio d'Aministrazione,*" the "Round-table," or the "Inner Circle." This body serves as a combination board of business directors, legislature, supreme court, and arbitration board, but most of its functions are judicial, as we will show later. Members look to the Commission as the ultimate authority on organizational disputes, and each Commission member is sometimes called a "chairman" or an "*avvocato*" (advocate, counsel). The Commission is made up of the rulers of the most powerful "families," which are located in large cities. At present, eight such "families" are represented on the Commission, but the number of commissioners usually varies from nine to twelve. Thomas Gaetano Lucchese, head of a New York "family," died in 1967. For a time, it looked as though leadership of his "family" was to be taken over by his deputy, Anthony Corallo. However, Corallo was arrested before he was "raised"—which is the Cosa Nostra term used to refer to selection as a member of the Commission. Three of the eight "families" currently represented on the Commission are in New York City, one in Buffalo, one in Newark, and one each in Philadelphia, Detroit, and Chicago.

The Commission is not a representative legislative assembly or an elected judicial body. Cosa Nostra "families" in cities such as . . . Kansas City, Pittsburgh, and Tampa do not have members on the Commission. It is probable, however, that the "families" in these and other areas have a specified Commission member, usually a regional neighbor, looking after their interests. The members of the Commission do not regard each other as equals. There are informal understandings which give one member authority over another, but the exact pecking order, if there is one, has not been determined. The Commission is not a recent invention. . . . A "Grand Council" of nine men was operating in 1940, and federal agencies knew for certain in 1959 that the ruling body of Cosa Nostra was a Commission made up of nine to twelve men. The Apalachin conference was a meeting of Commission members and their lieutenants.

In some sections of the country, the next level of authority, below the Commission, is a "council" made up of the more experienced members of each "family" in a particular geographic area. New York, Detroit, and Chicago (at least) have councils. The patriarch of the council may be called a "Don" or "chairman," and he might or might not be a member of the Commission. Council members are elected by the council. When a council member dies, the council chooses a new member from the men in his "family." The New York body is sometimes called a "council of six," sometimes, more mundanely, a "grievance committee." In Detroit, the Don is sometimes called "elected boss" or "chairman of the board," and the council is sometimes named the "high court." It has three members, called "elder statesmen," one from each of the three principal Detroit groups, which might be three distinct "families." Sam Giancana of Chicago was until recently both a Commission member and the Don of the Chicago Council or "Board." This policy-making Board has five members, each with his own territory—usually coinciding with a number of Chicago police districts.

Beneath the Commission and councils are at least twenty-four "families," each with its "boss." The wealthiest and most influential "families" operate in New York, New Jersey, Illinois, Florida, Louisiana, Nevada, Michigan, and Rhode Island. The "family" is the most significant level of organization and the largest unit of criminal organization in which allegiance is owed to one man, the boss. The number of members in a "family" varies from about 800 to about 20. The largest of the twenty-four known "families" operates in New York City and adjacent New Jersey cities. Only occasionally do members say "I am in Cosa Nostra." But it is commonplace for them to make statements such as "I am in Carlo's family," or "That damned Bonanno family has got to be watched." Italian words are used interchangeably with each of the English words designating a position in the division of labor. Rather than "boss," the words *"il capo," "don," "capofamiglia,"* and *"rappresentante"* are used. Moreover, the term "family" is not used in all communities. In Kansas City the apparatus is called "The Clique." Similarly, each Milwaukee member is affiliated with one of three cliques which, collectively, might or might not constitute a "family."

The boss's primary function is to maintain order while at the same time maximizing profits. Subject to the possibility of being overruled by the Commission, his authority is absolute within his "family," geographical area, and any sphere of influence which does not bring him into conflict with another boss. He is the final arbiter in all matters relating to his branch of the confederation. Some bosses are members of the Commission. Each boss who is not a Commission member probably has his designated *avvocato* on the Commission.

The members of a "family" are likely to believe that they elect their own boss, but this is only vaguely the case. The "family" ordinarily submits the name of the man of its choice to the Commission, but the Commission makes the final decision. When a boss, Thomas Lucchese, became seriously ill during the summer of 1966, law-enforcement personnel knew that there would have to be a meeting of the Commission, or some subcommittee of it, in order to designate a successor. They followed men for over three months, until they were finally led to the meeting in a Queens (New York) restaurant, La Stella.

Each boss knows each of the other bosses personally. Accordingly, each "family" is interrelated with every other "family." Alliances and agreements are usually formal, but sometimes they are merely based on the mechanism of "respect" the bosses have for each other, and the fear they have of each other. The boss also initiates any alliances or other arrangements necessary for living in conditions of peaceful coexistence with any nonmember organized criminals permitted to operate in his community. In Boston, for example, the boss (who lives in Rhode Island) until recently permitted an Irish group to conduct lottery and bookmaking operations in one section of the city, probably because the profits lost were not worth the bloodshed necessary to drive the Irishmen out of business. The Commission rejects or ratifies any treaty or other arrangement which a boss might make with non-Italian groups.

Beneath each boss of the larger "families," at least, is an "underboss," or "*sottocapo*," appointed by the boss. This position is, essentially, that of executive vice president and deputy director of the "family" unit. The man occupying the position often collects information for the boss. He relays messages to him, and he passes his orders down to the men occupying positions below him in the hierarchy. He acts as boss in the absence of the boss.

On the same level as the underboss there is a position for a "counselor," or adviser, often referred to as "*consigliere*," or in slang, "*consuliere*." The person occupying this position is a staff officer rather than a line officer. He is likely to be an elder member who has partially retired after a career in which he did not quite succeed in becoming a boss. He is appointed by the boss, but he gives no commands or orders. He is something of a neutral adviser to all "family" members, including the boss and underboss. The counselor also is a historian. Consistently, his advice is based on precedent, frequently reflecting the wishes of the boss, of whom he is a close confidant. He therefore enjoys considerable influence and power. Although the counselor has no subordinates reporting to him, he is given a piece of the action of many members, in return for his counsel.

Also at about the same level as underboss is another staff position, "buffer." The top members of the "family" hierarchy, particularly the boss, avoid direct communication with the lower-echelon personnel, the workers. They are insulated from the police. To obtain this insulation, commands, information, money, and complaints generally flow back and forth through the buffer, who is a trusted and clever go-between. However, the buffer does not make decisions or assume any of the authority of his boss, as the underboss does.

To reach the working level, a boss usually goes through channels. For example, a boss's decision on the settlement of a dispute involving the activities of the "runners" (ticket sellers) in a particular lottery game passes first to his underboss and buffer, then to the next level of rank, which is "lieutenant," "captain," "head," "*capodecina*," "*caporegime*," or, simply, "*capo*." This position, considered from a business standpoint, is analogous to works manager or sales manager. The person occupying it is the chief of an operating unit. The term "lieutenant" gives the position a military flavor, and it once was the rule that one could not go to an underboss or boss without the lieutenant's approval. This rule changed in the early 1960's. Each boss now has at least two or three "soldiers" who report directly to him and who are answerable only to him. Although "*capodecina*" is translated "head of ten," there apparently is no settled number of men supervised by any given lieutenant. All lieutenants in a "family" are of equal status, no matter how many men each supervises. The number of such leaders in a "family" varies with the size of the "family" and with the specialized businesses the "family" conducts. Each lieutenant usually has one or two associates who work closely with him, serving as messengers and buffers. They carry orders, information, and money back and forth between the lieutenant and the men belonging to his regime. They do not share the lieutenant's administrative power.

Beneath the lieutenants there might be one or more "section chiefs" or "group leaders." Messages and orders received from a boss's buffer by the lieutenant or his buffer are passed on to a section chief, who also may have a buffer. A section chief may be a deputy lieutenant. He is in charge of a portion of the lieutenant's operations. In most "families," however, the position of lieutenant and the position of section chief are combined. In general, the larger the regime the stronger the power of the section chief. It is advantageous, in the interests of security, to cut down the number of individuals who are directly responsible to any given line supervisor.

About five "soldiers," "buttons," "button men," "good fellows," "wise guys" (meaning "right guys"), or just "members" report to each section chief or, if there is no section chief position, to a lieutenant. The number of soldiers in a "family" varies from about twenty to over six hundred. The lieutenant and the men reporting to him are sometimes called a "clique," "circle," or "*nostra brigata*," but each of these terms also is sometimes used as a synonym for "family." In Chicago, the terms "soldier" and "button" are not frequently used. There, a "street man" or "operator" reports to a "district man" (who is either a button or a lieutenant), who reports to an "area man" (probably a lieutenant but possibly boss or underboss), who reports to the Chicago Council, whose chairman reports to the Commission. When Giancana was Chicago Boss, some district men reported directly to him.

This structure was illustrated in a bugged conversation between two Cosa Nostra members who were lamenting the fact that federal agents were learning a great deal about the structure and operations of the organization. In that conversation, a soldier (Mike) used the titles "boss" and "captain" in discussing Cosa Nostra with Pete, who is his own captain. Pete, it develops, was especially upset because he feared that the law-enforcement officers would embarrass his daughter, a nun, if he did not reveal what he knew regarding the whereabouts of the men who had assaulted a policeman. In a conversation about this potential embarrassment, Mike and Pete again made references to structural terms such as "family," "boss," and "head."

> MIKE. He was told specifically—
> PETE. To come and see me?
> MIKE. You're a *captain*. No, they don't want to come to you. They don't want to come to you to embarrass you with your daughter.
> PETE. Who did they tell that to?
> MIKE. They told that to Freddy.
> PETE. Yeah.
> MIKE. They don't want to embarrass you. Three of them called. To him. They said, "We don't want to go to Petey Pumps, we don't want to embarrass him with his daughter."
> PETE. They already did
> MIKE. They already went to you—er—this week—this is the bullshit.
> PETE. Yeah.
> MIKE. They don't want to give no—in other words, they are telling you they don't want to embarrass you. In other words they won't go to the convent. Well, I say, right now they are giving you the zing. "You want us to go to the convent? You want us to embarrass you? Well then, see that the right thing is done."
> PETE. Yeah.
> MIKE. Actually what it boils down to, they're looking to use a stick. "But now we'll go on midnight raids. We'll do this. We'll do that. We'll do the other thing. *You're a captain.* You belong to Carlo's *"family"*—(a man yells in the background and

Mike yells back, "Hey, Dope, cut it out.")—You belong to *"the family."*

PETE. Well, previous to that he hands me Carlo's picture. "You know him?" I said sure I know him. "How long you know him?" I know him twenty, thirty years. ["Carlo" is boss of a New York "family."]

MIKE. They didn't expect you to say nothing.

PETE. "Can you tell us anything about him?" The only thing I could tell you about him is that he is a businessman, been in business all his life. Brought up four kids. They had a good education. They're all in business. They all went to college and—married—a profession. I said, what else could you ask for? He's got a very nice family. See, over there what they do—they want to get a message through. I mean get a message through someplace. There's no question about it. (Inaudible. Both talking.)

MIKE. They want to put the heat on you, me.

PETE. Yeah.

MIKE. Because here is the proof of it. They've gone to every *captain.*

PETE. Yeah.

MIKE. And they call them *"captains."* One guy said *"foreman."* And the other guy said *"caporegime."* I mean, they're going right to each *head*. To the *head* of everybody they're going to. But for them to say this, when he told me this, I said, Jimmy, I think he already saw them.

PETE. Yeah.

MIKE. I think he already saw them, I said. Now to put the heat on him to go to his daughter, I said, this don't make no sense to me. I said, where the fuck does this come into the picture? Now they don't want to embarrass you.

PETE. What are they going to embarrass me for? What can they do? Go up there?

MIKE. Well, God forbid. They can't—they can't throw her out.

PETE. No.

MIKE. They couldn't throw Albert's brother out. How they going to throw her out?

PETE. Nah. They can't throw her out.

MIKE. Embarrassment, that your daughter is a nun. I mean, Jesus Christ. It's supposed to be an honor.

PETE. They can't do nothing. They won't do nothing.

A soldier might operate an illicit enterprise for his boss on a sharecropping basis, or he might "own" the enterprise and pay homage to the boss for "protection," the right to operate. All soldiers in good standing are guaranteed a livelihood and need not fear encroachment on their illicit operations by other soldiers. Further, they are guaranteed assistance in overcoming any threatened competition from nonmembers. They also are promised various social-security benefits such as near immunity from arrest and, when immunity cannot be maintained, bail, legal assistance, and unemployment compensation in case they go to jail. In short, blackjacks, bribery, and guns are used to protect soldiers and all other Cosa Nostra members from anyone who might want to harm them physically or harm their business, whether the business is licit or illicit.

It is not absolutely essential that a soldier or any other member engage in illegal activities, but each soldier must report to his lieutenant at least once a month, whether or not he has anything to report about. Some members have retired from active crime, but one can leave the organization only by death. Theoretically, one could be boss of a "family" and not engage directly in illegal activities. None of the twenty-four known bosses has chosen this course. The boss alone has the power to admit members, but he can do so only within limits set by the Commission, with the permission of the Commission, and at times designated by that body. "Suspension" of membership (but not stripping of membership) has been used as a punishment for swindling another member and for excessive indebtedness to another member.

Partnerships between two or more soldiers, and between soldiers and men higher up in the hierarchy, including bosses, are common. The partnership could be in a usury operation, a dice game, a specific lottery, a specific bet-taking establishment, a vending-machine company, or any other enterprise, legal or illegal, making it possible to turn a fast buck. Most soldiers, like most upper-echelon "family" members, have interests in more than one business.

"Family" membership ends at the soldier level. All members are of Italian descent. Members once had to be Italian by birth or by parentage on both sides of the family. This specification has, in one or two cases, recently been relaxed so as to admit men whose mothers are not of Italian descent. Similarly, a few men have been allowed to retain active membership despite the fact that they married women of non-Italian descent.

Membership in the Italian-Sicilian Mafia does not automatically make one a member of the American organization. This might not have been the case before World War II, but now even a Sicilian Mafia member must be recommended for membership.

In the old country, a man could not be a soldier (or a member of any rank) if his father were also a member. The idea was to avoid a blood line that would work to the disadvantage of men not in that line. Some American "families" follow this principle, some do not. Albert Anastasia, late boss of a New York "family," was the first of the American bosses to give up this taboo. Vito Genovese and Joseph Profaci followed it, but Thomas Lucchese and Joseph Bonanno did not. At least two current "families," both of New York, do not follow it. Although the sons of some bosses cannot be members of their father's "family," they might be members of their father-in-law's "family." There are no restrictions on the membership of other male relatives. In one "family," brothers are boss and lieutenant. There are complaints that the lieutenant takes advantage of his brother's power, just as there were complaints that Attorney General Kennedy took advantage of President Kennedy's power.

About five thousand men are known members of "families" and, hence, of the cartel and confederation which is Cosa Nostra. But beneath the soldiers in the hierarchy of operations are large numbers of employees, sharecroppers, franchise holders, and commission agents who are not necessarily of Italian descent. These are the persons carrying on most of the work "on the street." They have no buffers or other forms of insulation from the police. They are the relatively unskilled workmen who take bets, answer telephones, drive trucks, and carry messages. Bet-taking and usury are not confined to members of Cosa Nostra, but almost all the successful nonmember bet-takers and usurers either sharecrop for members or front for them. My guess is that 95 percent of all the bookies and lottery operators in the United States are either soldiers or nonmembers who are sharecropping for soldiers. In Chicago, for example, the workers in a major lottery business operated in a Negro neighborhood were Negroes; the bankers for the lottery were Japanese-Americans; but the game, including the banking operation, was licensed, for a fee, by a Chicago "family" member. The entire operation, including the bankers, was more or less a "customer" of the Chicago branch of Cosa Nostra, in the way any enterprise operating under a franchise is a "customer" of the parent corporation. In this area, as in many others, the "small fry" were Negroes and the "big sharks" were Cosa Nostra men.

The authority structure sketched out above constitutes the

"organizational chart" of Cosa Nostra as it is described by its members. Three things are missing. First, there is no description of the many organizational positions necessary to actual street-level operation of illicit enterprises such as bookmaking establishments and lotteries. As indicated earlier, some of the positions in such enterprises are occupied by persons who are not Cosa Nostra members. Second, and more important, the structure described by members of the cartel and confederation is primarily only the "official" organization, such as that which might be described by the organizational chart of a legitimate corporation. Cosa Nostra informants have not described, probably because they have not been asked to do so, the many "unofficial" positions any organization must contain. To put the matter in another way, there is no description of the many functional roles performed by the men occupying the formally established positions making up the organization. Third, the structure as described by members is the structure of membership roles, not of the relationships between members and indispensable outsiders like street-level workers, attorneys, accountants, tax experts, and corrupt public officials.

In the business of taking bets on the outcome of horse races and other contests, dozens of specialized positions—occupied by well-trained craftsmen, executives, financiers, and bookkeepers—are essential. There are at least six levels of operating personnel in such enterprises, and each of these levels except the lowest one is occupied by persons with a corresponding status in the "family" structure of Cosa Nostra. A soldier, for example, is likely to hold a position in one of the lower levels of a bet-taking establishment, while a boss or commissioner is likely to hold a position in one of the higher levels.

The gambler wishing to place an illegal bet on the outcome of a legitimate horse race usually gets in touch with a man occupying a "solicitor" position, one of the many positions making up the structure of the illegal betting organization. There are three types of solicitor positions. All three types may be subsidiary to a single "bookmaker" position. Occasionally a bookmaker also occupies the position of solicitor, and the street name for what I call "solicitor" is, in fact, "bookmaker." The two positions are distinct, however, even if one man fills both of them. Ordinarily, a solicitor serves a bookmaker, in exchange for a percentage of the profits or in exchange for a straight salary. The person playing the role of "stationary solicitor" accepts bets at a fixed location, such as a newsstand, store, office, house, or factory floor. Gamblers go to him. A few stationary solicitors operate "horse rooms," where wagers are accepted on each race just before it is run, as at the track. Horse rooms tend to be small operations because the solicitor, who also functions here as bookmaker, has no opportunity to reinsure his bets. We shall see that, accordingly, he must live in hope that his patrons will bet approximately like the bettors at the track will bet. He gets by because most bettors, at the track or elsewhere, simply bet on the "favorites" selected by morning newspapers and racing forms. The returns on the gambler's investment are small when a "favorite" wins.

Men occupying the position of "traveling solicitor," or "walking solicitor" go to the bettors. Each traveling solicitor has a rather fixed route, which takes him through office buildings and factories. He, like the stationary solicitor, is likely to think of himself as a bookmaker, and he is popularly, but erroneously, called a "walking bookmaker," or "walking book." He issues small slips of paper on which bets are recorded, keeping a duplicate copy which he later turns over to the bookmaker. The solicitor may set limits determined by the bookmaker: "I'm a ten-dollar man" means that his bookmaker is a small operator who permits him to take bets no greater than ten dollars.

The third type of street-level position, "telephone solicitor," is occupied by men who simply advertise their telephone number to bettors. Men occupying the position of "runner," which is similar to the position of traveling solicitor, go out of the telephone room to collect the bets and make the pay-offs. Unlike the traveling solicitor, however, the runner takes no bets. Each customer of a telephone solicitor has an account, and some of them are permitted to settle up on a weekly or monthly basis. Solicitors take bets at the odds appearing in the "morning line" provided as a public service by metropolitan newspapers and racing forms to "sportsmen" all over the nation. These odds are approximate. They are based on prognostication of racing outcomes by so-called "sports writers" or racing-form handicappers. The odds actually paid to men holding winning tickets depend on the pattern of the legitimate betting at the track where the race is run. Race results, and the amount of the pay-off for the persons betting on winners, are announced, in the late afternoon, by radio stations and newspapers. However, bookmakers usually put ceilings on the amounts they will pay off. In Philadelphia, for example, bookmakers consistently pay odds no higher than 20 to 1 on winners, no matter what the pay-off on the same horses at the track.

The bookmaker position is at the second level in the organizational hierarchy of bet-taking enterprises. Men occupying this position have title to a neighborhood, which they divide up among their solicitors. It is not unusual for a bookmaker to employ six to ten telephone solicitors and a similar number of runners, who rarely are members of Cosa Nostra. The bookmaker, sometimes called a "handbook operator," or "handbook," ordinarily is in business for himself, as a sharecropper for his Cosa Nostra boss. If he is not his own solicitor, he can expect a little trouble from the solicitors who gather bets for him. These men, like the bookmaker, are cheats. Sometimes they book the bets solicited, rather than handing them in or calling them in to the bookmaker. In Chicago, this system for cheating the bookmaker is called "holding the cream," presumably because the solicitor holds back those bets which he believes are sure losers. If the bookmaker, who is likely to be a soldier in a Cosa Nostra "family," suspects that all bets are not being turned in, he notifies his lieutenant, who, in turn, might call out a man to occupy the position of enforcer. The solicitor loses his job, and his head is broken as a deterrent to others. Unauthorized soliciting of bets in a bookmaker's bailiwick is also severely frowned upon. Four Cosa Nostra "executioners," under orders from an "enforcer," called on an unauthorized solicitor-bookmaker in one city, telling him that henceforth he was to call all his bets to a specified telephone number. When he failed to do so, he was beaten up on three different occasions. He finally saw the light, and henceforth was permitted to "knock down the business," meaning that he got 25 percent of the profits (or losses) on the bets he called in. As in usury, Cosa Nostra finds it sound fiscal policy to keep the victim bringing in money.

The bookmaker does not gamble. His profits are established by the same procedures as are the profits of the legitimate track operators, who deduct 15 to 20 percent of the gross before calculating the amount to be paid on any winning horse. For example, suppose that only two horses are running in a race and that five hundred persons each bet $2 on Number 1 and five hundred persons each bet $2 on Number 2. Assuming that in this state the track operators are allowed to keep 20 percent of the gross, the five hundred persons who bet on the winning horse would share $1600 between them, for a pay-off of $3.20 for each $2 invested.

The matter is not this simple because about eight horses run in each race and because gamblers can bet that a given horse will come in first, or second, or third. But the essential point is that the money bet on losers, less a percentage, is used to pay off the persons betting on the winners. The 15 to 20 percent of the gross deducted by legitimate track operators goes for taxes, expenses, and profits. The bookmaker pockets the entire 15 to 20 percent, less salaries or commissions for solicitors and runners, less a percentage paid to a "family" member for a license to operate or for the cost of reinsuring some bets, less unspecified sums (sometimes a percentage) for corruption of police and political figures, and less small amounts of "employee welfare funds" to be used for bail and attorney fees in time of need. His personal profit, after these expenses are paid, runs about 10 percent of his gross. A run-of-the-mill bookmaker in New York City grosses about $5 million per year; a small-town bookmaker who acts as his own solicitor has about $5000 a year left after he pays his winners, his police chief, and his Cosa Nostra "protectors."

There are three conditions under which the bookmaker cannot lose: (1) he pays track odds; (2) the proportion of all money bet with him on winners is the same as the proportion of all money bet on winners at the track; (3) the proportion of all money bet on losers with him is the same as the proportion of all money bet on losers at the track. Bookmakers usually have little choice about the first condition—gamblers insist that they pay track odds because doing so keeps them somewhat honest. But the last two conditions do not always obtain. That is, the bookmaker's customers do not always bet, collectively, like the persons at the track do. Were this situation allowed to go uncorrected, on any given day the amount bet with the bookmaker on losing horses might not be enough to pay off those of his customers who have selected winners. The bookmaker would then have to dig down into his wife's household funds or, God forbid, down into the funds he has been saving up for a gambling holiday in the Bahamas. This will never do.

Suppose that while the thousand race-track aficionados were betting their money as indicated in the oversimplified example given above, sixty bettors gambling with a bookmaker each bet $2 on Number 1, and forty bettors each bet $2 on Number 2. Should Number 1 win, the bookmaker would have only $160 (after deducting his 20 percent) to divide among the sixty holders of winning tickets, for a pay-off of only about $2.70. Unless odds different from those at the race track had been announced in advance, a hue and cry would be raised in the late afternoon when the local radio "sportscaster" announced that the winning horse had paid $3.20. If the bookmaker paid $3.20 to each of his sixty holders of winning tickets, it would cost him $192, leaving him only $8 (4 percent) for the day's work. Considering his overhead, this would mean a loss. Moreover, under this kind of arrangement the bookmaker would be engaged in gambling, to which he and everyone associated with him is opposed.

Another arrangement must be made. If the bookmaker can make the proportions of his "outs" and "ins" (losers and winners) correspond with the proportions of "outs" and "ins" at the track, he can merely deduct his 20 percent like the track does. And the closer he can get to the track proportions of "outs" and "ins," the closer he gets to an "automatic" 20 percent gross profit. As a first stab at accomplishing this trick, he juggles the odds a bit. For example, he might have announced in advance that he never pays more than 20 to 1 on a horse, even if the track pays 30 to 1 or even 40 to 1. These "house odds" help a little, but not much. He finds a better solution to the problem in reinsuring some of his bets, just as a casualty-insurance company reinsures a risk that is too great for it to assume alone. This takes him to a man occupying a position in the third level of the bet-taking hierarchy, the "lay-off man," who is likely to be a lieutenant or an underboss in the "family" hierarchy. Persons occupying this position are bookmakers' bookmakers.

Stated simply, the bookmaker places with the lay-off man a bet equal to the amount of his "overload," which is the amount needed to pay off winners minus the amount bet on losers. Even those bookmakers who pay off at their own preannounced odds, rather than at the odds paid by the track, must lay off the overload in order to minimize risks. In the oversimplified hypothetical arrangement mentioned above, for example, the bookmaker would deduct twenty of the sixty Number 1 bets from his pool, giving them to the lay-off man. His pool then contains $80 bet on the winning horse and $80 bet on the losing horse. He can't lose. He has what gamblers call a "middle," which is another name for a sure thing. He deducts his 20 percent ($32) and pays $3.20 to each of the holders of winning $2 tickets. Moreover, the lay-off man gives him a percentage of the profits, usually 50 percent, on all bets he calls to him. The lay-off man pays a percentage to a Cosa Nostra boss for the privilege of doing business, and he has other expenses. It is obvious that men occupying this position need larger bankrolls than do bookmakers. Lay-off men take bets exclusively from bookmakers and exclusively by telephone. Each bet is recorded in the bookmaker's name, and the account is settled at the end of each week or each month. The few bookmakers who do not have the 50–50 arrangement must pay a fee for each bet made with the lay-off man. The establishment administered by a lay-off man is likely to be called a "clearinghouse," "master book," or "lay-off room."

But it should be noted that the lay-off man, like the bookmaker, might be confronted with an unbalanced relationship between his "outs" and his "ins." Since he also, like the bookmaker, is interested in a 20 percent gross return (before expenses) on his investment rather than in gambling, he seeks the services of a man occupying a position at the fourth level of the bet-taking hierarchy, "large lay-off man," or "big lay-off man." Large lay-off men accept lay-off bets from all the lay-off men in a large metropolitan area. The operation here is like that of a city or county clearinghouse.

There is no known special name for the positions at the two highest levels of the bet-taking corporation. The men occupying these positions are also called large lay-off men. One type services all the metropolitan large lay-off men in his state or region, operating a kind of intrastate clearing house. Another set of positions is occupied by large lay-off men who service the state men, serving as a national clearinghouse. One large lay-off man operating at the national level works out of Chicago. Others live in Las Vegas and other cities. A large lay-off man who lives in Las Vegas but who operates on a nationwide basis takes in about $20 million a year, and his annual profit is about 4 percent of the gross, or $800,000.

By means of the lay-off procedure, the proportions of "outs" and "ins" bet with each bet-taker can be made to balance each other or to resemble the proportions of "outs" and "ins" bet at any given track on any given horse race. When the thousands of bets made by off-track gamblers all over the country are filtered up to the large lay-off man operating on a nationwide basis, the statistical biases in betting which occur in any given local book-maker's shop cancel each other out. In other words, when the number of bets is large, the probability is high that the proportions bet on losers will offset the proportions bet on winners, as at the track. This can be readily seen in betting on athletic contests. Bookmakers nowadays handle bets on baseball games, football games, basketball games, and boxing matches as well as horse races. In central New York State, in fact, only about 40 percent of the bookmaking business is concerned with horse racing. When the New York Yankees play the Los Angeles Dodgers in the World Series, everyone patronizing a bookmaker in New York wants to bet on the Yankees and everyone in Los Angeles wants to bet on the Dodgers. If, in this situation, New York should win, the New York bookmakers would lose their shirts, and if Los Angeles should win the Los Angeles bookmakers would lose their swimming pools. But if the bookmakers in the two cities can pool their business, they have a "middle." Neither set can lose, for then the statistical biases stemming from a desire to bet on one's home team balance each other off. The money bet on the loser can be used to pay off the persons betting on the winner, minus a percentage. In sports betting, the various levels of lay-off men function to set various local and regional betting biases against each other. In horse-race betting, they function to insure that all bookmakers operate as one nationwide bookmaker whose customers bet just like the gamblers at the track setting the odds. This solitary nationwide bookmaker, who handles both sports bets and horse-race bets, is Cosa Nostra.

But Cosa Nostra also cheats. In sports betting it cheats by bribing athletes, generally by means of an organizational position for a "corrupter," to be described below. In horse-race betting it cheats by "fixing" the outcome of races. No reasonable man bets on trotting races nowadays because it is so easy to bribe the drivers. It also cheats in horse-race betting by means of a set of positions rationally designed for cheating and ordinarily occupied by employees of national-level large lay-off men. If, just before a horse race, it looks like there is some possibility that the persons occupying positions for national-level large lay-off men might lose huge sums because their books are out of balance with the legitimate books at the track, they employ the services of a man occupying a position called "come-back man." The men occupying this position function in such a way that the legitimate track bettors themselves reinsure the bets taken by large lay-off men. The come-back man is an "odds changer" who stands by at the race track. Just before each race, he or his assistant opens a telephone line to a representative of the syndicated large lay-off men. When the latter's books are out of balance with those at the track, the person serving in the position of come-back man is instructed to bet large amounts (say $50,000) on specific horses, thus making the track odds the same as they would be if based on the proportions bet with the large lay-off men on each of the horses. Miss Virginia Hill, a favorite companion of organized criminals in the 1940's, was employed as a come-back man.

The division of labor necessary to conducting a successful illegal lottery closely resembles the structure essential to profitable bet-taking. Lottery games are called "numbers," "policy" (from "*polizza*," the Italian word for the lottery ticket), or, in Spanish-speaking communities, "*bolita*." The basic idea is simple enough. The player bets that he can guess which three-digit number, like 2-7-9, will come up in an agreed-upon tabulation such as the total of all money bet at a race track on a given day. Players could once bet pennies and nickles, but today a quarter usually is the minimum, and $1 bets are the rule. Regular $10 bets are accepted in some locations, and some lotteries have no limit on the size of bets. The gambler has one chance in a thousand to guess right. If he does guess correctly, he gets paid at odds of about 500 to 1, and certainly not higher than 600 to 1, leaving a nice margin of profit. There are variation bets, such as a "boxed" or "combination" number, where one bets on 2-7-9 but, at the same time, on 2-9-7, 7-2-9, etc. It is also possible to play a "bleeder" (last two numbers only) at odds between 60 and 80 to 1, or a "leader" (first numbers only) at odds between 5 and 8 to 1. In "single action," which is popular in Harlem, the player bets on, say, 2-7-9 and then also bets, at odds of about 8 to 1, that the first number will be 2 or the second number will be 7 or the third number will be 9. The odds are reduced on popular numbers. For example, 0-5-7 would in the Heinz pickle factory be a "cut number." "Repeaters," "triples," or "trips" such as 4-4-4 are always cut numbers. A number like 5-6-7 might be cut only during May, 1967, and 1-2-3 might be cut on December 3 of every year.

Two or three different lotteries are run each day in large

cities. Pittsburgh has four "houses," as its citizens call their illegal lotteries: Old Stock, New Stock, Early Race, and Late Race. In the Old Stock lottery, the three lucky digits are determined by the totals of the daily New York Stock Exchange transactions—the last digit in the figure representing total stock advances is selected as the first number, the last digit in total declines is selected as the second, and the last digit in the total of unchanged stocks is selected as the third number. The New Stock "house" is similar, but winners are determined by the digits fifth from the right in the numbers reporting total volumes of stock trading of various kinds. Early Race and Late Race numbers are determined by adding the total amounts bet in the horse races run at a given track on that day. For example, in Early Race the "leader" is the first digit to the left of the decimal point in the total of all money bet on the first five races.

"Policy" is like the Pittsburgh lotteries except that one can bet on a single number or any combination of numbers up to five digits. The normal "gig" is a three-digit bet. Some cities still use a "Treasury Number," which is the final digits of the United States Treasury cash balance. In this lottery, as it is played in Syracuse, New York, the player does not select his number. For a fixed sum he receives a printed ticket which is pasted or stapled so that the five-digit number cannot be seen until after the purchase has been made. There is more profit in Treasury Number than in other lotteries because the odds are less favorable to the bettor. Occasionally, a lottery with numbers determined by throws of dice, the spin of a fortune wheel, or draws from a hat crops up. In Chicago, "*bolita*" is run this way. But such systems are so susceptible to fraud that people play them only if they are very stupid or if there is no relatively honest place to gamble.

The person who sells the lottery ticket to the bettor holds a positon called "writer," "policy writer," "pick-up man," "walking writer," or "runner." The duties of the men in this position resemble those of stationary solicitor and traveling solicitor. Usually the writer works in a fixed location, called a "spot," where he is free from arrest except in most unusual circumstances. A spot may be a tenement hallway, a newsstand, an elevator, a bar, a grocery store, or a street corner. In New York in 1960, each of the three police patrolmen serving a day-time shift collected $2 from each spot daily. Higher-ranking policemen had their own bag men, who called at each spot weekly or monthly and collected much more than a mere $2 per day. The total minimum payment for "police protection" was about $2500 monthly per spot. Ninety spots in one section of Harlem alone paid police about $2,500,000 a year. A writer working on a spot sells about $1000 worth of bets a day, six days a week, so the police were taking about 10 percent of the gross. In Buffalo, New York, writers collectively sell about $7 million worth of illicit lottery tickets a year; this amounts to about $11 for each of Buffalo's citizens.

Writers ordinarily get a percentage of all the money they take in. This ranges from 10 to 25 percent, depending upon the city. New York writers get 25 percent of the gross from their employers and winning bettors hand them 10 percent of the amount of each winning ticket. Some writers work for a salary, but even when they are on salary, some kind of commission usually is paid them. In 1938 the salaried writers in Chicago went on strike and got their salaries increased from $30 to $35 a week. Nowadays, the writer usually works on a "cash basis," meaning that each day he turns all the money over to a supervisor, who later pays him for any hits his customers have had, plus his commission. An occasional writer may be permitted to "go on the gamble" rather than take a commission on the gross. If he works under this arrangement, he shares the risks on the numbers he writes, and he receives a share of the profits. To "go to the gamble" is not much of a gamble because, as indicated, the pay-off is 600 to 1 or less on a 1000 to 1 chance. A writer "on the gamble" must have sufficient capital to pay off lucky hits of large bets. If he doesn't, he may find it necessary to borrow from a usurer, which is not a business-like way to try to accumulate a fortune.

A "field man," or "controller," who is likely to be a Cosa Nostra soldier, supervises about ten writers, who turn the day's slips and money over to him. He watches the writers for dishonesty, and in time of need he assists them by paying court fines, attorney fees, bail bonds, etc. The field man and his bookkeepers and messengers are likely to be called a "turn-in station," or "substation," even if they conduct their business in an automobile. In some cities, writers turn over their money and slips to a central location called a "drop." The "drop man," who might be a lunch-stand owner or simply a housewife, is a paid employee who merely receives packages. Another paid employee, "pick-up man," takes the packages to the field man. Field men, like writers, ordinarily work on a commission basis, usually 10 percent of the amount of bets sold by his writers.

A "manager," "owner," or "banker," often a Cosa Nostra lieutenant, receives the slips and money from each of the field men. Some managers have up to sixty' or seventy field men working for them, but eight or ten is customary. The manager does business at a fixed location called the "main office," "bank," or "wheel headquarters." Each branch of the policy-lottery business, especially, is likely to be called a "wheel," which is the operating unit in which the money bet by losers is used to pay off the holders of winning tickets. Each wheel has a name, and religious terms are sometimes used—"The United Sacred Heart Society" or "The Saint Anthony Society." The profits on "The Silver Wheel" are not used to pay off the winners in "The Saint Anthony Society" even if the latter on a given day has so many "hits" that its operators are scrounging around for ready cash. The two wheels may, in fact, use different systems for determining the lucky number. One man may own more than one wheel, however. If a wheel or bank is "independent," in the sense that it is operated by nonmembers of Cosa Nostra, the owner must permit a Cosa Nostra soldier or lieutenant to check his "ribbon" (adding-machine tabulation) of each day's play so that the Cosa Nostra boss can be sure he is getting his cut, usually one percent "off the top." In some cities, even soldiers and lieutenants are "independents," who give their boss a percentage of the gross for the privilege of doing business in his territory. A manager who believes that he cannot handle all the bets coming in on a given day may lay off some of them with the same lay-off men that service bookmakers.

When the day's slips and receipts have been turned over to the manager, he sets a crew of about six employees to work on them. I do not know the special terms used, if any, for each of these occupational specialties. Someone tabulates the amounts bet with each writer and, indirectly, with each field man. Someone determines which slips are winners. Someone serves as payroll clerk for all the commission agents and employees working for the manager. Someone hands winning slips and a bundle of money to a messenger (usually a man who also serves as a writer) who goes out and "drops drawings" (distributes winnings) to field men, who distribute them to writers, who distribute them to bettors.

12
Rules to Live By

RALPH SALERNO and JOHN TOMPKINS

While the code of the Mafia is unwritten, it can be broken down into a number of universal rules. Except for his East Harlem pronunciation, Joseph Valachi beautifully summed up their meaning in a phrase worthy of a philosopher or a judge. Adhering to the code meant you had done "da right t'ing." But a member who disobeyed orders or who hit another member, simply hadn't done the right thing.

Secrecy

Most members reveal as little as possible to the police, but the silence of the Mafia segment of organized crime has been so complete that until the famous Apalachin meeting in November 1957, many law-enforcement officials doubted its very existence.

Secrecy surrounding the ritual and older practices of a social or political group is, of course, nothing new. It is part of the attraction of joining. And it is essential to the operation of groups like the Communist Party and the Ku Klux Klan. But Cosa Nostra is different: its secrecy was so pervasive that it concealed not only the operation of the group, but the fact of its existence.

In spite of television shows and movie plots about police officers on undercover assignment, the security of Cosa Nostra has been so tight that there is no record of its successful penetration by someone who was in fact serving another master. There have been covert defections by Mafia personnel, and some of them have become established sources of information as defectors in place. There have also been business contacts and intercourse with members by undercover agents or special employees, but in the true meaning of the word there has not yet been penetration—no honest police officer has ever become a member of an organized criminal group. Considering the success we have enjoyed in penetrating the Ku Klux Klan, the Communist Party, Negro extremist groups, foreign governments and in counterespionage, this fact says much about the security of organized crime.

Law-enforcement men have often contributed to the secrecy of organized crime by their approach to it. Until recently, many policemen and prosecutors did so unwittingly by treating each case as though it concerned an individual crime, completely unrelated to any other. They knew that certain criminals seemed to associate with each other, but they did not see evidence of an organized criminal conspiracy because they were not looking for one. The Apalachin affair and the Valachi hearings did a lot to change this attitude.

What has not changed is the political risk that intelligence policemen run in handling information on organized crime. Police department lists of known burglars, car thieves, gamblers and others are widely kept and available to any other law-enforcement agency that asks to see them. But few departments have lists of the men in organized crime and those that do keep the information locked up and rarely give it out to anyone. This practice, of course, contributes to the secrecy of organized crime.

The reason for the careful handling of intelligence data on organized crime is simple. Surveillance reports on a jewel thief, for example, will show that he associates with certain criminals, women, receivers of stolen goods and the like. But surveillance of a Cosa Nostra figure may reveal that he dined with a judge one night and entertained a city councilman the following weekend. Such information is political dynamite, and if it were to leak back to the politicians involved that their criminal associations were known, the policemen who uncovered the facts might find themselves looking for new jobs.

As Valachi described, there used to be an induction ceremony for Cosa Nostra, involving an oath and a symbolic burning of paper and shedding of blood. When Joseph Valachi broke the rule of silence, the organization was only moderately upset by most of his revelations. They were particularly incensed, though, that he described the ritual. This was unforgivable—almost as it would be for a member of Skull and Bones to talk.

The Organization Before the Individual

As in the case of secrecy, this rule is one that many in the outside world subscribe to. In military service the individual is expected to put the good of the organization ahead of his own, even if his life depends on it. Our gallery of national heroes is made up of people who made such a choice; the heroes of organized crime are those who went to the death house with their mouths shut.

It is infuriating and baffling to police, judge, and jury that a known criminal, caught in the act of committing a crime in which he must have had accomplices, will often refuse to cooperate with the authorities, or "cop a plea" (i.e., plead guilty) in return for a lighter sentence. Such men are not being heroic. They are influenced to put the organization ahead of themselves by an awareness of the alternatives.

If a man breaks the rule and cooperates, he will at best become a pariah among his fellows. At worst he will be killed. If he subscribes fully to the code and keeps his mouth shut, he will be in line for a number of fringe benefits. He will get bail and the services of a good lawyer. He will get help during the trial, including the intimidation of witnesses and the possible subversion of jurors. If he's convicted his family will be taken care of while he's in prison and he will likely have a soft job while there.

In addition, the United States Constitutional ban against punishing a man's family for his wrongdoing (no laws "working corruption of the blood") does not apply in the Mafia. If a man talks, his relatives will be shunned. But one of the rewards of accepting a death sentence in silence is that one's family will always be "in good standing." There are now a number of men who are members because their ancestors obeyed the rules.

The choice between these alternatives is obvious to most organized criminals—the more so since the government has officially admitted that the best it can offer in exchange for cooperation is a concentration camp or a life of exile. In September 1963, during the Valachi hearings, the then Attorney General of the United States, Robert F. Kennedy, discussed how the government could protect cooperative members of Cosa Nostra from reprisal:

> We have taken steps, Senator, to even move people out of the country. We have provided them positions and work in areas where nobody will really have any contact with them. We have arranged to move their families and have their names changed . . . .

Nearly three-and-a-half years later, in January 1967, the President's Crime Commission Report recommended that:

> The Federal Government should establish residential facilities for the protection of witnesses desiring such assistance during the pendency of organized crime litigation. After trial, the witness should be permitted to remain at the facility so long as he needs to be protected. The Federal Government should establish regular procedures to help Federal and local witnesses who fear organized crime reprisal, to find jobs and places to live in other parts of the country, and to preserve their anonymity from organized crime groups.

In effect, the Crime Commission put its imprimatur on the established practice, except that it did not go along with exile to another country. Apparently, the report had some impact. Within three months after it was issued, the Department of Justice announced just such an arrangement. In addition to changing the identity of witnesses and relocating them, it had arranged with the Department of Defense to house them, their families, and in some cases even prosecuting attorneys behind the barbed wire and chain mesh fences of military bases where they could be guarded around the clock by U.S. Marshals and military police while trials were in progress.

Life on an Army post is not quite what the words "residential facilities" implied, but no matter what euphemisms are used the plain fact is that witnesses are being asked to surrender their freedom of movement and activity as though they were going to prison. The only basic difference is that the sentence would be voluntary. Thus, in 1963, witnesses were offered freedom in permanent exile; by 1967 they were advised to surrender their freedom for the privilege of remaining within the United States.

Some of them chose not to remain here.

Late in 1967, Joseph Barboza, also known as Joe Baron, a member of the Raymond Patriarca family in New England, was developed as a witness against his Boss while in prison. Underworld intelligence established that he was revealing everything he knew about the organization. His lawyer was contacted and told to relay a message to Baron to keep his mouth shut, but Baron continued to inform. A short time later, the lawyer started his car one morning and had his legs nearly blown off by a bomb connected to the ignition. He lived and was put under guard. His testimony and that of his client, Baron, helped convict several Cosa Nostra members including Patriarca for conspiracy to commit murder.

Early in 1969, the Justice Department announced that the lawyer was voluntarily going to live "somewhere in Europe" and that it would arrange for some protection for him for at least his first year of exile.

The remarkable thing about these admissions is that they got almost no publicity. The government of the most powerful nation on earth had admitted that it was virtually unable to protect its citizens from criminal reprisal except by methods so extreme as to make the protection a punishment.

The message was not lost on the men of organized crime.

Other Members' Families Are Sacred

In most social groups it would be considered unnecessary to specifically prohibit members from making seductive approaches to their associates' wives and daughters. But Cosa Nostra is an organization of Italian-Americans and, as Luigi Barzini has observed, all Italian males, married and unmarried, are in a constant state of courtship. The rule helps protect the organization from vendettas over such "matters of honor." It makes it possible for a member to be inattentive to the female relatives of another member without this lack of interest being considered unmanly. This sense of chivalry does not, of course, extend to the families of strangers. They can be, and often are, taken advantage of. . . .

The protective attitude toward women also means that they

should not be exposed to a situation that might involve physical violence, but if they are exposed everyone will try to keep them from being harmed. If a woman is killed with a man in a gangland execution, it is presumed that it was no accident and both were marked for death. Hiding behind a woman, or using her sex as a shield in a fight is, of course, considered unmanly and if she gets hurt it is the fault of the man who used her.

As with the rest of society, though, there are signs that the new emancipation of women may be changing the old mores. During the Gallo-Profaci war in 1962, women were used to "spot" enemy soldiers on the street and to carry weapons from one location to another. There was also at least one case of a man being shot at while a woman was in his car—an unusual thing by past standards.

An aspect of organizational regard for the family that can be admired is the attitude toward divorce. While the breakup of a marriage is condoned, there is a very specific rule concerning the husband's responsibilities. If he was at fault in any way, she and the children must be provided for as a matter of honor and regardless of any civil court ruling in the case.

In sum, the part of the code that deals with the family is quite literally a reflection of a specific, Latinate cultural heritage. Problems in this area can unleash more passion than in any other. Punishment for violations of the rule on families has often been particularly barbarous.

Reveal Nothing to Your Wife

There are three reasons for this rule.

In the first place, a member might become estranged from his wife and—since "Hell hath no fury . . ."—it is important that she not know anything that she could use to hurt him. But it is hard to keep everything from your wife, as several well-known members have discovered.

Keeping wives in the dark about illegal activities diverts law enforcement attention from them and the rest of one's family. Actually, though, wives are bound to have dangerous knowledge even without knowing anything about particular crimes. The up-

per echelon of organized crime is only vulnerable in complex conspiracy cases, and wives would be in a position to corroborate
testimony concerning contacts between different individuals, their
comings and goings and their relationships with each other.

The overall policy that business is not discussed with one's
wife is part of a general desire to dissociate the home and family
from criminal activities. A member's home is always off limits
except to relatives and his closest business associates. Thus, a man
can in the Mafia be said to have arrived in status when the Boss
has him "out to the house." As with some of the other rules, this
one is not so different from the practices of the upperworld, and
it is observed just about as successfully in both places.

It should be noted that members much resent occasional
efforts by police to gain information from their families. Such
tactics are considered underhanded and indecent.

No Kidnaping

The rule against kidnaping for ransom is probably a holdover
from Sicily where this form of coercion and extortion was widespread. When the rules were promulgated a generation ago, a
recent incident had just occurred in New York that served as a
reminder. John Bart Salvo had been kidnaped and held for ransom
by a Jewish gang from the Bathgate Avenue section of the Bronx.
After he was ransomed, three of the kidnapers were murdered
and two others ran to a police station to plead guilty to a long
series of burglaries and stickups that would ensure prison terms
and safety.

In 1967 this rule was spectacularly violated by some Negro
Cosa Nostra associates and rebellious white members in East
Harlem. Angry at their small share of the profits from narcotics
and numbers, they began kidnaping members and holding them
for ransoms averaging $40,000 apiece. The kidnapers were well-
informed enough to time their crimes just after the victim had
made a large narcotics sale and had plenty of cash on hand. One
was murdered and the corpse found with the head and hands cut
off. Enraged at this violation of the code, the Cosa Nostra groups
involved have posted a $50,000 reward for the identity of any

one of the kidnapers who could then be induced to reveal his associates. In the spring of 1968 two Negro associates of the Cosa Nostra in New York were found dead upstate and the police believe they were members of the kidnap gang. Later a grand jury summoned three of the alleged victims, but all of them chose to accept contempt citations rather than answer questions.

The anti-kidnaping rule is no longer as important as it must have seemed in the early 1930s when this form of extortion was widely used, not only on rival gangs, but on wealthy people generally. In both cases it has almost died out. Nowadays, an underworld kidnaping is usually for some reason other than ransom.

In the case of Joseph Bonanno, formerly one of the New York Bosses, kidnaping was a brusque form of summons before the Commission. It happened in the style of an old gangster movie. Bonanno was standing on Park Avenue talking with his lawyer (he had been scheduled to appear before a grand jury) one evening in October 1964, when two men with guns forced him into a long black car and drove away. The scene was a cliché in every respect: Bonanno's lawyer reported that one of the gunmen said, "Come on, Joe. My Boss wants to see you," and then fired a shot at the lawyer when he tried to follow his client.

You Don't Strike Another Member

This is another rule designed to avoid internal vendettas that could easily arise if an argument were allowed to turn physical. The restraint of often fiery temperaments that it demands is a graphic demonstration of the authority that the code carries.

An interesting example of it occurred several years ago on a Brooklyn street. Two young men, Carmine, nineteen, and Frank, twenty, neither a member but both in training and bound by the rules, got into a heated argument while standing with a group of friends. Suddenly, Carmine hit Frank in the face, challenging him to fight. Frank, trembling and white-faced with rage, said that he could beat Carmine easily any day of the week, but he refused to hit him because Carmine was on parole from Elmira State Reformatory and a public fight might get him in trouble. In addition, the incident took place in front of an olive oil refining business owned by a member of the family both young men wanted to join. Frank pointed out that a fight might bring "heat" to the place from the police.

Later the same day Frank registered an official complaint over the affair with a Caporegime. He demanded action. Within a few days it was decided that Frank had, indeed, done the right thing and Carmine was ordered to apologize to him in front of the same eleven young men who had witnessed the humiliation. The apology was to include an expression of gratitude for Frank's wisdom in handling the situation.

The result of this Solomon-like decision was that thirteen young men had demonstrated for them the power of the law and the rules and the proprieties.

The injunction against violence, of course, also includes a ban on coercion and intimidation of other members, even when no blow is actually struck. There was the case of a somewhat drunken young member who approached an older Don in a tavern and asked for a loan. He was persistent about needing money and got so pugnacious that he had to be slapped. The young man left the place, came back with a gun and, holding it to the Don's head, forced him to kneel down and lick the floor all the way from the bar to the door.

A few days later the young man was found dead in the trunk of a car with several bulletholes in his head. As in the first example, all those who knew about the incident and then read what happened to the young man were forcefully impressed that one does not do the wrong thing with impunity.

Orders Cannot be Disobeyed

While self-explanatory, this rule is much broader than similar injunctions found in military or religious organizations. Orders must not only be obeyed, they must be properly carried out. Going through the motions, or hewing to the letter of one's instructions is not enough. This is true even though orders are not detailed or explicit.

A man will often be told to "handle it," or "straighten this out," or "take care of it." The vagueness is characteristic and means that the superior will always be right no matter what happens. If things work out well, the superior can take credit for having ordered someone to take care of it. If they go wrong he can blame the underling for having chosen a bad way of handling the problem.

Take murder, for example. When a Boss orders a "hit" he is not interested whether the man he gave the order to does the killing himself, or turns around and orders a subordinate to do it. He also does not care how and when the job is done. His only interest is that the order be carried out. While organization has tended to create a certain amount of job specialization in this area, there is still an aura of prestige surrounding a man who is willing to execute a "hit" order personally. Until recent years, in fact, it was the surest road to promotion.

The Mafia at Home

THE RULES THAT MAFIOSI LIVE BY affect not only their own lives but the lives of their wives, children, mistresses and friends as well. The section that follows deals with those who are not criminals themselves, yet whose lives are dramatically touched by the Mafia.

The first chapter offers a sweeping look at the lives of Mafia women—wives, sisters, daughters, mistresses. It depicts the restricted and unglamorous life of a Mafia wife and describes how some of the younger women, including Mafia daughters, are beginning to rebel against their narrow existence. It also describes how some women have paid with their lives for their relationships with members of the Mafia.

The second chapter focuses on an incident in the tragic life of one woman who married a Mafioso. The woman, Ann Drahmann, married Trigger Mike Coppola, a brutal Mafia *capo* who made her life a living hell. In this account, taken from the biography of Ann written by Hank Messick from her diaries, she learns that her daughter by a previous marriage has been introduced to drugs by Trigger Mike.

A more representative insight into Mafia home life is given by Gay Talese in the third chapter which is taken from his book, *Honor Thy Father*. The scene is a gathering in California of some members of two important Mafia dynasties. Years before, Salvatore

Bonanno, son of Mafia boss Joseph Bonanno, had married Rosalie Profaci, niece of Mafia boss Joseph Profaci. Now members of both families are gathered to meet the fiance of Rosalie's youngest sister, an independent-minded girl who has picked as her future husband someone who not only is not a Mafioso but is not even Italian.

In the final chapter, "Gangster Chic," Charlotte Curtis of the *New York Times* discusses the sudden popularity of Mafioso Joseph Gallo, who became a social lion cultivated by some of New York's well-known society and show-business personalities in the months before his murder on April 7, 1972. Gallo, who specialized in breaking arms, legs and heads while making a name for himself in the Mafia, found it easy to captivate Broadway and Park Avenue with his wry humor and his familiarity with the works of such writers as Sartre and Camus.

13
Mafia Women

NICHOLAS GAGE

The Mafia is the surest stronghold of male chauvinism in America.

In the Mafia a woman may be a means to a profitable alliance with another Mafia "family"; a showcase for displaying her husband's wealth, status, and power; a valuable piece of property; a loyal helpmate; a good cook; a showy and ego-boosting mistress. But what she must never be is a liberated woman.

Joseph Valachi, the Mafioso who turned informer, made clear the degree to which a woman is considered a piece of property. He testified that two offenses bring the death penalty in the Mafia: "Talking about the Cosa Nostra or violating another member's wife."

To an outsider the life of a Mafia wife, mistress, or daughter might seem to be surrounded by an aura of glamour. There is the constant threat of violence, the profusion of big money, stolen jewels, and furs, the thrill of belonging to a man who faces danger every day. Unfortunately the reality is a good deal drearier.

Only rarely do tales of wife-beatings, nervous breakdowns, suicides, and even the occasional murders of Mafia wives leak through the tight security of the underworld. But in spite of the all-important law of silence—the first law every Mafia woman learns—reports of the misery of Mafia women sometimes reach

223

the outside world through wiretaps, informers' stories, court battles, and even occasionally through the desperate actions of the women themselves.

Mafia women responsible for major infractions of the rules have been killed or have had relatives or friends killed as punishment. Joseph Valachi told federal officials of one case in which a Mafia wife had had a brief liaison with a lesbian during a long absence of her husband. When the husband returned and found out what had happened, he could not bring himself to kill his wife; he took his revenge instead by having one of her friends shot to death. The friend's only crime was that he owned the club where the two women had met.

The social life of a Mafia wife is usually dull and restricted. When mobsters gather at the bars, casinos, nightclubs, restaurants, and racetracks where they do business, they would never dream of bringing their wives. The Mafia women live lives of inconspicuous luxury in homes that are clustered in certain neighborhoods of highly respectable suburbs.

Mafia wives are expected to limit their friendships to other Mafia wives. (To most of them this seems natural, since they are often related.) They keep busy with a constant round of weddings, baptisms, funerals, church functions, and charities. Some, however, occasionally rebel against such restrictions. Once the wife of a leading gangster called me in tears. The day before, a newspaper story of mine had appeared in which the address of her husband's $150,000 Manhattan townhouse was mentioned. Now, she said, two men were standing outside on the sidewalk surveying her house, and she was afraid of the effect the publicity might have on her children. I inquired gently why she did not live at Sands Point, Long Island, a fashionable suburb where there was a considerable settlement of Mafia homes. "Who wants to live out there," the woman exploded, "with all those creeps?"

Although she may have nearly unlimited money available to her, a Mafia wife cannot spend it on things that will show. The Internal Revenue Service is constantly on the alert for expenditures by known or suspected Mafia members that seem out of line with the "legitimate" income that they report on their income tax forms. So, excessively palatial homes, extravagant cars, jewels, fur coats, and designer clothes bought through legitimate stores are all taboo for the Mafia woman.

As one sympathetic friend remarked about Joseph Colombo's platinum-blonde wife at the $125-a-plate testimonial dinner held for him in March, 1971, by the Italian-American Civil Rights League, "Poor Lucille has to walk around in rags because of those IRS jerks." (Nevertheless, "poor Lucille" and her family have two luxurious homes, one in Bensonhurst, Brooklyn, and another in Blooming Grove, New York. The latter includes tennis courts, stables, and a swimming pool.)

Not only must a Mafia wife spend money with one eye on the IRS, but she must be very careful to observe internal protocol. A Mafia family (*borgata*) is headed by a *capo famiglia*. Under him are an underboss and a *consigliere*. Next in line come a number of *capos*, who are each responsible for a certain number of soldiers. And a woman must be sure never to have a more expensive dress or car or house than her husband's superior or his wife.

Any kind of ceremony—wedding, funeral, baptism—is an occasion for lavish gifts, but a Mafia wife must be very careful not to spend more on a gift than the wife of the man who is ahead of her husband in the pecking order. "We once came across a list of gifts brought to a Mafia wedding," says a former member of the New York Police Department who specialized in organized crime, "and we used it to check the status of the various people who had given them. The price of the gifts coincided exactly with the status of each man in the hierarchy."

Overshadowing all the other problems of being a Mafia wife is her constant knowledge that her husband may suddenly disappear or be murdered and that there is nothing she can do about it, even if he is killed before her eyes. Joseph Valachi quoted a Mafioso, known to him only as Buster from Chicago, who once shot an errant member while the man was with his wife: "He came out of his office with his wife. He kissed her in front of the office and I was worried I couldn't get a shot. But he turned and went for the corner. She was just standing there watching when I got him. I don't think I missed once. You could see the dust coming off his coat when the bullets hit."

One of the unwritten laws of the Mafia, however, is never to attack a man by harming his wife and children. Only if a wife has herself in some way broken the rules of the Cosa Nostra does she have to fear for her own life.

The Mafia is the last place a woman is likely to achieve an

equal footing with a man, although occasionally a Mafia wife displays a drive and toughness equal to that of her husband. A good example was Constance Rastelli, whose husband, Philip, is now one of the leaders of a New York Mafia family. According to federal law enforcement sources, Constance showed great initiative in involving herself in her husband's jobs. She would drive the getaway car during robberies, keep the books on gambling operations, and run the abortion rackets set up by her husband. Once when her husband was charged with robbery, she visited the key witness in the case a dozen times trying to bribe her not to testify against her husband. "That Constance has the balls of a man," one Mafioso said about her admiringly.

Her husband, however, seemed to prefer a less independent type of female and once, while hiding out in Canada, he started living with a younger woman. When Constance found out, she traveled to Canada, located her husband, and beat his mistress senseless. She then told her husband that if he continued to play around she would kill him.

Rastelli did not take her threat very seriously and continued his wandering ways on his return to New York. One day Constance confronted him on a Brooklyn street and fired several bullets at him, hitting him twice but not wounding him seriously.

Rastelli, not surprisingly, refused to go back to her after that, and she threatened to talk to the authorities about him and his friends. At that point, she later told officials, she was visited by John "Big John" Ormento, a leading Mafioso who warned her against carrying out her threat.

Undaunted and still furious at her husband, Constance began to talk to federal authorities, giving them valuable information. At that time the government was investigating Ormento and half a dozen other major Mafia figures for narcotics violations. Constance warned the officials that the Mafia was planning to kill their key witness. To prove the accuracy of her information she told them the address of the house in New Jersey where the witness was being held—a secret known only to a few government agents.

The government saved the witness's life and ultimately won its case against the high-powered Mafiosi, who were convicted and received heavy sentences. But before they could make a case against Philip Rastelli, the irrepressible Constance was shot to death, a victim of Mafia vengeance.

The life of a Mafia girl friend is even less enviable than that of a Mafia wife. For one thing, the girl friends seem much more likely to come to a bloody end along with their inamoratos. Anthony Colombo, for example, the father of the Joseph Colombo who founded the Italian-American Civil Rights League, was found strangled in an automobile in 1938. With him was the body of a woman friend, Christine Oliveri, who had also been garroted.

One Mafia girl friend showed such admirable presence of mind in a difficult situation that it eventually won her a highly placed underworld husband. The girl was spending a weekend in Florida with her gangster boy friend, when he suddenly died of a heart attack. Before doing anything else, according to police, she called two Mafia friends to come over and search his still-warm body for any evidence that might incriminate fellow family members. Only then did she call an ambulance. This display of cool thinking under stress so impressed a major New York gambling figure that she is today the gambler's wife.

The vast majority of Mafia girl friends, however, soon discover the sad truth: although a Mafioso may be a very generous lover, he will almost never divorce his wife for his girl friend. This, of course, is a universal tendency of the married male, but the Mafioso, especially, respects the old double standard that holds that there are good women (one's wife and mother) and bad women (who are fun to sleep with) and each must be carefully kept in a separate niche.

The old-time Mafiosi—the Mustache Petes, who were born in Sicily and brought the Cosa Nostra to the United States—had very strict sexual codes and frowned on members having mistresses at all. Mustache Petes, Giuseppe Masseria among them, even blocked the entry of Al Capone into the Mafia for a good many years because they disapproved of the fact that he made money from prostitution.

The modern Mafia leader, however, finds a good-looking mistress—preferably several—as important an accessory as a diamond pinky ring or a Miami Beach suntan. One such interesting revelation emerged when the FBI, under court order, released conversations picked up by a bug in the office of Sam "The Plumber" De Cavalcante, the boss of a small New Jersey Mafia family, and a married man. In addition to more significant facts about the life of a Mafia boss, the transcript revealed that Sam was carrying on an affair with his secretary, Harriet Gold, who was also the sister of Larry Wolfson, Sam's partner in the plumbing business. Not only was Sam cheating on his wife with Harriet, he was also cheating on Harriet with a number of other women. He frequently told each of them, including his wife, how much he loved her. He also got a kick out of talking to Harriet's husband on one telephone line while whispering endearments to her on another.

As the affair progressed, Harriet complained to Sam that she was uncomfortable when she and her husband and Sam and his wife were together, that Sam did not call her as often as he promised, that she did not get along with her husband any longer, and that she was no longer sleeping with him. Sam, meanwhile, continued to take discreet weekend trips with other women and emphasized to Harriet, when necessary, his respect for his wife, Mary, and their children.

The tapes also revealed Sam in his "godfather" role. He arranged for his Mafia family to pay for the wedding of his under-boss's daughter. He also attempted to help sort out the troubled marriage of one Frank Perrone, who had left his wife. Both were children of alleged members of his Mafia family. Sam agreed, in a conversation with a friend, that both Frank Perrone and his father were rotten because they had both assured Sam that the marriage would be a success. The friend suggested that Sam get together with a relative of the Perrones' who might persuade Frank to do the right thing by his wife. This interest by a Mafia boss in an underling's private life and the lives of his sons and daughters is not unusual. Even the marriages of a soldier's children are sometimes subject to veto by the soldier's *capo*.

Sam also took a godfatherly interest in close friends who were not Mafia members, such as his partner Larry Wolfson. Larry told Sam that he was trying to turn a young female relative of his into a lady, and he asked for Sam's advice. Should he bring the girl to New York from California, where she was living? Sam replied that he had already had the girl investigated and that she was no good: she was out every night with a different man. "She steals, she drinks, and she doesn't care who she goes out with," said Sam. He added that he loved Larry like a son, "so take my advice and leave her in California." Sam's motivation for having Larry's relative investigated was not solely altruistic. Any unstable person, such as a woman who drinks and runs around with men, can become a potential chink in a Mafia family's armor.

The Mafia woman most deserving of pity is the Mafia daughter. She did not choose her way of life, but she has difficulty escaping it. Her love life and her virtue become matters of great interest to everyone in her father's Mafia family. Until recently her marriage was likely to be arranged for political reasons to bolster the strength of the Mafia family, and she might not have known the groom who had been selected for her.

Today, however, according to law enforcement authorities, more and more Mafia daughters are meeting and marrying men outside the Mafia. One reason is the increased tendency of all young people to travel. Another is the fact that Mafia daughters are, as a rule, sent away to college. "Their fathers tend to use the college level more as a finishing school than as a first step to a career," said one federal agent. But some daughters will later go into a serious career, such as buyer for a large department store, often with a little behind-the-scenes boost from Daddy.

There are other advantages to being a Mafia daughter. Joseph Profaci, the late Brooklyn Mafia boss also known as the Olive Oil King, named his olive oil for his daughter Carmela. A Boston Mafioso set aside $10,000 annually for his daughter and gave her the whole bundle when she turned twenty-one. And many Mafia leaders are particularly solicitous of their daughters' virtue. For example, when Carmine Lombardozzi, a married Mafioso, started a relationship with the daughter of a reputed Mafia soldier, the girl's irate father complained to the leadership. The leaders in turn issued an ultimatum to Lombardozzi: either marry the girl or leave her alone. After thinking it over, Lombardozzi decided to divorce his wife of nearly thirty years and go through with the wedding. His ex-wife proved remarkably amenable and the pair remained on good terms.

Some daughters inherit the toughness of their fathers along with a dangerous independence of spirit. One such girl, the daughter of a Florida-based underworld racketeer and financial genius, shook the entire underworld with her doings several years ago. Used to having her way, she threw over her Mafia boy friend for a passionate affair with a singer well known in the Miami area. The rejected Mafioso did not take kindly to the slight.

Before long, the door of the singer's plush hotel room was found peppered with bullet holes. Although no one was hurt, this made the girl so angry that she did the one thing the underworld cannot accept—she went to the police. Ultimately the rejected suitor was severely reprimanded and the girl was left in peace with her singer, but not before her father had received a harsh tongue-lashing from his fellow racketeers. Only his very high position in the hierarchy prevented bloodshed.

Few daughters of Mafiosi are as assertive as the Miami girl. Most of them accept the rules that go with the life into which they were born. Until recently, when marriage outside the Mafia became acceptable, those rules called for dutiful Mafia daughters to become dutiful Mafia wives.

Some Mafia daughters were coaxed into marrying sons of Mafiosi who belonged to groups with which their fathers wanted to cement business ties. Others fell in love and married within the groups to which their fathers, brothers, uncles, and cousins belonged. All this resulted in many Mafia groups becoming closely inbred. In one case, for example, two daughters of a Mafioso married two brothers who were part of the same Mafia group that their father belonged to. The brothers were distant cousins of the girls. Twenty-five years later a son of one of the couples and a daughter of the second fell in love and married. They had five children, three of whom were born mentally retarded. "There are many instances of defective children in Mafia families because of the inbreeding through the years," says a federal agent. "I'm sure that is one reason why Mafiosi now allow their children to marry outside the Mafia."

Those women who have married within the Mafia, however, are expected to possess two qualities above all others—loyalty and silence. But even a good Mafia wife can come to grief if she makes the mistake of knowing too much about her husband's rackets. "Trigger Mike" Coppola, an important figure in the New York numbers racket, had a dark-eyed wife named Doris, whom he loved. She was present on the day that Mike and a friend discussed a certain Republican district captain in Mike's home. The next day the district captain was beaten, and six days later he died.

During the investigation of the murder, Mrs. Coppola vanished. A search for her as a possible witness in the case was launched and she eventually surrendered. On the basis of her testimony before a grand jury, she was charged with perjury. Now she was in a difficult position: if she told the truth, her husband would go to jail; if she refused to talk, she would go to jail. To make matters worse, Doris was pregnant. While she was still under indictment, a daughter was born, and the next day Mrs. Coppola died, thus solving everyone's problems. Her husband, contrary to his religion, had the body cremated.

Everyone assumed that Doris had died of complications of childbirth, but many years later, Trigger Mike's second wife claimed she found papers in a safe that indicated that Mike had had his beloved wife killed. According to acquaintances, he never quite got over her death.

Any man who puts his love for his wife before his sense of "justice" loses face with his fellow gangsters. This is what happened to Vito Genovese, one of the most powerful Mafia figures in the United States before his death in Atlanta Penitentiary in 1970.

In December of 1952 Genovese's wife, Anna, left their home in New Jersey and sued for divorce on the grounds that his cruelty "endangered her health and made her life extremely wretched." During the divorce proceedings she portrayed her husband as a vicious mob leader with a vast income. She talked about the location of safe-deposit boxes full of cash in the United States and in Europe. She discussed his involvement in gambling, nightclubs, loan-sharking, and labor-union kickbacks. The Mafia could hardly believe that she was being allowed to give such testimony, but Genovese, who was still in love with her, did not have the courage to kill her.

"The word was all around, why didn't he hit [kill] her," Joseph Valachi later recalled. "But he must have really cared for her . . . I remember when we—Vito and me—were in Atlanta [Penitentiary] together later on, he would sometimes talk about her, and I would see the tears rolling down his cheeks. I couldn't believe it."

But Genovese had no compassion for the man he had assigned to keep an eye on Anna, Steve Franse. Valachi said Genovese had had him killed for not performing this duty adequately.

Franse was not the only man connected with Anna to meet

a violent death. Her first husband, Gerard Vernotico, was murdered twelve days before Anna married Genovese in a civil ceremony. Valachi said that Genovese had ordered Vernotico killed so that the beautiful Anna would be free to marry him.

Genovese's passion for Anna weakened him in the eyes of the mob because few Mafia husbands are so soft-hearted toward their wives. Indeed some of them carry home with them the violence and sadism that make them so feared in the underworld, as Ann Drahmann, Trigger Mike Coppola's second wife, discovered.

Ann was born to Italian parents in 1921 in Cincinnati. She grew into a dark-eyed, dark-haired beauty and at the age of sixteen found herself pregnant and married to a young sailor. As soon as a daughter was born, the marriage was over. Ann became a waitress in a mob-owned restaurant-bar-casino in Covington, Kentucky. She caught the eye of the casino manager, Charles Drahmann, a small time gangster, and eventually they were married.

When Ann was thirty-one, Drahmann and his boss were killed in the crash of a private plane, and Ann was left a widow without much money. She opened a dress shop and frequently gave parties at which local gangsters were guests.

In 1955 Ann was invited to attend the Marciano-Moore fight in New York in the company of three Newport, Kentucky, gangsters and their wives. Although they did not mention it to her, the real purpose of the trip was to introduce Ann to Trigger Mike Coppola, the fat, swarthy, five-foot-five boss of the numbers racket in East Harlem and an overlord of the Eastern Syndicate. His first wife, Doris, had met an untimely death, as we have seen, and Mike was looking for a replacement. His gangster friends had picked Ann as a likely candidate after making sure that she was not promiscuous or otherwise unsuited to be the wife of such an important man.

Trigger Mike was enchanted with Ann. After a short courtship, during which he bombarded her with jewels, candy, and flowers, they were married on December 28, 1955, in Lawrenceburg, Indiana. When it was all over Mike paid for the reception with a $1,000 bill.

Because New York had become a bit too hot for him, Mike had moved to a luxurious house in Miami Beach, and it was there that he installed his new bride. Unfortunately, Ann was too nosy for her own good and unearthed a number of "plants"—secret hiding places behind walls and sliding bookcases—where her husband secreted vast amounts of cash, as most important mob figures do. Mike rewarded her for her discoveries with a vicious beating, the first of many. Soon she discovered that he had a strong sadistic streak that included rather bizarre practices.

When Ann became pregnant, her husband insisted on calling in an underworld doctor, who performed an abortion on her while she lay on the kitchen table and Trigger Mike helped. She quickly realized that this was her husband's idea of a really good time. He assisted at four abortions in all until, during the fifth pregnancy, she managed to fake a miscarriage, which was then treated at a hospital.

In spite of the beatings and abortions, Ann felt that her life as the wife of an important Mafia figure had its compensations. They traveled annually to the Kentucky Derby and on occasion to Las Vegas on gambling junkets. Whenever Ann would say "the girls and I want to do a little gambling," Mike would call friends in pre-Castro Havana to get them the best hotel suites and un-limited credit. Mike, eager to show off his status, gave her jewels, furs, and cars. He also handed her large sums of money for her own use, which she carefully stashed away after noting down the amount in a little black book. In four years her hoard of cash amounted to $277,100.

By this time Ann had come to feel that life with Trigger Mike was no longer tolerable. After her daughter from a previous marriage graduated from private school at the age of eighteen, she had come to live with them, and Ann felt that Mike was show-ing an unhealthy interest in the girl. During one of their violent fights Mike revealed to Ann that he had been providing her daughter with drugs. (See next chapter.)

In 1960, after one last bloody fight, Ann and her daughter moved out. Mike filed for divorce, charging that her "vile and abusive language" would make delinquents of his children by his previous marriage. She filed a cross-claim charging him with ex-treme cruelty. Their final divorce decree was signed on March 25. He agreed to pay her $25,000 in cash and another $25,000 under the table.

At about this time, an agent of the Internal Revenue Service approached Ann and asked if she would help with an audit of her husband's tax returns by giving information on his income and expenditures. For the sake of vengeance, she agreed. Trigger Mike, who had given her $277,100 in four years, had reported his income to the IRS as $15,000 in 1957 and $31,087 in 1958. He claimed that these sums had been earned at the racetrack.

Ann poured out every detail of her life with Trigger Mike as the IRS prepared its case against him. She estimated Mike's income from the rackets to be at least $1 million a year. In 1961 he was indicted on four counts of income tax evasion.

When the trial finally opened, Mike unexpectedly pleaded guilty before Ann could testify. It was generally believed that the mob had decided that this was the course he must take in order to prevent damaging secrets about his rackets from being aired in court. He was condemned to serve a year and a day on each of four counts, the sentences to run concurrently, and he was ordered to pay a $40,000 fine. He was also placed on four years probation when his sentence expired.

Mike served his time in the federal prison near Atlanta, where Mafiosi like Vito Genovese and Joe Valachi were among his fellow prisoners. After his release, most of his underworld friends made it clear that they regarded him as a fool, both for allowing his wife to learn his secrets and for being unable to stop her from talking. In October of 1966 Trigger Mike died of undisclosed causes in an expensive Boston hospital room.

After Mike's trial Ann returned to Rome, where six months later she committed suicide by washing down an overdose of Nembutal with a lot of scotch. She had been marked by the mob as a stoolie and an outcast, and she was to have been killed.

With her pen still clutched in her hand, she was found dead on her bed in an ultrafashionable Roman hotel. On the wall above the bed she had written: "I have always suffered. I am going to kill myself. Forget me."

14
Mrs. Trigger Mike

HANK MESSICK

The Coppolas dined alone on December 23, 1958. The children had left for a party. Joan had a date and was taking her usual good time about dressing.

Mike had spent the afternoon at his favorite hangout, the Midtown Social Club, playing cards with Joe Massei. Ann had been busy finishing preparations for Christmas and checking the family Christmas list to make sure no one had been forgotten. It was a long list and most of the names were friends of Mike.

Several years later, after Joe Valachi spun tales about La Cosa Nostra to the McClellan Committee, the author compared the names listed by Valachi with those on Ann's Christmas list. Among the "soldiers" said by Valachi to owe allegiance to Trigger Mike, the following were on Ann's list five years earlier:

Philip Lombardo, Frank Livorsi, Teddy De Martino, Tony Salerno, Dan Scarglatta, Ben De Martino, Joseph Torrice, Anthony De Martino, Joey Rao, Joe Stacci, and Al Rosato.

Also on Valachi's charts and Ann's lists were a lieutenant, Vincent "Jimmy Blue Eyes" Alo, and the man identified as the former "boss of all the bosses," Charles "Lucky" Luciano. The Coppolas listed his address as 464 Via Lasso, Naples, Italy. . . .

Had Ann needed additional assurance of Mike's standing in the rackets, the events at dinner provided it. Suddenly Mike slapped his open hand against his face. Cursing loudly in Italian, he pushed back his chair and rushed to the telephone.

"That stupid bastard," he exclaimed, as he dialed the number of the social club he had left an hour before.

Demanding to speak to the club manager, Coppola loosed a new torrent of profanity when the man answered. Finally he calmed down enough to issue orders. In a quiet voice more menacing than his curses, Mike commanded:

"Look in the deep-freeze unit and get the package I left there. The one that came in today. Send it over here right away."

Apparently the manager gave satisfactory assurance the package would be delivered. Mike returned to his meal, still cursing quietly. Ann didn't dare ask questions. Mike was obviously in no mood to answer them. But her mind raced. It was almost Christmas. Their third wedding anniversary was at hand too. Was this some special gift the unpredictable Coppola had ordered for her? Whatever it was it had to be valuable. She had never seen Mike so upset.

George the Wop, a flunky at the social club, arrived by taxi with the package before Mike finished eating. He must have set a new record getting there. Ann's curiosity was redoubled—it was such a large package. Perhaps another mink, she thought.

Without a word to her Mike put the package on a side table and completed his dinner. With the box in his possession, the emergency was past. Ann was too excited to eat her dessert.

"What's in it?" she asked. "Please, Mike."

Obviously amused by her excitement, Coppola threw down his napkin and picked up the heavy package.

"Let's take it up to the bedroom," he suggested.

Ann quickly followed him and sat on the bed as Mike began fumbling with the cords. The box had been well sealed and he had trouble opening it. When at last he turned back the lid, Ann could scarcely believe her eyes. Money, tons of it. Loads and loads and loads of money.

Delighted with her reaction, Mike suggested she help him count it. Eagerly she agreed. As they worked, Mike condescended to explain.

"The courier came in from New York today and found me at the club. I was right in the middle of a big hand so I told him to stick it in the deep freeze. And, by God, I forgot all about it. I'm going to fire that manager. He's supposed to take care of details like that for the members."

Details like that? There were so many details her hands were becoming tired. "You count the little stuff awhile and let me count the big ones," she suggested.

The "little stuff" was $10's and $20's. The "big ones" were $100 bills with quite a few $500 and $1,000 ones included. Ann was exhausted when they finished. The total count was $219,000.

"Not bad," said Trigger Mike.

Big money was no longer a novelty to Ann as Mike supposed. Over the years she had become accustomed to it by counting Mike's hoard. He had given her large sums as well and even designed a special plant for her own use. But so much in one package was a little hard to accept. And to think Mike had been so preoccupied with a card game he had forgotten all about it.

Feeling well satisfied with the impression he had made, and perhaps as a reward for her help, Mike gave her $10,000 for Christmas. She put the money away and noted the amount in her little black book. As of the end of 1958, it listed some impressive totals:

In 1956—January, $2,000; February, $3,500; April, $2,000; May, $2,500; June, $3,500; August, $2,200; October, $2,500, and December, $5,000, for a yearly total of $23,200.

In 1957—January, $2,700; February, $5,000; March, $3,200; April, $7,500; May, $8,300; June, $5,000; July, $6,200; August, $4,000; September, $1,000; October, $5,000; December, $10,000, for a yearly total of $57,900.

In 1958—January, $3,800; February, $5,900; March, $3,600; April, $7,900; May, $10,000, June, $6,500; July, $7,500; August, $9,700; September, $3,300; December, $10,000, for a total of $68,200. . . .

With money matters settled, the Coppolas could relax. Soon it was Derby time again, the social event of the underworld. Off to Louisville and the Brown Hotel they went. Gil Beckley and his wife, June, shared the excitement as Tommy Lee won the run for the roses, and the Beckleys then accompanied them to Cincinnati-Newport. They had dinner at the Beverly Hills Club.

Beckley had ended his long exile in Canada and was operating the biggest layoff betting business in the nation from the Glenn Hotel on Monmouth Street. Ann obtained a certain satisfaction in hearing that her old friend was living much of the time at Jimmy Brink's mansion on Dixie Highway. A handsome ex-football player, Tito Carinci, who wore his black hair in bangs and operated the Glenn Rendezvous on the first floor of the hotel, also lived there. It would appear, Ann decided, that the widow of Charley's old boss was operating a rooming house for hoods.

There was tension in Newport these days although no one appeared really worried. Those "sneaking preachers," as one gambler put it, were still trying to cause trouble. They had appeared before the October grand jury and, despite a brush-off, had returned in February. No one would have paid them much attention except that the *Courier-Journal* in Louisville sent a reporter up to cover both sessions and his stories created a degree of heat.

The reporter happened to be the author.

A very funny thing happened in December, Ann was told. The same reporter had gone with some preachers and a state beverage agent into the Flamingo. Fortunately, said Louis ("Sleepout") Levinson, he had been tipped in time. The party found a sedate scene. Years before the Flamingo had lost its liquor license, so to prepare for the visit Sleepout had to clean out the bar. A vase of flowers replaced the row of bottles. All the customers were asked to cooperate. The preachers found them seated at the tables drinking milk—or trying to down the stuff. The reporter tried to lead the way into the casino at the rear, but Kenny Bright—the Cleveland Syndicate representative—neatly blocked them.

"The back room is closed, gentlemen," said Kenny, "but could I offer you a glass of milk?"

It was all very funny, Ann agreed. Fifteen minutes after the preachers left, the bar was open and the milk had been poured down the drain.

The reformers were undiscouraged. They continued to visit gambling joints and brothels despite a February grand jury report which had been specially written for them. The report said, in part:

"Our experience, reason and personal evaluation of human failings incline us to the oft-repeated belief that man's frailties and weaknesses cannot be completely legislated away. Mankind having been born in sin will ever be a prey to the temptations of sin."

If the gamblers were inclined to shrug off the ministers, Newport officials with an eye to the elections were not. The *Courier-Journal's* stories, first of their kind in many years, had been widely read. If the stories continued, the Cincinnati newspapers would be forced to start crusading in self-defense. The situation was potentially dangerous.

In an effort to cool the zeal of the preachers, City Manager Oscar Hesch arranged a meeting with the Reverend Harold Barkhau, most influential of the ministers. Barkhau reported later he was told by Hesch:

"I asked you to meet with me because you have been here longer, you are older, and I think you know the situation better. Would you ask your group to withhold going to higher authority for a couple of months? Mr. Wise and I have had a conversation and we are determined to wipe out prostitution. You really don't want all the handbooks closed, do you?"

Reverend Barkhau, whose church had been once destroyed by fire and rebuilt with help of gambler's money, was willing to compromise. Other and younger ministers, such as Dudley Pomeroy of the First Baptist Church and George Bennett of the First Presbyterian Church, were opposed. Ultimately they won the debate and with Chris, the patient postman, leading the way, the Social Action Committee continued its unhurried campaign. It soon became apparent even to Barkhau that any promise by Wise or Hesch to close brothels was an empty one—city officials could not control police who had made their own deals with pimps and madams. Reverend Bennett was able to write in his diary:

"Strange, how little we know each other, how different our backgrounds, our denominations, our lives—yet in one thing so solidly united and close."

That unity was the one thing the syndicate could not beat.

Ann listened to the gossip with only half an ear. Ever since her marriage she had been planning a big party for her relatives, a party to which everyone of importance in the Newport-Covington area would be invited. Her sisters and brothers would be able to see how important, how successful, she had become. Mike had not wanted to be bothered, but when Ann insisted he grudgingly gave his consent. The Beverly Hills Club as the location appealed to her though Beckley advised against it. With so many preachers and reporters snooping around, such a famous person as Trigger Mike might be recognized and featured in a newspaper story. Better go to some fine restaurant that didn't have a casino. There were a few, you know. Ann agreed and selected Retschultze's, a nice place outside Covington on the road to Louisville.

The turnout wasn't quite as large as Ann hoped. An ex-Newport city commissioner was opening a new joint over in Campbell and a lot of guests left early to attend. It was satisfactory, nevertheless, and the food was good. Even though it wasn't the Beverly Hills or the Fontainebleau, her relatives seemed impressed. As usual, however, when things were going well, the only bad chip in the game was Mike. He began drinking early and continued at a heavy pace. Her sisters avoided him, a fact that did not escape his attention and only increased his bad humor. Ann accepted the situation philosophically—it seemed that Mike never wanted her to be happy unless he was the cause of it. The bastard was so self-centered.

Noting his growing annoyance, Ann decided she'd better quit table-hopping and give him some attention. After all, she was just trying to show him off. But it was too late. When she returned to her seat beside him, Mike swayed toward her and leered:

"I'm going back to Miami on the next plane."

"You can't do that," said Ann. "You promised we would stay two more days."

"Can't help it," said Mike in a guttural whisper. "Got to get home. Joan needs me. She can't get her snow without old Trigger Mike, you know."

"Joan?" Ann could not comprehend. "Snow? What ever in the world are you talking about?"

Mike's snigger was obscene. He was very drunk. "You don't know your darling daughter, do you? Your princess takes drugs. She may get hooked soon."

"Hooked?" Ann was still fumbling for understanding, but her stomach was turning to ice. All those old fears, old suspicions. She had suspected something but, dear God, not this.

Pleased with her reaction but a bit impatient, Coppola snarled: "She could turn addict, you bitch. You've been too busy spending my money to notice."

With that he stood up. Ann sat stunned as he motioned unsteadily to Jelly Wehby.

"I gotta catch a plane," he said. "Drive me to the airport."

Emil "Jelly" Wehby was a huge fat man, a flunky of Screw Andrews, who sometimes used him as a bouncer-bodyguard. For him an order from Coppola was the same as an order from Screw. He obeyed instantly. Ann, sitting numb and motionless, watched the two men leave the room. All eyes followed them out, then turned back to Ann.

The noise of a motor starting outside the building penetrated the hurt and shame. Ann came suddenly to life. Mike had to be stopped. Whatever had happened in the past couldn't be changed, but he had to be kept away from Joan. He couldn't go back alone. She jumped up, overturned her chair, and ran toward the door. Only Gil Beckley intercepted her.

"What's going on?" he asked quietly.

"Give me your keys," said Ann "I've got to stop Mike."

Beckley produced a car key. "It's the black Olds," he said. "I borrowed it from Roger Seith."

Ann didn't wait to hear more. Grabbing the key, she fled to the parking lot, her long gown pulled high to let her run. Mike had already vanished, but she knew Wehby's car—a new station wagon. Even though it was well after midnight Dixie Highway was still crowded. The night was young in Newport-Covington and a lot of suckers were still coming up from Louisville.

The Greater Cincinnati Airport is located, curiously enough, in Boone County, Kentucky, southwest of Covington, on level ground which stretches to the very edge of the Ohio River gorge. It can be reached from the front by driving down Dixie Highway. A shorter but narrow and more dangerous approach is River Road and the side street which climbs out of the gorge to the rear of the airport.

Ann went down Dixie Highway, hitting eighty miles an hour when the traffic thinned. Riding with her were memories— memories of Mike insulting the young swain who came calling to take Joan to a football game in the Orange Bowl; of Mike arranging dates for Joan with Lefty Rosenthal and Chuck White, the handsome son of Charles "the Blade" Tourine; of Mike buying a new car for Joan; of the beatings that never took place when Joan was present.

She reached the airport and followed the long detour around the public parking lot to the front of the terminal building. There was Jelly's car, illegally parked with the motor running. She stopped behind it. Through the large window she could see Mike at the ticket counter. Wehby stood behind him, holding a suitcase. So the bastard hadn't acted on impulse after all; he had brought his bag along when Wehby drove him to the party.

Ann rushed into the building. What she said, she could never remember. It was insulting. It was vicious. Even Mike became embarrassed as the girls behind the counter stared in amazement. He told her to come outside. The air felt cool on Ann's flushed face and she renewed the verbal assault. This time Mike said nothing. As Wehby, who had followed along still holding the suitcase, watched, Mike knocked her down. She fell against a concrete bench. Mike bent over her and Ann kicked up with all her strength. The kick landed and Ann scrambled to her feet. She was an animal now, fighting for life and something dearer than life, her daughter. However she was no match for Trigger Mike Coppola, who learned the arts of gutter fighting in East Harlem before she was born. He struck her again and again until she lay dazed, blood trickling from her nose and mouth.

Coppola stepped back satisfied. He glanced inside the terminal. The girls on duty at the ticket counter stared back. One of them was holding a telephone. Not even Coppola wanted to face them now.

"I've changed my mind," he said to the impassive Wehby. "Let's go back to the hotel."

Jelly put Mike's bag in the station wagon, held the door for Mike, and climbed under the wheel. Without a glance at the bloody face of his wife, Mike rode away.

"Step on it," he snapped.

Ann pulled herself up, shook her head to chase away the red blobs, and got back into the Seith-Beckley car. Wehby's taillights were vanishing around the corner of the parking lot. Recklessly she followed, gunning the motor hard. They were just outside the entrance to the airport when she caught up with the station wagon and cut in front of it. There was a crash of glass as the right window of Ann's car shattered under the impact. Both cars came to a stop.

Cursing wildly, Mike got out to meet her.

"Look, you bitch," he said. "You've got to stop this shit. Move over. We'll go somewhere and talk."

Wehby watched them drive off in the Seith-Beckley car. Instead of taking Dixie Highway, Mike turned left toward River Road. It was a lonely area. Back in bootleg days a lot of people were taken there on their last ride. . . .

. . . Ann sat stiffly. She felt physically and emotionally exhausted. Having achieved her objective in turning back Mike at the airport, she felt incapable of further effort. Mike, sobered by the action, made the twisting descent into the gorge without difficulty. As they drove on through the blackness, Ann felt a surge of hope. Maybe this was just one of Mike's attempts at humor. The bastard was capable of telling such a lie just to hurt her.

"Oh, Mike," she said, grasping his arm. "Tell me it was just a joke. You didn't mean it, did you?"

Coppola braked the car to a stop. On their left the roar of the river was loud. The darker bulk of the mountain on the right could be felt rather than seen. Mike reached across his wife and opened the shattered door.

"Get out, bitch," he said. "I'm sick of listening to you."

Ann didn't move. With a curse, Mike shoved her from the car. She stumbled and fell into a ditch. Lights of an approaching automobile touched the scene. The oncoming car slowed, then speeded up and went by fast. Coppola slammed the door and drove off in the direction of the lights of Cincinnati far ahead. Ann lay whimpering in the ditch.

Reaction to hope so quickly born and so speedily dead left her weak. Fear came to give new strength as Mike's taillights vanished around a curve. The bastard might change his mind again and go back to the airport. She had to stop him. Joan's life might depend on her. Somehow she staggered up and started walking.

It was along River Road that Gil and June Beckley found her. Mike had returned to Retschultze's and given Beckley the key to the car. It took the smooth Beckley only a minute to persuade Mike to tell where he had left Ann. Someone volunteered to take Mike to Sleepout's house in Fort Thomas. Beckley got into Seith's car and started down River Road in search of Ann. He found her outside a fish house which was closed for the night. She was pounding on the door, hoping to awaken someone and borrow a telephone to call Joan in Miami Beach. When Beckley assured Ann that Mike had gone to Sleepout's home for the night, Ann consented to be taken to her hotel.

The evening wasn't over. Someone at the airport had reported the fight. And Covington police got an anonymous call from the driver who had seen Ann pushed from the car on River Road. A radio message alerted the two police cars in the area to watch for the Olds and the station wagon.

Fort Mitchell police spotted Seith's car on Dixie Highway and ordered it to the police station. Fort Mitchell was only a wide place on the road, but it had a station and it was there Beckley stopped.

The situation was complex enough but Beckley knew how to simplify it. The whole affair was simply "domestic trouble," he explained, and it was all settled. The officers knew Beckley by reputation and they remembered Ann as Charley Drahmann's widow. They wrote no names and made no detailed report. "Just routine," they said.

When asked about the episode later, the officers were vague. "Do you consider it a normal thing that a woman has been beaten up, thrown from a car, picked up, and later apprehended?" one officer was asked.

The man admitted it was not normal. He also agreed the report on the incident was "very incomplete," but he had an excuse:

"It was lack of prosecution," he said. "Nobody wanted to do anything about it."

Beckley was permitted to take Ann to her hotel. A doctor was called. He couldn't do much about the black eye but he treated her cuts and abrasions and assured her no bones were broken.

Next day the sophisticated Beckley assumed the role of peacemaker. He persuaded Mike to tell Ann he had "exaggerated" Joan's habit. She really wasn't on the heavy stuff—just a few "bennies" and "yellow jackets" like all kids try. And, promised Mike, he would see she didn't get any more. All he had to do was spread the word and Joan wouldn't even be able to buy, beg, or borrow a pep pill of any kind.

Beckley was successful in his appeal to Mike only because he knew his man was desperately afraid of the Internal Revenue Service. For years he had gone to elaborate extremes to conceal his income. He warned Coppola:

"Ann's not just another dame. She's tough and she's mean. You get her mad enough and you'll have an old-country vendetta on your hands. She'll go to the feds and talk. You can't afford that, Mike."

Ann accepted the truce for several reasons. It was good to believe that Mike had exaggerated. Not to think so would be too terrible. And she knew he did have the power to cut off Joan's drug supply. There was still hope if Mike would keep his word.

The couple, still not talking very freely, returned to Miami Beach and the stormy marriage continued much as before. Ann began a conscious effort to reach her daughter, to establish a better relationship, but Joan resisted. It would take time, Ann decided, a lot of time. Fortunately, Mike remained in a reasonable mood. Ann was able to postpone her date with reality.

Joan accompanied her on a trip to Cincinnati in November 1959. Ann hoped the visit would soften her daughter but she could note little change. The visit itself was unsatisfactory. Too many people had questions they were afraid to ask. It was almost a relief to return home. The women got in late. It was after midnight when Ann entered the master bedroom. Mike was asleep but stirred as she was undressing.

"I've got a headache," he complained. "Look in the dresser drawer and get me some aspirins."

Ann obeyed. There were no aspirins in the drawer but there was a small box that had not been there before. She picked it up.

"Open it," said Mike.

Inside the box was a pair of diamond earrings. They sparkled in the night-light's glow.

"Who are they for?" asked Ann.

"For you," said Trigger Mike.

"You darling," said Mrs. Trigger Mike.

15
A Family Gathering

GAY TALESE

Rosalie's mother flew to San Francisco from New York carrying among her luggage a box of live snails that she had personally selected at a Brooklyn fish market, live lobsters from Maine, special Italian sausages stuffed with cheese, and other delicacies that were rare in California and that she intended to serve at a large family gathering on the following day, the first Sunday in March.

The dinner, to be attended by a dozen people, would be held at the home of her daughter Ann, who was in her seventh month of pregnancy, and with whom Mrs. Profaci would be staying in San Jose until after the birth; she would help with the cooking, would look after Ann's two young children, and would also be available for whatever assistance she might provide her eldest daughter, Rosalie, and her youngest daughter, Josephine, who was twenty-one and would be getting married in June, shortly after her graduation from Berkeley.

Josephine would be married in the chapel on the Stanford campus to a non-Catholic, non-Italian, hazel-eyed young man with long blond hair named Tim Stanton, the son of an upper-middle-class family in Westchester County, New York. Josephine had met Tim Stanton at a college barbecue exchange in the spring of 1966 when she was a student at Santa Clara, and during that summer in New York she went with him to the suburbs to meet his parents, an encounter she had dreaded in advance even though,

early in their dating, she made it clear to him who her relatives
were, learning to her surprise and relief that this precaution was
unnecessary; he already knew. The meeting with his parents turned
out to be unexpectedly pleasant, because the Stantons succeeded
in making her feel welcome and comfortable.

During the next two years, after Josephine had transferred
to Berkeley and as her relationship with Tim Stanton became closer
and there were plans for marriage, it was not Tim's family, but
Josephine's, that seemed the more concerned. That it was to be
a non-Catholic wedding ceremony was most disappointing to Josephine's mother and older brother; but when they sensed how determined Josephine was and how inseparable the young couple
obviously were, they accepted the inevitable and Josephine's
brother agreed to escort her up the aisle on her wedding day.

The extended family, however, which included Bill Bonanno
and his friends in addition to other in-laws and relatives of the
Profacis', still expressed doubts about the wisdom of such a marriage; and by the time of the large family dinner, Tim Stanton
had been the subject of several conversations and debates in Brooklyn and San Jose. They had all met him by now, inasmuch as
Josephine had introduced him at various times during the last year;
and since he was so different from anyone who had ever approached the family threshold before, he was a subject of both
fascination and confusion.

Some of Bill's friends, reacting to Stanton's long hair and his
casual style of dress, and having heard him denounce the war in
Vietnam and hint at his own refusal to fight if drafted, regarded
him quickly if incorrectly as part of a radical new generation that
wished to overthrow the system; and in any showdown with the
new generation, Bill's men would be curiously on the side of the
system—the government, the police, and "law and order." These
men did not want the system to collapse, for if it collapsed they
would topple with it. While they recognized the government
as flawed, hypocritical, and undemocratic, with most politicians
and the police corrupt to a degree, corruption was at least something that could be understood and dealt with. What they were
most wary of and what centuries of Sicilian history had taught
them to mistrust were reformers and crusaders.

Bill Bonanno's view of the younger generation, however, was

less rigid, and he agreed with Tim Stanton on many issues—except when he learned that Stanton was thinking of registering as a conscientious objector or of joining the Peace Corps and serving in Malaysia with Josephine after the marriage. Bill believed that joining the Peace Corps was "copping out" since it was subsidized by the same government leaders who were fomenting war in Vietnam. If Stanton did not wish to engage in an immoral war, then, according to Bill, he should be willing to pay the price and should go to jail. Jail was the place for many honorable men these days, Bill believed, including himself in such company.

Rosalie was not upset by any of Stanton's political views, but she was distressed that Josephine was marrying outside the church; she preferred that her youngest sister agree to "go along" with the Catholic wedding and the religious beliefs that she had grown up with and ostensibly had accepted until recently. But in this instance, Bill supported Josephine's decision not to give the appearance of believing what she did not; and yet Bill was bothered by Josephine for other reasons, vaguely definable ones that were inspired by his suspicion that Josephine privately detested him. He was perceptive enough to sense that Josephine remembered well certain raging scenes between himself and the Profaci family after Rosalie had left him in Arizona in 1963 and had returned to New York. Josephine had since then seemed quiet in his presence, occasionally suggesting her disapproval by certain gestures and remarks; and Rosalie herself recently said that Josephine had probably decided on a different course with regard to marriage and religion because Josephine had seen how Rosalie had suffered by following the ways of the past. Bill knew of course that he could count on Rosalie not to miss an opportunity to portray herself as some sort of martyr; but he also knew and took pride in the fact that Rosalie's sister Ann had never held a grudge against him—Bill and Ann always got along splendidly, and he had often said in jest at family gatherings that he had married the wrong Profaci.

Ann, though a bit heavy like her mother, had a beautiful face, expressive eyes, and, uncharacteristic for a Profaci, a sense of humor. Ann was an efficient homemaker, a wonderful mother, and, while she was intelligent, she deferred to her husband's judgment; her husband was clearly in charge. But Josephine, Bill was sure, would lead a different life, she was the product of another time.

She was the first daughter to finish college, and, without being a feminist, she undoubtedly identified with the cause of modern women seeking greater liberation, which was probably one reason, Bill thought, why she disliked him, for he typified everything that she as a modern young woman undoubtedly rejected—he was the dominant Sicilian male who did as he pleased, came and went as he wished, unquestioned, the inheritor of the rights of a one-sided patriarchal system that the Bonannos and Profacis had lived under for generations.

But at this point, in March 1969, with his mother-in-law visiting San Jose, Bill Bonanno was not eager for any further friction with the Profacis; and at the Sunday dinner that Mrs. Profaci was preparing, and at which Josephine would be present and perhaps also Tim, Bill decided that he would be on his best behavior.

In the morning, however, Bill woke up with a mild headache, and as he went out to the patio with the Sunday newspapers and a book under his arm he noticed that two of Charles's rabbits had broken out of their pens, had dug into the flower garden, and were now chasing one another wildly around the backyard. The yard was also littered with toys and pieces of wood.

"Rosalie!" Bill yelled to his wife in the kitchen. "Is Chuckie getting out of bed today?"

"He's not feeling well, and I thought I'd let him sleep for a while."

"I want him to clean up this mess out here and catch these rabbits!"

"He's not feeling too well," she repeated, her voice rising. "What do you want me to do?"

"I told him three times this week I wanted this place fixed up," Bill said, sitting down on a patio chair in the midmorning sun and putting on his dark glasses. He had stayed up half the night reading the book that he held in his hands, a new novel about the Mafia called *The Godfather*. He was half-finished, and so far he liked it very much, and he thought that the author, Mario Puzo, had insight into the secret society. Bill found the central figure in the novel, Don Vito Corleone, a believable character, and he wondered if that name had been partly inspired by "Don Vito" Genovese and by the town of Corleone, which was in the interior of western Sicily southeast of Castellammare. Bill believed that his own father possessed many of the quietly sophisticated qualities that the writer had attributed to Don Vito Corleone, and yet there were also elements in the character that reminded Bill of the late Thomas Lucchese. Lucchese in real life, like Don Vito Corleone in the novel, had influential friends in Democratic political circles in New York during the 1950s, men who reportedly performed special favors for generous political contributions; and in 1960, Lucchese went to Los Angeles to mingle with some of these friends who were attending the Democratic National Convention. Lucchese favored the nomination of John F. Kennedy, but other dons such as Joseph Profaci, influenced partly by an immigrant Sicilian's traditional suspicion of the Irish, were against Kennedy. Most Irish politicians, like Irish priests and cops, would do no favors for the Italians, whom, in Profaci's view, they privately abhorred—a view that Lucchese did not share, nor did Frank Costello, who had been on intimate terms with William O'Dwyer. But after Kennedy became president and after the Irish Mafia rose to power, and when only Valachi among Italians achieved fame in Washington, many mafiosi asserted that Profaci had been right.

The Sicilians described in *The Godfather*—not only Don Vito Corleone and his college-educated son Michael (with whom Bill identified) but other characters as well—were endowed with impressive amounts of courage and honor, traits that Bill was convinced were fast deteriorating in the brotherhood. The novel was set in the years following World War II, and in those days the Mafia was probably as the novelist described it; and as Bill continued to read the book, he became nostalgic for a period that he had never personally known. He read on the patio for nearly an hour, then was interrupted by the sound of Rosalie's impatient voice coming from the kitchen.

"Joseph," she yelled, "stop blowing that balloon—I don't want you exerting yourself today!"

Bill resumed his reading, but was interrupted again by Rosalie who stood at the patio door saying that she was going with the children to Ann's house to help prepare dinner. Bill, who had an appointment with a man at noon, would join her there later.

"Now don't be late," she called, as she turned to leave.

"I won't," he said, waving at the children, and saying nothing to Charles about the condition of the yard or the fact that the rabbits were running loose somewhere behind the small bushes and plants. Bill would deal with that tomorrow.

He read for another half hour, then got up to shave and get ready for his appointment. He was dressed casually on this Sunday, looking as if he were headed for the golf course. He wore light blue slacks and brown loafers, and glaring from under his gray sweater was a Day-Glo orange shirt. In the kitchen, after pouring himself a cup of coffee, he decided to telephone Brooklyn and say hello to his aunt Marion and his uncle Vincent Di Pasquale, with whom he would again be staying when he reappeared before the Kings County grand jury in a few weeks. That the phone was tapped was of no concern to him now, since he would be saying nothing of importance on this call; but after his aunt Marion had picked up the receiver, Bill heard a series of clicking sounds and various extensions being picked up, and he called out, "Hey, how many people are on this phone?"

"Hello," his aunt said in a voice he could barely hear, and he also heard his cousin Linda on the bedroom extension in the Brooklyn house, with a child crying in the background.

"Is that you, son?" his aunt Marion asked, a childless woman who had always called him son. "Is that you?"

"Yes," Bill said, "it's me and the FBI on my end, and on your end it's you and Linda and the baby and probably Aunt Jeanne upstairs and the New York detectives, right?"

"Hello," said Linda, "how's everybody there?"

"Fine," Bill said. But before he could say much to Linda, his aunt Marion, a woman in her late sixties who kept abreast of nearly every trivial detail concerning the several relatives of the Bonannos, the Labruzzos, the Bonventres, and other kin and *compare* at home and overseas, had several things to say; among them was that her back ailment was improving, that Bill's uncle's cold was no better, that her nephew was doing well in art class, that the weather was chilly, that the television set needed a new tube, and other bits of vital information that Bill knew would fascinate the federal eavesdropper who was recording this conversation for posterity.

Mrs. Profaci stood at the stove cooking the snails, the lobsters, and preparing the ravioli, while Rosalie and Ann helped her, and Josephine sat in the living room with the men. Ann's husband,

Lou, was serving drinks, and the six children were running through the house, which was handsomely furnished and had a guitar near the fireplace that Lou used to play, along with the bass, when he sang professionally in small clubs where he was thought of as a second Russ Colombo. A relaxed, genial man approaching forty, Lou was now in business and sang only in the shower. But he appeared to have no regrets, was happily married and on good terms with his mother-in-law, delighted that another child was expected, and seemed to be unaware of the noise the children were now making as they scampered through the room out toward the patio. Lou noticed that his little son Lawrence was waving a toy pistol that Bill had given him; and while Lou knew that his wife did not like even toy guns in the house, he said nothing.

Bill was not yet at the house, nor was Tim Stanton. Tim would probably be late and they would not wait for him before starting dinner; but there was no question of going ahead without Bill. Until he arrived and greeted the assemblage, all would wait and talk among themselves, never thinking of sitting around the table without him, for in many subtle ways Bill was regarded as the head of the family.

He walked in shortly before 2:00 P.M., followed by another man and also by Catherine's husband. Catherine was in Tucson with her children visiting the elder Bonannos; she would be returning by plane later in the evening. Bill greeted his mother-in-law and Ann cordially in the kitchen, nodded toward Rosalie, then continued into the living room, where Lou got up to pat him on the back and mix him a drink. Josephine, who sat wearing bell-bottomed trousers, a white sweater, and the round-toed shoes that were the latest fashion, focused her dark eyes on Bill momentarily, then announced with just the slightest edge, "Well, the man has arrived, and now we can eat."

Bill forced a smile, ignoring a reply, and then Rosalie, removing her apron, came in and sat down, and Lou fixed her a drink. From the kitchen could be heard the rattling sound of snail shells cooking in the pot, reminding Rosalie of the large family feasts from her girlhood days when her uncles Joseph Profaci and Magliocco had been alive, and she remembered that when the live snails were left in the sink and ignored while other food was being prepared, they would sometimes slowly crawl up from the sink and would begin to climb the walls. Bill reminisced about those days too, about Magliocco's voracious appetite, and the extraordinary sight of Magliocco, who weighed about 300 pounds and was not very tall, gracefully mounting a horse each morning and galloping around the estate at East Islip.

When Mrs. Profaci stood smiling in the doorway, indicating that dinner was ready, everyone was seated, and steaming plates were passed around the table. Bill inhaled the aroma of the food spread before him, and after tasting the snails, he complimented Mrs. Profaci and lifted his wine glass in a toast. Then he proceeded to tell everyone about the new book that he was reading, *The Godfather*, which none of the others had heard of; and after describing a few dramatic passages, Ann said, "Boy, that sounds like a wonderful organization—I'd like to join it as a gun moll."

"You should," Bill said, "you've got good recommendations."

Everybody laughed except Josephine, who did not look up from her plate.

Mrs. Profaci said that she had recently seen *The Brotherhood* at Radio City, starring Kirk Douglas, but before she could offer her opinion of it, Bill interrupted to say that it was one of the most stupid films ever made.

"There's this ridiculous scene in the end where two brothers kiss, and then one brother takes a gun and shoots the other," Bill said. "It's real Hollywood crap."

Mrs. Profaci, without refuting him, said nonetheless that she had been moved to tears during one scene when a character was identified as Turiddu, which was what her late husband had been called. Even as she repeated the name now, at the table, her voice became soft, and she said, "May his soul rest in peace."

Her husband had been a kind and loving man, Mrs. Profaci continued, after a pause, although she did admit that he had been extremely strict and that his rules had been especially hard on Rosalie, the first-born daughter. Mrs. Profaci remembered one evening many years ago when, because her husband was expected to be out of town for a few days, she permitted Rosalie to accept a date to attend a dance with a West Point cadet. But just as Rosalie was about to leave the house, dressed in a beautiful gown, her father unexpectedly appeared, and he immediately demanded to know where she was going. Mrs. Profaci, trying to seem casual, had explained that Rosalie was joining other young girls at a dance, adding that she would be home early; but Mr. Profaci, furious, insisted that his daughter return to her room and change her clothes—she would be going nowhere on this evening.

As Mrs. Profaci recounted the incident now, more than fifteen years later, there was silence at the table. Then Rosalie stood and turned toward the sink, carrying a few dishes.

The next course was ravioli, and Lou poured red wine in the glasses as Bill tasted the ravioli. His expression changed slightly, and he said to Lou, who sat next to him. "I think it's not cooked enough. Mine is a little hard."

Lou tasted the ravioli from his plate, and agreed that it was hard. Mrs. Profaci, who did not seem at all perturbed, offered to cook the ravioli a bit longer, but Josephine from the opposite side of the table disagreed, saying after she had sampled it, "It's very good, Mom. I like it hard."

Bill looked at Josephine, measuring her for a moment, and then he said with a grin, "Oh, you like it *hard*, do you?"

Josephine looked directly at Bill, having caught the double entendre immediately, and she replied, "Yes, Bill, I like it hard."

Ann laughed and then changed the subject by focusing on Bill's Day-Glo orange shirt: "That's some shirt you're wearing, Bill, that's quite a color."

"It's designed for men who stand on aircraft carriers, and flag down planes," he said, "It makes a wonderful target, which is why I don't wear it in New York."

This got a laugh around the table, and then Bill asked one of the men if he had heard any news from New York. When the man said he had not, Bill frowned and said, "I'm going to make a call."

Ann again addressed Bill, asking in a good-humored chiding way, "Why do you people spend so much money on phone calls? Why don't you write a letter once in a while?"

"*What*," Bill exclaimed, laughing, "and put it in writing!"

They continued to eat the ravioli, which Bill had not permitted his mother-in-law to cook longer, preferring to drop the subject. And then Mrs. Profaci noticed a car pulling up in the driveway—Tim had arrived, and Josephine stood to greet him at the door. While the others continued to eat and Bill told a joke, the young couple spoke between themselves for a few moments in the vestibule; then Josephine, followed by Tim, returned to the table. Lou and Bill and the other men stood to shake hands, and Tim greeted them by name. He had met Bill and Lou many times before and he seemed poised and particularly pleased to see Mrs. Profaci, who had already met his parents and was on friendly terms with them. A chair was obtained for Tim, and he squeezed in next to Josephine. He was wearing chinos and boots, and a button-down shirt under his sweater, and his blond hair was long but neatly barbered. As Bill looked across the table at Tim, he was reminded of the fact that Tim resembled the photographs of Robert F. Kennedy years ago when Kennedy had been the attorney general.

As Mrs. Profaci got Tim a plate of food, and Lou poured him a glass of wine, the conversation became more general; but Josephine, who was holding Tim's hand underneath the table, turned to him and soon they were speaking softly to one another, ignoring the other conversations. They were a typical young couple about to be married, completely absorbed in themselves and only remotely aware of the rest of the family around them. Occasionally Mrs. Profaci or Rosalie or Ann would pass a serving dish of food toward Tim but they tried not to interrupt the private conversation. They were very happy that Josephine seemed happy, were pleased about the coming marriage despite whatever reservations that they had once expressed. Josephine Profaci was going off in a new direction, was breaking with many traditions and customs of her family, but her older sisters and her mother were secure in their belief that the love they shared with Josephine would keep them close no matter how far she moved in the future from the familiarity of their past.

After coffee was served, Josephine and Tim stood and said that they had to be getting back to their respective campuses. Both had schoolwork to do that night, they said, and Tim, an English major, further explained his hasty departure to the Bonannos and Profacis: "I've got a paper due on Lear."

16
Pal Joey
—A Study in Gangster Chic

CHARLOTTE CURTIS

"People like me are a plague on people like you"—Joey Gallo.
"No, Joey. The reverse is true"—Marta Orbach

He spilled spaghetti sauce on Thomas H. Guinzburg's shoes. He played pool with Bruce Jay Friedman's sons. He cleared the dinner plates at Marta and Jerry Orbach's, and emptied their ashtrays. He probed "the meaning of life" in a deep discussion with the ever fashionable Mrs. John Barry ("D.D.") Ryan III.

The he, of course, was Joseph ("Crazy Joey") Gallo, the tough Mafioso, convicted extortionist and suspected murderer who exuded what his newest friends have described as "refreshing insight and intelligence in a world of cliches."

He didn't make it to Park Avenue, or even El Morocco, but in his final days, he unknowingly had become something of a sought-after social pet.

"Everyone talked about it," said Mrs. Richard Clurman, an authority on such matters who refused to meet him. "It was the thing to do. You'd go somewhere and people would say, 'Have you met Joey Gallo?' and it was like Stravinsky or Yevtushenko. If you hadn't met him, you weren't in."

Eleven years ago, in the prelockup days when the Gallos were kidnaping the Profacis to get their way in the rackets, you could see, if not actually meet, Joey Gallo in Greenwich Village

Joseph Colombo, in dinner jacket, being applauded as he walks across the floor at a dinner of the Italian-American Civil Rights League. *Camera 5—Ken Reagan*

Father and Son: Joseph Colombo (seated) and his son, Anthony, before the plaque of the Italian-American Civil Rights League, seated at the conference table in the League's headquarters. *Camera 5—Ken Reagan*

Right: The Colombo Family: Members of Joseph Colombo's family in a group portrait at a testimonial dinner. From left to right: Vincent Colombo; Joseph Sr. and wife Lucille; sons, Anthony and Joseph Jr.; in foreground: daughter Catherine and son Christopher. *Camera 5—Ken Reagan*

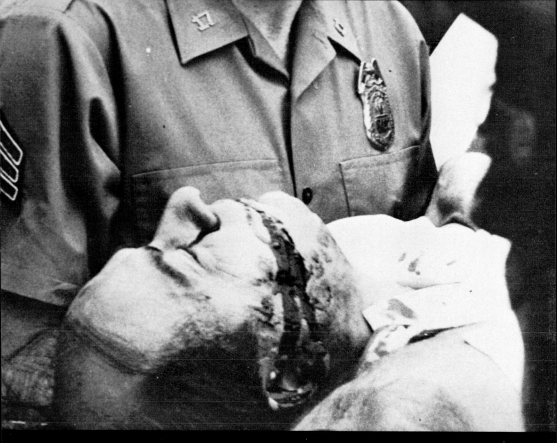

Wounded Joe Colombo being moved into ambulance after shooting at 1971 rally.
N.Y. Daily News Photo

Left: During Italian-American civil rights demonstration, Joseph Colombo (in striped shirt) is seen atop police van with high-ranking New York police officer.
Camera 5—Ken Reagan

Joseph Bonanno and son, Joseph Jr., walking together outside the Federal Building in Tucson, Arizona, where the elder Bonanno was scheduled to be arraigned on a grand jury indictment in 1969.

HUGH ADDONIZIO IN MIXED COMPANY. *Above:* With Italian motion picture actress Sophia Loren at a Washington party.   *Below:* With U.S. Marshals in Newark, New Jersey, on his way to begin a 10-year prison term in 1972. *Wide World Photos*

Above: New York's Mayor, John V. Lindsay, acting as godfather at the baptism of the son of N.Y. Water Commissioner James Marcus (far left). Mrs. Lily Lodge Marcus looks on, as Lindsay holds the baby. *Below:* Commissioner Marcus looking into courtyard at federal prison at Lewisburg, Pennsylvania, at the start of his 15-month jail term for bribery conspiracy. *Wide World Photos*

bars. There, often in the company of literate journalists, he was as likely to cite Celine, Hugo or Kafka as to talk the events of the neighborhood or joke bitterly about what would become of his family.

Then came the nine-year stretch. By 1971, when Mr. Gallo was released, the Village bars were changed or gone. It was another world. In January of 1972, when he telephoned the Orbachs because friends had admiringly described Jerry's movie role in the Mafia spoof, *The Gang That Couldn't Shoot Straight,* he called from Brooklyn.

"We weren't sure what to do at first," Mrs. Orbach said. "We wanted to meet him—more out of curiosity than anything else."

What may have started for them as the tingling excitement of knowing a real live hood quickly turned into what they considered friendship. They accepted his invitation to dinner in a Brooklyn restaurant and were surprised to discover that the notorious Joey Gallo was "only about 5 feet, 6 or 7." They found him "charming" and "brilliant." It was at that first meeting that he casually asked Mrs. Orbach whether she preferred Camus or Sartre. As she tells it, "I almost fell into a plate of spaghetti."

After that, he'd drop by the Orbachs' late at night, sipping coffee laced with anisette or a brandy while talking mostly with Mr. Orbach.

"He once told me to shut up," Mrs. Orbach said. "I'm Italian and I understand that. We had to make it very clear that in our family and our world women are bright and they talk, too, and he began to understand."

The conversations, hardly evidence of anyone's brilliance, ran to casual discussions, occasionally punctuated by Mr. Gallo's humor. He argued that people who broke the law should expect to go to jail, which rather startled the Orbachs. He said it was tragic that men like Van Gogh weren't recognized and rewarded in their lifetime rather than years after death.

"Liberals," he explained, "are the first to dump you if you fail them or get into trouble. "Conservatives are better. They never run out on you."

If he had lived in Italy, he once said, he might have been a Fascist. He was interested in power and money. Within weeks

of meeting the Orbachs, Mrs. Orbach, herself a writer, was working with him on his memoirs and a "prison comedy." He believed
the ventures could be profitable. The friendship had obviously
blossomed.

Between January and April 7, when he was gunned down
on his 43rd birthday in a Little Italy restaurant, the only way
to meet Joey Gallo—unless, of course, you were his parole officer,
the cops who followed his violent career or his South Brooklyn
business associates—was to know the Orbachs and get invited to
one of their regular five o'clock Sunday "brunches."

The rub was that the actor and his wife were purposely protective of him. They didn't invite just anybody.

"We knew his background and he knew we knew and nobody
pretended it didn't exist," Mrs. Orbach said. For them, it was
enough that "he'd read in prison." They believed he was "rehabili-
tated." "He said he wanted to go straight," Mrs. Orbach added.
"I know it sounds outrageous, but he was shy."

Shy? Indeed that does sound outrageous, particularly about
a man who jabbed one enemy with an ice pick and broke a protec-
tion-money victim's arm. But the Orbachs simply shake their heads,
argue that people just don't understand and insist: Joey Gallo was
shy.

"He'd sit around my kitchen with those sad, sad eyes," Mrs.
Orbach recalled. "He wanted to talk about things—everything.
He needed people who were as bright as he was. We never invited
anyone who wouldn't understand this. Just our closest friends."

Those who did go, and they're now caught somewhere between affection for the man, the horror of what he represented,
and the notoriety of being publicly identified as acquaintances—let
alone friends—of a gangster, found themselves at a typically informal family gathering.

What with the Orbach youngsters, the family cat and what
Mrs. Orbach calls "our rude dog" (he jumps on people), it was
pretty much of a do-your-own-thing afternoon.

Everyone wore comfortable clothes (which in that set can
include $200 pants suits), sipped red wine or made their own drinks
while Mrs. Orbach, often in blue jeans and an old sweater, put
the finishing touches on dinner. Then everyone, including the children, gathered around the big dining room table to help themselves
to spaghetti and green salad.

"Everybody I know is tired of the dressing up and the sitting down, with the servants waiting on you and the Baccarat crystal," Mrs. Orbach explained. "I was raised on spaghetti. I hadn't had Sundays like this since I was a child and my grandmother cooked. Joey liked it that way."

After dinner, there were lingering political debates over the last of the wine and espresso or somebody off shooting pool at one end of the living room. At the other end, twos and threes clustered on the elegant white brocade sofas to talk.

Comedian David Steinberg went to these parties. So did playwright Neil Simon, Broadway producer Harold S. Prince, actress Joan Hackett (who loved it when he called her a "broad") and Richard Mulligan, her actor-husband, the Friedmans, the Ryans, assorted wives and girl friends, the Guinzburgs and nearly everybody else on the "best friends" list.

"Joey would sit at the poker table with his back to the wall and listen," Mrs. Orbach said. "Sometimes, he'd head for the sofas. I'd see him playing host, making sure everybody was included."

What's unusual about these parties and all the conversations is that virtually none of the celebrated guests, not even the literate Mr. Guinzburg, who became his publisher, can remember anything Mr. Gallo said. Try as they will, those who are eager to talk about him (and some friends are not—mostly because of the old notoriety thing) really haven't much to say.

"He was as bright and interesting as people said," according to Mrs. Ryan, with whom he had one of his lengthy brocade-sofa talks. "He'd done a lot of thinking. It was nice to talk with somebody who'd had the time to think. I'm sorry I didn't know him better."

We know, Mrs. Ryan, but what did Joey Gallo say.

"Well, I know it's a cliche, but we talked about life. He knew so much about life's value. . . ."

Aside from the brunches, Mr. Gallo's last delicious days with the Orbachs have been somewhat exaggerated. If they were, as one report suggested, "part of the theatergoing, nightclubbing celebrity set," not many people noticed. In the 12 weeks the friendship lasted, they went to three Broadway shows and two nightclubs. They were twice at Elaine's literary saloon and twice at Sardi's, where Mrs. Peter Stone, the writer's wife, distinctly remembers meeting Mr. Gallo's mother.

"She seemed very nice," Mrs. Stone said.

Like the Orbachs, Mrs. Stone met Mr. Gallo on the telephone. Mrs. Orbach told him the Stones' dog had been stolen. Mr. Gallo offered to help find it.

"He called me up," Mrs. Stone said, "and I told him I'd had answers to my ads in the paper, and he said he'd check them out. He thought there might be a dognaping ring. I didn't meet him until he came to the apartment to go with me to see people who'd answered the ad. He wouldn't let me go alone."

Besides the nights out, the last days included Mr. Gallo's wedding at the Orbachs' townhouse—with the priest getting his name wrong and Allan Jones singing "The Lord's Prayer"—and two small dinner parties. One was at the Guinzburgs'. The other was at the Ben Gazzaras'.

When the Orbachs asked Mr. Gazzara if they might bring their friend to dinner, he knew precisely who Joey Gallo was, and he agreed.

"He served his time, didn't he," he said rhetorically.

Of such nights out and the brunches was the post-prison image of the new Pal Joey legend made. Those who met him liked him. Those who didn't either schemed, fumed privately or declared themselves unalterably opposed to dinner with a gangster. Once again, there was the question of radical chic.

While Mr. Guinzburg says, "Gangsters have always exercised a certain fascination for Society," he insists that "somehow this wasn't the same. Each of us who knew him well tried to keep him away from people who would take him up and use him badly."

To a certain extent, they succeeded. Yet the relationships remind Mafiologists of the days when Hollywood stars, including Jean Harlow, lionized "Bugsy" Siegel, and Meyer Lansky was something of a wheel in Miami society. They also smack of naiveté.

His new friends can say all they want about his "loyalty and sense of honor," his patience with little children at the pool table, his wit, his charm and his obvious intelligence, all of which may well be true—right down to the possibility of his rehabilitation. But in the end, one of the fascinations Joey Gallo held for these people was that he was a gangster, and nobody seems to have come to grips with that.

Friends in High Places

T HE MAFIA COULD NOT OPERATE so openly in many areas
of the country if it did not have friends at all levels of
government looking after its interests. These friends include cops, councilmen, mayors, state legislators and, in a few instances, congressmen. Their friendship doesn't come free, and
enormous amounts are set aside by the Mafia for corrupting
officials. In just one Harlem numbers operation, for example,
$25,000 a month, or 7.5 percent of the profit, was set aside for
graft.

In return for Mafia favors, some officials bend over backwards
to help their Mafia friends. In Florida some years ago a local sheriff
not only provided "special policing" for certain illegal gambling
casinos; he even deputized the men who drove the armored cars
carrying the casinos' profits to the bank.

In another case, in 1968, three federal agents went to Columbus, Ohio, to investigate reports of illegal gambling operations
there. No sooner had they arrived than the local police arrested
them and charged them with being drunk in public. The agents
were eventually acquitted and eight of the city policemen were
finally indicted for taking $8,000 in bribes from gamblers.

In the following chapters we are introduced to some of the
powerful friends of the Mafia. The first is James Marcus, a popular
but naive former New York City commissioner. In pursuit of the

good life Marcus turned to loansharks for money, couldn't pay back his debts and soon found himself in the pocket of the Mafia.

The second chapter demonstrates that not only individuals but entire administrations can be corrupted by the Mafia. Thomas Hoge, a reporter for the Associated Press, writes about the State of New Jersey where underworld elements have been able at times to take over entire communities, thanks to the willing cooperation of public officials.

Not all the Mafia's friends in high places are corrupt public officials. Sometimes, as in the case of Frank Sinatra, its members can use the friendship and loyalty of a man who enjoys public respect and fame to achieve what one investigator calls "innocence by association." The last chapter in this section examines the friendship of Frank Sinatra with some of the most notorious Mafiosi in the country.

17
A Good Friend at City Hall

WALTER GOODMAN

In the middle of his life's journey, James Marcus found himself in a dark wood. He entered it after a fine bright year of success, the only completely successful year that he was to know. That came in 1965, when he was 35 years old and a volunteer in John Lindsay's campaign to be mayor of New York City. The Lindsay candidacy, an attack on the city's political masters, had to be run by outsiders, many of them new to municipal give and take, and James Marcus was one of these. He did the odd jobs that came his way—mainly following up potential sources of funds and support—and he won, along with the friendship of the new mayor, a place in the City Hall establishment. For the first time in his life, he could look forward to a position of consequence.

Until that good year, Marcus had played the part of the charming failure. He grew up in Schenectady, only child of a middle-class Jewish family. His father was a lawyer and sometime assistant district attorney; his mother a busy worker in a variety of causes. In his teens, owing to parental hopes for his future or exasperation with his scholastic past, he was sent off to military school, one of those places where characters are supposedly built. His later years at Union College and at the University of Pennsylvania were a blend of social success and academic failure. He found that he was better suited to the softer pleasures of the campus than to the rigors of the classroom; his record spotted with Fs

271

and cuts, he was dropped from both institutions. The jobs he held after finishing with college were of the sort that make impressive reading on a fellow's resume but are not otherwise sustaining. He was president of a short-lived investment firm in Chicago called James, Martin & Co., which never made any money. "It was a one-man operation, overhead extremely limited, a 10-by-10 office," reports the firm's secretary-treasurer. In 1960, according to the information released when he joined the Lindsay team, he became president of Chlorodyne Chemical Company, an organization that no one has been able to track down. In 1962 he got his fanciest connection, becoming head of a subsidiary of the large and famous advertising agency, Interpublic, Inc. The subsidiary, however—called Investors Marketing Services and designed to "assist" investors—was another small operation that did not last very long. Still, it had its uses. In a press release a few years later, which Marcus carried personally from City Hall to newspaper offices, this connection would be splendidly embellished by memory: Marcus described himself as having been "president of the I.M.S. subsidiary of Interpublic, Inc., a world-wide advertising and public-relations concern." Like a new wine in an old bottle, the Marcus career seemed inviting until uncorked.

Yet Marcus had charm. He cut a handsome figure, his boyish face improved by the early gray of his hair. He took pains with his grooming and his tailoring, his style up to date but not unduly innovative, appropriate, say, to a knowing young executive in a stock-brokerage house. An acquaintance of the time describes him: "He was nice and neat. Always had a suntan, always looked like he just came out of the shower."

Marcus was naturally attracted to affluent and swinging young New Yorkers. He gained entrance into their delectable ambiance with his marriage, in June, 1962, to Lily Lodge, daughter of John Davis Lodge, former governor of Connecticut and ambassador to Spain. (Thereafter, Marcus would sometimes have himself introduced as "the son-in-law of former Connecticut Governor John Davis Lodge," or a mouthful of words to that effect. The former governor, for his part, is not known to have advertised the new connection.) Jim and Lily had met at a theatrical colony in Maine.

Among the new friends whom he owed to Lily was John Lindsay, then Congressman from New York's Silk Stocking District. They met in 1964, and Marcus, free of worldly commitments, became a volunteer in the estimable young politician's 1965 mayoralty campaign. He was no major strategist, but his social talents served him well in making contacts in his candidate's behalf. Without the Lodge key, we may fairly assume, the doors of New York Republicanism would not have opened so wide to Marcus, so disastrously wide. "I thought he was the very nice son-in-law of a wealthy Christian family," a Lindsay aide of the time recalls dryly. Though short of the stamina that would have been required to work his way up through established party ranks, in the Lindsay camp he found a ready welcome. He owed his quick progress to the lack of an operating political machine, as well as to Lindsay's predilection for young men cast in his own handsome mold; he was in fact one of the earliest products of 1965 reform politics in New York City. Once Marcus won the friendship of John Lindsay and became a person to be reckoned with, he was doomed. He might have been spared the tribulations that lay ahead if only no one had considered him worth corrupting.

New York's depleted water reservoirs made a lively campaign issue in the summer of 1965, and John Lindsay promised that, if elected, he would oust the water commissioner and replace him with a professional engineer. Regarding the water shortage, campaigner Lindsay declared, "Let the responsibility fall where it should—at the highest level," and he promised to "clean out the whole crew and get qualified professional engineers in the water department from the top to the bottom." At the top, Mayor Lindsay decided to install James Marcus. Why Marcus? Three or four qualified men were offered the post, but all declined. "Marcus was available," shrugs an important member of the early Lindsay team. "He was hanging around. No doubt there were better people for the job, but we were busy and they weren't on hand. Jim was."

What Lindsay hoped to find in Marcus in 1966 was a mayor-loyal commissioner, with perhaps some undeveloped skills. He had assisted in the campaign; he was young and personable; he was a friend; he was, more or less, a Lodge. Turning him into a commissioner was at once politically sound and personally satisfying. If John Lindsay, the Republican in a Democratic city, could trust anyone, he could trust Jim Marcus. Although he became an official assistant to the mayor in March, 1966, charged with running the

Department of Water Supply, Gas and Electricity, with its 3,000 employees, Marcus would not go onto the city's payroll until he was sworn in as commissioner the following September. For the time being, therefore, he was on no one's payroll. "I never knew what he did for a living," says a co-worker. "I just assumed he had money." It was not a question of going hungry—but the situation did have its delicate aspects. The reward of marriage to a Lodge and friendship with Lindsay (who perhaps got a feeling of security from having at his side an associate who could scorn salary) was a welcome to a very expensive stratum of New York society. To live up fully to his own appreciation of his new role, Marcus needed a lot of money.

In 1966, the unsalaried Marcus did what any smart young fellow would do under the circumstances—he played the stock market. Having discovered early that he was not cut out for workaday accomplishments, yet smitten with visions of high-riding success, Marcus was drawn insensibly to the magic of the market— that Great Reformatory for Crooks, in Finley Peter Dunne's opinion—and all that it promised. A friend recalls: "He was talking in the beginning, he was going to make five or six million dollars before two years were out." Though his investment-firm connections came to nothing, the rising stock prices of the early 1960's enabled him to do well enough with his own speculations to carry on the game at quite high stakes for a man without an income. In the spring of 1966, at the height of his career, he apparently received the ultimate tip, and went after it with everything he had and quite a bit that he didn't have. The company in question, named Xtra, was in the business of leasing piggyback containers to railroads, but for the go-go investor, the details of what a company actually makes, what services it performs, are irrelevant to the dream symbolized by its stock. On April 4, 1966, Marcus reached for that banal dream: he bought 1,000 shares of Xtra, at about $96 a share. Within a week, the stock jumped 10 points, and so Marcus, having made a fast $10,000 went all the way; he took another thousand shares, this time at about $106 a share. He did not, to be sure, have the more than $200,000 needed to pay in full for these purchases, but he did have credit with a finance company. At an interest rate of one percent a month, Koenig & Co. laid out 80 percent of the cost of the stock—around $160,000.

Marcus' account at the time held $43,000, which went toward the remaining 20 percent. Koenig kept the stock as collateral. And then, that cruel April, as though the gods of the American Stock Exchange had nothing better to do than play jokes on James Marcus, Xtra began a precipitous drop. By the end of the month, it was down to the low eighties and getting lower; by fall, it would be hovering shakily at around $40 a share. There went Marcus' millions.

As the value of the shares fell, his friends at Koenig & Co. began pressing him for cash to keep up the value of his collateral, with the regrettable but businesslike alternative that he would otherwise be sold out. Marcus had no resources of his own and no means of raising on short notice the thousands required as the stock kept slipping and the interest charges, of about $1,600 a month, kept adding up; he did borrow from relatives, friends, and friends of his wife, but the sums proved insufficient, and his relations with his father-in-law were not such as to encourage him to seek assistance in that direction. So he turned to his new, special friend, Herb Itkin.

In many ages and varied climes, the legal profession has found room for men whose careers consist of skirting, manipulating, and torturing the law. Some spend their lives in offices, more or less well appointed, pondering how the letter of a provision of the tax code may be twisted to subvert the code's spirit. Others take the courtroom for their stage and there, on any weekday afternoon, they will grind out a tear for any Mafioso who can meet their fee. Whatever our reservations as to their callings, these young men on the make and middle-aged men grown sanctimonious are part of our system; they are the testers of the law— devil's advocates perhaps, but advocates withal.

No such plea can be advanced on behalf of Herbert Itkin. Like some of his more legitimate professional kin, he practiced a law that was all fancy deals and contortionist logic—but he went further, past the hazy fringes of legality, into the bush where the lawyer does not merely stand between his client and society but becomes part of the criminal tribe.

Investing other people's money in unwholesome ventures took up more of Itkin's energies that the conventional practice of law. He seems to have gone through around $100,000 belonging to his mother-in-law. One of his early promotions involved drilling for gas in the Catskills. By the end of 1963, he concedes, he was "doing very little legal work." He was on to more exotic lines, pursuing wealth in Central America. Although his commercial connections in that part of the world remain elusive, they seem to have had to do with unsettled political conditions in Haiti and the Dominican Republic. From 1963 to 1964 he was registered with the Justice Department as a foreign agent in behalf of interests in both those lands, representing, on paper at least, an exile group known as the Provisional Government of the Republic of Haiti, based in San Juan, Puerto Rico, the Ministry of Education of the Dominican Republic, and the Dominican Ambassador to the United States. He also represented himself as attorney for Westrade, Inc., a Coral Gables, Florida, outfit which purportedly was to play a role in an effort by the Dominican Republic government to float a bond issue of $35 million. It is understood, too, that Itkin had something to do with an unsuccessful attempt in 1963 to invade Haiti from the Dominican Republic and depose the tyrant Duvalier. His interest in this enterprise was connected with the possibility of obtaining lucrative contracts in the event that Papa Doc fell and democracy triumphed.

These dashing activities, like his later activities inside the Dominican Republic around the time of the 1965 civil war, may have been sponsored, to some extent, by the Central Intelligence Agency. Itkin claims to have been recruited personally in the mid-fifties by CIA Director Allen Dulles, on the recommendation of Senator Joseph R. McCarthy, to whom he says he sent information about "crucial areas of the Far East" obtained on trips for the law firm he was connected with at the time. Later, when his area of interest shifted to Central America, he says that he found Mafiosi everywhere. They showered attentions upon him because "in their eyes I was a scheming lawyer." He became a "money-mover" for them. He claims to have remained a salaried CIA "illegal" through 1967, code name "Portio." CIA spokesmen have let it be known that Itkin's account of his relationship with the agency goes far beyond anything in their records. By their unattributable account, Itkin first came to the attention of a CIA "intelligence source" in New York City in the spring of 1962. The CIA man, a lawyer who had private business dealings with Itkin, responded to his tales of adventures in Haiti and the Dominican Republic and encouraged him to look into things down there. It was a rather casual association, Washington officials insist, which lasted for only about a year and from which Itkin derived no income. Indeed, he is reported to have complained that the CIA still owes him about $90,000 for out-of-pocket expenses.

All of the preceding, however, falls into the category of avocation. Itkin's main line of work during the 1960s was as a most untypical sort of "labor lawyer." If he was not widely known among members of the city's labor bar, that was probably due to the special nature of his specialty. He served as a conduit for the passage of bribes from needy businessmen to racketeers and accessible union officials who would then arrange for large and shakily secured mortgage loans to the businessmen out of union funds. "We couldn't say no to the hoods," explains Itkin—the "we" taking in the U.S. government. "We were using them in CIA activities." In these cases, Itkin endeavored to keep one and a half to two percent of the amount of the mortgage for himself. "He was really making it in 1961 and 1962," recalls his first wife. "He would bring home stacks of bills and he would give me half and say, 'This is for you. Put it in the safety-deposit box.'" At one time, she reports, there was $100,000 in that box. (On the occasion of his wife's birthday in 1962, Itkin presented her with a Macy's shopping bag filled with $25,000 in $5 bills.)

The greater part of the many billions of dollars now invested in private pension and welfare plans for the nation's workers is, we may presume, in honest hands, but government regulation in the area is distinguished by its loopholes. Through these have leaped such labor irregulars as Herbert Itkin.

He developed a reputation as a man with connections who, for a price, could obtain a mortgage. But perhaps Itkin began to feel some intimations of mortality and thought of the FBI as a kind of insurance firm. J. Edgar Hoover, after all, might protect one from the vengeance of the lawless as well as from the retribution of the law. "I was in with the hoods," says Itkin. "What a shot! Who else was going to take the chance?" And so in March, 1963, he was passed along to the FBI by the CIA, rather as sportive aristocrats once traded mistresses, and became a "voluntary federal informant," which the FBI defines as "an individual, a citizen, who offers to furnish us information on a confidential basis, with no promise of a reward of any type."

Such was the delicacy of his relationship with the FBI that during their five years together he was able to collect tens of thousands of tax-free dollars from illicit operations. He relayed "just highlights" of his activities. The deals he reported, he reported after the fact; he elaborated upon the parts that others played, but scanted his own contribution. No one can remember his ever giving up any of his share of the payoff money; the closest he came was the time he handed over to his FBI contact the wrappers from two piles of bills. Generally, reports the contact, he "told me about these deals after they were completed and he had disbursed the proceeds." The FBI, which acknowledges giving him only a few thousand dollars for expenses, accepted what he chose to tell.

So happy a resolution between the appetites of the body and the needs of the spirit is not given to many men. A couple of times a week, Itkin, voluntary unpaid informer No. 3936C, code name "Mr. Jerry," would make partial confession to an FBI agent. "We met in a restaurant," reports the agent, "public places generally, for short periods of time generally. He was constantly on the move. He was meeting so many people and dealing with so many people." With no injunction to do penance, lawyer Itkin would at once return to his trade. Not, we may be sure, without a sense of honor. Asked whether, in setting up escrow accounts for loan-seeking businessmen and then using the funds therein as bribes to union functionaries, he was not violating his trust as an attorney, Itkin replies in the negative on the grounds that the escrow accounts were fraudulent to begin with and he was only doing what was expected when he milked them. Asked how he could reconcile his attachment to the FBI with the fact that he profited from the criminal conspiracies he had undertaken to wipe out, he replies: "I had to live and I had to further my infiltration. . . . Either you go to the Copa with them [Mafiosi] and spend money or they won't go along with you." In his heart Itkin knew he was doing right: "I felt in my heart that every bit of information that I finally accumulated I would eventually turn over to the FBI."

Marcus and Itkin came together first in the early summer of

1965, just a few weeks after John Lindsay's announcement that he was a candidate for mayor. The intermediary was Oscar A. Bloustein, one of the lawyers who shared offices with Itkin at 300 Madison Avenue. Bloustein wanted to help in the campaign but preferred to do so "behind the scenes," out of regard for the position of his brother, then a member of the city's Planning Commission. "Where do you need help?" he asked, and when Marcus mentioned union endorsements, not often bestowed on Republican candidates in New York City, Bloustein introduced him to Itkin—"I am sure he can help you with labor unions."

Their friendship took fire at once. To Itkin, Marcus must have seemed a prize from the gods. The relationship with the Lodges and with the Lindsays, which Marcus took no pains to conceal, suggested large quantities of money and pull, basic ingredients in the Itkin way of life. Marcus was irresistible. But Itkin was not without appeals of his own for the neophyte politician and faltering operator. Itkin *knew* things. He knew people and powers and where the action was and where the bodies were buried and whose closets housed which skeletons. Where tips were to be had, Itkin would have them, and Marcus, the eternal outsider who wanted more than anything to be inside, had faith in tips. Soon, Itkin was a frequent visitor to Lindsay headquarters in the Hotel Roosevelt, and by November, election month, he and Marcus would be seeing one another almost daily. On Fridays, Marcus would pick up Itkin's children by his first wife and deliver them to their father for their weekend visit.

Itkin, if one may believe him on this inconsequential point, early invested $6,000 of his second wife's money in Xtra on Marcus' promise that the stock was about to "skyrocket." When it began its descent toward the end of April, 1966, and Koenig & Co. pressed Marcus for more cash to keep up his margin, Marcus turned for advice to Itkin, who had become his mentor in many things. Itkin's advice in 1966 was to this effect: instead of selling out and taking his loss—which at that stage would have been in the neighborhood of $40,000, substantial but manageable—Marcus should hold on, keep faith, and borrow in prospects that "perhaps the stock will come back." Moreover, Itkin the insider would undertake to arrange the needed loan. This he would do as a sign of their abiding friendship, with the understanding that should the stock one day indeed rise, he, Itkin, would share equally in the profits. Infatuated with the prospects of Xtra, determined not to take his loss and quit, Marcus could not appreciate what he did to himself when he agreed to this course. By giving up half his profits and by committing himself to months of interest payments over and above what he was already paying to Koenig & Co., he reduced drastically the possibility that he could still, somehow, come out ahead. Itkin, for his part, could hardly come out behind. If there were a loss, Marcus would suffer the brunt of it. If there were a gain, Itkin would share as a full partner. Yet what choice did James Marcus have? How could he admit defeat again? Casting about for the money needed to keep this young partnership afloat, Itkin turned to Daniel J. Motto.

At the age of 57, when he was arrested for his part in the Marcus-Itkin affair, Motto's face held the story of his career, the tough, soft, twisted face, the tight mouth, the slitted untrusting eyes. During World War II, he was convicted of black-market operations in gasoline-ration coupons, getting off with a suspended sentence of a year and a day and a fine of $1,000. He was a creature of racketeers; in their behalf he lent his radiant name to the executive board of the American-Italian Anti-Defamation League, an organization established to spare the Cosa Nostra a bad press. He complained of ulcers. It was fated that the labor consultant Itkin and the labor official Motto, president of Queens Local 350 of the Bakery, Confectionary and Food International Union, should find one another, even in so large a metropolis as New York. They existed in the same element and operated by the same rules. Local 350, which has about 900 members in bakeries around the city, was separated from labor's mainstream some years ago, owing to its Mafiosic propensities. On a recorded annual salary of $13,250, Motto had managed to acquire a $57,000 house in Greenwich, Connecticut, and a stable of trotters, as well as a new-model Oldsmobile, with his initials on the license plate. He and Itkin met, probably at a union dinner, around 1964, and soon they were collaborating on small pieces of business.

Motto was able to supply some of the money that Marcus needed in the spring of 1966 to replenish his fast-deteriorating account with Koenig & Co. The approach was made by Itkin, Marcus' new partner in Xtra. He asked for $25,000. Motto agreed to a loan of $20,000, in words, as Itkin recalls, more or less like these: "Well, maybe I will lend you the money, but I want to know something first. Lindsay hasn't done a thing for me up to now, and I have been trying to get to see him and can't even get to see him." Motto put two conditions on his loan: a specific one—a guarantee that his friend Charlie Imperial would be kept in his job; and a general one—assurance that Marcus intended "to play ball with me."

Motto had to be pressed to come up with the promised sum—but by May he had handed over $19,500 in two installments to Itkin and to Itkin's young helper Charles Rappaport. This counted as a loan of $20,000, the remaining $500 serving as Motto's interest, deducted in advance in the manner of lending institutions the world over. In addition, according to Itkin, Motto demanded to be shown a letter from Marcus and Itkin stating that $15,000 worth of stock was being purchased in Itkin's behalf, with the thought that the lender would share in the profits if, by some chance, the stock should go up. The terms were exceedingly generous by Motto's standards of moneylending, interest being computed at just 13 percent per annum. Later in the year, the Marcus-Itkin combine would borrow another $5,000 from him; for this, according to Marcus, they would pay the more customary two percent a week interest, or "vigorish" as it is known in the trade. Motto was but one of the lenders who helped keep the commissioner afloat. Through the services of Itkin, Marcus was able to borrow at least $5,000, at the prevailing rate of 104 percent a year, from a loan shark in the fall of 1966—and feel himself fortunate since this entrepreneur was at about the same time charging 260 percent for loans to another of Itkin's associates.

In June, 1966, when Motto was already dunning him for repayment of the lately loaned $20,000, Marcus agreed to attend a convention of the regional council of the bakery-workers union. Motto was up for the presidency of the regional group, which took in locals in six Eastern states, and he thought it might make a good impression on the boys to have a pal of John Lindsay at his side. So it came to pass that on the afternoon of June 18, 1966, Mr. and Mrs. Marcus drove to Atlantic City from their summer home on Long Beach Island and joined Mr. and Mrs. Motto at the Colony Motel. There Mrs. Motto told of her troubles in getting her daughter into a good school in Greenwich and asked the former Lily Lodge whether she might help out. For an hour or so, Motto shepherded the Marcuses around the motel lobby, introducing the delegate bakery workers to the commissioner presumptive, and then he took his guest alone into a corner and, as was his custom, pressed him for favors. By now, in June, the main favor on Motto's mind had to do with the Jerome Park reservoir.

In November, 1965, hard upon John Lindsay's election as mayor, residents of the Bronx and parts of Manhattan were annoyed to find dirt in their drinking water. It was altogether appropriate that there be muck at the bottom of the reservoir, which serves as a storage basin for water from the Croton watershed; that is one of the reasons for its existence. It holds the water—which would otherwise go to waste, but may now be delivered to householders' faucets at peak need—long enough so that organic and inorganic material carried down from Croton can settle to the bottom. Leaves, dust, and soot also settle and undergo natural decomposition. Over the decades, this material, 175,000 cubic yards of it, had turned into a fluid grayish-black sludge blanket for the reservoir bottom, and bits of that blanket were finding their way into the drinking water of Bronxites.

In February, 1966, the Water Department's chief engineer recommended that for the first time in its existence the reservoir be drained and the muck removed. The draining and cleaning of a reservoir that covered more than 96 acres, was 23 feet deep, and held 773 million gallons of water represented a project of considerable proportions. Such an undertaking was beyond the capacity of the department; a private contractor would have to be hired.

The City of New York uses three main methods for hiring contractors. By the first, a formal contract containing plans and specifications and approved by the city's Corporation Counsel is publicly advertised for bids from private firms. By the second, where the sum involved is less than $2,500, the contract is informal; several firms are invited to bid and the job goes to the low bidder. The third method, in which James Marcus would receive an education, employs an emergency contract, the job being awarded by the commissioner of a department without public advertisement—on a cost-plus basis.

In March, Acting Water Commissioner Marcus received from

his engineers the recommendation that an emergency contract be issued for the cleaning and repair of the Jerome Park reservoir. Marcus seems not to have understood immediately the quality of the gift that was being handed to him. Like a freshly developing maiden, he required the attentions of new admirers before he could put a proper value on his own endowments.

No sooner did the hustling Itkin hear of the big emergency contract than he hustled back to Marcus. We have Itkin's version of their conversation:

"I said, 'Jim, Danny wants us to work on a big reservoir contract. I understand it is something that is going to be the biggest ever given out. Are you going to play with us?'

"And Jim said, 'How did you hear about it?'

"And I said, 'I don't know. I guess it is all over the street. The people in the know know.'"

Marcus did not miss the drift of Motto's message: "I understood him to mean that he would find a contractor or negotiate with a contractor and there would be a kickback." Perhaps it can be taken as a sign of residual grace that Marcus had not brought the emergency contract to Itkin's attention during the preceding weeks, and that even now he sought to hedge, although escape was out of the question for him. "I just heard about it myself," he protested, feebly and untruthfully. Then, according to Itkin, he added: "Let us not push too hard. Danny waited on the money. Let us wait a little on this."

But Itkin was nothing if not a hard pusher: "I don't know what good that is going to do us. Do you want to play ball with him or not?"

They talked, and whatever qualms or hopes of redemption Marcus may have had fell away. Inevitably, he said, "Yes, I will."

The fact was that Daniel Motto, despite his fine house, his trotters, and his political connections in Queens, was a small star in the Cosa Nostra universe. No *capo* he; not even a *subcapo*; not even a *caporegime*. His position relative to the dominant Mafia families was something of an in-law. He could arrange a brokerage fee on a union insurance plan, steer a client to an Itkin, make a two-percent-a-week loan, put in a good word for a pal in the municipal employ—but when it came to a serious swindle, he would defer to his betters. Motto's particular mover was Antonio (Tony

Ducks) Corallo. Despite a mythology which pictures the Mafia as a centralized bureaucracy of crime, its politics owe less to Rome than to Florence. Friends and cousins and sons-in-law move in on one another as opportunity permits, make alliances and ignore them, take sides in feuds, cultivate old grudges—that is, they conduct themselves more like kinsmen than like statesmen. We may think of Daniel Motto as a small city-state existing by the grace of Tony Ducks.

Known to some of his associates as "The Doctor" and described by one student of Cosa Nostra affairs as "a loan shark's loan shark," Corallo had a considerable reputation in the Motto-Itkin circle and beyond. He is 53 years old when he enters our story, and his life's progress can be measured by his record of convictions. He served time in his youth for trafficking in narcotics and in his maturity for attempting to bribe a judge in a bankruptcy proceeding. Depending on the story one prefers, the sobriquet "Tony Ducks" commemorated his escape from an attempted assassination or from merited convictions. Such was his distinction by January, 1967, that he was ejected from England by Scotland Yard on the basis of reputation alone shortly after his arrival in the company of his new friend, Herbie Itkin, and a reputed strong-arm type named Tommy Mancuso, the three of them apparently drawn to those shores by the opportunities inherent in legalized gambling.

In May, 1966, Itkin had his first meeting with Antonio Corallo at the Pancake House in Queens. Itkin, who knew Corallo by reputation, received a candid introduction. Motto presented him as "the guy that's going to handle these contracts with the city with us." No matters of substance were discussed at this first meeting—but, at parting, Corallo somewhat patronizingly confirmed the fresh relationship. He said, "I'm glad you're going to work on the contracts with us." Itkin reported back to Marcus that he had met "a high guy"—which Marcus understood to mean "the top of the Mafia."

A few days later, at the diner near Motto's office, there was a more substantive meeting of Itkin, Motto, and Corallo. Corallo announced: "Here's what we're going to do. Joe Pizzo, who is the labor-relations consultant for Henry Fried and Mackay Construction, is going to handle this for us. He's been in a lot of deals with Henry."

Henry Fried, proprietor of Mackay Trucking Co. and S. T. Grand, was big-time. To intercede for him with the commissioner, he chose no less an emissary than Vincent Albano, the Manhattan Republican Party chairman and political patron of John Lindsay. In the weeks preceding his inauguration, Marcus was contacted "on numerous occasions" by Albano with reference to Fried and the reservoir contract. He knew and valued the uses of personal contact and Vincent Albano obliged him in October by inviting Marcus for a drink at the Hilton Hotel, where the Republican organization was then quartered for the 1966 Rockefeller gubernatorial campaign. There, in the Bourbon Room of the Hilton, the introduction was made.

Marcus provides the gist of the conversation: "Mr. Albano said that if I could give the job of Jerome Park reservoir to Mr. Fried, he would be very appreciative. That Mr. Fried had always been a heavy contributor to the Republican Party, and any work that I could give Mr. Fried, he would be very appreciative." No money payment was alluded to at this meeting; the solicitation was political. As Marcus explains, ". . . when you get called in by the county chairman and asked to give the job to a certain company, you get the message." Marcus acted upon the message by recommending Fried and firm to other city officials.

The dropping of the name of Vincent Albano in among such names as Corallo and Motto at the June, 1968, trial caused agitation in the city's Republican establishment. A response was called for, and so an "informal study" was undertaken by two of Chairman Albano's more prominent peers on the G.O.P. county committee, Judge Bruce Bromley and Peter M. Brown, a Wall Street lawyer. They took care to note that no criminal act was involved, but concluded that "so far as considerations of propriety are involved it seems to us unwise and probably unethical for political leaders in the position and of the stature of Mr. Albano to introduce substantial contributors or any person to government officials for the purpose of aiding the persons involved in doing business with the city or government agency." Yet it came as something of a puzzle when Mayor Lindsay issued a statement commending Judge Bromley and Mr. Brown for their public service and agreeing with them as to the desirability of precluding "even the impression of impropriety or ethical compromise"—only to add: "Their finding of no wrong-doing confirms the personal and political integrity of

Vincent Albano." The Mayor went further: "Mr. Albano has underscored this by his progressive approach to public affairs, his complete cooperation with Judge Bromley and Mr. Brown, and by his public endorsement of their recommendations." With a stroke of the pen, the compromised had been transformed into the occasion's guest of honor, an exemplar to us all.

Although the act of bestowing a medal on a politician for helping to lead a public official astray was unbecoming in a man of John Lindsay's quality, his predicament was not easy. Vincent Albano had sponsored him at the outset of his political career, when he ran successfully as an insurgent Republican for the congressional seat from New York's 17th district. Eleven years later, after the liberal Lindsay lost his party's mayoralty nomination to a conservative from Staten Island, Vincent Albano stood by him. One does not subject such a friend, particularly when he still holds his party post, to the discourtesy of public criticism.

At the dinner meeting in May, Corallo asked Itkin, "How much do you want?" Itkin, relaying the question to his partner, confessed: "I don't know what the going price is. I really don't know how much to ask." And if Itkin, the professional, was puzzled on this point, what could have been expected of the amateur Marcus? The two resorted to simple arithmetic to calculate an answer for Corallo. Their partnership had debts outstanding at the time of about $75,000. Estimating that the reservoir contract would come in at around a million dollars, Marcus settled on a cut of seven and a half percent as being just enough to meet his needs. In Itkin's phrase, "$75,000 in green."

It was now June of 1966, the beginning of a summer lull in the conspirings. Marcus and Itkin met twice more with Motto. At the end of June, Marcus accompanied Itkin to the Dominican Republic for the inauguration of President Balaguer. They returned home for the weekend of July 4th, and Marcus joined his family on holiday while Itkin went off on one of his mysterious journeys for most of July. The first weeks of August found Marcus vacationing in Maine, and so it was not until the middle of the month that he began to receive hints that all was not going well, that the fee he had set for his compliance might prove unrealistic.

In September the case was put to Itkin bluntly by Motto and Corallo. They met at the Loren East restaurant on the East Side of Manhattan and at the Pancake House in Queens. At one of these sessions, Itkin was told, "Look, 15 percent is just too much for Henry Fried to pay, and we can't get this amount. We just can't get it." Itkin was taken aback. It had not occurred to him, nor certainly to Marcus, that their associates would tack another seven and a half percent onto their seven and a half percent and make a demand of Fried which even they in their hopefulness recognized was excessive. In fact, it seems not to have occurred to either Marcus or Itkin that the Corallo-Motto team planned to ask for anything above the somewhat arbitrarily set fee. Itkin confesses that he was reluctant to bring the 15 percent news back to Marcus, but after a while, under Motto's naggings, he did.

Tuesday, September 27, 1966, was an important day for James Marcus, a day of ceremony and conspiracy, when in the space of a few hours he swore allegiance to the people of New York and took part in a meeting dedicated to betraying the trust he had barely assumed. That Tuesday, at eleven o'clock in the morning, Marcus, generously described for press purposes as "a 35-year-old banker and businessman," was sworn in as the city's Commissioner of the Department of Water Supply, Gas and Electricity, at an annual salary of $25,000 and perquisites. He issued a call to civic consciousness: "I hope and urge that New Yorkers will conserve water to the best of their ability." Itkin, who had spent the morning with Motto, attended the solemn event in the Board of Estimate room at City Hall. As the congratulations died away, he whispered to his friend that a meeting had been set up for that afternoon with their accomplices.

At the Loren East that afternoon, Marcus and Itkin and Corallo brooded together over the difficulties of coming to an agreement with S. T. Grand. Corallo, who did the talking for his half of the combine, suggested that the other half was asking for too much money. The conversation, as received from Itkin, then went as follows:

"Jim said, 'I understand you are asking for 15 percent. No wonder we haven't got a contract.'

"Tony said, 'Don't you think we deserve it too? We are the ones taking the risk. We are picking up the green.'

"Marcus said, 'Well, I guess it is all right, but what about the loan Herb has talked to you about?'

"Tony said, 'Well, if you come down, I think there is going to be a deal, and I will lend you the ten.'

"I think I was the one who said, 'All right, Jim, what about five percent?'"

"And Jim said, 'Okay, five percent.'"

Corallo, a frequent visitor to Itkin's office now, dropped by a day or so after the inauguration to tell him that the deal was dead. Henry Fried had turned down the 10-percent figure—five percent for Marcus-Itkin, five percent for Corallo-Pizzo-Motto.

A few days later, in a luncheonette near where he customarily parked to pick up his wife after her day's work, Motto repeated this message at a meeting with Corallo and Itkin. He wanted a go-ahead from Corallo: "Look, Tony, I know I can get it, and there is no doubt in my mind—but I can't get more than five percent. Now, is this going to be satisfactory to the commissioner and is it going to be satisfactory to you?"

Corallo, The Doctor, replied, "If that's the best you can do, that's the best you can do, and the commissioner will just have to go along with us." For many years Corallo had made a livelihood out of knowing who would go along and under what circumstances; he needed only two conversations with Marcus to make his judgment.

Still, on receiving the dismaying news from Itkin, Marcus threatened halfheartedly to back out. But Itkin had only to remind him of Corallo's promise of the $10,000 loan and he succumbed. He did, however, add that there was one thing he wanted understood: "I want three percent and the rest of you can share two percent." Such was the force of his personality that Itkin would wait some weeks before relaying this proviso to Corallo. At first, early in October, at the Loren East, he merely reported to Tony that Marcus had given his okay, and received for the news an envelope containing $10,000; this, together with $5,000 more from Motto, went to Koenig & Co. (In a break with ordinary business practice, Corallo's loan was apparently repaid without vigorish.)

The second business meeting between Corallo and Marcus took place in mid-October, soon after Motto had triumphantly notified Itkin, "You've got your deal. It is closed at five percent with Henry Fried." Marcus and Itkin drove together, in the commissioner's official car, to the Tower East restaurant at 72nd Street and Third Avenue, where Itkin went inside to "see if everything is clear." Everything was not clear; the busy Corallo had some friends or associates with him, and he told Itkin to wait. This scene, of the New York City commissioner waiting in his car outside a restaurant at the pleasure of a Mafioso, encapsules the Marcus-Corallo relationship. After 15 or 20 minutes, Corallo came forth to confirm the $10,000 investment and to make the point for which Marcus had been summoned uptown: "Well, now that we have done Jerome Park, can we do some other things?"

The commissioner replied, "Yes, we can." According to Itkin, he added, "Thanks, Tony."

So it came about that shortly before Thanksgiving Day, 1966, S. T. Grand, Henry Fried presiding, was awarded the contract to clean the Jerome Park reservoir. The Jerome Park deal had now been made, the contract let. On December 5, 1966, S. T. Grand's bulldozers began their attack on the long-accumulated sludge of the drained reservoir; and, in Marcus' words, "We were looking to get paid."

The total contract, as it turned out, would amount to $841,316—five percent of which, owed by Fried to the combine, came to something over $42,000. The Marcus-Itkin share was to be roughly $28,000, down somewhat from the $75,000 that had danced in their heads the previous spring. And even this reduced sum would never find its way to them in full.

On the occasion of the fifth payment, in the middle of May, Corallo directed that Motto bring $5,000 to Itkin's office. There, with Itkin present and Marcus waiting in another room, Corallo made his move: "Put the money down on the table and let me explain something. I haven't been getting my share. I've laid out a lot of money in other things. I want it off the top now." Then, amid some bickering, he coolly pocketed most of the cash, leaving just $500 for Marcus-Itkin.

"This is insane!" protested Itkin, and he warned that the commissioner, who was pacing without, would be displeased.

Not noticeably affrighted, Corallo said, "Well, go tell him, and tell him that we just had a lot of expenses."

Marcus, as foreseen, was displeased. He roused himself to a boyish threat: "That's the last deal I'm going through with these fellows."

The end of Itkin's fading relationship with James Marcus was foreshadowed in September, 1967, when the district attorney invited the commissioner in to discuss certain matters to which investigators had been drawn. Their interest was piqued in particular by a deposit of $55,000 which had been added to Marcus' account with Koenig & Co. in October, 1966. When Marcus told Itkin of his visit to the district attorney—"They are asking me questions that I am going to find impossible to answer"—Itkin replied with one of those exquisite sentences that become classics at the moment they are uttered. Said Itkin to Marcus: "You're in a lot of trouble."

In the weeks that followed, Itkin became more helpful. Marcus attributes to him the inspiration for his explanation to the district attorney that the $55,000 had come from his father. (Itkin refuses credit for this limp tale. It was Marcus' brain child, he maintains—which, if so, makes it one of the few original ideas that Marcus seems to have come up with during their entire acquaintance.) In December, 1967, when Marcus, back to the wall now, was ready to go to the FBI—"All I wanted to do was go there and tell my story"—Itkin was more than ready to go with him. They went together to the office at 201 East 69th Street, where Itkin presented Marcus to his Special Agent. Though Marcus insists that the decision was his alone, the fact that he chose to tell his story to the FBI rather than to the district attorney (and, in fact, perjured himself before a New York County grand jury) bespeaks Itkin's influence. On the model of Baron Munchausen, who was able to leap from cannonball to flying cannonball until he was carried safely back to his home camp, Itkin had managed to ride his criminal deals as long as possible, and when that became impossible, he jumped onto his deals with the law. James Marcus was the trophy that Herbert Itkin brought home from the jungle.

The tale of the amiably vicious alliance that feeds upon our cities does not begin and end with James Marcus and Herbert Itkin. Indeed, what makes this pair special is that they were *unsound*. Had they only known how to behave, Marcus might still be a municipal official and Henry Fried, the contractor, would be a happier man. We owe our glimpse into the enduring system of favors, pressures, and bribes to an odd set of circumstances—and the reader may be left wondering how many deals are completed around the land each day in which no revealing accident intervenes.

18
New Jersey
—The Friendly State

THOMAS A. HOGE

On July 22, 1970, Hugh J. Addonizio, mayor of Newark, New Jersey's biggest city, was sentenced to ten years imprisonment on kickback conspiracy charges involving the Mafia.

In 1971 Thomas J. Whelan, mayor of Jersey City, was convicted of conspiring with the Mafia to extort money from companies doing business with city and county governments in that state.

The same year, Mayor John R. Armellino of West New York, New Jersey, was sentenced to four years on charges of conspiring to protect gambling operations of the Cosa Nostra.

These cases and half a dozen others involving Jersey public officials have brought to light the most sweeping domination of local government by the Mafia that has been uncovered in many years. It is a classic example of how the Mob can eventually take over a state—lock, stock and barrel.

The first indication that the Mafia had reached Jersey politicians on such a wide scale came in 1969 when tapes secretly planted in the headquarters of several of the state's leading racketeers by the FBI were made public on orders of a federal judge.

One revealing recording carried a conversation between Angelo "Ray" De Carlo, a Mafia captain, and one of his aides, Joseph "Little Joe" De Benedictis. At one point, De Carlo was overheard telling De Benedictis, "Hugie (Addonizio) helped us along. He gave us the city."

The tapes also told how the Mafia went about scaring off rival candidates who planned to run against Addonizio. De Carlo warned one such hopeful that unless he desisted at once, "I'll be the guy to break your legs."

It was the same story all over Jersey. In Old Tappan, Police Chief Charles G. Shuh and all four members of his force were indicted in 1970 on charges of taking payoffs from a Mafia enforcer. In Elizabeth, District Court Judge Ralph De Vita was convicted the same year of offering a $10,000 payoff to a prosecutor to dismiss a case against two underworld figures.

In 1971 the minority leader of the State Assembly, David J. Friedland, was barred from practicing law for six months after he had been accused of acting as middleman in obtaining dismissal of criminal charges against a Mafia enforcer and loan shark.

The widespread corruption in New Jersey and the dominant role played by the Mafia moved former federal prosecutor Frederick B. Lacey to declare that "The plunder was unmatched by anything in my experience."

What shocked the people of New Jersey most perhaps was the case of Addonizio who, before his election as mayor of America's 13th largest city, had served for 14 years in Congress.

A wave of revulsion swept the state when a federal grand jury indicted Addonizio and 14 others, including 10 public officials and a Mafia leader, on charges of sharing $1.5 million worth of kickbacks extorted from contractors doing business with the city of Newark.

Prosecutor Lacey declared in his summation that the defendants had been guilty of "cold-blooded, calculating, contemptuous corruption. . . ."

Replying to the defense contention that Addonizio had "built a wall of ignorance" around the mayor's office, the prosecutor asserted that "the stench of corruption would have penetrated any such wall."

In pronouncing sentence, Federal District Judge George H. Barlow declared that Addonizio had committed crimes of "monumental proportion that tore at the very heart of our civilized society and our form of representative government." He concluded that "the corruption disclosed here is compounded by the frightening alliance of criminal elements and public officials."

How was such an alliance born? Why was the Mob drawn in the first place to New Jersey, a small state which had been laughingly referred to as a cow pasture between New York and Philadelphia? Whatever the reason, FBI tapes made clear that Jersey had long been the playground of the Mafia.

Some hold the view that Prohibition started it all, since Jersey has a long coastline—ideal for running in liquor by night. One imaginative plan dreamed up in bootleg days was to run a pipeline to shore from beyond the three-mile limit, but like many enterprising schemes, it never got off the ground. The Prohibition theory may explain why the late Mafia chief, Vito Genovese, settled in the Atlantic Highlands, a community originally organized by the Methodist church, but one which is on the highest point on the Atlantic Coast south of Maine and provided an excellent view of rum-running ships at sea.

Other Mafia-watchers blame the completion of the George Washington Bridge which provided easy access to New York and may have accounted for some of the baronial estates Mafia bosses have along the Palisades.

Still others say that the Mob headed for New Jersey in the 1930s when they were fleeing from New York's gangbusting District Attorney, Thomas E. Dewey. In this context, it will be recalled that when New York's crusading mayor, Fiorello H. La Guardia, set out to clean up his city before World War II, he announced over the radio that he was chasing all the "tinhorns" out of New York "over the bridge" into Jersey.

There was one flaw in La Guardia's crusade: The "tinhorns" were actually the elite of the underworld, millionaire barons who found the pickings delightful and the climate salubrious in New Jersey.

The early settlers in New Jersey had few common ideas about government and no alliances by which to govern themselves. As a result, they settled into separate pockets to preserve their own identity. They included Swedes who had crossed the ocean to settle in Delaware and the Dutch who had conned the Indians out of Manhattan. Gradually both Swedes and Dutch spilled over into the cow pasture that was Jersey—the Swedes in the south and the Dutch in the north. They were followed by Englishmen fed up with the Puritan fanaticism of New England. In later years, there came the Irish fleeing the potato famine in their homeland, and finally, Italians.

These ethnic groups stuck together to preserve their cultural identity, and from the potpourri was grown the doctrine of home rule. Under this system, the county emerged as a dominant force in Jersey politics, undermining the authority of the governor and the attorney general. The system gave power to a nonelective county boss who, if he was corrupt, could provide an effective shield for organized crime.

The union between organized crime and civic dictatorship reached full flower during the 30-year reign of Frank "I Am The Law" Hague, mayor of Jersey City. Hague could perform miracles with money that no one has since matched. On an official income of $7,500 a year, he was able, over a seven-year period, to save enough to purchase real estate worth $392,910.50. It included, incidentally, a mansion on the Jersey shore and one in Florida.

Hague's counterpart in southern Jersey was Enoch L. "Nockey" Johnson who for 29 years ruled Atlantic County, Atlantic City, as county treasurer until he was packed off to jail in 1941 for tax evasion.

"When I lived well, everyone lived well," said Nockey, an outspoken soul whose take from gambling, bootlegging and prostitution was said to have exceeded half a million dollars a year. He tooled around the countryside in a chauffeur-driven $14,000 limousine painted powder blue.

The Jersey mobsters began to thrive after Prohibition went into effect in the 1920s. For them, the Noble Experiment was manna from heaven. The good citizens of New York and Philadelphia developed a colossal thirst for illegal spirits, a thirst rivaled by the yearning of the people of New Jersey itself. And the state, with its numerous creeks and rivers that meandered deep into pine forests, provided an ideal refuge for the rum-runner.

How many thousands of gallons of whiskey and gin flowed in across the isolated beaches or were unloaded onto trucks at sites up remote streams will never be known. Suffice it to say the traffic was huge and there reportedly was considerable cooperation from the law. One legend has it that a convivial county sheriff used to ride shotgun on the bootleg trucks as they rumbled past the courthouse.

Newark was only a short truck haul from the speakeasies of Manhattan and soon became the bootleg capital of the eastern seaboard. With such a lucrative racket, competition was more than keen. It was deadly. Dutch Schultz, the beer baron, was gunned down while washing his hands in a Newark tavern.

From the gangland wars of the era, two powerful figures emerged—a Jew named Abner (Longie) Zwillman and an Italian, Ruggiero (Richie the Boot) Boiardo, who had worked his way high up in the ranks of the Mafia. Zwillman, who had become one of the most powerful bootleggers along the East Coast, soon began to feel himself crowded by Boiardo, a flashy Mafioso who sported a $5,000 diamond-studded belt buckle and wielded political control in Newark's old First Ward.

The blowoff was inevitable, but before it came, Longie and the Boot announced in 1930 that they had settled their differences. The two Mob chiefs sealed their newborn friendship by throwing a party that lasted two days and is still being talked about. Among the politicians who helped celebrate were a former U.S. commissioner and a candidate for the State Assembly. Another guest was a Democrat running for Congress who lived to regret that he had ever attended the bash and been indiscreet enough to have his picture taken with the Boot resplendent in his bejewelled belt buckle. The Congressional candidate was Paul Moore, and his rival, the late representative Fred Hartley, had thousands of copies of the picture distributed in the Eighth Congressional District. Moore commented later that the photograph of him and the Boot had played a large part in his defeat at the polls.

The Boot was having troubles of his own. Shortly after his feast of friendship with Longie, he stepped out into Broad Street and was promptly riddled by a hail of bullets. Sixteen slugs entered the Boot's body and he doubtless would have been a candidate for the undertaker except for the diamond belt buckle. "The shot that almost certainly would have killed him, ripping through his intestines, hit that belt buckle and ricocheted away," said a man who remembered the incident.

Richie recovered, but, ironically, he was sent to prison for 2½ years because he had been carrying a gun himself when he was attacked. Out again after 16 months, he returned to his old job as leader of the First Ward. At this point he and Longie apparently agreed to split up Newark between them and there was no more intramural warfare. Years later, Longie was found hanging in the basement of his elegant home in West Orange. It was ruled a suicide although there was nothing nearby that he could have jumped from.

The law's effectiveness in Jersey in the days when Longie and the Boot were dividing the spoils was illustrated in 1939 when the State Alcoholic Beverage Control office homed in on Richie. It seemed that the A.B.C. felt that, as a convicted gangster, the Boot had no business operating a tavern (called the Vittoria Castle). In the hearings that ensued, however, Boiardo received sterling character references from some high police officials. Acting Captain Joseph Cocozza of the Essex County Prosecutor's staff testified that he and his wife frequently had dinner with Boot and his spouse, adding that "We have never connected him with any gang in our work." The deputy police chief in Newark and the sergeant in charge of the morals squad joined in, testifying that Richie was only "trying to earn an honest living."

In sharp contrast to this chorus of praise were government transcripts covering four years of surveillance of Mafia boss Simone Rizzo (Sam the Plumber) De Cavalcante. These tapes gave an enlightening picture of the Boot. One tape, according to the FBI, recorded a conversation involving the Plumber, Ray De Carlo and Ànthony (Tony Boy) Boiardo, son of the Boot. It went thus:

> TONY BOY: How about the time we hit the little Jew. . . .
> RAY: As little as they are, they struggle.
> TONY BOY: The Boot hit him with a hammer. The guy goes down and comes up. So I got a crowbar this big, Ray. Eight shots in the head. What do you think he finally did to me? He spit at me and said, "You ———."

The tapes also gave a chilling picture of the goings on at the great stone mansion inhabited by the Boot on a wooded plot of several acres in Livingston, New Jersey. They explained perhaps why the house was set so far back from the road and was screened so thoroughly by shrubbery. The estate boasted lifesize statues of Richie and his family on a series of pedestals in the garden, but more significant, the tape carried a graphic description of an incinerator for human bodies that was situated at the rear of the

Joseph Gallo ("Crazy Joe") contemplating his bride, Sina, as she is cutting their wedding cake on March 16, 1972, less than a month before Gallo was killed.
Pictorial Parade—Tim Boxer

Joey Gallo was shot at Umberto's Clam House in New York's "Little Italy" section on April 7, 1972. *Above:* Exterior of the restaurant that was the scene of the murder. *Right:* View of the restaurant's interior; in foreground, right, is the table at which Gallo sat at the time of the shooting. *Wide World Photos*

...asket containing the body of Joey Gallo, being carried out of St. Charles Church, Brook-
...n, on April 10, 1972. Mrs. Gallo, the widow, stands in the entrance wearing dark glasses.

Joseph Profaci, key figure in the prolonged conflict between the Profaci and Gallo families, seen here in a photograph taken

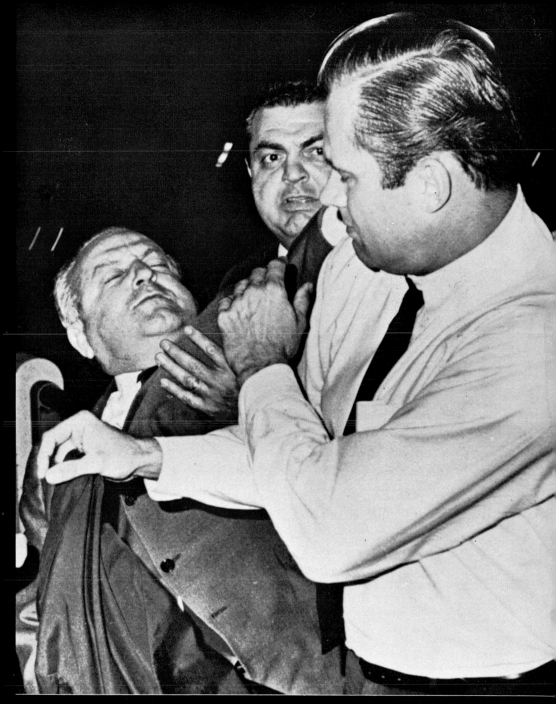

Carlos Marcello, arriving at New Orleans airport in 1968, punches an unidentified F.B.I. agent who stood among newsmen and photographers awaiting Marcello on his arrival from New York. *Wide World Photos*

Right: Joe Adonis, one time alleged gambling king in U.S., on his way to court in Milan, Italy, on June 4, 1971. Below: Johnny Dioguardia, handcuffed and under guard by court officers in New York.

N.Y. Daily News Photo and Wide World Photos

302

Willie Bioff, as head of the International Alliance of Theatrical Stage Employees, walking out of Federal Building in New York in 1941, released on bail (see following page). *Wide World Photos*

Body of Willie Bioff, at the end of his career as a Hollywood labor racketeer, lies in front of a truck that blew up as Bioff stepped on the starter button. Bioff had been living in Phoenix, Arizona, in apparent retirement and under an assumed name. *Wide World Photos*

estate behind the Boiardo greenhouse. The conversation was between De Carlo and Anthony (Little Pussy) Russo.

> RUSSO: Ray, I seen too many. You know how many guys we hit that way up there?
> DE CARLO: What about the big furnace he's got back there?
> RUSSO: That's what I'm trying to tell you! Before you go up there. . . .
> DE CARLO: The big iron grate.
> RUSSO: He used to put them on there and burn them.

According to the tapes, Russo warned De Carlo never to go near the place alone if the Boot tried to lure him there. Both concluded that the Boot was "a nut" because he not only disposed of bodies resulting from his own operations, but also those any other Mafia chief happened to pass on to him. Russo claimed that the late Thomas (Three-Finger Brown) Lucchese, onetime boss of one of New York's five Mafia families, used to turn the bodies of his victims over to Boiardo for burning. "He'd give them to me and we'd take them up," Russo told De Carlo.

In addition to the Boot, other important Mafiosi who became politically powerful in New Jersey included Willie Moretti, Joe Adonis, Gerardo Catena, Albert Anastasia, Vito Genovese and Sam De Cavalcante. Most of them made their initial forays into the state during Prohibition, but went on to establish their power during the 1930s and 1940s.

Adonis set up a series of plush gambling casinos in New Jersey in the late 1930s, and high rollers from New York were soon flocking to Mafia gambling dens just over the bridge in Bergen County. Fleets of glittering limousines purred across the bridge each night, carrying their cargoes of hopeful bettors. The chauffeurs had strict orders not to speed or run lights and soon became known as the safest drivers in three states. Ensconced in ornate surroundings, the players could be fleeced in comfortable barber's chairs or at the tables.

The operation was so far-flung that Adonis set up a headquarters in the closely guarded back room of a tavern known as "The Duke's" almost opposite the entrance to Palisades Amusement Park. In this room a daily conclave was held by a working crime council consisting of Joe Adonis, Frank Costello's partner;

Albert Anastasia; the brothers Willie and Solly Moretti; and Anthony (Tony Bender) Strollo, the right bower of Vito Genovese. One day a week the council met with top figures in the national syndicate, like Frank Costello from New York or Meyer Lansky from Florida. Law-enforcement agencies outside Jersey were painfully aware of the significance· of Duke's Restaurant. The Federal Bureau of Narcotics, District Attorney Frank Hogan's office in New York, the New York Police Department's Bureau of Criminal Identification and others kept a close check on the place. But when many of these agencies sent scouts over to Jersey to do some snooping, they were often chased away by local policemen.

The threat of a federal investigation finally blew the lid off in Bergen County and the resulting scandal rocked the New Jersey State House in the early 1950s. One indictment for payoffs was against Harold John Adonis, no relation to gangster Joe, who managed to buy a $40,000 home in cash, despite the fact that he had earned only $4,100 a year as executive clerk to then Governor Alfred E. Driscoll. But Harold Adonis was small potatoes. A few years later thè people of New Jersey were horrified to learn that one of their most beloved governors, Harold G. Hoffman, had embezzled $300,000 and juggled $16 million in state funds involving 68 bank deposits and 38 forgeries. The startling revelation came out in a posthumous letter to Hoffman's daughter urging her to "do what you know must be done."

"In order to be elected," the letter continued, "you must necessarily accept favors from a large number of people. If you attempt to repay them later, after being elected to office, it becomes wrong doing. If you do not try to help those who have helped you, you become an ingrate."

The lid blew off again in August 1968 when *Life* magazine published what purported to be the transcript of telephone conversations between Representative Cornelius E. Gallagher, a Hudson County Democrat, and Joseph (Joe Bayonne) Zicarelli, said to be the Mafia boss of the city of Bayonne. *Life* charged that Gallagher was the "tool and collaborator of a Cosa Nostra ganglord." The Congressman denied the charge, denounced *Life* and was reelected by his followers in Hudson County.

At this point Henry Ruth, a law professor at the University

of Pennsylvania who was a member of President Lyndon B. Johnson's task force on crime, told a legislative hearing that "official corruption in New Jersey is so bad that organized crime can get almost anything it desires."

Ruffled Jersey legislators ordered a state investigation and appointed William J. Brennan III, son of a Supreme Court Justice, to head it. Brennan had been probing crime since he had been appointed as an aide in the state attorney general's office a year earlier. Placed in charge of a Mercer County grand jury empowered to look into official corruption, Brennan had access to state police files and to a number of federal investigative dossiers. It made fascinating reading and prompted Brennan to tell a group of newsmen that "organized crime in New Jersey manages to work its way into . . . almost every area of our society except the church." Asked if that included the legislature, Brennan said some legislators "are a little too comfortable with organized crime."

Indignant legislators denounced Brennan for besmirching the name of their august body and demanded that he submit names with proof. Brennan retorted that he had what he deemed significant information on three members of the legislature and later said there were indications that three others might be "too comfortable" with the Mob. The investigation went on, but Brennan, at his own request it was said, was removed from further contact with criminal investigations. Meanwhile, a special legislative committee reached the conclusion that nothing illegal had happened and blasted Brennan for making what it called flimsy charges.

Then came the first FBI tapes indicating a broad range of Mafia activities centering around Simone (Sam the Plumber) De Cavalcante, a Princeton contractor and alleged Mafia family chief who was indicted for extortion. The entry of a new U.S. Attorney, Frederick B. Lacey, also changed things. Aided by his able team of assistants, particularly Herbert Stern, who later succeeded him, Lacey waded through a mountainous pile of indictments that outlined the most complete network of crime and official corruption that had ever been projected in an American courtroom. An example was the case of the financial maneuvers of a Newark insurance broker, Louis Saperstein, who had gone to his Maker in 1968, loaded with "enough arsenic to kill a mule." The money for these machinations in high finance had been obtained,

Lacey said, from Angelo De Carlo, alias "The Gyp," who was identified as a capo in the Mafia family formerly headed by the late Vito Genovese. De Carlo and three associates were accused of trying to collect thousands of dollars a week in usurious interest from Saperstein. They allegedly used persuasion on the broker "until his face turned purple and his tongue bulged out."

The prosecution of such cases triggered a smear campaign against Lacey. Aside from the vicious smears against himself and his family, Lacey was approached by cynics who echoed the theme, "You are always going to have crime and corruption, so why get so excited about it?" But reformers see the recent attacks on the alliance between New Jersey politicians and the Mafia as a firm foot in the door for change. Several of them have expressed hope that it will mean the end of the appointive prosecutors, some of whom had taken a too benevolent view towards organized crime. There was also hope it would spell the downfall of county leaders whom one former law enforcement official had described as "absolutely unresponsive to the public."

William J. Brennan, who has since moved into private practice, expressed the opinion that the power of the county bosses was waning precipitously. "Five or ten years from now, the boss system as we now know it will be finished," he said.

But until such elements are eliminated, the Mafia will probably continue to flourish in New Jersey.

19
Frank Sinatra is a Pal

NICHOLAS GAGE

"Friendship is everything," says the Mafia don in Mario Puzo's novel *The Godfather*. "Friendship is more than talent. It is more than government. It is almost the equal of family. Never forget that."

The Mafia leader addresses this advice to a character named Johnny Fontane, an Italian singer who revives his sagging career with a straight acting role. Many readers consider the career change to be one of the numerous similarities between the fictitious Johnny Fontane and singer Frank Sinatra, who revived his career in 1953 with his Academy Award-winning performance in *From Here to Eternity*. (The successful comeback allowed Sinatra to announce his retirement early in 1971 while at the top of his profession.)

But those who know Sinatra well would realize that the similarity between Johnny Fontane and Frank Sinatra is superficial. Frank Sinatra, for instance, would not need the lecture on friendship from the Mafia don. For Sinatra has, for thirty years, honored his friendships with Mafia leaders even though they have tarnished his image, damaged his business interests, and cost him his amiable relationship with the late President John F. Kennedy.

It is not at all unusual for singers to have to deal with gangsters, who have a stake in many of the nightclubs where entertainers get their start. But no other entertainer has ever built such acquaintances into enduring friendships. Although Sinatra has never been accused of participating in any illegal Mafia enterprises, he has visited the homes of Mafiosi, introduced them to women, and apparently allowed them to use his name to try to win favors from government officials.

Even at the peak of his fame, Sinatra did not hesitate to fly to Cuba to pay his respects to the exiled Mafia boss Lucky Luciano, nor, on the eve of appearing at a New York rally to improve the image of Italians in America, did he neglect to visit the nearby home of Dave Iacovetti, a major East Coast Mafia figure.

Sinatra did not limit his friendships with gangsters even after they shattered his carefully constructed contacts with John F. Kennedy. When Kennedy won the Democratic presidential nomination in 1960, the singer raised money for the young Senator, joined him on campaign trips, and praised him to everyone who would listen.

When Kennedy was elected, Sinatra redoubled his efforts and devoted ten exhausting weeks to planning a gala party in Washington for the eve of the inauguration. Tickets cost $100 to $10,000, and Sinatra's efforts erased $1.4 million of campaign debts in a single night.

The extravaganza, which featured performers ranging from Jimmy Durante to Sir Laurence Olivier, was an unforgettable "opening night" for the glamour of the Kennedy years. No one doubted that Sinatra would be the favored entertainer at the White House. But after a time things began to sour.

The singer's relations with the President began to deteriorate after Robert Kennedy took office as Attorney General and launched a campaign against organized crime in the United States. Before long, veteran investigators at the Justice Department complained that they did not understand how the administration could both wage war on the Mafia and welcome at the White House a man as closely tied to Mafia leaders as Frank Sinatra.

Robert Kennedy ordered the organized crime section at the Justice Department to give him a report on Sinatra's Mafia associations. Although the department had never investigated Sinatra himself, surveillance of many of the leading gangsters in the country had produced indications of a relationship between the gangsters and the entertainer, and a Justice lawyer was set to work compiling all the scattered information into one special report.

After studying the Justice Department report, Robert Kennedy felt it was significant enough to take to his brother. While President Kennedy was examining it, an incident took place that fueled the fire.

A friend of Sinatra's—Sam "Moe" Giancana, a leader of the Mafia in Chicago—became irked at the continual close surveillance of FBI agents. He sent an aide to tell the agents that he, Giancana, wanted to confer with Robert Kennedy himself about ending the surveillance. As for the mechanics of setting up such a high-level meeting, the aide told the agents: "Moe says that if Kennedy wants to talk, he should get in touch with Frank Sinatra to set it up."

According to one of Robert Kennedy's assistants, the Attorney General not only disregarded the invitation but took the FBI report of the incident to the President.

The honeymoon between the President and Frank Sinatra was over. This became all too clear when JFK visited Palm Springs and stayed at the home of Bing Crosby. The special wing that Sinatra had added to his Palm Springs home, in anticipation of President Kennedy's visits, was to remain unoccupied.

Sinatra soon learned from friends in the Kennedy circle that it was Bobby Kennedy who had persuaded the President to break with him, and the singer never forgave him. As his mother once said of Sinatra, "My son is like me. You cross him, he never forgets." Peter Lawford, the President's brother-in-law, was no longer a welcome member of Sinatra's court. And no one who knew the singer well was at all surprised when, in 1968, he announced his support for Hubert Humphrey for the Democratic presidential nomination soon after Robert Kennedy declared that he would be a candidate. "Bobby's just not qualified to be President," Sinatra said.

There has been much speculation as to the contents of the Justice Department report on Frank Sinatra. As standard procedure, the department will not reveal its contents or even acknowledge that such a report exists. However, I have been able to secure a copy of the report through special sources.

It is a nineteen-page document dated August 3, 1962, and titled "Francis Albert Sinatra, a/k/a Frank Sinatra." The information in it is based partly on the reports of FBI agents who followed gangsters associated with Sinatra and monitored their telephone conversations, and partly on information supplied by government informants, who are identified by code names like "LA T-79."

The report establishes the fact that Sinatra was in contact with about ten of the best-known gangsters in the country in the late 1950's and early 1960's. It details exact dates when some of these gangsters telephoned Sinatra's home, using his unlisted number, and it enumerates special favors that Sinatra performed for some of them.

One of these favors involved a car dealer named Peter Epsteen. He tried to persuade Sinatra to record a singing commercial for his Pontiac agency in Skokie, Illinois, but the singer refused. Then Epsteen brought the matter to the attention of Joseph and Rocco Fischetti, cousins of Al Capone and leading Mafia figures, "after which Sinatra made the commercial as a favor without charge," the report quotes Epsteen's former wife as telling FBI agents. (Sinatra did, however, agree to accept two Pontiacs as a gift from the grateful Epsteen, the report adds.)

Spokesmen for Sinatra later said that the commercial was done as a personal favor to Epsteen and had nothing to do with the Fischetti brothers. But the Justice Department report does point out that after the commercial was made, Joseph Fischetti and a close lady friend of Rocco Fischetti's were seen driving Pontiacs "bearing Epsteen's dealer's license plate and label."

Sinatra's favors to the Fischetti brothers went beyond his willingness to sing a commercial for their friend. The Justice Department report indicates that Sinatra arranged for Joe Fischetti to receive payments as a talent scout from the Fontainebleau Hotel in Miami Beach whenever Sinatra performed at the hotel.

The report quotes an informant as saying that as of April, 1962, "Joe Fischetti, under the name of Joe Fisher, had received 71 checks from the Fontainebleau Hotel, each in the amount of $540.00 (Total: $38,340.00)." It is difficult to double-check such a statement, but the report does point out that Joe Fischetti, in his income tax returns from 1959 and 1960, listed fees of $12,960 from the Fontainebleau Hotel as a "talent agent."

The report adds that in Miami Beach "Fischetti is Sinatra." It says that Sinatra usually entertained there for a contract price plus a cash deal and that the cash deal was generally handled by Fischetti. The report also says that Sinatra reportedly lent Fischetti $90,000 to help the gangster buy a secret interest in a large Miami restaurant.

Sinatra's favors to his gangster friends have not been solely of a financial nature. The report indicates that sometime in 1961 a twenty-eight-year-old divorcée acquaintance of Sinatra's was introduced to Chicago mobster Sam Giancana, the man who later complained about the FBI agents tailing him. Giancana, a short, bald man with a harmless-looking smile and a mild manner, was rejected by his draft board in 1944 as a psychopath. At fifteen he was sent to jail for auto theft, and by the time he was twenty he had been questioned in connection with three murders.

Giancana does not look like a Don Juan, but he has an eye for beautiful women. He has been widely seen and photographed in the company of Phyllis McGuire, of the singing McGuire sisters. He was so pleased with the companionship of the young divorcée to whom Sinatra introduced him that he showered her with expensive gifts, including a new Thunderbird sports car.

The Justice Department report also indicates that Sinatra may have been involved with gangsters in business dealings in Nevada. Early in the 1960's he owned a controlling interest in the Cal-Neva Lodge, a resort complex and casino on Nevada's beautiful Lake Tahoe. The report quotes Sam Giancana as bragging to friends that he owned a piece of Cal-Neva through Sinatra. While the singer owned the lodge, he employed Paul Emilio D'Amato, a New Jersey underworld figure, as an overseer. The report says that D'Amato's actual purpose was to protect Giancana's interest in the lodge.

The Cal-Neva Lodge was the setting for some dramatic encounters in Sinatra's life. The Justice Department report says that in the summer of 1962 the singer made "improper advances" to a cocktail waitress at the lodge who happened to be married to a local deputy sheriff. The lawman warned Sinatra to leave his wife alone, the report says, but the singer persisted in his advances. On or about June 30, 1962, the angry deputy sheriff walked up to Sinatra in the casino and punched him in the face so hard that he had to cancel his singing engagement.

The bruises healed, but a year later Sinatra ran into real

trouble at the lodge. The cause of it was his powerful friend from Chicago, Sam Giancana, who arrived at the Cal-Neva with his traveling companion, singer Phyllis McGuire.

Giancana was missed by his faithful shadows in Chicago, and the State Gaming Control Board in Nevada soon traced him, through informants, to Chalet 50 of the Cal-Neva Lodge. Giancana happened to be one of eleven gangsters on the gaming board's blacklist—a black folder circulated to all casinos with the names, pictures, and backgrounds of the men considered *personae non grata* in the state.

The gaming board had warned that if any of the gangsters on the blacklist were allowed into any casino, its license would be revoked. Therefore, when Giancana was traced to Cal-Neva, the chairman of the gaming board, Edward A. Olsen, called Frank Sinatra to his office for an explanation.

Olsen says that Sinatra admitted having seen Giancana at the lodge, but denied having invited him there. He promised not to associate with the gang leader in Nevada anymore, but said that Giancana was a friend and that if he wanted to see him outside the state, it was his own business.

Olsen says he replied that as long as Sinatra associated with gangsters at all while holding an interest in Nevada casinos, it reflected badly on gambling in the state. But Sinatra refused to yield, Olsen says, and the gaming board began to amass evidence to file a complaint against the entertainer.

Several days after the meeting with the singer, according to Olsen, Sinatra telephoned him at his office and invited him to Cal-Neva for dinner "to talk about this thing." Olsen replied that he did not think such a visit appropriate, since the board was investigating the lodge. "But he kept insisting," Olsen says, "and I kept refusing. The more I refused the madder he got, until he seemed almost hysterical. He used the foulest language I ever heard in my life."

Finally, Olsen says, Sinatra declared that if his invitation was refused, he would never talk to anyone from the board. Olsen says he was angry himself by this time and told Sinatra that if the board wanted to talk to him, it would subpoena him.

"You subpoena me," Olsen quotes Sinatra as replying, "and you're going to get a big, fat, fucking surprise."

"It was clear to me he meant that as a threat," says Olsen.

The gaming board never subpoenaed Sinatra, but not because of the threat. After the board initiated formal proceedings to revoke his gaming license, the entertainer turned it in voluntarily and promised to sell his Nevada gambling interests, worth $3.5 million.

Before events reached that stage, however, gaming board officials and Nevada's Governor Grant Sawyer were subjected to pressures of a different kind. Paul D'Amato, Sinatra's right-hand man at Cal-Neva, tried to slip two $100 bills to gaming board agents who were making a routine inspection of the lodge. The agents returned the money and reported the offer.

Then Governor Sawyer got several phone calls from people who spoke about making large contributions to his upcoming campaign while at the same time discussing the Sinatra problem. "I told them that the rules were made for everyone, including Mr. Sinatra," he says. (Sawyer, who served two terms as governor, lost the election and is now practicing law in Las Vegas.)

Sinatra's involvement in Las Vegas ended in 1963, although he continued to appear as an entertainer there. But his involvement with underworld figures has persisted unabated despite the adverse publicity he has received and the financial losses he has suffered as a result of it. In 1963, Sinatra and singer Dean Martin turned up as directors of the Berkshire racetrack in Massachusetts. No one thought much about it until it was discovered some time later that Raymond Patriarca, the Mafia boss in New England, and Thomas "Three-Finger Brown" Lucchese, the late head of one of the five Mafia families in New York, had secret interests in the track.

In 1967 Sinatra performed at a big rally given in Madison Square Garden by the American-Italian Anti-Defamation League. However, in view of his underworld contacts, the choice of Sinatra to head a movement to improve the image of Italians in the United States shocked everyone. "The American-Italian Anti-Defamation League, in picking Frank Sinatra as their national leader, has chosen to add fire to fire," said The *New York Times* in an editorial. Before long, Sinatra resigned from the league. (Later, when Joe Colombo founded the Italian-American Civil Rights League in 1970, Sinatra gave it his full support.)

In 1968 Sinatra tried to make a political comeback in the Democratic party. He joined the campaign drive of presidential contender Hubert Humphrey and scheduled a series of fund-raising concerts for his benefit. But a *Wall Street Journal* article enumerating some of the singer's underworld contacts moved Humphrey to quietly cut him out of his campaign. (The dismissal, added to the treatment he had received under the Kennedys, soured Sinatra on many Democrats, and in 1970 he supported Republican Ronald Reagan for re-election as governor of California.)

In 1969 Sinatra's name was linked to several more gangsters. A Mafia figure named Angelo "Gyp" De Carlo was put on trial in New Jersey on charges of extortion. The FBI released some twenty-one thousand pages of recorded conversation De Carlo had had with other Mafiosi, and Sinatra's name figured on several of these pages. At one point a loan shark claimed that he would get money from Sinatra to buy a hotel in Jamaica. At another, De Carlo, whose sister-in-law is married to a cousin of Sinatra's, described an incident involving a woman Sinatra apparently wanted to see: "Russo says that while in Miami, Tony Bennett came over to the Racquet Club and says he's looking for this broad," De Carlo related. "I says, 'What do you want?'

"He says he wants this job [girl].

"I says, 'What are you talking about? Frank Sinatra sent a telegram wantin' this broad.' She was a beautiful thing, a real job.

"I called her up. I told her . . . [about] the telegram. It was a request by Frank for her to come to the coast, his telephone and all. I told her, 'Call him. Tell him to wire the money and go out there.' "

The De Carlo conversations were publicized at the same time that Sinatra was trying to avoid appearing before the New Jersey State Commission of Investigation, which had been looking into organized crime in that state, and the impact of the two events seriously hurt the singer's reputation. When he finally appeared before the commission, however, the furor had subsided.

Whether De Carlo really knew Sinatra or was just bragging (a frailty not uncommon among second-string Mafiosi) is uncertain. But it is clear that Frank Sinatra has long had relationships with a number of gangsters in his native New Jersey.

When he left his Hoboken home to pursue his dream of becoming a singer, performing for practically nothing in local roadhouses and clubs, he became fast friends with Quarico "Willie Moore" Moretti, a leader of the Mafia in New Jersey who, before his violent death, was involved in extortion, dope pushing, and murder.

While singing with Harry James's band in 1939, Sinatra made his first hit recording: "All or Nothing at All." When band leader Tommy Dorsey offered him $125 a week to be his vocalist, it seemed like a princely sum to Sinatra and he took the job. But his star continued to shoot upward, and crowds of bobbysoxers followed him everywhere.

The contract he had signed with Dorsey was shackling him. He could not take full advantage of his new-found fame. Suddenly and inexplicably the contract was canceled and Sinatra was a free agent. Dorsey never explained why he let such a valuable property go, but the story, much repeated among the underworld, was that Willie Moretti showed up at Dorsey's dressing room one night, put a gun into the band leader's mouth, and suggested that he sell Sinatra's contract. The price was one dollar.

Moretti continued to take a paternal interest in Sinatra, and eleven years later when the gossip columns were full of the news that the singer was going to divorce his first wife, Nancy, and marry Ava Gardner, the gangster fired off a telegram of advice to Sinatra: "I am very much surprised what I have been reading in the newspapers between you and your darling wife," Moretti wrote. "Remember you have a decent wife and children. You should be very happy. Regards to all. Willie Moore."

Shortly thereafter, Moretti, his mental health weakened by advanced syphilis, was shot to death by fellow Mafiosi, who feared that he would talk.

Sinatra may have reflected on the fate of his old friend with some trepidation, but long before this his contacts with the underworld had reached to the very top of the Mafia ladder—namely to Salvatore Lucania, the Mafia boss who was better known as Lucky Luciano. Luciano was deported to Italy after World War II and spent his final years in Naples, but he did not give up his influence in Mafia affairs, even in exile. During one of his absences from home, Italian police found in Luciano's Naples apartment a gold cigarette case with this inscription: "To my dear pal Lucky, from his friend, Frank Sinatra."

In 1947 Luciano flew to Cuba from Naples in the vain hope

of finding some way to get back into the United States. The arrival
of the Mafia boss, only ninety miles from the United States, was
such an important occasion in the underworld that thirty-six hotel
suites were required to accommodate all the important gangsters
who came to Havana to pay their respects. And along with the
gangsters came Frank Sinatra to pay his respects to his "dear pal
Lucky."

On the same plane with Sinatra were Joseph and Rocco
Fischetti, the cousins of Al Capone. Federal investigators later
claimed that Rocco carried a bag with $2 million in "very large
bills" to Luciano as part of his dividends from United States
rackets.

The tremendous publicity generated by Sinatra's visit to
Luciano moved the singer to offer an explanation: "I was brought
up to shake a man's hand when I am introduced to him without
first investigating his past," he said. Luciano's past, however, was
not much of a secret, and the adverse publicity continued at such
a pitch that Sinatra tried again to explain his presence in Cuba.
He said he had run into one of the Fischetti brothers in Miami
and mentioned that he was planning to make a little trip to
Havana. The Fischetti brothers had also made plans to go to
Havana and changed their reservations so they could fly down
on the same plane with Sinatra.

When he got to Havana, Sinatra said, he was introduced to
a large group of people who asked him to join them for dinner.
And when he arrived at the dinner he discovered that Lucky
Luciano was a guest as well. "It suddenly struck me that I was
laying myself open to criticism by remaining at the table," Sinatra
told the press, "but I could think of no way to leave in the middle
of dinner without creating a scene."

In spite of his explanations, United States investigators learned
from informers in the city that Sinatra did not just have dinner
with Luciano and his friends, but spent four days with them,
gambling and partying until the early morning hours. The only
periods when Sinatra was not with the gangsters were when they
held "business" meetings.

Sinatra continued to keep in touch with Luciano after the
1947 meeting, and he cultivated his association with the Fischetti
brothers. Often when visiting Chicago the singer was seen paying

a call at the home of Rocco Fischetti (who has since died), and whenever he was in Florida his entourage always included Joseph Fischetti, who became one of his most devoted associates.

The comments of a man who has often been part of Sinatra's entourage reveal just how close the singer's friendship with Joseph Fischetti became. "Frank is very touchy about his baldness and tells everyone to leave when he's going to change hair pieces," the man told me. "But if Joe Fischetti wants to stay, he stays."

A spokesman for Sinatra once berated a reporter who asked to interview the singer about his underworld contacts. "These reports are rumors and vicious, unnecessary attacks," the spokesman said. "Mr. Sinatra has associated with presidents, heads of state, and hundreds of personalities much more interesting and copy-worthy. Why don't you write about those associations?"

It is precisely because of such associations that Sinatra's contacts with gangsters affect American society, suggests Ralph Salerno, a specialist on organized crime formerly with the New York Police Department. "People say to themselves, 'If Frank Sinatra, who knows presidents and kings, is friendly with Joe Fischetti, Sam Giancana, and all the rest, they can't be all that bad.' That's the service Sinatra renders his gangster friends. He gives them innocence by association. You'd think a guy like Sinatra would care about that. But he doesn't. He doesn't give a damn."

Dollars and Death

THE HAND OF THE MAFIA touches nearly everyone in America, from the housewife in the supermarket to the longshoreman on the waterfront to the numbers player in the ghetto. Mafia power is the more insidious because the Mafia is increasingly involved not only in illegal rackets but in a variety of legitimate businesses as well. This final section of the book is devoted to illustrating just how far Mafia infiltration into legitimate businesses can go.

Many products on the supermarket shelves are made by companies in which Mafia leaders have either an open or a hidden interest. And in some instances the Mafia promotes the distribution and sales of its products using the same deadly techniques that proved so effective in underworld activities. As a result, many legitimate businessmen, restaurant owners and the like have found themselves faced with such persuasive techniques as the well-phrased threat or the well-placed bomb.

In the first chapter in this section, Joe Demma and Tom Renner, veteran reporters for *Newsday*, document the involvement of many Mafiosi in food businesses across the country. In the second chapter, Stanley Penn, a Pulitzer Prize-winning reporter with the *Wall Street Journal*, examines how the Mafia muscles in on a thriving business. The case in point is the Murray Packing Company, a New York firm that was taken over by a Mafioso, quickly bled of most of its liquid assets and then abandoned to bankruptcy. In the third chapter, Penn illustrates how Mafiosi are sometimes welcomed, even invited, onto the payroll by companies who feel they could use an underworld edge over their competitors.

One major way in which mobsters affect business is through labor unions. Some years ago, for example, several heirs of Al Capone took control of a key motion-picture union. The havoc this raised within the movie industry is related by Malcolm Johnson in the fourth chapter of this section.

Next, Charles Grutzner, who retired from the *New York Times* in 1971 after covering the Mafia for many years, discusses how businessmen sometimes make themselves willing victims of the Mafia and offers suggestions on how its infiltration into legitimate business can be prevented.

Finally, Fred J. Cook analyzes the underworld enterprises of Joe Colombo's Mafia family.

20

The Mafia in the Supermarket

JOE DEMMA and TOM RENNER

From southern New Jersey to Virginia and West Virginia, supermarket patrons buy cheese, milk products and juices produced by M. Maggio Co., Milk Maid Dairy Products, Michael's Dairies and Vineland Cheese, all of Philadelphia. Sailors and workmen at the U.S. Navy Yard in Philadelphia drink milk produced by the companies, as do Coast Guardsmen in the area. The Philadelphia school system buys fruit juices from them. Restaurants and pizza parlors buy ricotta cheese and milk.

The companies' annual sales are estimated at more than $10,000,000. All the companies are owned by Peter Maggio. And the Pennsylvania Crime Commission and federal authorities say that Maggio is a captain in the Mafia crime family of Angelo Bruno of Philadelphia.

One of the more popular brands of Italian bread on Long Island is baked by Sapienza Bakery of 553 Meecham Ave., Elmont. The bakery's annual sales are more than $650,000. Its president is Andrew Sapienza, a baker who is proud of his product. Its vice president and part-owner is Salvatore (Sally the Sheik) Mussachio, of 2947 Murdock Ave., Wantagh. Police and federal agents say that Mussachio is a captain in the Joseph Colombo crime family.

In March, 1971 the Food and Drug Administration seized 938 cases of a detergent called Ecolo-G and a similar product sold under a Bohack label, charging that the products should have been labeled as dangerous to users. Ecolo-G and the Bohack brand were manufactured by North American Chemical Co. and its subsidiary,

Ecology Corp. of America, both of Paterson, N.J. In 1964, North American hired Best Sales Co., to sell its detergent. Best Sales is now out of business, but during and after its unsuccessful attempts to sell the detergent to the Great Atlantic and Pacific Tea Co., federal officials say, the supermarket chain was hit by a rash of arsons topping $60,000,000 in losses, two of its store managers were murdered, others were beaten and two committed suicide. North American's sales, meanwhile, grew from $3,000,000 a year to $8,000,000.

The Port of Newark receives 200,000 tons of meat a year. All of that tonnage plus the meat shipped to the Port of Philadelphia is handled by the Erb Strapping Co., which inspects, stamps, straps, boxes and arranges shipments of the meat to supermarkets. In 1955, Vito Genovese, then the nation's most powerful crime boss according to the federal government, bought 49 percent of the $1,000,000-a-year firm for $245. Since then, the company has more than doubled its business. By 1968, Vito and his brother, Michael, had, according to New York Waterfront Commission testimony, collected more than $170,000 in salaries. Vito is dead, but Michael still has a contract that guarantees him an additional $198,000 by 1977 for selling his share (once Vito's) of the firm.

An investigation into the food industry nationwide has uncovered more than 50 figures from 12 organized crime syndicates involved in more than 30 food and food service companies. These figures influence, control or own firms that supply American consumers with more than $400,000,000 in products annually.

The presence of these racketeers does not appear to be part of a conspiracy by any single group to take over the industry. But there is evidence that racketeers from different areas work together to further their profiteering, using ruthless competitiveness and salesmanship and utter contempt for laws.

In some cases, racketeers have been in the food business for generations. In others, they have been brought in by businessmen to help increase sales, overcome competition or obtain favorable terms from racketeer-dominated unions. The names read like a who's who of organized crime: Genovese, Colombo, Maggio, Joseph (Joe Bananas) Bonanno, Carlo Gambino, Simone (Sam the Plumber) De Cavalcante, Joseph (Joe Peck) and Thomas Pecora, Thomas (Tommy Ryan) Eboli, John (Johnny Dio) Dioguardi, Aniello Dellacroce, Gerardo Catena and his late brother, Eugene, Nicholas (Cockeyed Nick) Rattenni and Murray Kessler, all from the New York-New Jersey area. In New Orleans, the investigation found the name of crime boss Carlos Marcello involved with a tomato wholesaler; in Chicago it was Ross Prio infiltrating the business world, and in Detroit, it was crime boss Joseph (the Old Man) Zerilli and his aide William (Black Bill) Tocco.

Bonanno is sometimes called the "King of Mozzarella" because of his interests in the old Colorado Cheese Co. and the more current Grande Cheese Co. of Fond du Lac, Wis. Canadian authorities also say that Bonanno owned part of Giuseppe Saputo & Sons Ltd., of Montreal, a major supplier of Italian-style cheese to restaurants and supermarkets throughout the U.S. and Canada. The owners of Saputo deny that Bonanno is a partner, but they admit that they offered him a partnership in their $4,000,000 firm for only $8,000. Canadian law enforcement agencies, however, list Frank Cotroni, a soldier in the Giuseppe Cotroni family of Canada, as a Saputo salesman.

And the owners of the Falcone Dairies of Brooklyn said that they at one time shared ownership in Cloverdale Dairies and Gourmay Cheese Co. with Bonanno's and Prio's representatives. The Falcone owners claimed that they divested themselves of the interest, without collecting a nickel on their investment, after they and their general manager, a salesman for Grande for nine years, learned that Bonanno was a mobster because of the 1957 raid on the Apalachin crime conclave.

Then there is Paul Gambino, who the New York State Investigations Commission and a U.S. Senate rackets subcommittee say is a captain in the family of his brother, Carlo. He was cited in testimony before the state commission for infiltrating supermarkets through a butcher's tool business that offered less than $1,000 worth of equipment for more than $300,000. He also operates the Blue Star Market in Flushing and sells cheese through the Ferro Cheese Co. of Brooklyn, the owners of Falcone Dairies said. At his Blue Star Market, the commission said, Gambino's prices were less than those of competitors. A partial explanation became apparent when the FBI raided his market, arrested him and carried off a large quantity of Polish hams that had been hijacked.

The P&H Rendering Co. of Brooklyn is one of a group of New York firms picking up fats and unsaleable products from meat stores, processing them and reselling them to stores and other companies as cooking fat or material for soap, glue, fertilizer and dog food. One of its most astute business deals was consummated with the help of the U.S. District Court. The court permitted the company to contract with the now-defunct Dilberts Supermarket chain to buy its offal then sell part of it back to another rendering firm which was a subsidiary of the supermarket chain. The principal officers of P&H are Joseph Castellano, president, and Paul Castellano, Jr., secretary-treasurer. They are the sons of Paul Castellano, Sr., described by federal authorities and police as a captain in the Gambino family. Castellano, Sr., is listed as a salesman for his sons' firm. His sons claim that they are harassed and followed by police and tax agents because of their father. The senior Castellano, police sources say, controls meat markets of his own and is influential with supermarket butchers.

In 1963, Porko Pork of Jamaica, Queens, was averaging $500,000-a-year processing Italian sausages, pork burgers and Chinese-style pork products. New York City police say that the firm's president, William Musto, whose salary was $200 a week, hired Anthony (Tony the Sheik) Carillo and Ciro Perrone as "truck spotters" at $250 a week and Carillo's brother, Salvatore, as a $250-a-week "sauce maker." Police say that Tony Carillo and Perrone were "soldiers" in the Genovese family and Salvatore was an "associate."

In testimony before the State Joint Legislative Committee on Crime, police said that Porko Pork's business rose after the hirings to more than $2,000,000 a year but not before the company fell $145,000 in hock to the ANR Leasing Corp., a firm owned by Genovese soldier-loanshark John (Gentleman Johnny) Masiello. Today, Porko Pork is bankrupt and out of business.

Racketeers also have managed to make contacts with some major corporations and brand names in the food industry.

The whipped cream topping called Reddi-Wip is owned, produced and sold by Hunt & Wesson Corp., a subsidiary of the $350,000,000-a-year Norton Simon Co. Reddi-Wip Corp. and its patents were bought by Hunt & Wesson from Marcus Lipsky, of Beverly Hills, Calif., identified in U.S. Senate rackets subcommittee testimony as a former front man for the remnants of the Al Capone mob and formerly a partner with high-echelon Chicago crime figure Ross Prio in the Blue Ribbon Dairy Co. and

L (for Lipsky) & P (for Prio) Milk Co. Hunt & Wesson agreed in July, 1970, to buy Reddi-Wip for $6,000,000, plus interest. Lipsky received $1,200,000 down and the balance to be paid in five equal installments. Lipsky also receives royalties of one and a half percent on products and processes he has developed, including Reddi-Bacon, as well as rights to European sales of Reddi-Wip. Lipsky, Los Angeles police sources say, had Angelo Polizzo, a captain in the California family of Nicola Licata, on his payroll as a salesman until he sold the company.

Progresso Foods, Inc., of Jersey City, has a long-time family tradition in the Italian-American community, but there was a period during World War II when it owned part of Grande Cheese Co. Police say that Grande was formed by Prio and later partly owned by Bonanno.

The president of Progresso, John F. Taormina, said that the officers of his company, when it was called Uddo & Taormina, did not realize in buying part of Grande that they were associating with a firm controlled by racketeers. He said that his firm's officers were merely attempting to obtain Italian-type cheese for their products at a time when such cheeses could not be obtained from Italy. The association was discontinued in 1949 when, according to Taormina, Progresso suspected that something was wrong with the firm and pulled out. Grande, he said, paid back in cheese for Progresso's investment.

Until 1970, Progresso's general manager for its New Jersey operations was Anthony Baressi, identified by a Kings County grand jury as an associate of the Bonanno family when he was subpenaed in 1968. Baressi was responsible for helping Progresso obtain its valuable waterfront site for $180,000 from Jersey City and, according to testimony at a Joint Legislative Committee on Crime, his helper was Walter Falcetta. The committee said that Falcetta, who testified that he received more than $31,000 from Progresso for land appraisals, was a partner of Salvatore Bonanno in the Republic Finance Co., a firm identified in federal hearings as a loanshark front.

The Hoffman soda label is an old and reputable one, now owned by the $28,000,000-a-year American Beverage Corp. of College Point, Queens. American, a reputable firm, bought the Hoffman label from Hoffman Products, Inc., of Newark, N.J. Hoffman Products, Inc., has been described in State Investigation

Commission hearings as a mob-dominated subsidiary of 20th Century Industries, a firm accused last year of fronting for the Philadelphia Mafia boss Angelo Bruno, in an attempt to take control of a Caribbean casino. The president of Hoffman Products is Martin Goldman. Goldman was convicted in 1970 with Gambino soldier Michael Catalano of conspiracy in a $100,000 scheme to shake down a platinum dealer. The state commission said that Goldman's adviser and salesman was Aniello Dellacroce, the Gambino underboss.

An FBI bug revealed how Simone (Sam the Plumber) De Cavalcante became an entrepreneur in the shrimp trade.

On Feb 26, 1965, the New Jersey Mafia boss was called by one of his soldiers, Gaetano (Corky) Vastola, who wanted a storage warehouse for 1,100 pounds of shrimp which was about to be hijacked. Vastola asked De Cavalcante to find a place that could be rented for $1,000 a month.

De Cavalcante did better. He called a Roselle Park, N.J., food dealer, who said that he not only could store the shrimp, but could sell the whole load for more than $1.90 a pound. The hijacker was selling the shrimp to Vastola for only 30 cents a pound.

For the racketeer to be interested in food, federal experts say, there has to be that large profit potential. And hijacking, they say, is only one small way of food profiteering. There are other methods for infiltrating the food business, including strong-arm tactics, threats of labor trouble, loansharking, guarantees of labor peace or simply, being invited in. . . .

In New Orleans, Joseph (Baby) Matassa, vice president of Pelican Tomato Co., said that Louisiana crime boss Carlos Marcello collects a third of the company's profits because "he sells tomatoes."

Matassa said that Marcello became involved with the firm because "I went to him . . . in 1962-63." Matassa added: "I had been trying to sell a big customer who was a friend of his . . . I knew he owed Carlos a favor."

The executive director of the New Orleans Metropolitan Crime Commission, Aaron Kohn, said that the customer was Louisiana State Sen. John Schwegmann, a leading Democratic candidate for governor this year and president of Schwegmann Brothers Giant Supermarkets. Matassa said that he also has A&P Supermarkets and the U.S. Navy as customers.

"Marcello got me the [Schwegmann] account and said he could get me other companies," Matassa said. ". . . Before he [Marcello] came in, I was doing $400,000 to $500,000 a year in business. When he came in, it jumped to $700,000 . . . and now it's almost two million . . . I'll hire a Red Chinese if he'll do that for me."

Schwegmann denied that Marcello sold him on Pelican. "I never had any dealings with Marcello that I know of," he said. "He might own a hundred companies I don't know of. He's never given me a dime. He don't have anything to do with the store."

Similarly, North American Chemical Co. had sales of $3,000,000 in 1964 when it hired Best Sales Co. of Newark to sell its detergents. Now its sales top $8,000,000, the firm's executive vice president, Louis D'Almeida, says.

Federal authorities say that Best Sales was operated by the late Eugene Catena [brother of Mafia boss Gerardo Catena]. They say that Catena expected to sell the detergent to A&P Supermarkets as a private label and believed the sale would be easy because of his labor connections. One of Catena's connections in 1964 was Irving (Izzy) Kaplan, the leader of Local 464 of the Amalgamated Meat Cutters, the union which was negotiating a contract with A&P at the time. . . . Another connection was Joseph (Joe Peck) Pecora, who federal officials say is a Catena captain and is secretary-treasurer of the International Brotherhood of Teamsters Local 863. That local in 1946 conducted a two-month strike against A&P that cost the company more than $4,000,000 a month. Both men, federal sources say, endorsed the detergent and suggested to A&P executives that it would be wise to use it.

In 1965, federal sources say, Kaplan arranged to have Nathan Sobol, president of North American, make a sales pitch to A&P. He followed it up with a personal recommendation. Pecora also did his part, federal sources say, urging a trucking firm executive who dealt with A&P to "tell your boss [an A&P executive] to keep his word." A&P, however, after testing the product, turned it down as inferior. Catena was furious, and FBI bugs recorded him promising to "kick A&P's brains out."

Suddenly the chain's stores and warehouses were hit by a series of arsons. Two store managers were shot to death, one in Elmont, within a month of each other. Others were beaten, and, police sources say, arson losses mounted to $60,000,000, including a

$7,000,000 fire in New Jersey last year. Behind the violence, the federal sources say, was Nicholas (Cockeyed Nick) Rattenni, a crime captain who controlled a group of enforcers in Westchester. The sources say that one of Rattenni's enforcers was Joseph Maselli, who is now serving a life plus three-year prison term for the torture murder of an elderly widow. Maselli was identified by A&P store manager John Mossner of Elmont as one of two men he found in his Brooklyn store twice in December, 1964, trying to set a fire. On Feb. 5, 1965, Mossner was killed by gunfire in Elmont.

D'Almeida denied that Sobol was aware that force was used to sell his product. "If we asked them [Catena] how they were selling, they would tell us, 'You make it, we sell it. Don't ask what we are doing,'" he said. Sobol refused to talk to reporters, but he told the New York Waterfront Commission that he signed a binding, 10-year contract with Catena because of "big promises" of sales. Federal sources say that the only way Best Sales agreed to stop as a sales broker for Sobol was if Catena was paid $25,800 a year for 13 years. Payments are still being paid to Catena's estate.

D'Almeida said that his company supplies three-quarters of the major 100 food chains in the nation. Last March, the Food and Drug Administration seized a large quantity of North American's products including its best-selling Ecolo-G. The government charged that the detergents were "corrosive to intact skin and a severe eye irritant" and should be labeled dangerous to users.

While Best Sales was pushing North American's products, Thomas (Timmy Murphy) Pecora, a soldier in the Genovese family, was using North American facilities to house an office for the firm he owns, All Purpose Chemical Co., police say.

Pecora was business agent and director of the maintenance division for IBT Industrial and Allied Workers Local 97 of Newark. All Purpose's product is intended primarily for warehouses, and its sales have been to such buyers as the Division of Purchase and Property of the State of New Jersey. The president of the firm is Frank Vasfailo, described by law enforcement officials as a Catena family associate with a minor record.

When the New Jersey State Commission of Investigations held public hearings in 1970, it found that Pecora had used his labor influence to sell his detergent, known by the brand name

"Poly-Clean." The New Jersey commission found that the firm's sales pitch was based on guarantees of labor peace.

One witness, Emil J. Bevacqua, a window-cleaning firm employe, recalled a conversation he had with Vasfailo and Buddy Evangelista, regional manager for Great Eastern, in which he said: "You're doing pretty good getting in on a supermarket shelf. That should make Timmy [Pecora] pretty happy." He said Vasfailo replied: "That makes Timmy happy, it makes Great Eastern happy because they have no union problems." Pecora has been missing since the hearing, and Vasfailo refused to testify.

Unlike other rackets members, Peter Maggio came into his milk and cheese products firms in the Philadelphia area legitimately. He inherited them.

The firms were founded in Columbus, N.J., by his father, his grandfather and his uncles when they emigrated to the U.S. in 1912. At first, the business was only a farm in Columbus, N.J., but the Maggios started to market their cheese in the Trenton and Hightstown areas. In 1920, his father, Michael Maggio, moved to Philadelphia. The business now bottles milk and cream under the Milk Maid label and distributes cheese under the Vineland and M. Maggio labels. Michael's Dairies, his fourth firm, is a distributor.

Maggio is the brother-in-law of Angelo Bruno and has been identified by the Pennsylvania Crime Commission and federal authorities as a captain in Bruno's family. FBI bugs disclosed that Maggio's father sponsored Bruno as a member of Cosa Nostra. Maggio, himself, has been called before seven grand juries but has never been indicted or arrested. He says that he sells his products to the Navy Yard in Philadelphia, the U.S. Coast Guard, the Philadelphia School District, and several supermarket chains.

In a recent interview, Maggio said of Cosa Nostra: "This is an opera written by Bobby Kennedy, orchestrated by J. Edgar Hoover and sung by all the attorney generals throughout the country . . . I have no knowledge of the Mafia or Cosa Nostra." He admitted that he was formerly a partner in the G (for Carlo Gambino) & M (Maggio) Realty Co. of Florida in control of 110 acres in Broward County, Fla. He describes Gambino as a gentleman, not a mob boss.

A racketeer who can threaten strikes and offer labor peace or a sweetheart contract to a merchant has a pronounced advantage in selling a product. John (Johnny Dio) Dioguardi had that advantage. Nassau District Attorney Cahn once said that Dioguardi's income from the kosher meat business, for example, rose from $250 a week when he entered the field in 1963 to $250,000 a year in 1966.

Dioguardi entered the rackets as a youth on Manhattan's Lower East Side, under the patronage of Louis (Lepke) Buchalter and Jake (Gurrah) Shapiro of Murder, Inc. He has been convicted of labor shakedowns, extortion, tax evasion and bankruptcy fraud and is now serving the fraud sentence. He was accused by FBI and U.S. Senate investigators of establishing paper unions, ordering the 1956 acid blinding of labor columnist Victor Reisel and other crimes.

Herman Rose, president of Consumer Kosher Provisions, hired Dioguardi as a $250-a-week salesman in 1963. The State Investigations Commission said that Rose hired Dioguardi because he had been losing business to American Kosher Provisions, Inc., of Brooklyn. American Kosher had on its payroll ex-labor racketeer Max Block, and Lorenzo (Chappie) Brescio, a Catena soldier. Block was a $50,000-a-year vice president, Brescio was a $500-a-week salesman.

After Rose died in 1964, Dioguardi and his cousin, Thomas Plumeri, took over the business and set out to obtain control of the low-priced kosher meat field.

Essentially, Dioguardi's method was to gain control of a company and milk it by buying supplies on credit, selling the products and failing to pay his suppliers until the firm went bankrupt, at which point he would move on.

During a merger agreement with American Kosher, the company milk it by buying supplies on credit, selling the products were instructed to deliver Consumer products to the supermarkets with the stipulation that they could not be returned. One salesman testified in 1969 that the meats were "sometimes light green and sweaty" and were "an atrocity to perpetuate on our consumers." The Consumers company went bankrupt, but not before Dioguardi moved its remaining assets to another firm marketing a product called Tel Aviv. Eventually, that firm, too, went bankrupt and Dioguardi set up a new sales company, Finest Kosher Provisions, which entered into an agreement with the failing Mizrach

Kosher Provisions Co. of New York. The agreement, later vacated by a court order, gave Dioguardi the title to the brand name Mizrach if Mizrach went bankrupt. Mizrach's president, Louis Zeleznik, refused to talk about his deal with Dioguardi, or whether Dioguardi or his associates sell Mizrach products.

American Kosher is now back in business under Jerry Kleinberg who took over its operation from his father in 1966 after the firm declared bankruptcy. "At one time our business was grossing $16,000,000, but last year we grossed only $6,200,000." Kleinberg said. "We are just about shut out of the New York area. . . . Nobody tells us why, they just say they are getting a better price [from Mizrach]. Of course the prices are the same."

Among the supermarket chains, the attitude toward infiltration is sometimes hostile, sometimes defensive and, very often, indifferent.

King Kullen is one of a few chains maintaining a security system for checking on its suppliers. The president of the firm with 44 Long Island stores, Walter Miller, said that he is adamantly opposed to dealing with any organized crime figures.

Except for A&P, King Kullen was the only food chain to refuse to handle any of the detergents of North American Chemical Co., products that were pushed by the racketeer-owned Best Sales Co.

"We have a responsibility not to carry the products of any gangster," Miller said. "I can't see us promulgating these people . . . putting bad money on top of bad money. We have made attempts [to discover mob influence] through our security system, and we continue to do so . . . to run our own security check on each product." If pressure ever was applied on the firm to carry a racketeer's product, Miller said, he would go straight to the Justice Department. "I think markets should go to the FBI if they thought they were under any pressure," he said. "I know we would, but we've never had any trouble."

A spokesman for A&P said that the firm also runs confidential checks if it has any misgivings about a product or a name. If the checks turn up racket connections, he said, "We get rid of it pretty quick, and you know from the detergent thing that those guys have a hell of a job getting in."

Although some supermarket executives were unaware of the

racket connections of some of their products, a chain store food buyer who requested anonymity said that many supermarketmen are well aware of the connections. After the A&P squeeze, he said, mob names began showing up on lists of salesmen and on corporate records.

"If a product like clams or bread or soap or what have you is being sold by a salesman with the last name of Dioguardi or Gambino or Pecora, you know damn well who they are and what they represent," he said.

"I'm not saying all their products are bad or good for that matter, but you know what they represent. If you hear Dioguardi [crime figure John Dioguardi] is recommending a kosher meat or a bagel or Gambino [crime captain Paul Gambino] is selling a knife-sharpening service, it's just not smart to say I'm not going to take it.

"Who the hell can stand 10 or 50 million bucks in losses? Testify? You got to be crazy. You'd lose your job, your contacts and you'd worry about every car that passes you by, not to mention the pressure they'd bring to bear on the labor front."

Several chain store executives, including a spokesman for A&P, were critical of the federal government for not alerting firms about the activities of racketeers in the food industry.

"The federal government does a lot about publicizing fraudulent check pushers and wanted criminals . . . they get their faces plastered all over the place," the A&P spokesman said. "But you never see them saying, 'Don't do business with the Mozzarella Cheese Company of Upper Aspic, New Jersey.' "

When the Waldbaum Supermarket president, Ira Waldbaum, was asked about products that may be manufactured or sold by racketeers, he said: "Do I know who owns Borden's or Reyers? I don't want to get involved."

U.S. District Judge Edward Neaher said that, when he was U.S. attorney for the Eastern District of New York, there was much publicity about the terror campaign against A&P, but the giant food chain never filed a formal complaint with federal prosecutors. The firm did make an informal complaint with former U.S. Attorney Robert Morgenthau in New York, and Morgenthau called Gerardo Catena before a grand jury for questioning. The campaign against A&P promptly ended.

21
Muscling In

STANLEY PENN

Murray Packing Co. became a dead duck the moment Joseph Pagano was named president in 1961. The Weinberg and Newman families that controlled the Bronx meat processor seemed powerless to control their new president. Testimony in Federal District Court in New York reveals he bought large quantities of supplies on credit, then made quick sales to customers at cut-rate prices. He pocketed nearly $750,000 of Murray funds, the testimony indicates. The company, some $1.3 million in debt, went bankrupt a short time later.

The owners didn't know it, but they had turned over control to the Mafia.

A 1964 Senate subcommittee report on racketeering identified Pagano, who was sent to prison for his now-celebrated activity at Murray, as a member of the feared Mafia gang, or "family," of the late Vito Genovese. The family operates in the New York-New Jersey area and is one of the largest of the 26 similar Mafia groups around the country, law enforcement officials say.

It was unusual that the Mafia could get control of a legitimate business like Murray, but it is becoming less unusual. By various methods, organized crime is infiltrating a growing number of legitimate businesses. According to the Justice Department, organized crime now has links with tens of thousands of businesses and businessmen in such widely ranging fields as electronics, trucking, banking, construction, real estate and food and health services.

335

One motive, surprisingly, is to establish a money-making front to justify the criminals' luxurious way of life. Without such a front, the Internal Revenue Service would be constantly investigating Mafia members to find out where they get the money for their high living. The front, the criminals hope, provides the answer. The Mafia has plenty of cash to invest in these legitimate enterprises. Its yearly revenue from gambling, narcotics, usurious loans, prostitution and the numbers game has been estimated at as much as $50 billion.

How does the Mafia work its way in? There are several methods. Pagano had worked for a Murray affiliate and knew the parent firm was short of capital. According to court testimony, he told the owners that if made president he'd invest $35,000 in the firm for a one-third interest and would bring in new business through his connections in the wholesale meat field. The owners bought the deal.

Joseph Weinberg, one of the principals of Murray, found to his dismay that once gangsters get control it's difficult to force them out. Weinberg tried vainly to get Pagano to discontinue withdrawing Murray's funds for his own use, testimony indicates. "Look at the hole you are putting us into," Weinberg complained to Pagano, according to the court testimony. "Don't worry, I'll get the money back to you," Pagano lied.

Weinberg was asked in court why he didn't remove Pagano. After all, he and David Newman, another principal in the company, controlled two-thirds of Murray's stock. Weinberg's reply: "I didn't know what steps to take." For their role in violating the Federal bankruptcy laws by defrauding creditors, Weinberg and Newman in 1965 were given 12-month and 15-month jail sentences, respectively. Pagano got a five-year sentence.

Extortion is another favorite device for gaining control of a firm. Witness the ordeal of Irving Holzman, a New York juke box distributor. According to documents on file with the New York Court of Appeals in Albany, Mr. Holzman was asked by Salvatore Granello, a Mafioso, to meet with him at a Manhattan restaurant. There, testimony indicates, Granello got right to the point: He said Mr. Holzman should surrender one-fourth of the profits of his firm and, in return, the Mafia would see that no physical harm came to Mr. Holzman. "If at the end of a week, you have $1 left, I'll take 25 cents and you keep 75 cents," Granello explained. When Mr. Holzman resisted, the pressure intensified. Court documents described how several men entered his home in Roslyn, N.Y., and beat up his wife. He said their married daughter, who was expecting a child, got a phone call at her home in Oyster Bay, N.Y., warning: "If your father doesn't cooperate, we'll come and kick your pregnant belly in."

But Mr. Holzman didn't cave in. He went to Nassau County District Attorney William Cahn and allowed authorities to tap his phone conversations with Granello. The mobster, convicted on an extortion plot, was given an 18-month jail term in 1967.

Because the Mafia pays no taxes on its income from illegal rackets, its members must be circumspect when they buy into legitimate businesses. They can't appear to pay more than the amount of money they could have amassed through legitimate enterprises. Otherwise, they would arouse the suspicions of the Internal Revenue Service, and that could lead to criminal charges of tax evasion.

A real estate operator who is in a position to know tells how the Mafia often dupes the IRS. "Suppose John Smith, a legitimate businessman, wants to sell a building for $1 million," he says. "The hoodlum has the money to pay for it, but he can't show he got it all legitimately. So he says to John Smith, 'We'll make the legal papers show it as a $500,000 deal, and I'll give you the other $500,000 in cash.'" The legitimate businessman agrees not to pay taxes on the cash, because if he did the IRS easily could trace the money back to the gangster.

"You take a Mafia man who owns 10 night clubs," says Ralph Salerno, a former investigator for the New York City police. . . . "He'll use front men as owners for nine of the clubs, and he'll show ownership for the 10th. Each club, supposedly a separate business, pays a smaller tax bill than if the Mafia man admitted ownership of all 10." He explains that under the arrangement, profits of the individual clubs are taxed at a lower rate than would prevail if the profits were pooled in one sum.

The mere charge of Mafia penetration can prove a headache to nationally known firms. In 1959, for example, Sen. John McClellan's committee on racketeering was told that Carlos Marcello, a Mafia chieftain in the New Orleans area, had a "sub-

stantial financial interest" in a motel franchised by Holiday Inns
of America, Inc., now one of the nation's largest motel chains.

Aaron Kohn, director of the Metropolitan Crime Commission
of New Orleans, told the Senate panel that the motel—in Jefferson
parish in the New Orleans metropolitan area—had been purchased
in November 1958 in the names of New Orleans businessmen Roy
and Frank Occhipinti and others, but that Marcello had a concealed partial interest.

Mr. Kohn says he called the alleged Marcello part-ownership
to the attention of Holiday Inns management. "They were deeply
concerned, and they reacted immediately," Mr. Kohn says. A
Holiday Inns executive went to New Orleans to investigate, but
the company took no further action. Mr. Kohn says he was informed by Holiday Inns that the Occhipintis had committed no
violations of the franchise charter to provide grounds for revoking
the franchise.

In 1964, the Occhipintis sold the motel, together with another
Holiday Inn they controlled in New Orleans, to a group headed
by Leon Poirier, a former tax accountant for Marcello. Recently,
a spokesman for Mr. Poirier, asked whether Marcello was a hidden
owner in the two motels, said Marcello had no financial interest
in them during the period the Poirier group operated them.

Later, Holiday Inns tried to revoke the licenses of the Poirier
group on the ground that the operation of the two motels didn't
meet company standards. The Poirier group protested that without
licenses the motels couldn't be identified as part of the national
chain, and that a mortgage loan on one of the motels would be
jeopardized. In a suit filed in Federal District Court in New
Orleans, Mr. Poirier charged harassment and sought to block Holiday Inns from carrying out its threat.

The suit dragged on. Then came a series of transactions that
ended the controversy. The Poirier group sold the two motels to
a Topeka, Kan., firm. The firm, which owns other Holiday Inn
motels, was acting strictly on its own initiative, maintains a Holiday
Inns spokesman. Recently, Holiday Inns announced plans to buy
all the motels owned by the Topeka concern. Holiday Inns insists
this move isn't connected with Mr. Kohn's charge of 1959 alleging
a hidden ownership by Marcello.

A Mafia-controlled enterprise, though it may operate within

the law, has definite advantages over the ordinary firm against which it competes. The Mafia firm is likely to be capitalized in part with untaxed funds. Often it has no union trouble while a competitor may find itself struck by a Mafia-dominated union. And the Mafia enterprise may get bargain rates by using a Mafia-controlled trucking firm. A hearing in New York in 1969 heard testimony suggesting that a Mafia-controlled concern can sometimes win customers away from reliable, independent firms.

A spokesman for some knife-sharpening companies told the State Commission of Investigation that steady customers switched in 1959 to a new company formed by Paul Gambino, a member of the Mafia gang headed by his brother Carlo Gambino. To get back their customers, the independent knife sharpeners raised $175,000 and bought out the Mafia enterprise, the commission was informed. Commission members listened with skepticism as one of the customers said he didn't know that Paul Gambino was a Mafioso when he switched to the Gambino firm. He said he switched because he was offered two weeks of free service.

After listening to this and similar testimony, Commissioner Goodman A. Sarachan asked: "Does anyone really believe that an individual like Paul Gambino could persuade large chain supermarkets to switch to his company the services they were buying from well-known and reliable persons, simply by arranging to meet with executives of such chain supermarkets and offering two weeks' free service?"

22
On the Waterfront

STANLEY PENN

Ross Trucking Co. has a good thing going: A guarantee that about half the bananas imported into the New York area must be hauled from the docks in Ross trucks. Three of the four major U.S. banana importers see to it that no competitor muscles in. The importers say Ross gets the work because the company is fast, efficient and reliable. Others, including a representative of the Waterfront Commission of New York Harbor, suspect it's because a key Ross employe is well-connected to the Mafia.

Law enforcement agencies are concerned about the proliferation of Mafia-owned and Mafia-controlled businesses, resulting from the reinvestment of the vast profits of organized crime. But Ross, with its employe who has been tied to the Mafia, raises a related question: Does the mere suggestion of a Mafia link give a firm a competitive advantage?

There isn't any evidence that Ross used illegal tactics to get its exclusive position at Port Newark, N.J., and Pier 13 on New York's East River. The three banana importers unload at these docks, and they won't sell their bananas (which include such brand names as Bonita and Cabana) to jobbers unless Ross gets the delivery work. The jobbers pay Ross' entire bill.

Jobbers are middlemen who buy green bananas from the importers and sell to retailers after the bananas ripen. The 23 trucks Ross operates haul bananas to jobbers within a 50-mile radius of

New York City. (Ross' monopoly at the two piers doesn't apply to bananas going to more distant points.) Ross deals with 25 or more jobbers, it is estimated. Some jobbers who use Ross get nervous when the name is mentioned. "Leave me out," says one. "This is strictly a cement-overcoat situation." Another says, "Look, I don't question the system." A third, asked whether he thinks importers would face reprisals if they didn't insist on Ross, says, "You said it. I didn't."

The Waterfront Commission of New York Harbor, a bi-state group formed in 1953 to combat crime and corruption, isn't so reticent. Ross charges "exorbitant rates" and its trucks aren't insulated to protect the fruit, says William P. Sirignano, the commission's executive director.

The commission is particularly interested in Ross' highest-paid employe, Pete De Feo. Mr. Sirignano says the Federal Bureau of Investigation has described Mr. De Feo as a member of the Mafia "family," of the late Vito Genovese, who directed Mafia activities in New York and New Jersey. The commission says Mr. De Feo also is an associate of Gerardo Catena, who succeeded Genovese as family boss.

Mr. De Feo's brother-in-law, Frank Aquilino, founded Ross. Mr. Aquilino died in January 1969 and his widow and sons operate the company now. But the real power may lie with Mr. De Feo, whose mug shot cropped up in a 1964 Senate committee report on racketeering. Police records show Mr. De Feo has had several encounters with the law, but no convictions. In 1947 he was arrested on a homicide charge, but was found innocent. In 1965 he was arrested on a charge of disorderly conduct, but was acquitted. In 1968 U.S. Attorney Robert Morgenthau obtained an indictment against Mr. De Feo and five others, charging they conspired to receive a kickback for arranging a $1.9 million loan from a Teamsters Union pension fund to a New York builder. The case hasn't yet come to trial.

The commission says it has stamped out much of the gambling, loan-sharking and extortion that plagued the waterfront before 1953. But now "criminals have moved into fringe areas, including warehousing," says Mr. Sirignano. He explains that he considers Ross a warehouser, at least technically, because loaded Ross trucks sometimes sit on the pier overnight before the bananas are delivered. He asserts that "it is obvious from the rapid and tremendous growth" of Ross and a few other small waterfront firms that these concerns "are part and parcel of the underworld's branching out into areas free from any effective government control which would protect the public interest."

Documents on file with the Interstate Commerce Commission show that in 1968 Ross revenue was about $429,000. That hardly qualifies the company as a business giant. However, Ross earnings in 1968 totaled about $89,000—a 21% profit margin that most blue-chip companies might well envy.

Ross officials don't want to be interviewed. One indicated over the phone that written questions would be answered, so a list was promptly mailed. But no answers were received. Company headquarters at 219 Mulberry St., in a drab working-class section on Manhattan's Lower East Side, reinforces the impression that curious outsiders aren't welcome. Black curtains cover the front windows of the office, which is in an old tenement.

The three big importers that unload at Port Newark and Pier 13 are Standard Fruit & Steamship Co., New Orleans; Pan American Fruit Co., New York; and West Indies Fruit Co., a subsidiary of Del Monte Corp., San Francisco. All speak highly of Ross.

One concern likes Ross because Ross trucks handle only bananas, "and not meat or fish or any obnoxious material to bananas, which could give bananas a bad odor," according to an official. This official says Ross never has attempted to coerce his firm into using Ross trucks.

"Years ago," an official at a second importer says, "we had a number of truckers doing our work. Some went out of business. Others didn't have decent equipment. Ross performs a good service."

The importers also argue that if competing truckers were allowed, costly tieups and traffic jams would result. However, United Fruit Co., Boston, the fourth major importer, allows competing truckers at its unloading operation, and observers say there are no traffic jams or long delays there. (United Fruit unloads at Weehawken, N.J. As a result of a Government antitrust suit, the company signed a consent decree in 1958 that, among other things, prohibited it from having an exclusive trucker like Ross.)

Some jobbers complain bitterly about Ross' hold on the two

piers. "It costs me 22½ cents a box of bananas if Ross delivers," says one. "I could save 10 cents a box by sending my own truck down to the dock. But, no, I'm forced to use Ross." Another jobber says he recently asked one of the three big importers why he couldn't use his own truck. Recalls the jobber: "The importer said, 'This is the way it's got to be.' I say it smells."

One authoritative source maintains that the importers use only Ross because they "just don't want to take any chances." He explains: "They believe, rightly or wrongly, that Ross has connections. Nobody knows if Ross has connections with the Longshoremen's union, but I guess the importer feels that he shouldn't take a chance that his bananas will be mishandled on the pier." A New York spokesman for the International Longshoreman's Association says he knows of no "dealings or connections" between the union and Ross.

But other jobbers say they like Ross, and insist they're saving money by using the company. Years ago, when a group of jobbers tried breaking Ross' grip by refusing to buy bananas at Port Newark, the effort collapsed when other jobbers continued buying there. One jobber argues that even though Ross trucks aren't insulated, bananas don't stay in the trucks long enough to be damaged by heat or cold.

Mr. Sirignano of the Waterfront Commission, however, cited Ross' "underworld connections" when he argued before a New Jersey legislative committee for passage of an anti-crime bill aimed at the New Jersey waterfront. The bill passed. It requires licensing of warehouses and other pier facilities not now regulated by the Waterfront Commission. Under Mr. Sirignano's view that Ross is technically a warehouser, the trucking company, too, would have to get a license. . . .

23
In Hollywood

MALCOLM JOHNSON

Of all the gangsters who flourished during prohibition, few attained such power and wealth as Scarface Al Capone. This deceptively mild-looking little man with soft brown eyes migrated from Brooklyn to build an empire of crime in Chicago with influential underworld connections throughout the country. It was one of the ironies of the times that Capone enjoyed complete immunity from the law for the reign of terror he invoked. He was never brought to trial for any of his major crimes, including innumerable murders committed by his paid gunmen on orders from himself. When the law finally nailed Capone it was for income-tax evasion. He was convicted in 1931, served seven years in prison, then retired to a life of luxury in Florida until his death, of paresis, in January, 1947. Capone's lieutenants carried on his organization, which is still active in Chicago.

Though its chief source of income during prohibition was from the sale and distribution of liquor and beer, the Capone mob owned brothels, gambling establishments, and night clubs. In addition, the mob perfected the "protection" racket as it is now known—the device of levying tribute from businessmen for the privilege of staying in business. The protection, of course, was from the gangsters themselves; if the victim did not pay, a bomb . . . was exploded in his place of business. The racket usually was worked through a trade association, so-called, to which the victims were compelled to belong.

When the Capone gangsters invaded the labor field after the death of prohibition in December, 1933, they applied the same technique of intimidation against the unions and their members. One of the gang's first and most successful ventures in labor forms an almost incredible story of extortion in the motion-picture industry. The story is now a matter of public record through the court testimony of a convicted labor racketeer who squealed against his gangland bosses. It is a story with strong political implications, with hints of bribery in high places. It is a story of how the most notorious gang in the country, working through union officials, brought the entire Hollywood movie industry to its knees.

The story properly begins in Chicago in 1932 as the prohibition law was on its way out. It was a bleak year in the depth of the nation-wide depression: a year of soup kitchens, bread lines, bank failures, shuttered factories, and of jobless, despairing men tramping the streets in a vain search for work. It was a bad year even for labor racketeers. Nevertheless, a paunchy little man of boundless cupidity named Willie Bioff was doing his best to turn a dishonest dollar by organizing and preying upon Chicago's kosher butchers. Bioff was a panderer, a thief, an extortionist, and an all-round racketeer and gangster. His name a few years later was to strike terror in the hearts of the Hollywood movie moguls.

In that year, 1932, Bioff met a professional unionist, one George E. Browne, business agent of Local 2 of the International Alliance of Theatrical Stage Employees, an American Federation of Labor union with jurisdiction over motion-picture-theater projectionists and allied theater workers. As a sideline, times being what they were, Browne was organizing chicken dealers. It was a fortuitous meeting—for Bioff and Browne. Both had only one interest in the labor movement: to gouge money out of it. Each was quick to appreciate the talents of the other. As a labor leader, Browne, tough and thoroughly corrupt, was more than willing to accept the aid of a smarter racketeer. He found one in Willie Bioff. While Browne was a good front man, Bioff was the schemer, the planner, the strategist with an utterly ruthless talent for extortion. Bioff and Browne joined forces, abandoned the kosher market, and concentrated on the theatrical union as offering greater possibilities. Nominally, Bioff became Browne's assistant. Actually, he was the brains of the combination.

Browne's union local was in a bad way. Out of 400 members, 250 were unemployed. There was no profit for Browne and Bioff in unemployed union members. They decided to mix charity with business by setting up a soup kitchen where a working member could get a meal for thirty-five cents and the unemployed could eat free. They persuaded politicians and theatrical celebrities to drop in frequently for meals and contribute $20 to $50 to a good cause. The contributions served the double purpose of keeping the local alive and providing Browne and Bioff with a small income. The contributions also gave Browne and Bioff the idea for their first successful shakedown. In 1934 the pair went to millionaire Barney Balaban of the Balaban & Katz theater chain with a demand that he restore a pay cut imposed on IATSE members in the Balaban & Katz theaters in 1929. They had no illusions about getting the cut restored, nor did they want it. Their interest never was in the welfare of the workers except when it was a means of extorting money from them in dues, initiation fees, and assessments.

Balaban appeared to give their request serious thought. He said he might be willing to comply, but was afraid that if he did so, other unions would jump in with similar demands. That would be too costly. Browne and Bioff then casually mentioned the soup kitchen, observing that it cost $7,500 a year and was serving a humane cause. Balaban got the point. He saw immediately that paying for the kitchen would be much cheaper than restoring the pay cut. His attitude reflected that of many businessmen who paid off labor racketeers. In permitting themselves to become extortion victims they nearly always were seeking some advantage for themselves, usually at the expense of the workers. Obviously the large sums paid to labor gangsters were never passed on to the workers. In any event, Balaban volunteered to pay for the soup kitchen in lieu of restoring the pay cut. He quickly discovered that Browne and Bioff had no intention of letting him off so lightly.

"I figured right then I might as well kill a sheep as a lamb," Bioff boasted in court. "Barney turned out to be a lamb. When he agreed to our suggestion I knew we had him. I told him his contribution would have to be $50,000 unless he wanted real trouble. By that I meant we would pull his projectionists out of the theaters. He was appalled, but we turned on the heat. He finally agreed to pay us $20,000. The restoration of the pay cut was forgotten. We were not interested in that then or at any other time. We didn't care whether wages were reduced or raised. We were interested only in getting the dough, and we didn't care how we got it."

From the day that Balaban coughed up $20,000, Browne and Bioff knew that they were on top of a lucrative racket. Joyously they celebrated the knowledge by spending $300 at a night club and gambling resort operated for the Capone mob by Nick Circella, alias Nick Deane. As they wined and dined on the money that they had extorted at the expense of their members, they boasted of their recent good fortune. A few days later, Frank Rio, a leader in the Capone gang, accosted Browne and demanded to know how the union was making out. Up to this point the mob had let Browne alone; the "take" wasn't enough to interest it. But the first big shakedown changed the picture entirely. Browne spun a woeful tale of his union's impoverished state, but Rio was unimpressed. "From now on," he said, "we expect 50 percent of the take. Everything you get. Understand?"

Browne and Bioff understood perfectly. The Mafia had muscled in on them, as it had on so many other union locals. It was a case of the big fish swallowing the small fish. Browne and Bioff knew that they had been served with the usual "or else" proposition. They agreed to cooperate, for they had no choice. On the one hand they hated to surrender half their union booty. On the other hand they were smart enough to know that, with the Capone mob's backing, the "take" should be much larger and that future expansion would be made easier. The gang's reputation for terrorism, built up over the years, would take care of that.

It should be remembered that the mobsters at no time had any official connection with this or any other labor union except insofar as they were able to plant their own stooges in union offices. Their sole interest in a union was the profit in it for them. They operated behind the scenes, issuing orders and directing policy through their captives in the union. In this instance they took over by intimidating two thieving union officials who were not too unhappy about being taken over. The capture of Browne's local was just the beginning. The mob was determined to expand and gain control of the international union. They intended to do it by using

Browne as a front man. A meeting was held. Present were Browne and Bioff; Frank Nitto, or Nitti; Louis Campagna, Paul De Lucia, and Rio—all top men in the Capone circle. Nitto, a first cousin of Capone, was known as the Enforcer. When Capone went to jail on income-tax charges Nitto was regarded as the number one man in the gang's underworld enterprises. Campagna was one of Capone's ex-bodyguards.

The gang chieftains knew that Browne had been defeated in 1932 for president of the international union. They told him he was to run again and get elected. There must be no mistakes this time. Where were the weak spots, the places in the national organization that had failed to support him? New York City, New Jersey, Cleveland, and St. Louis, Browne said. The gangsters explained that their out-of-town connections would help this time—
. . . Louis (Lepke) Buchalter and Charles (Lucky) Luciano in New York, and lesser known gangsters in Cleveland and St. Louis. For another meeting, two weeks before the June, 1934, convention of the IATSE, Lepke was summoned from New York. Nitto gave Lepke a message for Luciano . . . "Local 306 (the New York projectionists) was to vote for Browne for president."

"I won't have to see Lucky on that, Frank," Lepke replied. "I can handle it myself. I'll also see Kaufman of New Jersey [Louis Kaufman, business agent of the big Newark local] and see that Longy [Zwillman] delivers that outfit."

The campaign went exactly as planned. The Capone syndicate's representatives in the key cities spread the word: "Vote for Browne." As a final gesture to insure success, the syndicate's far-flung representatives gathered in Chicago and from there descended on the international union's convention in Louisville. The presence of the nation's top gangsters and their gunmen at the convention, circulating among the delegates and openly backing the candidacy of Browne, created such an atmosphere of intimidation that opposition wilted. Browne was elected without a single dissenting vote. Democratic processes were forgotten and the best interests of the dues-paying union members were ignored. Everybody at the convention knew that the Capone gang had made a successful bid for power and was now in control of the union.

President Browne's first official act was to announce that Willie Bioff was his "personal representative." The convention delegates knew what that meant too: Bioff was giving orders for Browne and through Browne. Backed by the Capone gangsters and their powerful out-of-town connections, Bioff and Browne were quick to solidify their control of the entire union. The Capone group appointed Nick Circella to oversee their activities and to report back. . . . From then on they were tools of the mob in a major racket venture, and the stakes were high.

When Bioff and Browne departed for New York to chart a campaign of extortion and to "confer" with theater owners and other union officials, they were told to feel free to call upon Luciano or Frank Costello any time they needed help. "They are our people," gangster De Lucia explained, according to Bioff's testimony. . . .

In Chicago the mob, through Browne and Bioff, extorted $100,000 from motion-picture theater chains by threatening to force them to hire two projectionists in each theater booth instead of one. The Balaban & Katz circuit paid $60,000; Warner Brothers $30,000; and an independent chain, the S. & S., $10,000. Here again the racket fee was at the ultimate expense of the union workers. There would have been more work for more members had the union's demand been on the level. When one theater representative protested bitterly that putting two projectionists in a booth would drive him out of business, Bioff replied, "I can't help that. If this is going to kill drama, then drama has got to die." After this shakedown, the Capone mobsters gave Browne and Bioff the bad news that henceforth the gang's take was to be 75 percent instead of 50 percent; Browne and Bioff could divide the remaining 25 percent between them.

The mob's brazen method of operation was further demonstrated in the case of a burlesque-theater owner named Jack Barger. When Barger opened a new theater in Chicago, Bioff called on him and calmly announced that Barger would have to surrender half his profits. "Barger raved and said it wasn't fair, but I told him that was the way it had to be if he wanted to stay in business," Bioff recalled in court. "He went along."

On orders from Bioff, the wages of union members were slashed and stagehands were laid off so that the profits would be bigger for division with the mob. This was during the worst part of the depression, when work of any kind was hard to get and

good men and their families were going hungry through no fault
of their own. Yet a union whose ostensible purpose was to better
the living conditions of its members was deliberately and pitilessly
throwing men out of work and cutting wages. Not content with
this abuse of the members, Bioff milked another $200 a week from
the theater owner, Barger, when he discovered that Barger was
drawing that amount for himself in salary. The gang promptly
put one of its own men on the payroll for a like amount for doing
nothing. They closely scrutinized Barger's books to see that they
got their full share of the money. In fact, they ran the business.
Every time Bioff saw Barger, he would taunt him by asking,
"How's *our* business, partner?"

Like other labor racketeers before and since, Bioff and Browne
extorted money from their victims by a variety of methods. They
sold "strike prevention insurance" for whatever they thought the
traffic would bear. They threatened wage hikes and shorter hours,
demands which were promptly withdrawn and forgotten when
payment was made directly to them. They ruthlessly sold out their
members by agreeing to wage cuts or longer hours. One of Bioff's
greatest triumphs in the field of "strike prevention" was the
$150,000 he extorted from Charles Moscowitz of the Loew's
theater chain in New York in 1935.

By 1936, two years after seizing control, the Capone gang's
power in the union was such that it was ready to launch a daring
offensive against the billion-dollar industry of Hollywood itself.
Millions in extortion fees were the stake. The union had only a
small membership on the West Coast, but that did not deter the
mob. They persuaded the West Coast studios to give the IATSE
jurisdiction over labor by exerting pressure against movie outlets,
notably the Balaban & Katz theater chain, a subsidiary of Para-
mount Pictures.

It was necessary, however, to close every theater from Chicago to St. Louis before the theater officials saw the light and influenced the West Coast companies to give the IATSE jurisdiction.
That done, Bioff in the fall of 1936 went to Nicholas M. Schenck,
president of Loew's and spokesman for the movie industry in dealings with the union.

"You have a prosperous business here," Bioff told Schenck.
"I elected Browne president of this union because he will do what

I say. I am the boss and I want $2,000,000 out of the movie industry."

"I was shocked," said Schenck, recalling the conversation. "At first I couldn't talk. But Bioff said, 'You don't know what will happen. We gave you just a taste of it in Chicago. We will close down every theater in the country. You couldn't take that. It will cost you many millions of dollars over and over again. Think it over.'"

The movie bigwigs, including Schenck, Sidney Kent of Twentieth Century–Fox, and Leo Spitz of RKO, thought it over and decided to pay. An agreement was reached by which the major companies were to pay $50,000 a year and the minor companies $25,000 a year to the racketeers. The payments were to continue indefinitely—forever, if Bioff and the mob had their way. A first payment of $75,000 in cash was made to Bioff and Browne in a room in the Hotel Warwick, New York. Schenck brought $50,000 and Kent $25,000. Bioff and Browne dumped the money on a bed and carefully counted it, while Schenck and Kent watched, squirming.

The full story of the audacious Hollywood shakedown is well-known history today because Willie Bioff out-smarted himself. Otherwise the conspiracy might never have been revealed. Juggled bookkeeping and a dummy loan finally started Federal investigators on his trail. Bioff, like Capone before him, first attracted the government's attention in connection with income-tax evasion on a transaction of $100,000.

Bioff's talent as an extortionist had won him a bankroll of $100,000 which he was anxious to conceal from the government. He yearned to buy a ranch in California, but knew an investment of that kind would arouse the curiosity of the tax agents. So in 1938 Bioff pretended to borrow $100,000 from Joseph M. Schenck, then chairman of the board of Twentieth Century–Fox and a brother of Nicholas M. Schenck. Bioff realized that it would look curious for Schenck to make him a loan of that amount. Therefore he arranged with Schenck for the latter's nephew, Arthur Stebbins, to give him a check for $100,000. Bioff gave Stebbins the cash in return. On the books, however, the transaction appeared as a loan, guaranteed by Schenck, with Bioff giving a note. In the eyes of the government it appeared that Schenck had derived an income of $100,000 in a deal he had not reported. In the chain of investigations which followed, other irregularities were discovered. Schenck was indicted for income-tax evasion and sentenced to three years in prison. The sentence was reduced to one year and a day for perjury after Schenck gave evidence against Bioff and Browne leading to the discovery of the extortion conspiracy and the union's backing by the Chicago mob.

Browne and Bioff were indicted for extortion and conspiracy, tried, and convicted in 1941. Bioff was sentenced to ten years in prison, Browne to eight years, and each was fined $10,000. In prison the two racketeers squealed on their Mafia bosses. The mobsters were indicted by the government on March 18, 1943, on charges of conspiracy, extortion, using the mails to defraud, and of having extorted more than $2,500,000 from union members and motion picture producers.

Frank Nitto, the Enforcer, named in the indictment, committed suicide. Nick Circella pleaded guilty. Frank Rio had died in 1935. The defendants brought to trial were Louis Campagna and Paul De Lucia (mentioned previously), Phil D'Andrea, Francis Maritote, Ralph Pierce, Charles Gioe, John Roselli, and Louis Kaufman. Except for Kaufman, they were all members of the Chicago Mafia. Each had a long police record. Maritote, for instance, had been arrested twenty-seven times.

The gangsters were tried in New York. Willie Bioff was the principal witness against them. He testified with gusto, his hard, pig-like eyes gleaming from behind thick glasses. For days Bioff was on the stand, spilling out the story of the mob's control of the union and of the extortion plot. Obviously relishing his role, he boasted of his own part in the plot and implicated all the defendants. His attitude was that he was a gone goose anyway and that the gangsters deserved punishment, too. He, Bioff, was going to see that they got it. The gangsters listened impassively as Bioff, smirking and leering at them, gave evidence that was to convict them. Browne, though less flamboyant, corroborated Bioff's testimony.

Their testimony, together with that of the movie producers who admitted the payments to the union racketeers, convicted the Capone gangsters. They did not take the stand in their own defense. The defense lawyers contended that the sums paid to Bioff and Browne were straight bribes to influence their actions as union officials, and not an extortion plot involving the defendants. It was shown that Bioff was on friendly terms with the producers, despite the fact that he was extracting huge sums of money from them. They deferred to him, entertained him in their homes, and wined and dined him on lavish trips to Europe—all at company expense, of course. The money expended in this manner was not denied, but the jury refused to swallow the bribery defense. At one point when Bioff was telling how frightened the producers were during the shakedown negotiations, he was asked if they were afraid that the money they paid him was a bribe, making them liable to prosecution. Bioff said he didn't know anything about that. Didn't he know that under New York law it was a criminal offense to offer a bribe to a union official to influence his action?

"No, I didn't know that," Bioff replied. "I wish I had. I could have used that."

"How?"

"Why, to get more money out of them. That would have given me another hold on them."

Boasting of his talents as a chiseler, Bioff told, among other things, how he obtained $5,000 worth of furnishings for his new Hollywood home from Leo Spitz, RKO executive.

"I hadn't collected the money his company owed us and I figured I might as well get something out of them," said Bioff. "So I went to Leo and I said, 'Leo, I gotta have some drapes and other things for my new home and I thought maybe you could get them for me wholesale through RKO's purchasing department.' Of course, I didn't intend to pay for them," he added parenthetically.

"Did you get the furnishings?"

"Yes, but unfortunately I am still charged with them and I understand they are going to sue me now."

"Did you get any other gifts?"

"No, but I hinted."

"Did any of these defendants get any share of those gifts?"

Bioff flashed the gangsters a triumphant smile. "No, sir!" he replied. "That's one spot where I beat them."

Bioff said that once when things looked tough he threatened to quit the racket. The mobsters told him that anybody who resigned from the syndicate resigned from life as well. "That is why I never resigned," he said.

Bioff's fears were justified. The gang's rule of the union was marked by warfare in the old Chicago style. Tommy Malloy, tough business agent of Local 110 of the union, balked at splitting his take with the Mafia, and was promptly and permanently removed. In February, 1935, Malloy was shot to death with sawed-off shotguns. Clyde Osterberg, who tried to organize apprentice operators in defiance of the gang's ruling, was eliminated in a similar manner. Fred Blacker, nicknamed Bugs because he scattered bedbugs in the theaters of recalcitrant exhibitors, was killed when the gang felt that he was on the verge of talking.

The fear instilled in the movie producers was described by Major Albert Warner, vice-president and treasurer of Warner Brothers. Knowing the background of these people, Warner said, he was afraid of personal injury as well as property damage when Bioff first approached the producers in 1936. Warner and other executives testified that they did not feel that they could afford to fight the union and the gang behind it.

The ever-present subject of political influence cropped up several times in Bioff's long-winded recital, but was never developed by the prosecution. In 1937 the California legislature began to investigate labor conditions in the movie industry. Bioff claimed in court to have paid $5,000 to a certain Colonel William Neblitt, an influential California politician and law partner of the late Senator William G. McAdoo, presumably to arrange a quick end to the legislative inquiry. Bioff's accusation was never followed up, but in 1941 Colonel Neblitt sued some twenty-five defendants—Bioff among them—for "malicious and unfounded attacks." "Good old honest Colonel Neblitt," as Bioff facetiously termed him in court, lost the case.

Usually Bioff and Browne had to threaten the movie executives into buying protection and cooperation. In at least one instance, however, a theater executive took the initiative and sought out the services of Bioff. It was another case of a businessman eager to sit down with the lowest type of criminal in order to obtain some financial advantage. This particular executive was so anxious for the opportunity that he secured the services of a prominent lawyer with high political connections to arrange a meeting with Bioff.

Bioff swore in court that Sol Rosenblatt, a New York lawyer, formerly general counsel to the Democratic National Committee and administrator under the NRA for the movie industry, received 25 percent of a $25,000 bribe paid to him (Bioff) in 1937 by George Skouras of the Fox theater chain in New York. "It was a bribe, sir, and a welcome one," was the way Bioff put it. He said that Rosenblatt invited him to a meeting with Skouras in Rosenblatt's plush New York office. There Rosenblatt told Bioff that Skouras was in a "kind of trouble" and that perhaps Bioff could remedy it. Bioff's nose for money began to twitch. Just what was Mr. Skouras's trouble? Skouras explained carefully. He operated a chain of eighteen movie houses, similar to a rival chain, the Frisch-Rintzler outfit in Brooklyn. They showed the same kind of pictures at the same time, even dealt with the same banks. But there was a difference which Skouras found embarrassing. The competing chain was able to operate its projection booths for $60,000 a year less than it cost Skouras. The banks were chiding him for this seeming extravagance and inefficiency. If Bioff could put the competing chain on a "comparable basis" it would be worth $50,000 to Skouras. Bioff complied. His method was characteristically direct and unorthodox.

"As a result of that conversation I called up the heads of the Frisch-Rintzler circuit and *increased* their scale $60,000 a year," testified Bioff, the great equalizer, in court. That was his idea of a comparable basis, but Skouras was "a little disappointed," Bioff admitted. It wasn't quite what Skouras had in mind and he didn't think the method was worth $50,000, so they compromised for $25,000.

"And you got 75 percent of this $25,000?"

"Yes, sir."

"And did Sol Rosenblatt get the other 25 percent?"

"I believe he did."

"That was his fee?"

"Yes, sir."

Bioff said that his share, in cash, was delivered to him by Rosenblatt.

Christmas presents for "the boys" in Chicago came high that year, 1937, and the Hollywood producers played Santa Claus. Bioff was the collector, explaining that "the boys" would be expecting something for Christmas and that he didn't want to disappoint them. It might not be safe. He said he collected a Christmas fund of $7,500 from Harry M. Warner, president of Warner Brothers. . . .

Bioff's brother-in-law, Norman Thaw Nelson, shed some more light on the manner in which the extortion payments were covered up on movie-company books. From June, 1937, until early in 1939, he was the nominal recipient of $77,448 paid to him through a film agency, but he actually kept only $125 a week for himself. Ostensibly the money was for commissions on the sale of raw film to Metro-Goldwyn-Mayer; actually it was a bookkeeping device to conceal payments to Bioff. Nelson got the money as a collector for Bioff. It was paid through the firm of Smith & Allar, Ltd., distributors of motion-picture film. Nelson was introduced to one of the agency officials by Louis B. Mayer, production chief of M-G-M, who said, "This is Mr. Bioff's brother-in-law. I want you to put him in the film business." Thereafter Nelson collected weekly checks for Bioff totaling from $2,000 to $3,500 a month.

Six of the Capone gangsters and Kaufman, the Newark union official, were convicted after a trial of six weeks. D'Andrea, De Lucia, Campagna, Gioe, Maritote, and Roselli were sentenced to ten years each in Federal prison and fined $10,000 each. Kaufman got seven years and a fine of $10,000. . . .

. . . Four of them, D'Andrea, De Lucia, Campagna, and Gioe, were released on parole by the Federal Parole Board on August 13, 1947, after serving the bare one-third minimum of their sentences required to make them eligible for parole. . . .

On November 4, 1955, Willie Bioff, who had squealed on the Chicago Mafiosi, left his Phoenix, Arizona, home, got into his car and stepped on the starter. The car, rigged with dynamite, exploded and he was killed instantly. No one was ever arrested for his murder.

24
The Businessman as Victim

CHARLES GRUTZNER

Despite the efforts of law enforcement agencies and such business organizations as the U.S. Chamber of Commerce, the National Industrial Conference Board, and others, the flood of underworld money, muscle, and managerial activity seems to be spreading faster than it can be drained off. A large part of the explanation is businessmen's reluctance, for one reason or another, to turn over to official investigators and prosecutors their specific suspicions and evidence of infiltrative attempts. The reticence of this "silent majority" has made matters far easier for the underworld—and far more difficult for legitimate business. Perhaps the best way to illustrate the role played all too often by uncommunicative businessmen is to take an actual example from recent experience:

The Progressive Drug Company in New York, a respectable family enterprise that prospered into a $10 million-a-year wholesale business, was sold after the founder's death to the Pawnee Drug Company. Strange things began to happen. As the New York State Investigation Commission found out later, Twentieth Century Industries, a giant conglomerate whose top officers had dealings with identified members of the Mafia, had created Pawnee for the sole purpose of acquiring Progressive. Under the new ownership, Progressive was milked dry for the benefit of underworld figures and other subsidiaries of Twentieth Century Industries. It went into bankruptcy with losses to creditors.

The weird sequence of events in the rape of the Progressive Drug Company begin with a switch in the company's labor contract, which had been with a reputable AFL-CIO union, to a local of the unaffiliated Teamsters Union. The ploy, listed in the Chamber of Commerce's *Deskbook on Organized Crime* as a telltale indicator of possible hanky-panky, went apparently unnoticed by Benjamin Goldfinger, who had been a vice president of Progressive and whom the new owners kept in the same post after the sale.

Goldfinger was directed by one of his new bosses to put one Dominick (Nicky) Bando on the payroll at $150 as a guard at the company's warehouse in the Bronx, and to hand to Bando an additional $100 in cash each week "to insure labor peace." Testifying as a subpoenaed witness before the State Investigation Commission after the bankruptcy, Goldfinger swore he had been ignorant that Bando was an ex-convict and an associate of Mafiosi. . . .

It developed that Goldfinger had also made cash payments in amounts of $100 to $200 at a time to a man he said he knew only as "Abe," who was neither an employee nor a creditor of Progressive but who was connected with another subsidiary of Twentieth Century Industries. There were other payments that Goldfinger knew were, to use the kindest word, "irregular"— $13,405 to an affiliate company for "merchandise" never delivered, and $2,000 to the comptroller of another affiliate firm for nonexistent "services rendered."

Goldfinger, a slightly built man who had receding gray hair and who wore glasses, was unable to hide from himself the obvious illegality of these and other transactions. Although he kept silent until the State Investigation Commission people called him in (too late to save the company and its creditors), he was keeping a private journal in which he listed the cash payments against a possible day of reckoning. The Commission induced him to testify at open hearings in 1969 after giving him immunity from prosecution. Other witnesses, from ex-convict Bando to Martin Goldman, Vice President of Twentieth Century (which controls or has interests in mining, drug, soft drink, and plastics companies), invoked the Fifth Amendment against self-incrimination in refusing to answer questions at the hearings.

The Progressive Drug case was one of more than a dozen in different industries laid bare by the Commission in seven days of public hearings in New York City. Each case made clear one or another of the ways in which organized crime gains an interest or complete domination of a hitherto legitimate business and either operates it in unlawful or unethical ways to increase its profits and destroy competitors, or else bankrupts the captive company by siphoning off its assets. . . .

In not a single case did the legitimate entrepreneur who was the target of the illegal maneuver step forward to inform federal or local law enforcement agencies of the obvious evidence. Such early information, along with a willingness to testify, *could* have thrown the invasion strategy off balance, saved many businesses from ruin, averted puffed-up costs for legitimate competitors and inflated prices for consumers, and transferred some of the underworld agents from executive offices to prison cells.

Of course, *some* of the invaders have gone to prison, along with the businessmen and public officials they corrupted. There have been convictions for fraud, labor racketeering, income tax evasion, extortion, larceny, perjury, conspiracy, and other specific crimes connected with business take-overs. But these convictions represent only a fraction of the cases known to enforcement officials. An even larger number of flagrant cases of underworld infiltration gather dust in prosecutors' files, often until statutes of limitation wash them out, while investigators search desperately for witnesses whose testimony is essential for a court case.

The public, including businessmen, frequently wonders why disclosures by Congressional committees and state investigation commissions of clearly illegal activities fail so many times to result in criminal prosecution. The answer is simple. It is one thing to produce the testimony of investigators and subpoenaed books, records, and bank accounts at public hearings, with the public drawing its conclusions from the repetitive invoking of the Fifth Amendment by the principals. But it is an altogether different thing to get people involved in or innocently affected by the criminal acts to mount the witness stand in a courtroom and give the kind of testimony required for conviction.

Some of the information about the infiltration of legitimate business has resulted from routine surveillance of known members of the criminal organization, some from tedious checking of corporate records, some from wiretaps and electronic bugs, some from underworld informers. But *almost none* has been supplied voluntarily to official agencies by legitimate businessmen who became unwilling or willing associates of criminals.

How do the leaders of "America's number-one growth industry," as it has been called, get inside legitimate businesses? In answering this question, which has an obvious bearing on the strategy of counteraction by legitimate companies, it would be well to keep in mind the two principal motives of the underworld's "top management":

1. It wants to put the profits of its illegal enterprises to work earning more money. The huge take from gambling and loan sharking, for instance, cries for reinvestment in other ventures. This need is so pressing that every major Mafia borgata has its own "money mover"—a member or associate whose function it is to find the weak or willing spots in the business community where the ill-gotten gains can be used as seeds for further profits.

The idea of unemployed capital is as repugnant to the bosses of organized crime as it is to any banker or captain of legitimate industry. And the infusion of tainted capital into the nation's business and industrial fabric requires an underworld organization and highly skilled "money movers. . . ."

2. Many underworld leaders want to seed legitimate businesses with the profits from criminal rackets in order to provide a visible source of earned income. Their principal channels of wealth remain underground. Income from reputable corporations provides a basis for income tax filings, however false in terms of total income, as well as a veneer of respectability.

Like guerrilla campaigners in other fields, the agents of organized crime infiltrate their target areas along devious trailways where possible. In the guise of labor relations consultants, they entice businessmen who are willing to pay a price for substandard labor contracts into making deals with labor racketeers. Or they offer to supply merchandise at prices so far below market quotations that only a merchant blinded by avarice doesn't spot it as stolen goods or sequestered stock from a fraudulent bankruptcy.

Once a businessman has compromised himself with the underworld, he is vulnerable to further advances. These may take the form of a suggestion that the labor consultant, the phony union leader, or the cut-rate supplier has a friend with some idle funds he would like to invest in the business. Or the seducer may suggest making a loan to expand the business or to handle an influx of new business which he can guarantee.

The loan-shark approach is used to entrap hard-pressed businessmen who would not otherwise have any dealings with racketeers. This is widely employed in industries like garment manufacturing where competition among small entrepreneurs produces a rags-or-riches business climate. Because of the high business mortality, garment makers often find it difficult to get bank credit for the capital they need each season to try their luck with a new fashion line. They borrow from usurers, confident that their line will become a popular success and that they will be able to repay the loan with exorbitant interest and still come out ahead. But if the season isn't a smashing success and the businessman is unable to meet his obligation to the loan shark, the racketeers settle for a partnership—and then they are on their way.

Contrary to a popular impression, the foregoing approach is not limited to high-risk industries. The loan sharks and their underworld bosses like nothing better than to hook onto a substantial, long-established business whose owners may be hard up for ready cash to ride out a temporary emergency. The New York State Investigation Commission learned that certain bank employees were tipping off Mafia money men whenever a business customer had exhausted his line of credit and was unable to get further conventional financing.

Sometimes, as indicated earlier, business executives take a more active role in becoming associated with the Mafia. Once again, though, an apparently simple liaison may lead to an unintended result for the company:

A large Detroit corporation was willing to do business with the local Mafia to get a mortgage loan from a teamster union pension fund. As a consequence it found itself in the middle of a dispute between two criminal groups. The strange involvement came to light with the indictment of 13 men, 10 of them identified by the government as Mafiosi, on charges of conspiring to pay kickbacks to a pension fund officer. The defendants are awaiting trial in federal court.

The Mid-City Development Company of Detroit, according to the government, needed a large loan to buy an industrial building complex in Warren, Michigan, in 1964. Management sought help from Dominick Corrado of Grosse Point Park, a top Mafia figure in the Detroit area. Samuel Marroso, a public relations man in Warren, who is also under indictment now, was drawn into the orbit of the scheme and became instrumental in getting a mortgage loan of $1,050,000 from the Teamsters Central States Southeast and Southwest Areas Funds.

Later, according to the government, Mid-City Development sought Mafia help to obtain an additional loan, that one for $200,000. But there was some bickering with the Detroit Mafia over terms. The company allegedly tried then to make a deal for mortgage money through James Plumeri, a captain in the New York Mafia family of the late Thomas Lucchese. This led to a dispute between the Detroit and New York Mafia groups.

The Mafia's nine-man national commission . . . ruled that the dispute should be settled on neutral ground by a neutral referee. Frank Amato, 75-year-old alleged Mafia boss of southwest Pennsylvania, sat in judgment at a hearing in a Pittsburgh suburb, according to federal investigators, and made this decision: Detroit, having priority on the local deal, would handle the entire matter; after the loan was received by Mid-City Development, the New York Mafia would get a cut of the take. The indictment alleges that an illegal kickback of $5,000 was paid to David Wenger, a certified public accountant and auditor of the teamster pension fund, to influence his decision on the mortgage application. The $200,000 loan never materialized from the pension fund despite the alleged conspiracy and kickback payment, according to the government.

Organized crime uses some of its illegal profits to set up its own companies, usually under false fronts or proxies. What appears to be a legitimate mortgage and loan company is sometimes a blind for loan sharking and unorthodox transfers of real estate. Or a trucking company and a union local, both established by the same criminal group, may work in cahoots in the pilferage of millions of dollars of cargo at piers and airports. For instance, large scale infiltration along the waterfront and at Kennedy International Airport has been uncovered by the New York-New Jersey Waterfront Commission and by the New York Investigation Commission.

Further, Mafia-controlled companies having branches in Latin America and interests in Europe serve as conduits for the outflow of profits from illicit operations in the United States. Some of the funds go to the smugglers of raw opium from the Near East; some to the refiners of heroin in France and Italy; others to coded accounts in Swiss banks whence some of the money comes back, through U.S. banks, in the form of untraceable investments in major American corporations or equally untraceable "loans" to the very underworld bosses who started the funds on their roundabout journeys. In the latter instance, a gangster, sending his illicit profits deviously into a Swiss bank account, "borrows" his own money from his unidentifiable Swiss account and gets it back as "clean" money to be used in becoming a shareholder in any legitimate U.S. business in which he wants a stake.

A highly profitable form of infiltration is that practiced by some "money movers":

An agent of a criminal organization ingratiates himself with a branch manager of a large bank or a top executive of a medium-sized bank by placing the accounts of the borgata's businesses in the selected bank. Through strategic deposits and social cultivation of the bank executive, the "money mover" manages to be made a director in the bank (such instances have been verified by law enforcement investigators). He eventually attains an eminence where he can approve, or get a higher bank official to approve, the lending of large amounts, sometimes unsecured, at perhaps 8%. The borrower, a fellow conspirator, is a loan shark who puts the money out on the street at interest of anywhere from 120% to 500%.

I could describe other methods, but the foregoing should make the point that underworld leaders today usually present a business-like appearance and do their business by negotiation. Gone, for the most part, are the days of frontal attacks on business when gangsters walked into nightclubs and saloons and declared them-selves partners, with their shares to be handed over each week—refusal to be followed by beatings, bombings, vandalism, and other acts of terror and destruction. *Some* vestiges of terror tactics have survived (e.g., in garbage collection and waste removal), but they no longer are characteristic.

Now let us look at several cases that highlight typical tactics of criminal infiltrators, all-too-characteristic patterns of response of target businessmen, and likely results of such a response for the victims and their companies.

A classic in the annals of infiltration began in August 1967 when Maurice Minuto, the president of the Nylo-Thane Plastics Corp. at Farmingdale, New York, was looking for capital to ex-pand his operations, which were built around a formula for speed-ing the vulcanizing of rubber. Alan Morrell (not identified further in the subsequent testimony) telephoned Minuto to say he had an investor who wanted to meet with him alone that evening in his office. Instead of an investor, there arrived five or six thugs, two of whom put knives to Minuto's sides while a third put a gun to his head. (In this respect, at least, the criminals' approach lacked contemporary finesse.) The leader, identified later from a rogue's gallery photo as Julius (Julie) Klein, a notorious Long Island racketeer and ex-convict, announced: "We're going to kill you unless you give us $25,000."

Minuto was held overnight in a motel, where he wrote a check for $25,000. He was released next day after one of the kidnappers had cashed the check, according to testimony he gave to the State Investigation Commission nearly two years later. (The Commission happened to learn about Minuto's involvement with members of organized crime during the course of another investigation.) Minuto said he did not report the kidnapping and extortion to the police because of Klein's threat to kill his wife and children. But, he did go to see "Gentleman Johnny" Masiello, a major loan shark who had been publicly identified by the FBI as a "soldier" in the Genovese borgata of the Mafia. Minuto's move was a common type of mistake by businessmen victims; hoping to save himself by backstage maneuvering, he succeeded only in making matters worse.

The circumstances of the visit to Masiello, as related by Minuto to the Commission, remain somewhat clouded. Minuto said he had previously borrowed money from Masiello but swore he had not known that the dapper "Gentleman Johnny," who wore striking ensembles of electric blue and a huge diamond pinky ring, was a loan shark or a Mafioso. Minuto said his reason for calling on Masiello was to enlist help in preventing further forays against him by Klein and his desperadoes. He said also he went to borrow $25,000 from Masiello in order to reimburse his company, Nylo-Thane Plastics, for the check he had written against its account.

Masiello agreed to arrange a loan. He sent Minuto to the Royal National Bank, whose president and board chairman, William Goldfine, was a friend of the Mafioso's, with instructions to Minuto to take out a loan of $50,000 and "lend" half of it to Masiello. Minuto said he did just that, hoping that his "loan" to Masiello would "get the Long Island hoodlums off my back." Masiello got *most* of the $50,000, instead of half the amount.

Neither Klein nor his gang ever bothered Minuto thereafter. But the manufacturer, already out $50,000, was far from free of the toils of organized crime. Masiello repeatedly induced him to take out new loans from Royal National, to pledge Nylo-Thane shares for the loans, and to sign over other shares of Nylo-Thane to the Mafioso and his associates. In testimony about one transfer of 25,000 shares to the president of the Masiello-controlled Setmar Holding Company, Minuto explained: "I felt an obligation to Setmar. I just handed this [stock] over to Mr. McKeever and said: 'Thank you for everything you've done for me in the past.' Later Mr. Masiello called me and said: 'Thank you for the shares.'"

Nylo-Thane, which had been offered at $4 a share when it first went public, began in 1967 a meteoric rise to $88 a share. After trading in it had twice been suspended by the SEC, the stock had leveled off at about $22 by March 1969, when the State Investigation Commission hearings were held. By November it had plummeted to 2¾.

As for Minuto himself, the Commission's hearings revealed that he had become obligated for $515,000 in bank loans, of which he had received only $13,500 for himself. A total of $292,500 had gone to Masiello and his associates, and $179,000 had been eaten up by interest, bank discount, premiums on a policy issued by an Oklahoma insurance company, premiums on a fidelity bond of a Florida surety company for collateral for some of the bank loans, other fees, and $45,000 given by Minuto to two Las Vegas hotels to liquidate the gambling debt of a known racketeer. In addition, $1.3 million of Minuto's Nylo-Thane stock was either held by the bank as collateral on unpaid loans or had been given to Masiello and his associates.

The Commission's chart showing all this was captioned: "The High Cost of Protection."

Not content with his mulcting of the Long Island businessman, Masiello managed also in 1967 to get $466,000 from the United States Government in the form of Small Business Administration loans. In this, as in his dealings with Minuto, the Mafioso had help from the banker Goldfine. The Royal National Bank put up 25% of the amount of the loans to meet the federal requirement for Small Business Administration outlays. As Paul Kelly, Associate Counsel to the State Investigation Commission, later declared, this chain of events in effect "put the federal government in the position of financing Masiello's loan-shark activities." Masiello, a jaunty witness, invoked the protection of the Fifth Amendment in refusing to answer any of the 21 questions put to him at the Commission's hearing, including whether he had used the federal loans for loan sharking.

Goldfine made an interesting witness. Although admitting to a first-name friendship of many years with Masiello, he swore that he never knew Masiello was a loan shark or a Mafioso—matters that had been reported prominently in newspapers over the years. And although Goldfine had sponsored Masiello for the federal loan, he said under questioning that Masiello and his companies constantly were overdrawn by more than $100,000 at the Royal National Bank. At that time, Setmar Holding Company (one of Masiello's organizations) owed the bank $106,000; and A.N.R. Leasing Corp., a truck company headed by Masiello's son, John, Jr., owed the bank $135,000.

Goldfine acknowledged that at a dinner marking his seventieth birthday, he had been pledged 5,000 shares of Nylo-Thane by Masiello. He said that the stock was turned over to the Hebrew Home for the Aged in Riverdale, beneficiary of the birthday dinner.

A red-faced Small Business Administration called in the loans to A.N.R. Leasing. The area administrator, pleading ignorance of Masiello's background, explained that the agency customarily relied on information supplied by the sponsoring bank about the prospective recipient. A.N.R. Leasing Corp. also had $2 million in contracts for truck rentals to the Post Office Department.

After the Chrysler Building was sold in 1960, there was a strike of service and maintenance men. The new owners, Sol Goldman and Alex DiLorenzo, hired S.G.S. Associates, a self-described "labor relations" firm, to help them. Subsequently, the strikers complained that "goons" with guns in holsters arrived at the building in Cadillacs and took over elevator operations. The strike was settled with the help of the Mayor's office, and the complaint about the "goons" went into limbo.

Five years later, when FBI agents were questioning clients of S.G.S. Associates in connection with another investigation, The *New York Times* revealed that the "G" in the firm's name was Carlo Gambino, boss of a Mafia family whose members operated in a wide range of legal and illicit enterprises. Gambino's partners of record in S.G.S. Associates were Henry H. Saltzstein, a convicted burglar and bookmaker, and George Schiller. The newspaper disclosed that S.G.S. Associates had been employed to handle labor relations for major industrial and business companies, among them Howard Clothes, Bond Clothes, William J. Levitt, most of whose massive building operations used nonunion labor, the Concord Hotel at Kiamesha Lake, New York, and Flower and Fifth Avenue Hospital in New York City.

These and other contracts with business companies had brought the Mafia-connected "labor consultants" an estimated $500,000 a year.

With Gambino's connection now made public, however, S.G.S. Associates lost clients as a maple loses leaves in a November gale. Spokesmen for most of the legitimate business companies involved professed ignorance of Gambino's partnership. Some revealing anecdotes of the infiltration process were given, of which the following is an example:

Dr. Ralph E. Snyder, President of Flower and Fifth Avenue Hospital, said S.G.S. Associates had first been called in during a strike of hospital employees in 1962. He told the story in these words: "We didn't know what to do. One of our doctors said he had a patient who was a labor relations expert and might help us. It was Mr. Saltzstein. With the settlement of the strike, hospital management and the union agreed on Saltzstein as impartial arbitrator of the contract. Since learning about Gambino I think we ought to eliminate Mr. Saltzstein as impartial arbitrator when the contract expires at the end of this year."

Why have members of the business community so often failed to respond to evidence of inroads into their companies by organized crime? Is the failure due to naïveté or inability to read the telltale signals? If so, why have the widely circulated warnings made by law enforcement agencies and other experts somehow failed to get across to businessmen? Or is the failure due to fear of physical or economic reprisal—or perhaps to the strain of larceny which is said to lurk in most humans? If so, do many businessmen *really* believe they can profit from a limited involvement with organized crime without eventually becoming its victims?

Whatever the explanation, it is not likely to hold up under analysis. And it is not an excuse for a businessman to say there is an absence of good alternatives. When signs of criminal inroads are observed, there *are* steps a businessman can take to cope with the problem without inviting reprisals against himself, his family, or his company.

To begin with, there is no good reason for failure of any businessman to recognize the first overture or stratagem of organized crime. The Chamber of Commerce's *Deskbook on Organized Crime* spells out how to recognize the different approaches and tells how businessmen, acting individually or through trade associations, can effectively counter such attempts. Similar information and advice is being given by the National Council on Crime and Delinquency, which has in the last two years sponsored, in city after city, meetings and conferences at which business executives and corporate security officers have discussed specific problems with experts such as Will Wilson, Assistant Attorney General in charge of the Department of Justice criminal division, state and county prosecutors, police officials, and investigators.

Among the situations listed in the Chamber's *Deskbook* and described at the conferences as indicators of possible infiltration

attempts, I believe the following should be singled out for
attention:

A change of ownership, not publicly announced, of a customer company.

A marked increase in a customer's orders unrelated to a
seasonal increase in business. This could be a tip-off to a fraudulent bankruptcy scheme.

A new account with a name very similar to that of an established company, perhaps even with an address in the same building as the offices of the better known company.

A sudden outbreak of bookmaking or numbers-game activity
in an industrial plant. This may mean that organized crime has
established a beachhead for other operations.

Picketing by nonemployees, followed by a visit from a "labor
relations consultant" offering to "take care of things" for a fee.

Any offer to arrange a labor contract with conditions less
favorable to the employees than those prevalent in the industry.
Such "sweetheart" contracts are often used by labor racketeers
as leverage to open the way to criminal infiltration.

Offers of loans from persons or companies of unchecked
background. Such an offer, coming when a legitimate business is
known to be in a credit squeeze, is frequently the opening gambit
of a loan shark who seeks to put a business man in his debt as a
prelude to a partnership to man.

Merchandise offered at less then wholesale prices, which is
likely to be stolen goods.

A series of incidents causing damage to a company's property
or equipment, followed by solicitation to join a "trade association" of unfamiliar background.

Discovery that pay checks of several employees are endorsed
over to the same person. This could mean that a loan shark or
bookmaker is at work and could be particularly dangerous if any
employees in sensitive positions become deeply indebted.

Suppose an executive notices warning signals like the foregoing. What is his next step?

He can get in touch immediately with the police and tell them
what has been going on. The trouble with this step is that other
agencies may be in a better position to help. Nevertheless, this step
should not be discounted; it has turned out to be safe and effective
many times.

As an alternative, the executive can consult with his lawyer or
with the executive director of his trade association. From them he
can gain information as to which law enforcement agency or regu-
latory body should be contacted for most effective results.

There is a third course of action which could be especially

effective. This approach has been suggested by Alfred J. Scotti, Rackets Bureau Chief for New York District Attorney Frank S. Hogan. Its virtues are that it preserves the business man's anonymity at the same time that it relieves him of the burden of trying to evaluate whether the suspicious situation he knows about is an isolated phenomenon or part of a larger picture. Scotti proposes that local commerce and industry groups set up committees to which businessmen could make confidential reports. Then, when a committee has reports from half a dozen or more sources in the same industry—as would be likely if infiltration were attempted—the complaints could be brought by it to the proper law enforcement agency without putting the spotlight on just one cooperative witness.

Establishment of such a committee is practicable because it can be done within the framework of the association or organization that exists in almost every industrial community. It is timely because increasing publicity about organized crime has made so many Americans uneasy. If the idea were supported by business leaders, it could be implemented quickly with existing personnel, at least in the beginning.

The need for such a step is *now*. All over the nation, judging from available reports, prosecutors are failing to get businessmen's cooperation. For two cases in point which I believe to be typical, let me refer to the experiences of Scotti and Robert M. Morgenthau, former U.S. Attorney for the Southern District of New York, where there are more business headquarters than in any other part of the nation. (Morgenthau resigned in January to become Deputy Mayor of New York City.) Both those prosecutors have sent bosses of organized crime and their associates to prison for bribery of public officials to get contracts, and for coercion, fraud, extortion, hijacking, perjury, and illegal business practices. Businessmen have testified for the prosecution in some cases, *but only after being subpoenaed to corroborate evidence the lawmen had dug up on their own.*

Where businessmen were found to have been in cahoots with the criminals, they testified in some cases after being named as co-conspirators. But *none* of the businessmen, whether innocent victims or bilked partners, came forward voluntarily at a time when the acts of infiltration could have been aborted. If industry committees such as those proposed were created, some real progress might be made in correcting this abysmal record.

25
A Family Business:
Hijacking, Bookmaking, Policy, Dice Games, Loan-sharking and Special Contracts

FRED J. COOK

It is the second largest and most powerful of the Mafia families of New York, according to one veteran investigator. It is without doubt the most turbulent and strife-torn. For more than a decade now, it has compiled an unparalleled record of violence and gore; kidnapping of gang leaders; all-out warfare with bodies dumped on the streets and in the sea; the public gunning down of its latest boss and his permanent incapacitation; and now again more warfare, more slayings, more contracts for more "hits."

This is the Colombo Mafia family of Brooklyn, torn during the early nineteen-sixties by the bloody rebellion of the Gallo brothers; pacified for a time by a new boss, Joseph Colombo, who brashly picketed the Federal Bureau of Investigation with followers of his Italian-American Civil Rights League; thrown into new turmoil when Colombo himself was shot down last June at the second annual rally of his league in Columbus Circle—but, through it all, surviving like some hydraheaded monster and lashing out April 7 in the slaying of its old trouble-maker, Joseph (Crazy Joe) Gallo.

The tale is as labyrinthine, as full of intrigue and violence, as any that marked the history of old Byzantium; and it is pocked with shadowed nooks in which the link of motive and deed is as yet only dimly perceived. What follows, then, is an account pieced together from a variety of official sources that attempts to give, as fully as one can, a picture of this underworld colossus and the men who run it.

"It's an extremely powerful mob, second only to the family ruled by Carlo Gambino," says one expert who has made a specialty of watching the clan. Denis Dillon, head of the Federal Eastern Strike Force in Brooklyn, puts its strength at about 185 members and associates. Other sources think it is much larger. One investigator, who is quite specific, says the family has 104 "made" members—that is, followers who have been formally inducted into the Mafia—and that, in addition, there are some 350 associates. "This is all based on observation," he says. "When we see a guy hanging around and doing business with one we know is a soldier in the family, we know he's connected. He's got to be."

What are the family's rackets? "Everything. They're into everything," this expert says. Hijacking. Bookmaking. Policy. Dice games. Loan-sharking on a fantastic scale. Legitimate businesses which they have taken over once the proprietors got in too deep to the sharks, especially bars and nightclubs and garment firms in Manhattan's garment center.

Just to run down the names of the nearly dozen capos—all subordinate to the family boss, or godfather, as he is also called—heading the different regimes within the family, as they appear on the charts of various investigative agencies, illustrates what this investigator means when he says the Colombo combine is deep into "everything." There is an old familiar, Johnny (Bath Beach) Oddo, a gambling kingpin who has been getting his name into the papers for more than 20 years and who still flourishes as a Colombo capo. There is Carmine (The Snake) Persico, now serving a long term in the Federal penitentiary in Atlanta but still the lord *in absentia* of one of the most powerful regimes in the family. "Whenever there was a major hijacking," a detective says, "you could almost bet the Persico gang had something to do with it." And then there is Nicholas (Jiggs) Forlano, probably the sharkiest loan shark in New York—a man who, with his partner, Charles (Ruby) Stein, was reported to have had as much as $5-million "on the street" at one time, according to a witness before the State Commission of Investigation in 1965.

There are five over-all Mafia families based in New York City. Such local structures are tied in with the larger, national interests

of crime through a national commission composed of major bosses
from strategic areas of the country—New England, the Philadelphia area, Detroit and Chicago. New York, however, is the only
city with five powerful, operating families. Control fluctuates. For
years, until his imprisonment and death, Vito Genovese was considered the most powerful of the New York bosses. Since his
demise, his mantle seems to have shifted families and to
have been donned, investigators agree, by Carlo Gambino, who
took over the family of the late Albert Anastasia, one-time
lord of Murder, Inc., and ruler of the Brooklyn docks. In this
never-ceasing struggle for power, the Profaci family (now the
Colombo family) has played many key roles. It has always boasted
some of the most efficient killers in gangdom and Genovese, among
other bosses, sometimes made use of its lethal *expertise*. One such
contract, which passed through the late Joseph Profaci to the Gallo
brothers, resulted in the blasting of Anastasia out of his chair in
the barber shop of the Park Sheraton Hotel in October, 1957, a
deed that removed a threat to Genovese and cleared the way for
the rise of Carlo Gambino.

The power of the subordinate capos who actually run the
multimillion-dollar rackets represents a prize plum. The severe
bloodletting in the Profaci-Colombo family began when the greed
of the Gallo brothers set them lusting after this power. Indeed,
it touched them with the kind of madness that drives a shark berserk in a blood-stained sea, and in the early nineteen-sixties, they
challenged the authority of the boss himself, then Joseph Profaci,
known as the "olive-oil king." The Gallos—Larry, Joseph and
Albert—had led a kind of maverick group within the family, and
evidently felt that such signal services as rubbing out Albert
Anastasia entitled them to a larger share of the Brooklyn rackets,
but Profaci disappointed them and continued to reward his personal favorites. The result was warfare.

The Gallos kidnaped four of Profaci's top henchmen, attempting to blackmail the boss, but Profaci talked them into releasing
his aides on his promise to negotiate. Then he negotiated in his
own way—with guns. The Gallos were no match for Profaci's
legions. They had some 20-odd followers, and they were soon
holed up in two barricaded tenements at 45-51 President Street
near the South Brooklyn waterfront.

The Gallo-Profaci war raged through 1961, 1962 and most of 1963. There were losses on both sides, but the Gallos, being outnumbered, suffered most. In the midst of the carnage, two significant events took place. In January, 1962, Crazy Joe Gallo was sentenced to a 7-to-14-year prison term for extortion, and on June 6, 1962, Joseph Profaci died of cancer.

Out of this tempestuous upheaval there finally emerged a new boss, the youngest and one of the most unusual figures ever to head one of the Mafia families of New York. He was Joseph Colombo, who was only 41 in 1964 when he was elevated to command, and he was so little-known to authorities at the time that he seemed to pop out of nowhere. In 1963, in hearings before a U.S. Senate committee, he had been identified as a capo in the Profaci family. He was, ostensibly, a prosperous real-estate salesman; he had never been convicted of anything. All that Inspector John J. Shanley, then head of the Central Investigation Bureau of the New York Police Department, had been able to tell the Senate committee was this: "Joe Colombo, also known as Joseph Lefore, he is a close associate of John Frances and Johnny Oddo. He has three arrests. He operates floating crap games."

This was the shadow man who was suddenly catapulted into command of the Profaci family. His ascendancy was attributable to three factors: He had the support of Carlo Gambino, by now clearly the successor of Anastasia in the realigned New York underworld; he held out the prospect that he could bring much needed peace to Brooklyn by giving the Gallos a fairer shake; and he met the need of the moment for a new-type, low-profile leader—a man with no police record of consequence, personable, likable, difficult to envision as a leader of hoods.

Detectives tailing this new mystery man soon observed him, as one said, "meeting with virtually every important hood in the city." They saw Colombo, the industrious real-estate salesman, conferring with the Gallos and other known criminals "on a daily basis" in the offices of Cantalupo Realty and Dart Realty in Brooklyn. They trailed the new boss over to *espresso* houses in the Spring Street section of Little Italy on Manhattan's lower East Side, and there they watched him enjoying a cup of morning brew with other mobsters who had just happened to develop a similar need for early-morning stimulant.

Wherever Colombo went in those early days, he was shadowed by his look-alike bodyguard, Rocco Miraglia, now a capo heading his own regime. "It's an amazing thing," said a detective who had spent many hours on Colombo's trail, "but Joe and Rocco were the same height, the same build; they even walked with the same swing to their step. I knew Joe well, but when you saw one of them come out of the realty office, I would say to my partner, 'Hey, is that Joe?' And he might say, 'No, that's not Joe; that's Rocco.' It might turn out it was Joe all the time, but from a distance it was almost impossible to tell them apart."

In the restructured family on which Joe Colombo solidified his hold as boss, another tantalizing figure emerged, Charles (Charlie Lemons) Mineo—a stolid, enigmatic figure around whom the storms and rivalries of the Colombo family would continue to swirl in moments of crisis during the years to come. Mineo has become a unique kind of underboss, one who is usually virtually inactive. According to some reports he was an important loan shark in his earlier years but had gradually withdrawn from illegal activities and was enjoying the fruits of retirement when Colombo elevated him to the No. 2 spot in the family. Colombo was said to have been suspicious of the designs of the powerful Carmine Persico and so desired as his chief lieutenant a man who was not so dangerously ambitious. But there may well have been another reason for the selection of Charlie Mineo. His strength then and now appears to be that he is a highly regarded "man of respect"; and whenever there is major trouble, capos of all persuasions turn to him. "Even during the Gallo-Profaci war," one investigator says, "he maintained such a strict neutrality that both sides trusted him; he was one of the few old-time leaders the Gallos respected."

Charlie Mineo is a squat figure, some 5-feet-9, 200 pounds, now in his middle 70's. He was born in Palermo, Sicily, on October 18, 1897. He lives quietly at 42 First Place in Brooklyn, and his favorite haunts are in the same area—a candy store at the corner of Court and First, the Stumble Inn Bar and Grill nearby, and (perhaps most important of all) a handy park bench on Court Street where he likes to sun himself on fine days and chat with friends who just happen to drop by, always with a bodyguard handy a few feet away to make certain that the friends stay really friendly. That park bench and its impassive "man of respect" were to become extremely important in the scheme of things after Joe Colombo started the Italian-American Civil Rights League.

The league was a startling innovation. Old-line mob leaders shunned publicity. Much experience had convinced them that the boss who stays healthiest is the one who attracts the least public attention. And so, when Colombo threw a picket line around New York F.B.I. headquarters on April 30, 1970, veteran Mafiosi were almost as startled as the Feds. Yet Colombo went brashly forward. He proclaimed that the F.B.I. was discriminating against all Italian-Americans; he ridiculed the whole concept of the Mafia and pictured himself as an honest businessman who was being persecuted because he was an Italian. Soon he was being interviewed by the press and appearing on television, wrapped in the new mantle—that of a civil-rights leader.

"According to our information," says one Federal investigator, "the older bosses didn't know at first what to think of it. This was contrary to their entire experience, but they weren't certain. It might work, and so they adopted a wait-and-see attitude."

It worked, at first, beyond wildest imagination. Much evidence seems to indicate that New York's large Italian-American community had developed its own persecution complex; it had begun to feel like a neglected stepchild. Much attention was being focused on other ethnic groups like the Negroes and Puerto Ricans; Italian-Americans felt that, by comparison, they were being ignored and treated like second-class citizens. Then along came Colombo, giving vent to their secret frustrations; and almost overnight thousands of honest Italian-Americans, ignoring the quality of the leadership they were being offered, joined his F.B.I. picket lines and swelled the ranks of his civil rights league.

The results stunned many. A following of this size represents a lot of votes, and politicians began to get jittery. The Justice Department in Washington issued instructions that prejudicial terms like Mafia and Cosa Nostra were no longer to be used. When motion-picture producers began to film *The Godfather*, Colombo insisted that all such offensive nomenclature be stricken from the film's dialogue—and it was. Colombo's league set up store-front headquarters in many sections of Brooklyn, and this, in the words of one investigator, "made it a new ball game." Police could no longer walk in and frisk a suspect as they might have done in the past; now they had to be very careful "about the civil-rights aspect of things."

"The impression made on our Government is one you wouldn't believe," one source says. "Take Nick Bianco, one of the capos—in my book one of the toughest hoods in the family. He was originally a Gallo man during the Profaci war, but he went over to Colombo and remained a Colombo loyalist. Well, you wound up with Nick Bianco having his picture taken with Governor Rockefeller and conferring with Mayor Lindsay in City Hall.

"For my money, Colombo did more for the mob than any boss had ever done. He gave them respectability. He claimed 150,000 members for his civil-rights league. Well, I'll give him even more than that. You know Greenpoint? The league's stickers are all over the section. If someone told me the league had 250,000 members, I wouldn't be surprised."

Such were the observable effects of Joe Colombo's magical hat trick by which the Mafia had been made to disappear like a magician's white rabbit. But for every success there was a penalty. Subterranean currents began to work, and the older mob bosses, just as they had originally feared, began to experience a fallout they did not like.

"The F.B.I. had been keeping track of Colombo and mob activities before he formed his civil-rights league," says one official, "but the F.B.I.'s efforts seemed, to gang leaders, at least, to have been greatly intensified after the picketing began. The capos and their soldiers found themselves shadowed wherever they went, whatever they did. It became more and more difficult to do business. Finally, even some of the soldiers in Colombo's own family began to rebel because they found they were being so closely watched they couldn't run their rackets as freely as they used to."

Into this nascent unrest, there now popped a catalytic agent that produced a fusion of highly volatile elements—the affair of the black attaché case. Colombo had been brought to trial for perjury in Manhattan Supreme Court, accused of making false statements when he applied for his real-estate broker's license. On the afternoon of Dec. 16, 1970, he was sitting with his ever-present bodyguard, Rocco Miraglia, in Miraglia's gold Buick station wagon, which had been parked cavalierly in the judges' parking space outside the State Supreme Court. As it happened, F.B.I. agents at that very moment were looking for Miraglia, who had been indicted for perjury, accused of lying to a Brooklyn Federal grand jury probing organized crime. Spotting Miraglia and Colombo, F.B.I. agents moved in and grabbed Rocco, who was holding the black attaché case.

Colombo began to scream at the top of his lungs. "That's mine, that's mine," he yelled, making a grab for the attaché case.

The agents shoved him aside. Since Rocco had the case in his hands, they argued, it must be his, and they hustled off their prisoner and the prize he was carrying. Colombo's storming and screaming attracted the attention of local patrolmen, and they slapped Miraglia with a $25 ticket for parking illegally in the judges' spot.

Denis Dillon recalls how Colombo, almost beside himself with fury, came storming into the offices of the Eastern Strike Force in Brooklyn, demanding the return of the attaché case and its contents. It contained only the records of his Italian-American Civil Rights League, he insisted, and the Feds had no right to hold it. F.B.I. agents weren't so convinced. They had had a chance to examine the contents, and they had found long lists of mysterious names—and, opposite them, figures indicating imposing sums of money. Names like "Tony the Gawk," "Frankie the Beast," "John the Wop" and just plain "Carl."

Federal investigators doubted that these gang-sounding aliases applied to innocent civil-rights workers, and they suspected that some of the five-figure amounts listed beside many of the names represented funds invested in the shylocking business. They told Colombo that, before he could get back the attaché case and its lists of names, he would have to testify before a Federal grand jury. He agreed.

He identified "Tony the Gawk" as Tony Angello, now serving 12 years in Federal prison for extortion and theft in interstate commerce. "Frankie the Beast" turned out to be Frank Falanga, a long-time associate of Colombo. And "Carl," Colombo admitted, was none other than Carlo Gambino. What did the $30,000 posted after Gambino's name represent? Oh, Colombo explained, that was the sum Gambino had raised by selling tickets to a league civil-rights rally. Aware that Gambino was supposed to be suffering from such a heart ailment that he could not stir from home, Federal officials were skeptical.

Colombo eventually recovered his papers, but the opportune snatch of the attaché case had raised all kinds of difficulties. Gambino and all the other mobsters whom Colombo had identified had to subject themselves to questioning before a Federal grand jury, and they couldn't be quite certain how much of their account was believed or what might return to haunt them later. There were other harassments.

Thomas (Tommy Ryan) Eboli, the New Jersey mobster who reputedly has shared with Gerardo Catena the command of the powerful Genovese family since the death of Vito Genovese, was returning from a trip to Europe. He expected to be treated like a man of stature and whisked right through customs. But his name had been among those on the lists in the black attaché case; he was taken aside, detained, questioned, and every seam of his baggage examined. Eboli was the very last passenger to clear customs, an indignity indeed. According to informants, he was furious—and blamed Colombo for his troubles.

Such embarrassments convinced Carlo Gambino and other mob leaders that, whatever Colombo's public-relations success with his league, the price tag on their operations was becoming prohibitive. The cooling off showed in the difference between the support given Colombo for his first Unity Day rally in Columbus Circle in 1970 and that accorded the second rally last year. In 1970, all work stopped on the piers so that longshoremen could attend the rally. Businesses in Italian sections of Brooklyn and lower Manhattan closed, giving their employes time off to whoop it up for Unity Day. Anthony Scotto, son-in-law of the late Tough Tony Anastasio and ruler of the Brooklyn docks, was an honored guest at the first rally. At the second, all this changed. Scotto didn't attend. The piers didn't close. Longshoremen kept right on working. Even many of Colombo's own soldiers didn't take the day off but continued operating their businesses, legitimate or otherwise, thus blackballing the second rally.

In addition to all of this, there was the revival of Gallo tensions. Larry Gallo who, many say, was the most capable of the brothers, had died of natural causes, but Crazy Joe Gallo, ever unpredictable, was once more on the loose, having been paroled from prison after nine years. He had returned to his President Street haunts and resumed control of his rackets. "He had lost nothing while he was in prison," one investigator says. And he was as arrogant as ever. When Rocco Miraglia came into South Brooklyn to put up posters for the second Unity Day rally, Crazy Joe ran him right out of the district and personally ripped them up.

So this was the over-all setting when, at 11:45 A.M., June 28, 1971, Joe Colombo was gunned down in front of thousands of his horrified followers in Columbus Circle. His assailant, a 25-year-old black named Jerome A. Johnson, of New Brunswick, N.J., was killed on the spot. Colombo, two bullets in his brain, survived five hours of brain surgery, but he has remained permanently paralyzed, incapable of exercising high command.

Colombo had hardly fallen when Nick Bianco was spotted rushing over to Brooklyn, his destination the candy store at Court and First. There he reported to Charlie Mineo; and Mineo, operating from the store and his favorite park bench in the days immediately following the shooting, acted out the role of the strong, silent "man of respect" to whom the capos reported. "Where he used to have one bodyguard standing near that bench, now he always had five or six others watching every move being made up and down the street, which in itself gives you some idea of his importance," an investigator says.

Who had shot Colombo? Why? There were all kinds of theories. One was that Carlo Gambino had approved the contract because Colombo's civil-rights activities were hurting the mob's businesses. Or, that Jerome A. Johnson was a loner, a psychiatric misfit who had tried to kill out of some dark inner compulsion of his own. Then there was the report that Colombo had issued a contract to get Crazy Joe Gallo, but that Crazy Joe, learning of it, moved first. There was the theory, very popular, that Crazy Joe had formed an alliance with black convicts while in prison; that Johnson was a new recruit of his—and hence Colombo's shooting was his handiwork. However rumor and speculation were pieced together, most reconstructions of what had happened seemed to circle back and point to Crazy Joe Gallo. "Our information is that practically everyone in the Colombo family exclusively blamed Joe Gallo for the shooting," Denis Dillon says.

An investigator from another agency that has kept close watch on the mob situation in Brooklyn disagrees for some plausible reasons: "There was no animosity when Joey came out of prison. When the capos were asked about him, they'd just shrug and say, 'The guy was in jail for nine years. Leave him alone.' When the shooting took place, there weren't any indications Joey was involved. After it happened, we watched him walking down the street alone every night, not even a bodyguard with him, and his whole crew would split and go home, just as if nothing had happened. We watched Joey going all over town to visit his girl friends, not bothering about protection. Now it's entirely different. The Gallo troops travel eight or nine together, and they go in two cars, one to protect the other. . . . No, Jerome Johnson was a real nut. There isn't anyone who can put Johnson anywhere near Gallo. If Joey had hit Colombo, you would have had the soldiers of every family after him because the bosses would have been saying to themselves, 'Hey, what about us? Are we next?' If the family heads thought he did it, Joey wouldn't have lasted two days."

While various police agencies were sorting out the tangled skeins of the Colombo shooting, the family itself was being regrouped around new leadership. Mineo, who seems to have played a pivotal role, would have appeared to be, as underboss, the logical man to assume control, but he felt that he was too old for the job. And so authority was exercised for a time by one of the less conspicuous members of the family, Joseph (Joe Yak) Yacovelli, the consigliere, or counselor.

"This is another highly respected veteran member of the family," a Federal investigator says. "But he had always been something of a mystery man. He had always managed to keep himself in the background and had maintained a very low profile." This low profile became a high profile almost the instant F.B.I. agents learned from their informants of Yacovelli's new importance. Yacovelli was subpoenaed to testify before a Federal grand jury; his picture was taken and appeared on the front pages of the press; and he found that he was being tailed wherever he went, his every activity watched. "This was a complete departure from his normal routine and way of operating," an investigator says, "and Yacovelli decided he didn't like it. He asked to be relieved of the responsibilities of command."

There is considerable evidence that Yacovelli's desires coincided with the personal preference of the family hierarchy. "The man they wanted all along was Vincent Aloi," a source close to the situation explains. "But he was under indictment in Federal Court on a stolen-securities charge. When he was acquitted a couple of months ago, he became available and almost at once they made him the acting boss of the family." Vincent Aloi is the son of Sebastian (Buster) Aloi, "a very respected member of the family" and a long-time bigshot in gambling and loan sharking in the Williamsburg section of Brooklyn. Buster Aloi lived in South Ozone Park, Queens, but about 1963 he began to suffer from ill health and turned his gambling operations over to Vincent. Buster Aloi now spends most of his time in Florida. Vincent Aloi, born Sept. 22, 1933, stands 6-feet-2 and weighs some 190 pounds. He has black hair, brown eyes and a dark complexion. A natty dresser, he looks and acts like a prosperous legitimate businessman. "If you met him at a cocktail party, you would like him at once," a detective says. "He's smooth, lots of class. A good family man with three children; goes to church on Sunday—the whole bit. This is why they gave him the family. They needed someone with his kind of image and his ability to handle people."

Vincent Aloi had been a capo in the organization since 1964, having been elevated in rank at the same time that Colombo took over. He lives at 6 Maurice Lane, Ramapo, N.Y.; and he is employed by Cameo Wedding Time, 149-03 Jamaica Avenue, Jamaica. Cameo Wedding Time specializes in services for elaborate weddings, and Vincent Aloi, investigators say, is a very well paid employe. His role: the furnishing of leads to the firm for weddings about to take place where arrangements must be made for flowers, tuxedos, receptions and other services. Vincent Aloi is also listed as part owner of City Carriers Corp., a trucking firm at 260 West 35th Street, Manhattan. His record shows a number of arrests for gambling, none of which hurt him very much. In 1952 he was fined $25 and given five days in jail on a gambling charge, and in 1958 he was fined $10 and given three days in jail on a dice-game charge. Other gambling arrests were either dismissed or resulted in suspended sentences.

With the high command of the family realigned in this

fashion, with Vincent Aloi in full command, the latest outburst
of violence began. In late March and early April, 10 gangland
slayings took place, some appearing to be connected with the
decade-old internal strife within the Colombo family, some not.
The most sensational deed of all, of course, was the rub-out of
Crazy Joe Gallo in the early morning of April 7 as he celebrated
his 43d birthday in Umberto's Clam House on Mulberry Street,
just a block east of police headquarters in the lower East Side's
Little Italy. With Gallo was his bride of three weeks, the former
Sina Essary, and his 10-year-old stepdaughter.

The blasting of Joe Gallo by a gunman who just walked in
from the street and began to blaze away revived all the old rumors.
According to some reports, there had been an "open contract"
on Joe for months—that is, virtually ever since the Colombo shooting. An "open contract" is supposed to mean that the man against
whom it is issued is fair game, and anyone who happens to spot
him with his guard down is at liberty to take him on the spot,
without any higher authorization. Some detectives insist, however,
that they never heard of any such thing as an "open contract"
until the phrase began to appear in the press; mob bosses, they
insist, don't leave such matters to chance. In any event, in early
May, F.B.I. agents got a break when a terrified mobster, who
feared he had himself been marked for death because he knew
too much, turned himself over to the bureau for safekeeping and
began to sing in accents reminiscent of the prize informer Joe Valachi. The new songster was Joseph Luparelli, a close associate
of Yacovelli's. He said that he had happened to be in Umberto's
when the birthday-celebrating Gallo and his party arrived.
Luparelli ducked out, he said, and, knowing of the contract on
Crazy Joe, he told Philip Gambino, a Colombo henchman, and
Carmine Di Biase, a former Genovese hood who had shifted his
allegiance to the Colombo group; Yacovelli was contacted by telephone and gave the go-ahead.

According to Luparelli's account, five hoods in two cars—the
second a "crash" car designed to protect the first—drove down
Mulberry Street and parked not far from Umberto's. Di Biase,
he said, did the actual shooting, pumping three bullets into Gallo
and wounding his bodyguard. Luparelli told F.B.I. agents that he
drove one of the cars, and that after the shooting, the killers then

drove to Yacovelli's apartment in Manhattan, informed him of the success of their mission and received instructions to drive to a hideout apartment in Nyack, N.Y., which had been rented several months previously in anticipation of just such a need. There Luparelli became violently ill after eating. He suspected an attempt had been made to poison him; and he gave his companions the slip, flew to California and there, still fearful, turned himself over to the F.B.I.

This reconstruction of events made it appear as if the Gallo slaying stemmed by a devious and delayed route from the shooting, some nine months previously, of Joe Colombo. Some detectives, however, are doubtful about any such cause-and-effect relationship. They point out that several mysterious developments had taken place in the days immediately prior to Crazy Joe's extinction. Joe himself had been playing a devious game. He pretended that he had gotten out of the rackets entirely. There was nothing there for him but death, he said, perceptively enough, and he was going straight. He had begun to hob-nob in show-business circles. He had become friendly with actor Jerry Orbach, and Orbach's wife, Marta, had started to collaborate with him on a book that would describe his reformation. After Gallo's murder, there was some wild speculation that he had been killed because the mob feared he might disclose too much in his memoirs; but this, like the Colombo revenge motivation, is discounted by some investigators who have been extremely close to the case. They give this rundown of events:

"Three weeks prior to Joe Gallo's getting killed, he, Frank (Punchy) Illiano and John (Mooney) Cutrone went out to the San Susan nightclub in Mineola, L.I., in which John Franzese [another powerful capo in the Colombo family] is reported to have a hidden interest. Joey is reported to have grabbed the manager and said, 'This joint is mine. Get out.' In other words, he was cutting himself in.

"This was the first sign we had that Crazy Joe was acting up again. Then we come to Easter week, and a lot of things began to happen. On Easter Sunday night or sometime into Monday morning, there was a safecracking at Ferrara Pastry Shop on Grand Street in Little Italy. [Ferrara's is a famous Italian bakery doing a multimillion-dollar business, a Little Italy landmark since 1892.]

It was reported that the safecrackers got $55,000. Now Ferrara's is a legitimate business, but Vinnie Aloi is always hanging out around there. It's reported that he does a lot of his shylocking in the immediate neighborhood.

"O.K. The story about the Ferrara burglary broke on Monday. Tuesday there is a hurry-up meeting at the up-state Saugerties farm of Carmine Persico. Vinnie Aloi called the meeting, according to our information, and there were eight guys there.

"The very next day, Wednesday, Alphonse Persico, Carmine's brother, and Jerry Angella, his bodyguard, fly to Atlanta to see Carmine in prison. Of course, it may have been just a brotherly visit, but on the other hand. . . .

"Well, anyway, on Thursday, we see Gennaro Ciprio on President Street talking to Joey. [Ciprio was a Colombo bodyguard. He had been on the platform at Columbus Circle when Colombo was shot and went nearly berserk. But he also had some money-making dealings with Gallo, a double tie that could be tolerated as long as just money-making was involved.] We hear during this same week that Joey and Johnny Cutrone have been marked for a hit shortly. At the same time, we notice a change in Joey's pattern. He isn't traveling alone so much. He always has a bodyguard with him, and sometimes he's accompanied by four or five guys in two cars.

"Friday morning, Gallo is hit. The way they did it is significant. If the killing had been the result of the Colombo thing, they could have taken him at any time; they wouldn't have had to do it this way. For months, we used to see him driving across the Brooklyn Bridge at night all alone and going down Centre Street; he always followed the same route. All they would have had to do was throw a truck across the road and take him. But, no. They banged him in front of his stepdaughter and his new wife. It shows they meant to disgrace him.

"Saturday morning, the day after Gallo is hit, we find the body of Grossman in the trunk of a car, with both eyes shot out. [Richard R. Grossman, 36, was found in the trunk of a car abandoned in a desolate section of Sheepshead Bay, Brooklyn. He had been beaten about the face before being killed.] The autopsy showed he had been killed probably on Wednesday, at least two full days before Gallo was hit.

"Now we hear Ciprio is carrying a gun. We also learn he had been hanging out in Ferrara's before the burglary. He knew everything about the layout there. Also, there is an association between Grossman and Ciprio. Both were burglars and safemen and had worked together.

"Sunday night—that is, early Monday morning, April 10—they bang Ciprio right in front of his sister. [Gennaro Ciprio was caught in a hail of bullets at 2:45 A.M. as he left his restaurant, Gennaro's Feast Specialties at 1744 86th Street, Brooklyn. He had $1,300 in cash in his pockets when he was killed.] Again, it's important to remember that they didn't have to do it this way unless there was a special reason. Carmine Di Biase was his godfather. If this all stemmed from the Colombo shooting and Ciprio's association with Gallo, all they would have had to do was to give Carmine the tip, 'Hey, tell your nephew to stop going down there to President Street.' No, there had to be a stronger reason than that; and the way they did it shows they wanted to disgrace him.

"Putting it all together, we believe Grossman and Ciprio went to Gallo and said they could take the safe in Ferrara's, and he gave them the O.K. That was the straw that broke the camel's back because, from our observation, all of this frantic activity started with the burglary of Ferrara's on Easter weekend."

Whether this is the right script, only time will tell. One thing, however, is certain: The powerful Colombo family, periodically strife-torn every since the days when Joe Profaci ruled it with an iron hand, is undergoing one of its recurrent and bloody spasms. Evidence of the all-out nature of this internecine strife was uncovered by the F.B.I. on April 24 when it went into a state court in Kingston and got a warrant to raid the Saugerties farm of Carmine Persico. The F.B.I. said it had reliable information that contracts had been issued to hit five more members of the Gallo faction: Albert (Kid Blast) Gallo, the last and least conspicuous of the brothers; Peter Diapoulas, the bodyguard who was wounded when Crazy Joe was gunned down; John Cutrone and Frank Illiano, who had reportedly accompanied Crazy Joe in his descent upon the San Susan; and Bobby Bongiove, another key member of the Gallo group.

In the Saugerties raid, the F.B.I. arrested four men and a woman just as they were driving away from the Persico home in two cars. In the front car were Alphonse Persico and Jerry Angella, the delegates who had made that sudden visit to Carmine Persico in the Atlanta pen just before all the fireworks began. At the farm itself, the F.B.I. found a veritable arsenal—a dozen rifles, shotguns and pistols in the main house, and a similar cache of artillery in the barn. The haul provided graphic evidence of how the power is weighted in this one-sided war. The powerful Persico regime is said to have seven soldiers connected with it, each with his own band of associated followers, and the weapons seized at the farm were enough to equip this army.

"And this is just one regime of the Colombo family," one expert says. "Against this, the Gallos were nothing. They have only one soldier left, Johnny Cutrone, and they have only 23 mobsters associated with them. If they think they can take on the whole Colombo family, they must be crazy."

The only man who may have been that crazy, Joey Gallo, is gone. Without him, with past misdeeds avenged, there are some signs that the strife which has again wracked this second most powerful of the Mafia families of New York is beginning to simmer down. In late April, watching agents noted that Mafiosi who had made themselves scarce were venturing back upon the streets, appearing in public for the first time since the shootings began. And Charlie Mineo, in fine weather, was enjoying the sun on his favorite Court Street bench, just one bodyguard hovering nearby. It was a portent, to some, that the latest upheaval had subsided and that the hoods were getting back to business as usual.

Editor's Epilogue

THE KILLING GOES ON

When Mafiosi kill in movies like *The Godfather*, they do it with a certain amount of public concern. They choose empty restaurants or deserted toll stations in which to gun down their enemies, careful not to injure any innocent bystanders. The continuing gang war in New York has shown how wrong such pictures of the Mafia are. On a warm August evening, four kosher meat dealers were standing at the bar of a Manhattan restaurant with the unlikely name of the Neapolitan Noodle when a short, stocky man walked up near them and ordered a Scotch and water. After taking one sip, he set the glass on the bar, pulled out two pistols, fired nine bullets at the businessmen and walked out of the restaurant. Two of the men were killed and the other two were seriously wounded.

The four businessmen had taken places at the bar which were vacated moments earlier by four members of the Mafia family of Joseph Colombo, Sr. While the Colombo men were at the bar, they were apparently spotted and a call went out to their enemies who entrusted the hit to someone who was evidently not familiar with the men he was expected to kill.

A few days later Mayor John Lindsay called the mistaken identity murders "an outrage which demands that the romanticization of the mob be stopped and gangsters be run out of town." He said he had instructed the police "to see to it that this city is no place for mobsters to do business." New York, of course, has always been one of the best places in America for mobsters to do business, as is witnessed by the fact that it is the only city with more than one Mafia family. It has five.

New York is also a good place for Mafiosi to gun down their enemies. The police, who know that gangland homicides are the most difficult to solve, have rarely tried very hard. Police Commissioner Patrick V. Murphy implied as much after the shooting at the Neapolitan Noodle when he pledged that his department would no longer be content to sit back and watch gangsters kill each other. For years, however, the police in most cities have done little but watch from the sidelines when gang wars raged in their communities. As a result, Mafiosi have rubbed each other out when and where they liked.

Traditionally Mafiosi have liked to choose restaurants for the scene of their assassinations, because they can catch their victims relaxed and off guard. But while restaurants may provide a convenient place for an ambush, they are also usually filled with innocent people.

When Joey Gallo was executed at Umberto's Clam House in the Little Italy section of Manhattan, for example, there were 20 other people in the place. It was only luck that none of the 20 bullets fired during the shooting hit any innocent bystanders. The incident demonstrated once again that while the public may be fascinated with Mafiosi, the Mafiosi don't give a damn about the public.

N. G.

Index

NICHOLAS GAGE is a veteran investigative reporter who has written extensively on the Mafia and other elements of organized crime. Currently on the staff of the *New York Times*, he previously worked for *The Wall Street Journal* and the Associated Press. His first book on organized crime, *The Mafia Is Not An Equal Opportunity Employer*, was published in 1971. His articles have appeared in leading magazines including *The Atlantic*, *New York*, *Cosmopolitan* and the *New York Times Magazine*. A graduate of Boston University and Columbia University's Graduate School of Journalism, Mr. Gage, 33, lives in Manhattan with his wife Joan, who is also a journalist, and their son, Christos.

Mafia Families in New York City from 1930 to 1972

MASSERIA GROUP

Boss:
Giuseppe Masseria
Murdered April 20, 1931 by unidentified
killer of Maranzano Group.
Boss:
Joseph Catania
Murdered Feb. 3, 1931 by Salvatore Shillitani
and Nick Capuzzi and "Buster" from Chicago.

Bosses:
Alfred Mineo
Steve Ferrigno
Both murdered Nov. 5, 1930 by Girolamo
Santuccio and Nick Capuzzi and "Buster"
from Chicago.

SUCCESSION OF GANG

Boss:
Salvatore Lucania
(Lucky Luciano)
Deported 1946, died 1962.
Underboss:
Vito Genovese
Fled to Italy in 1934 to
avoid prosecution for murder.
Chee Gusage
Died natural causes
approx. 1936-37.
Frank Costello
Attempted murder May 2, 1957
when deposed by Vito
Genovese.

Boss:
Vito Genovese
Returned to U.S. from Italy
in 1946. Convicted on
narcotics conspiracy
violation on April 17, 1959.
Acting Boss:
Gerardo Catena
Underboss:
Thomas Eboli
Murdered on July 16, 1972.
Consigliere:
Michael Miranda

Bosses:
Philip & Vincent Mangano
Philip murdered on order
by Albert Anastasia,
April 19, 1951.
Vincent missing &
presumed dead since 1951.

Boss:
Albert Anastasia
Murdered Oct. 25, 1957.
Conspiracy between Carlo
Gambino, Joseph Biondo
and Vito Genovese.
Underboss:
Frank Scalise
Murdered at direction of
Albert Anastasia June 17, 1957.

Boss:
Carlo Gambino
Underboss:
Aniello Dellacroce
Consigliere:
Joseph Riccobono